THE BAVLI'S MASSIVE MISCELLANIES

SOUTH FLORIDA STUDIES IN THE HISTORY OF JUDAISM

Edited by
Jacob Neusner
William Scott Green, James Strange
Darrell J. Fasching, Sara Mandell

Number 43
The Bavli's Massive Miscellanies

by
Jacob Neusner

THE BAVLI'S MASSIVE MISCELLANIES
The Problem of Agglutinative Discourse
in the Talmud of Babylonia

by
Jacob Neusner

Scholars Press
Atlanta, Georgia

THE BAVLI'S MASSIVE MISCELLANIES
The Problem of Agglutinative Discourse in the Talmud of Babylonia

BM
503.6
.N474
1992

Publication of this book was made possible by a grant from the Tisch
Family Foundation, New York City. The University of South Florida
acknowledges with thanks this important support for its scholarly projects.

Library of Congress Cataloging in Publication Data

Neusner, Jacob, 1932-
    The Bavli's massive miscellanies ; the problem of agglutinative
    discourse in the Talmud of Babylonia / by Jacob Neusner.
    p. cm. — (South Florida studies in the history of Judaism ;
    no. 43)
    Includes bibliographical references and index.
    ISBN 1-55540-698-X (alk. paper)
    1. Talmud—Criticism, Redaction. 2. Talmud—Sources. 3. Talmud.
Berakhot I—Criticism, interpretation, etc. 4. Talmud. Sanhedrin
X—Criticism, interpretation, etc. I. Title. II. Title:
Agglutinative discourse in the Talmud of Babylonia. III. Series:
South Florida studies in the history of Judaism ; 43.
BM503.6.N474
296.1'25066—dc20   92-4271
                                    CIP
Printed in the United States of America
on acid-free paper

Contents

Preface

The pages of the Talmud of Babylonia contain long stretches of apparently disorganized and disconnected writing, on one subject after another. In these miscellaneous entries we have the equivalent of paragraphs but none of those larger compositions of paragraphs setting forth sustained and connected arguments that in general characterize the Bavli. Partly because of these massive miscellanies, the Bavli appears to be disorganized or to adhere to no principle of arrangement that we can discern. If that were so, then the Bavli would radically diverge from the character of the other compilations that make up the canon of the Judaism of the Dual Torah in late antiquity. For prior writings[1] commonly exhibit traits of order and coherence, and none comprises vast conglomerations of free-standing thoughts. None but the Bavli contains sizable sequences that exhibit the appearance of a mere scrapbook – this and that, haphazardly thrown together. Here we analyze these massive miscellanies, and I demonstrate that they adhere to rules of discourse that we can discern, rules that show miscellanies to be anything but miscellaneous and haphazard. In the end, we shall find, to the contrary, the miscellanies, adhering to rules of agglutinative, not propositional and syllogistic, discourse, serve as Mishnah commentaries as much as do the cogent composites that predominate in the Bavli.

This seems to me to lay to rest the last shreds of the argument, so far as it is based on data, that the Bavli is disorganized or unorganized; that the document adheres to no clear principles of order and that it is really

---

[1]I am not sure that this statement would accurately characterize the Yerushalmi, not having done for that talmud studies equivalent to those on the basis of which I characterize, for example, the Mishnah, Tosefta, and all midrash compilations without exception. My impression, based on the work done for *The Talmud of the Land of Israel. A Preliminary Translation and Explanation* (Chicago, 1983: University of Chicago Press. XXXV. *Introduction. Taxonomy*), and also *Judaism: The Classical Statement. The Evidence of the Bavli* (Chicago, 1986: University of Chicago Press), is that the Yerushalmi contains much less miscellaneous material than the Bavli. But that is only an impression.

just this, that, and the other thing, all thrown together. Based on a profound misunderstanding of the document and revealing deep ignorance of all but the coherence of words and phrases into sentences and paragraphs, that opinion is broadly held and shows that, until now, the Bavli has really not been properly understood at all. Lest my claim prove implausible, I point to prior writings of mine, where I have extensively cited both received and contemporary statements of the theory that the Bavli is not a well-crafted and carefully edited document.[2] In fact the Bavli is a commentary to the Mishnah, and in this final work of literary analysis, I take up the most intractable type of material – vast stretches of the Bavli that appear to be little more than miscellanies – and I now show that that, too, is little more than Mishnah commentary, of a rather special kind to be sure.

In these pages I address a problem that, to my knowledge, has never before attracted attention. Before beginning my own work on the literary character of the rabbinic canon, over a period of years with my graduate students of that time I systematically reviewed the entire scholarly literature on the writings of Judaism in its formative age, with the results, for writers prior to our own age, presented in such works as *The Formation of the Babylonian Talmud. Studies on the Achievements of Late*

---

[2]Since Adin Steinsaltz has circulated this view in the public press, I have replied to him in the same media, specifically, in "An open letter to Adin Steinsaltz," *Moment*, December 1991. But the question is more systematically treated in such books of mine as the following: *The Integrity of Leviticus Rabbah. The Problem of the Autonomy of a Rabbinic Document* (Chico, 1985: Scholars Press for Brown Judaic Studies); *Comparative Midrash: The Plan and Program of Genesis Rabbah and Leviticus Rabbah* (Atlanta, 1986: Scholars Press for Brown Judaic Studies); *From Tradition to Imitation. The Plan and Program of Pesiqta deRab Kahana and Pesiqta Rabbati* (Atlanta, 1987: Scholars Press for Brown Judaic Studies) [with a fresh translation of Pesiqta Rabbati *Pisqaot* 1-5, 15.]; *Canon and Connection: Intertextuality in Judaism* (Lanham, 1986: University Press of America Studies in Judaism Series); *Mekhilta Attributed to R. Ishmael. An Introduction to Judaism's First Scriptural Encyclopaedia* (Atlanta, 1988: Scholars Press for Brown Judaic Studies); *Making the Classics in Judaism: The Three Stages of Literary Formation* (Atlanta, 1990: Scholars Press for Brown Judaic Studies); *Tradition as Selectivity: Scripture, Mishnah, Tosefta, and Midrash in the Talmud of Babylonia. The Case of Tractate Arakhin* (Atlanta, 1990: Scholars Press for South Florida Studies in the History of Judaism); *The Bavli that Might Have Been: The Tosefta's Theory of Mishnah Commentary Compared with that of the Babylonian Talmud* (Atlanta, 1990: Scholars Press for South Florida Studies in the History of Judaism); *The Rules of Composition of the Talmud of Babylonia. The Cogency of the Bavli's Composite* (Atlanta, 1991: Scholars Press for South Florida Studies in the History of Judaism); *The Bavli's One Voice: Types and Forms of Analytical Discourse and their Fixed Order of Appearance* (Atlanta, 1991: Scholars Press for South Florida Studies in the History of Judaism); *How the Bavli Shaped Rabbinic Discourse* (Atlanta, 1991: Scholars Press for South Florida Studies in the History of Judaism).

Nineteenth and Twentieth Century Historical and Literary Critical Research (Leiden, 1970: Brill), *The Modern Study of the Mishnah* (Leiden, 1973: Brill). I edited other such surveys, for example, *The Study of Ancient Judaism* (New York, 1981: Ktav. I. *The Study of Ancient Judaism: Mishnah, Midrash, Siddur.* II. *The Study of Ancient Judaism: The Palestinian and Babylonian Talmuds*). In addition, in my systematic book reviewing, collected in such books as *Paradigms in Passage: Patterns of Change in the Contemporary Study of Judaism* (Lanham, 1988: University Press of America. Studies in Judaism Series); *Ancient Judaism and Modern Category-Formation. "Judaism," "Midrash," "Messianism," and Canon in the Past Quarter-Century* (Lanham, 1986: University Press of America Studies in Judaism Series); *Ancient Judaism. Debates and Disputes* (Chico, 1984: Scholars Press for Brown Judaic Studies); *Ancient Judaism. Debates and Disputes. Second Series* (Atlanta, 1990: Scholars Press for South Florida Studies in the History of Judaism); *Struggle for the Jewish Mind. Debates and Disputes on Judaism Then and Now* (Lanham, 1987: University Press of America. Studies in Judaism Series); *Wrong Ways and Right Ways in the Study of Formative Judaism. Critical Method and Literature, History, and the History of Religion* (Atlanta, 1988: Scholars Press for Brown Judaic Studies). I have kept up on the academic side of scholarship on this canon. In none of my reading of work done in my own time –1960 to the present – have I seen a single line of thought on why the framers of the materials now found in the Bavli made the kind of composites that we shall examine in this book, or how come the framers of the Bavli included them, as they did over and over again, within the larger structure of their document.

I wrote this monograph during my tenure as Martin Buber Visiting Professor of Judaic Studies at the Johann Wolfgang Goethe University of Frankfurt. The facilities for research provided by that University are much appreciated, as is the friendship of my colleagues on the Protestant Theological Faculty and also on the Catholic Theological Faculty. Support for the work on this monograph was provided by the Alexander Von Humboldt Stiftung, Bonn, Germany, and I acknowledge with thanks the generous grant provided by that foundation.

Would that before my time, the great scholars of Judaism in Europe could have written such a sentence! Would that the scholarship of so many generations of great scholars of the Talmud, Jews and Germans, who lived out their lives in Germany, the masters who founded the modern, critical study of the rabbinic literature, had enjoyed the recognition and support of their fellow Germans such as I, a foreigner, an American and a Jew, was given generously and with much good will! And would that they had found for their work in what they thought of as their own country the appropriate, academic and University setting that it merited! Instead, they were neglected, their learning treated as null, as much as the massive tradition of worthwhile learning of Judaism was denigrated and treated as null. And, when the end came to them as it came to all of Jewish Germany, no one knew or cared or acknowledged the loss and the tragedy. Every day of what was a productive and tranquil sojourn in Germany, I remembered them all, the many who never enjoyed the opportunities lavished on me, the many who perished. Even bearing thoughts of a tragic past, it was a genuinely happy stay. The reason is what has happened, and is now happening. Today, by contrast, a new generation of Germans wants to know and chooses to treat with dignity and honor what their predecessors despised. Mine is the good fortune to live in this age, and not in a more difficult time, and I am grateful for my lot, but deeply cognizant that others, before me, earned but never got what has come to me for no merit of my own.

My students in my seminar on the Mishnah and in my public lectures on the canon of Judaism, theological students at Frankfurt, won my affection and esteem and respect. This was because of not only their intelligence and keen interest, but also, and especially, because of their unfailing effort to appreciate what was very often very strange to them. In my twenty years at a university that tells its students they are "the best," I never saw entire classes that joined intellect with character and conscience, such as these young Germans. Remembering, too, the burden of the past that they bear willy-nilly, I could not but admire their capacity to transcend an unwanted heritage and form for their heirs an honorable one.

I appreciate, also, the cordial hearing accorded to my ideas both in my public lectures and in my seminar. I thank all those whose hospitality and friendship made my stay in Germany memorable and happy. I identify with my German university, as I do with the University of Cologne, the honorary doctorate of which affords me membership on that faculty as well, and bear with special pride the name of Martin Buber. He was the first through word and deed to begin the work of reengagement between Germany and the Jewish people, and because of him, many Germans have found it possible to address the dreadful heritage left to them by their grandparents and parents.

I further express my genuine pleasure at the opportunity for a life of learning through both teaching and scholarly inquiry that is afforded to me by the University of South Florida. I express thanks to my University for its generous support of my scholarly work. I also thank my colleagues in the Department of Religious Studies for not only friendship but intellectual stimulus.

Finally, as always, I talked over my ideas with Professor William Scott Green, University of Rochester, and found in his responses important guidance for my own thinking.

JACOB NEUSNER

Graduate Research Professor of Humanities and Religious Studies
UNIVERSITY OF SOUTH FLORIDA
Tampa, St. Petersburg, Sarasota, Lakeland, Fort Myers

735 Fourteenth Avenue Northeast
St. Petersburg, Florida 33701-1413 USA

1

Defining the Givens of This Inquiry

Two conflicting characteristics mark the Bavli, or Talmud of Babylonia. It is, first, a disciplined and well-organized, carefully crafted piece of writing. Most of the document is formulated in accord with a few simple rules, so that it is well-organized and easily followed. The Bavli, viewed whole, is carefully set forth as a commentary to the Mishnah, and the vast majority of its composites are put together so as to elucidate the statements of the Mishnah. In Chapter One I shall spell out precisely what I mean by this description of the Bavli. But in the pages of the Bavli we observe, second, very large composites, not formed into Mishnah commentaries at all. These composites do not follow the rules that govern the formation of the composites that serve as commentaries to the Mishnah. In Chapter Two I shall define the character of these miscellanies. Mishnah commentaries proceed along orderly lines, treating a subject in a way that conforms to our logic, beginning with first things, moving onward, within the limits and logic of the subject, to more complex ones, ending then in subsidiary questions. But the miscellanies go from this to that to the other thing, and it is not easy to explain why one thing is joined to some other, or why one passage is presented before, or after, some other.

Not only so, but the large-scale aggregates to which I refer both have, and also give to the Bavli, when it is viewed by an undiscerning reader, a miscellaneous quality: this, that, the other thing, with no clear pattern or purpose much in evidence. These massive miscellanies – composites that on first glance seem to follow no clear rules of composition at all – are made up of a substantial number of free-standing compositions. They in no way serve the paramount purpose of the Bavli, which demonstrably is to explain the Mishnah. Whoever put the miscellanies together had a different program in mind. And if the framers of the miscellanies had in mind that they ultimately would be collected in a piece of writing of some dimensions, then that writing that they imagined bears no resemblance to the writing in which their miscellanies did end up, that is, the Bavli. In this monograph I shall set forth the rules of conglomeration and agglutination that govern the formation of these massive miscellanies and define their program. First of all, let me spell out what I conceive to be the principal modes of sustained discourse in the Bavli. Then I shall turn to the analytical givens that dictate all further work. Only with these basic facts in hand shall we be prepared, in Chapter Two, for the problem of the miscellany.

Two types of writing characteristic of the Bavli require clear definition and exemplification before the problem I address in these pages can be approached. That is because the problem at hand can be grasped, and solved, only within the analytical framework already defined by me, in both theoretical writings and also in my protracted translations. I myself did not see the problem of the miscellanies as susceptible of solution, treating it as an anomaly, until I had fully grasped the relationship of composition to composite, on the one side, and the definitive character of the Bavli, as a commentary to the Mishnah, on the other. We first have to master the way in which the Bavli, in general, formulates its commentary to the Mishnah, which is through sustained discourse, formed of both off the rack, ready-made, and also tailor-made, materials, the whole sewn together with remarkable skill and purpose.

I. The Bavli's Paramount Mode of Discourse:
Propositional and Analytical Composite

Most of the Bavli is made up of extended exercises of Mishnah exegesis and amplification, with, first, exegesis of the Mishnah's language, rules, sources, and authority; and, second, secondary discussions of laws and principles of laws pertinent to a given Mishnah paragraph. These sustained passages, running on for many pages at a time, are remarkably cogent. Even though made up of diverse materials, ready-made and rarely recast or rewritten for the occasion, nearly everything in a given composite will relate in some way or another to the purpose of the composite as a whole; will contribute facts; will provide examples; will address secondary or subsidiary issues; or will otherwise carry forward the analytical, and even propositional, program of Mishnah exegesis that is realized in the entire composite. Since the bulk of this book addresses a different kind of discourse altogether, one that is not analytical, not propositional, and sometimes not even topical in its mode of organization and coherence, we had best begin with one fine example, among countless candidates, of first rate Mishnah commentary in the Bavli's sustainedly excellent manner. In what follows, we begin with a Mishnah paragraph and proceed to a systematic commentary on its components. The passage marked **I.1** then cites a clause of the Mishnah; it further raises an analytical question, in this instance, the implications of the statement of the Mishnah. What serves our purpose – the identification of an already completed, quite cogent piece of writing – follows at C: a clear citation of a prior document.

1:1

A.   [There are] four generative causes of damages: (1) ox (Ex. 21:35-36), (2) pit (Ex. 21:33), (3) crop-destroying beast (Ex. 22:4), and (4) conflagration (Ex. 22:5).

B.   [The definitive characteristic] of the ox is not equivalent to that of the crop-destroying beast;

C.   nor is that of the crop-destroying beast equivalent to that of the ox;

D.   nor are this one and that one, which are animate, equivalent to fire, which is not animate;

E.   nor are this one and that one, which usually [get up and] go and do damage, equivalent to a pit, which does not usually [get up and] go and do damage.

F.   What they have in common is that they customarily do damage and taking care of them is your responsibility.

G.   And when one [of them] has caused damage, the [owner] of that which causes the damage is liable to pay compensation for damage out of the best of his land (Ex. 22:4).

I.1   A.   Four generative causes of damages:

B.   *Since the framer of the passages makes reference to* generative causes, *it is to be inferred that there are derivative ones as well.* Are the derivative causes equivalent [in effect] to the generative causes or are they not equivalent to them in effect?

C.   *We have learned with reference to the Sabbath:* **The generative categories of acts of labor [prohibited on the Sabbath] are forty less one [M. Shab. 7:2A].** *Since the framer of the passages makes reference to* generative categories, *it is to be inferred that there are derivative ones as well.* Are the derivative categories equivalent to the generative categories or are they not equivalent to them?

D.   *Well, there is no difference between one's inadvertently carrying out an act of labor that falls into a generative category, in which case he is liable to present a sin-offering, and one's inadvertently carrying out an act of labor that falls into a derivative category of labor, in which case he is also liable to present a sin-offering. There is no difference between one's deliberately carrying out an act of labor that falls into a generative category, in which case he is liable to the death penalty through stoning, and one's deliberately carrying out an act of labor that falls into a derivative category of labor, in which case he is also liable to the death penalty through stoning.*

E.   *So then what's the difference between an act that falls into the generative category and one that falls into the derivative category?*

F.   *The upshot is that if one simultaneously carried out two actions that fall
      into the class of generative acts of labor, or two actions that fall into the
      classification of a derivative category, he is liable for each such action,
      while, if he had performed simultaneously both a generative act of labor
      and also a derivative of that same generative action, he is liable on only one
      count.*

G.   *And from the perspective of R. Eliezer, who imposes liability for a
      derivative action even when one is simultaneously liable on account of
      carrying out an act in the generative category, on what basis does one
      classify one action as generative and another as derivative [if it makes no
      practical difference]?*

H.   *Those actions that are carried out [even on the Sabbath] in the building of
      the tabernacle are reckoned as generative actions, and those that were not
      carried out on the Sabbath in the building of the tabernacle are classified as
      derivative.*

I.2   A.   *With reference to uncleanness we have learned in the Mishnah:* **The
           generative causes of uncleanness [are] (1) the creeping thing, and
           (2) semen [of an adult Israelite], [2B] and (3) one who has
           contracted corpse uncleanness, [and (4) the leper in the days of his
           counting, and (5) sin-offering water of insufficient quantity to be
           sprinkled. Lo, these render man and vessels unclean by contact,
           and earthenware vessels by [presence within the vessels'
           contained] airspace. But they do not render unclean by carrying]**
           [M. Kel. 1:1]. And their derivatives are not equivalent to them, for
           while a generative cause of uncleanness imparts uncleanness to a
           human being and utensils, a derivative source of uncleanness
           imparts uncleanness to food and drink but not to a human being or
           utensils.

I.3   A.   *Here what is the upshot of the distinction at hand?*
      B.   Said R. Pappa, "There are some derivatives that are equivalent in
           effect to the generative cause, and there are some that are not
           equivalent in effect to the generative cause."

I.4   A.   *Our rabbis have taught on Tannaite authority:*
      B.   Three [of the four] generative causes of damage are stated with
           respect to the ox: horn, tooth, and foot.

I.5   A.   How on the basis of Scripture do we know the case of the horn?
      B.   *It is in line with that which our rabbis have taught on Tannaite authority:*
      C.   "If it will gore..." (Ex. 21:28) – and goring is done only with the
           horn, as it is said, "And Zedekiah, son of Chenaanah, made him
           horns of iron and said, Thus saith the Lord, with these shall you
           gore the Aramaeans" (1 Kgs. 22:11);
      D.   and it is further said, "His glory is like the firstling of his bullock,
           and his horns are like the horns of a unicorn; with them he shall
           gore the people together" (Deut. 33:17).
      E.   *What's the point of "and it is further said"?*
      F.   *Should you say that teachings on the strength of the Torah are not to be
           derived from teachings that derive from prophetic tradition, then come and
           take note:* "His glory is like the firstling of his bullock, and his horns
           are like the horns of a unicorn; with them he shall gore the people
           together" (Deut. 33:17).

G.   *Yeah, well, is this really a deduction out of a scriptural prooftext? To me it looks more like a mere elucidation, showing that "goring" is something that is done by a horn.*

H.   *What might you otherwise have supposed? That where Scripture makes an important distinction between an ox that was not known to gore and one that is a certified danger, that concerns a horn that is cut off [as in the case of the first of the two examples, that of 1 Kgs. 22:11], but as to one that is actually attached to the beast, all goring is classified as done by an ox that is an attested danger. Then come and take note:* "His glory is like the firstling of his bullock, and his horns are like the horns of a unicorn; with them he shall gore the people together" (Deut. 33:17).

I.6   A.   *What are the derivatives of the horn?*

B.   Butting, biting, falling, and kicking.

C.   *How come goring is called a generative cause of damages? Because it is stated explicitly,* "If it will gore..." (Ex. 21:28). *But then in reference to butting, it also is written,* "If it butts" (Ex. 21:35).

D.   *That reference to butting refers in fact to goring, as has been taught on Tannaite authority:* Scripture opens with a reference to butting (Ex. 21:35) and concludes with a reference to goring (Ex. 21:16) to tell you that in this context "butting" means "goring."

I.7   A.   *What, when the Scripture refers to injury to a human being, does it say,* "If it will gore" (Ex. 21:28), *while when Scripture refers to an ox's injuring an animal, it uses the language,* "if it will butt" (Ex. 21:35)?

B.   *In connection with a human being, who is subject to a star [planetary influence], will be injured only by [Kirzner: willful] goring, but an animal, who is not subject to a star, is injured by mere accidental butting.*

C.   *And by the way, Scripture tangentially informs us of another matter, namely, an animal that is an attested danger for a human being is an attested danger for other beasts, but an animal that is an attested danger for beasts is not necessarily an attested danger for injuring a human being.*

I.8   A.   Biting: *does this not fall into the classification of a derivative of tooth?*

B.   *Not at all, for what characterizes injury under the classification of "tooth" is that there is pleasure that comes from doing the damage, but biting is not characterized by giving pleasure in the doing of the damage.*

I.9   A.   Falling, and kicking: *do these not fall into the classification of derivatives of foot?*

B.   *Not at all, for what characterizes injury under the classification of "foot" is that it is quite common, while damage done by these is not so common.*

I.10   A.   *Now, then, as to those derivatives that are not equivalent to the generative causes [from which the derives come], to which R. Pappa made reference, what might they be? Should we say that he makes reference to these? Then how are they different from the generative cause? Just as horn is a classification that involves damage done with intent, one's own property, and one's responsibility for adequate guardianship, so these, too, form classifications that involve damage done with intent, one's own property, and one's responsibility for adequate guardianship. So it must follow that the derivatives of horn are equivalent to the principal, the horn, and R. Pappa must then refer to tooth and foot.*

I.11   A.   *Where in Scripture is reference made to tooth and foot? It is taught on Tannaite authority:* "And he shall send forth" (Ex. 22:4) – this refers to the foot, and so Scripture says, "That send forth the feet of the ox and the ass" (Isa. 32:20). "And it shall consume" (Ex. 22:4) – this refers to the tooth, in line with this usage: "As the tooth consumes **[3A]** to entirety" (1 Kgs. 14:10).

I.12   A   The master has said: "'And he shall send forth' (Ex. 22:4) – this refers to the foot, and so Scripture says, 'That send forth the feet of the ox and the ass' (Isa. 32:20)."

B   *So the operative consideration is that Scripture has said, "That send forth the feet of the ox and the ass." Lo, if Scripture had not so stated, how else would you have interpreted the phrase, "And he shall send forth" (Ex. 22:4)? It could hardly refer to horn, which is written elsewhere, nor could it mean tooth, since this, too, is referred to elsewhere.*

C   *No, the proof nonetheless was required, for it might have entered your mind to suppose that "send forth" and "consume" refers to tooth, in the one case where there is destruction of the principal, in the other where there is no destruction of the principal, so we are informed that that is not so.*

D   *Now that you have established that the cited verse refers to foot in particular, then how on the basis of Scripture do we know that there is liable for damage done by the tooth in a case in which the principal has not been destroyed?*

E   *It would follow by analogy from the case of damage done by the foot. Just as in the case of damage done by the foot, there is no distinction to be drawn between a case in which the principal has been destroyed and one in which the principal has not been destroyed, so in the case of damage done by the tooth, there is no distinction to be drawn between a case in which the principal has been destroyed and one in which the principal has not been destroyed.*

I.13   A   The master has said, "'And it shall consume' (Ex. 22:4) – this refers to the tooth, in line with this usage: 'As the tooth consumes to entirety' (1 Kgs. 14:10)."

B   *So the operative consideration is that Scripture has said, "As the tooth consumes to entirety." Lo, were it not for that statement, how might we have interpreted the phrase anyhow? It could hardly have been a reference to horn, for that is stated explicitly in Scripture, and it also could not have been a reference to foot for the same reason.*

C   *No, it was necessary to make that point in any event. For it might otherwise have entered your mind to suppose that both phrases speak of foot, the one referred to a case in which the beast was going along on its own, the other when the owner sent it to do damage, and so we are informed that that is not the case. [So we are informed that that is not the case.]*

D   *If then we have identified the matter with tooth, then how could we know that one is liable under the category of foot when the cattle went and did damage on its own?*

E   *The matter is treated by analogy to damage done in the category of tooth. Just as in the case of tooth we draw no distinction between a case in which the owner sent the beast out and it did damage and one in which the beast went along on its own, so in the case of foot, there is no distinction between a case in which the owner sent the beast out and one in which the beast went out on its own.*

I.14   A.   *Then let the Scripture make reference to* "And he shall send forth" (Ex. 22:4) *and omit* "And it shall consume," *which would cover the classifications of both foot and tooth? It would cover foot in line with this verse:* "That send forth the feet of the ox and the ass," *and it would cover tooth, in line with this verse,* "And the teeth of beasts will I send upon them" (Deut. 32:24).

       B.   *Were it not for this apparently redundant statement, I might have imagined that the intent was either the one or the other, either foot, since damage done by the foot is commonplace, or tooth, since damage done by the tooth gives pleasure.*

       C.   *Well, we still have to include them both, since, after all, which one would you exclude anyhow [in favor of the other], their being equally balanced?*

       D.   *The additional clarification still is required, for you might otherwise have supposed that the liability pertains only where the damage is intentional, excluding a case in which the cattle went on its own; so we are informed that that is not the case.*

I.15   A.   *What is the derivative of the generative category of tooth?*

       B.   If for its own pleasure the cow rubbed itself against a wall and broke it, or spoiled produce by rolling around in it.

       C.   *What distinguishes damage done by the tooth* [as a generative category] is that it is a form of damage that gives pleasure to the one that does it, it derives from what is your own property, and you are responsible to take care of it? *Well, in these cases too, one may say the same thing, namely, here we have* a form of damage that gives pleasure to the one that does it, it derives from what is your own property, and you are responsible to take care of it.

       D.   *It must follow that the derivative classes of the generative category of tooth are equivalent to the generative category itself, and when R. Pappa made his statement, he must have referred to the generative category of foot.*

I.16   A.   *What is the derivative of the generative category of foot?*

       B.   If the beast while moving did damage with its body or hair or with a load on it or with a bit in its mouth or with a bell around its neck.

       C.   *What distinguishes damage done by the foot* [as a generative category] is that it is a form of damage that is very common, it derives from what is your own property, and you are responsible to take care of it. *Well, in these cases too, one may say the same thing, namely, here we have* a form of damage that is very common, it derives from what is your own property, and you are responsible to take care of it.

       D.   *It must follow that the derivative classes of the generative category of foot are equivalent to the generative category itself, and when R. Pappa made his statement, he must have referred to the generative category of pit.*

I.17   A.   *Then what would be derivatives of the generative category of pit?*

       B.   *Should I say that the generative category is a pit ten handbreadths deep, but a derive is one nine handbreadths deep? Scripture does not make explicit reference to either one ten handbreadths deep nor to one nine handbreadths deep!*

       C.   *In point of fact that is not a problem, since the All-Merciful has said,* "And the dead beast shall be his" (Ex. 21:34). *And, for their part, rabbis established that a pit ten handbreadths deep will case death, one only nine handbreadths deep will cause only injury, but will not cause death.*

D. *So what difference does that make? The one is a generative classification of pit when it comes to yielding death, the other an equally generative classification yielding injury.*

E. *So R. Pappa's statement must speak of a stone, knife, or luggage, left in the public domain, that did damage.*

F. *How then can we imagine damage of this kind? If they were declared ownerless and abandoned in the public domain, then from the perspective of both Rab and Samuel, they fall into the classification of pit.* [3B] *And if they were not declared ownerless and abandoned in the public domain, then from the perspective of Samuel, who has said, "All public nuisances are derived by analogy to the generative classification of pit," they fall into the classification of pit, and from the perspective of Rab, who has held, "All of them do we derive by analogy to ox," they fall under the classification of ox.*

G. *What is it that characterizes the pit? It is that* to begin with it is made as a possible cause of damage, it is your property, and your are responsible to watch out for it. *So of these, too, it may be said,* to begin with it is made as a possible cause of damage, it is your property, and your are responsible to watch out for it. *It therefore follows that the derivatives of pit are the same as the pit itself, and when R. Pappa made his statement, it was with reference to the derivatives of the crop-destroying beast.*

I.18 A. *So what can these derivatives of the crop-destroying beast be anyhow? From the perspective of Samuel, who has said, "The crop destroying beast is the same as tooth [that is, trespassing cattle]," lo, the derivative of tooth is in the same classification as tooth [as we have already shown], and from the perspective of Rab, who has said, "The crop-destroying beast is in fact the human being," then what generative categories and what derivatves therefrom are to be identified with a human being! Should you allege that a human being when awake is the generative classification, and the human being when asleep is a derivative, have we not learned in the Mishnah:* **Man is perpetually an attested danger** **[M. B.Q. 2:6A]** – *whether awake or asleep!*

B. *So when R. Pappa made his statement, he must have referred to a human being's phlegm or snot.*

C. *Yeah, well, then, under what conditions? If the damage was done while in motion, it comes about through man's direct action, and if it does its damage after it comes to rest, then, whether from Rab's or Samuel's perspective, it falls into the classification of pit. And, it must follow, the offspring of the crop-destroying beast is in the same classification as the crop-destroying beast, so when R. Pappa made his statement, he must have been talking about the derivatives of fire.*

I.19 A. *So what are derivatives of fire? Shall we say that such would be a stone, knife, or luggage, that one left on one's roof and were blown off by an ordinary wind and caused damage? Then here, too, under what conditions? If the damage was done while in motion, then they fall into the category of fire itself. For what characterizes fire is that it derives from an external force, is your property, and is yours to guard, and these, too, are to be described in the same way, since each derives from an external force, is your property, and is yours to guard. And, it must follow, the offspring of fire are in the same classification as fire, so when R. Pappa* made his statement, he must have been talking about the derivatives of foot.

I.20   A   *Foot? Surely you're joking! Have we not already established the fact that the derivative of foot is in the same classification as the generative classification of foot itself.*

     B   *At issue is the payment of half damages done by pebbles kicked by an animal's foot, which we have learned by tradition.*

     C.   *And why is such damage classified as a derivative of foot?*

     D.   *So that compensation should be paid only from property of the highest class possessed by the defendant.*

     E.   *But did not Raba raised the question on this very matter? For Raba raised this question, "Is the half damage to be paid for damage caused by pebbles to be paid only from the body of the beast itself or from the beast property of the owner of the beast?"*

     F.   *Well, that was a problem for Raba, but R. Pappa was quite positive about the matter.*

     G.   *Well, if it's a problem to Raba, then from his perspective, why would pebbles kicked by an animal's foot be classified as a derivative of foot?*

     H   *So that the owner in such a case may be exempted from having to pay compensation where the damage was done in the public domain [just as damage caused by the generative category, foot, is not to be compensated if it was done in the public domain].*

I have now set forth twenty distinct, well-crafted statements, which we might call "paragraphs." Many of these paragraphs use available materials, but always, and only, for the purpose that the framer of the paragraph has in mind, that is, to make the point he wishes to make. Not only so, but the sequence of paragraphs is so orderly and inexorable that if we removed one item, we should destroy the coherence of all that follows; and if, obviously, we were to place the paragraphs into an order other than the one before us, the writing would be simply incomprehensible. So any notion that the Bavli is disorderly or fails to follow a discernible program and plan derives from an uncomprehending and superficial examination of this-and-that, not a close and thoughtful reading of the whole. We open with a sizable exercise in explaining the language of our Mishnah paragraph, in line with the same usage in other Mishnah paragraphs, I.1-3. No. 4 then turns to the amplification of the Mishnah's statement by appeal to other Tannaite materials; we start with a complement that locates in Scripture the generative categories that are before us. This complement forms an integral part in the exposition of No. 3, and the entire composite goes from No. 3 through No. 20. That the whole is a continuous, beautifully crafted composite, shaped into a single coherent and unfolding statement, is beyond all doubt. When, in Chapter Two, we examine our first miscellany, we shall see why the miscellany appears to form an anomaly in a writing of such remarkable power and determination as the one we have just now sampled.

II. The Composition and the Composite

Even my initial sample has shown the simple fact that the Talmud of Babylonia is made up of large-scale composites of already completed compositions. To begin with, the document draws upon the already completed writing, the Mishnah, being organized to present the appearance of a commentary to that writing. Second, it cites passages of another already completed piece of writing, the Tosefta. Third, very commonly we are able to identify a single cogent statement, with its own beginning, middle, and end, and furthermore we readily distinguish that statement from a larger framework in which, whole and complete, it is set to serve some larger purpose. When I say that the Bavli is made up of composites of compositions, I mean that for the most part, the framers of the whole have made use of (some) already completed pieces of writing, setting them out in such a way as to serve a purpose not contemplated by the author(s) of the original compositions but rather a purpose clearly dictated by the analytical and propositional program of the framers of the Bavli itself. The distinction between composition and composite is so fundamental that, before proceeding, I had best give a simple example of what I mean. Only then will the issue of this monograph be set forth in an intelligible context of literary analysis.

Let me explain to begin with how the materials that follow are meant to clarify the point at hand: what is a composition and what is a composite? A composition is a fully articulated, cogent statement, which contains everything we need to understand what the author of the writing wishes to say to us. A composite is a collection of such completed pieces of writing, worked out in such a way as to make the point that the framer of the composite, not the authors of the compositions that he uses, wishes to make. As I have explained in *The Rules of Composition of the Talmud of Babylonia. The Cogency of the Bavli's Composite,*[1] the author of a composition sets forth a proposition of his own, while the frame of a composite may make use of a variety of such compositions to make the quite different point that he has in mind. With this simple distinction in mind, we have, also, carefully to distinguish between glosses, such as – in the example to follow – are found at 2.B, D-E, and free-standing compositions that are utilized for a purpose other than that for which, on the face of it, they were written. What illustrates the classification, composition, in the sample at hand? The statement of Hisda, F, has been set down in its own terms. It is adduced to prove the point of E. So F is a composition, E-F a composite put together to clarify

---

[1] Atlanta, 1991: Scholars Press for South Florida Studies in the History of Judaism.

D, itself a gloss of C. Another example of the same is at W, glossed by X. X on its own makes good sense without reference to W or even to the purpose, signalled at X (*But how can they present such an argument, since*), that links Yohanan's statement to the context in which it now occurs. The same is to be said at DD, the gloss of AA-CC, which cites an already completed composition, with its own beginning, middle, and end, of DD, Joseph's statement. Another composition placed into the composite before us is at GG. Still a third is NN-OO. Simeon's statement, OO, is a free-standing one; but the compositor has introduced it as a footnote for the foregoing, NN. Another excellent example of a composition formulated in its own terms and then introduced here for the purposes of the compositor of the whole is at BBB-GGG. HHH contains a fine composition, Judah's citation of Rab, joined by "is this really so" to the larger composite. A still finer instance of the composite is at No. 3, the whole of which is worked out in a framework entirely autonomous of the larger composite in which No. 3 is now positioned. The same may be said of No. 4.

Abodah Zarah

1.2	A	R. Hanina bar Pappa, and some say, R. Simlai, gave the following exposition [of the verse,"They that fashion a graven image are all of them vanity, and their delectable things shall not profit, and their own witnesses see not nor know" (Isa. 44:9)]: "In the age to come the Holy One, blessed be He, will bring a scroll of the Torah and hold it in his bosom and say, 'Let him who has kept himself busy with it come and take his reward.' Then all the gentiles will crowd together: 'All of the nations are gathered together' (Isa. 43:9). The Holy One, blessed be He, will say to them, 'Do not crowd together before me in a mob. But let each nation enter together with [2B] its scribes, and let the peoples be gathered together' (Isa. 43:9), and the word 'people' means 'kingdom': 'and one kingdom shall be stronger than the other' (Gen. 25:23)."
	B.	*But can there be a mob scene before the Holy One, blessed be He? Rather, it is so that from their perspective they not form a mob, so that they will be able to hear what he says to them.*
	C.	[Resuming the narrative of A:] "The kingdom of Rome comes in first."
	D.	*How come? Because they are the most important. How do we know on the basis of Scripture they are the most important? Because it is written,* "And he shall devour the whole earth and shall tread it down and break it into pieces" (Gen. 25:23), and said R. Yohanan, "This Rome is answerable, for its definition [of matters] has gone forth to the entire world. [Mishcon: 'This refers to Rome, whose power is known to the whole world.']"

E.   *And how do we know that the one who is most important comes in first? It is in accord with that which R. Hisda said.*

F.   For said R. Hisda, "When the king and the community [await judgment], the king enters in first for judgment: 'That he maintain the case of his servant [Solomon] and [then] the cause of his people Israel' (1 Kgs. 8:59)."

W.   "They will say to him, 'Lord of the world, in point of fact, did you actually give it to us and we did not accept it?'"

X.   *But how can they present such an argument, since it is written,* "The Lord came from Sinai and rose from Seir to them, he shined forth from Mount Paran" (Deut. 33:2), *and further,* "God comes from Teman" (Hab. 3:3). *Now what in the world did he want in Seir, and what was he looking for in Paran?* Said R. Yohanan, "This teaches that the Holy One, blessed be He, made the rounds of each and every nation and language and none accepted it, until he came to Israel, and they accepted it."

Y.   *Rather, this is what they say,* "Did we accept it but then not carry it out?"

Z.   *But to this the rejoinder must be,* "Why did you not accept it anyhow!"

AA.   Rather, "This is what they say before him, 'Lord of the world, Did you hold a mountain over us like a cask and then we refused to accept it as you did to Israel, as it is written, "And they stood beneath the mountain" (Ex. 19:17).'"

BB.   And [in connection with the verse, "And they stood beneath the mountain" (Ex. 19:17),] said R. Dimi bar Hama, "This teaches that the Holy One, blessed be He, held the mountain over Israel like a cask and said to them, 'If you accept the Torah, well and good, and if not, then there is where your grave will be.'"

CC.   "Then the Holy One, blessed be He, will say to them, 'Let us make known what happened first: "Let them announce to us former things" (Isa. 43:9). As to the seven religious duties that you did accept, where have you actually carried them out?'"

DD.   *And how do we know on the basis of Scripture that they did not carry them out?* R. Joseph formulated as a Tannaite statement, "'He stands and shakes the earth, he sees and makes the nations tremble' (Hab. 3:6): what did he see? He saw the seven religious duties that the children of Noah accepted upon themselves as obligations but never actually carried them out. Since they did not carry out those obligations, he went and remitted their obligation."

EE.   *But then they benefited – so it pays to sin!*

FF.   Said Mar b. Rabina, [3A] "What this really proves is that even they they carry out those religious duties, they get no reward on that account."

GG.   *And they don't, don't they? But has it not been taught on Tannaite authority:* R. Meir would say, "How on the basis of Scripture do we know that, even if it is a gentile, if he goes and takes up the study of the Torah as his occupation, he is equivalent to the high priest? Scripture states, 'You shall therefore keep my statues and my ordinances, which, if a human being does them, one shall gain life through them' (Lev. 18:5). What is written is not 'priests' or 'Levites' or 'Israelites,' but rather, 'a human being.' So you have learned the fact that, even if it is a gentile, if he goes and takes up the study of the Torah as his occupation, he is equivalent to the high priest."

HH. Rather, what you learn from this [DD] is that they will not receive that reward that is coming to those who are commanded to do them and who carry them out, but rather, the reward that they receive will be like that coming to the one who is not commanded to do them and who carries them out anyhow.

II. For said R. Hanina, "Greater is the one who is commanded and who carries out the religious obligations than the one who is not commanded but nonetheless carries out religious obligations."

NN. "They will say before him, 'Lord of the world, the Heaven and earth have a selfish interest in the testimony that they give: "If not for my covenant with day and with night, I should not have appointed the ordinances of heaven and earth" (Jer. 33:25).'"

OO. *For said R. Simeon b. Laqish, "What is the meaning of the verse of Scripture,* 'And there was evening, and there was morning, the sixth day' (Gen. 1:31)? This teaches that the Holy One, blessed be He, made a stipulation with all of the works of creation, saying to them, 'If Israel accepts my Torah, well and good, but if not, I shall return you to chaos and void.' *That is in line with what is written:* 'You did cause sentence to be heard from heaven, the earth trembled and was still' (Ps. 76:9). If 'trembling' then where is the stillness, and if stillness, then where is the trembling? Rather, to begin with, trembling, but at the end, stillness."

PP. [Reverting to MM-NN:] "The Holy One, blessed be He, will say to them, 'Some of them may well come and give testimony concerning Israel that they have observed the entirety of the Torah. Let Nimrod come and give testimony in behalf of Abraham that he never worshipped idols. Let Laban come and give testimony in behalf of Jacob, that he never was suspect of thievery. Let the wife of Potiphar come and give testimony in behalf of Joseph, that he was never suspect of "sin." Let Nebuchadnezzar come and give testimony in behalf of Hananiah, Mishael, and Azariah, that they never bowed down to the idol. Let Darius come and give testimony in behalf of Daniel, that he did not neglect even the optional prayers. Let Bildad the Shuhite and Zophar the Naamatite and Eliphaz the Temanite and Elihu son of Barachel the Buzite come and testify in behalf of Israel that they have observed the entirety of the Torah: "Let the nations bring their own witnesses, that they may be justified" (Isa. 43:9).'

QQ.   "They will say before him, 'Lord of the world, give it to us to begin with, and let us carry it out.'

RR.   "The Holy One, blessed be He, will say to them, 'World-class idiots! He who took the trouble to prepare on the eve of the Sabbath [Friday] will eat on the Sabbath, but he who took no trouble on the even of the Sabbath – what in the world is he going to eat on the Sabbath! Still, [I'll give you another chance.] I have a rather simple religious duty, which is called "the tabernacle." Go and do that one.'"

SS.   *But can you say any such thing? Lo, R. Joshua b. Levi has said, "What is the meaning of the verse of Scripture, 'The ordinances that I command you this day to do them' (Deut. 7:11)? Today is the day to do them, but not tomorrow; they are not to be done tomorrow; today is the day to do them, but not the day on which to receive a reward for doing them."*

TT.   Rather, it is that the Holy One, blessed be He, does not exercise tyranny over his creatures.

UU.   *And why does he refer to it as a simple religious duty? Because it does not involve enormous expense [to carry out that religious duty].*

VV.   "Forthwith every one of them will take up the task and go and make a tabernacle on his roof. But then the Holy, One, blessed be He, will come and make the sun blaze over them as at the summer solstice, and every one of them will knock down his tabernacle and go his way: 'Let us break their bands asunder and cast away their cords from us' (Ps. 23:3)."

WW.   But lo, you have just said, "it is that the Holy One, blessed be He, does not exercise tyranny over his creatures"!

XX.   *It is because the Israelites, too – sometimes* [3B] *the summer solstice goes on to the Festival of Tabernacles, and therefore they are bothered by the heat!*

YY.   But has not Raba stated, "One who is bothered [by the heat] is exempt from the obligation of dwelling in the tabernacle"?

ZZ.   *Granting that one may be exempt from the duty, is he going to go and tear the thing down?*

AAA.   [Continuing from VV:] "Then the Holy One, blessed be He, goes into session and laughs at them: 'He who sits in heaven laughs' (Ps. 2:4)."

BBB.   Said R. Isaac, "Laughter before the Holy One, blessed be He, takes place only on that day alone."

CCC.   *There are those who repeat as a Tannaite version this statement of R. Isaac in respect to that which has been taught on Tannaite authority:*

DDD.   R. Yosé says, "In the coming age gentiles will come and convert."

EEE.   *But will they be accepted? Has it not been taught on Tannaite authority: Converts will not be accepted in the days of the Messiah, just as they did not accept*

	proselytes either in the time of David or in the time of Solomon?
FFF.	Rather, "they will make themselves converts, and they will put on phylacteries on their heads and arms and fringes on their garments and a mezuzah on their doors. But when they witness the war of Gog and Magog, he will say to them, 'How come you have come?' They will say, '"Against the Lord and against his Messiah."' For so it is said, 'Why are the nations in an uproar and why do the peoples mutter in vain' (Ps. 2:1). Then each one of them will rid himself of his religious duty and go his way: 'Let us break their bands asunder' (Ps. 2:3). Then the Holy One, blessed be He, goes into session and laughs at them: 'He who sits in heaven laughs' (Ps. 2:4)."
GGG.	Said R. Isaac, "Laughter before the Holy One, blessed be He, takes place only on that day alone."
HHH.	But is this really so? And has not R. Judah said Rab said, "The day is made up of twelve hours. In the first three the Holy One, blessed be He, goes into session and engages in study of the Torah; in the second he goes into session and judges the entire world. When he realizes that the world is liable to annihilation, he arises from the throne of justice and takes up a seat on the throne of mercy. In the third period he goes into session and nourishes the whole world from the horned buffalo to the brood of vermin. During the fourth quarter he laughs [and plays] with Leviathan: 'There is Leviathan, whom you have formed to play with' (Ps. 104:26)." [This proves that God does laugh more than on that one day alone.]
III.	Said R. Nahman bar Isaac, "With his creatures he laughs [every day], but at his creatures he laughs only on that day alone."

I.3	A	Said R. Aha to R. Nahman bar Isaac, "From the day on which the house of the sanctuary, the Holy One blessed be He has had no laughter.
	B.	*"And how on the basis of Scripture do we know that he has had none? If we say that it is because it is written,* 'And on that day did the Lord, the God of hosts, call to weeping and lamentation' (Isa. 22:12), *that verse refers to that day in particular. Shall we then say that that fact derives from the verse,* 'If I forget you, Jerusalem, let my right hand forget her cunning, let my tongue cleave to the roof of my mouth if I do not remember you' (Ps. 137:5-6)? *That refers to forgetfulness, not laughter. Rather, the fact derives from this verse:* 'I have long held my peace, I have been still, I have kept in, now I will cry' (Isa. 42:14)."

I.4	A	[Referring to the statement that during the fourth quarter he laughs [and plays] with Leviathan,] *[nowadays] what does he do in the fourth quarter of the day?*

B.   He sits and teaches Torah to kindergarten students:
            "Whom shall one teach knowledge, and whom shall
            one make understand the message? Those who are
            weaned from the milk?" (Isa. 28:19).

C.   *And to begin with [prior to the destruction of the Temple,*
            which ended his spending his time playing with Leviathan],
            who taught them?

D.   *If you wish, I shall say it was Metatron, and if you wish, I*
            shall say that he did both [but now does only one].

E.   And at night what does he do?

F.   *If you wish, I shall say that it is the sort of thing he does by*
            day;

G.   *and if you wish, I shall say,* he rides his light cherub and
            floats through eighteen thousand worlds: "The
            chariots of God are myriads, even thousands and
            thousands [shinan] (Ps. 68:48). Read the letters
            translated as thousands, shinan, as though they were
            written, she-enan, meaning, that are not [thus: the
            chariots are twice ten thousand less two thousand,
            eighteen thousand (Mishcon)]."

H   *And if you wish, I shall say,* he sits and listens to the
            song of the Living Creatures [hayyot]: "By the day the
            Lord will command his loving kindness and in the
            night his song shall be with me" (Ps. 42:9).

We see therefore the traits of the composite over all. To refer to materials
given only later, in Chapter Two, to make clear even now the purpose of
the composite over all, the Bavli at I.1 begins with a systematic inquiry
into the correct reading of the Mishnah's word choices. The dispute is
fully articulated in balance, beginning to end. No. 2 then forms a
footnote to No. 1. No. 3 then provides a footnote to the leitmotif of No. 2,
the conception of God's not laughing. We shall see in Chapter Two that
No. 4 returns us to the exposition of No. 2, at III. Nos. 5, 6 are tacked on
– a Torah study anthology – because they continue the general theme of
Torah study every day, which formed the main motif of No. 2 – the
gentiles did not accept the Torah, study it, or carry it out. So that theme
accounts for the accumulation of sayings on Torah study in general, a
kind of appendix on the theme. Now that the definition of a composition
and composite has been amply illustrated, let us go on with the problem
of this monograph: the anomaly of the miscellany.

2

The Bavli's Massive Miscellanies: The Problem of Agglutinative Discourse in the Talmud of Babylonia

To understand what I mean by a "miscellany" in the context of the Bavli, let me now set forth the traits of the document that, over all, classify the writing as anything but miscellaneous. Then the problem of the literary formations treated in this pages will become entirely clear. For until I have established that most of the Bavli follows easily discerned rules of composition and the formation of composites, and that these rules dictate the character of the document as a whole – a commentary to the Mishnah – my claim to identify and differentiate writing of a quite different character will not be fully understood. Since I propose not only to identify this other kind of writing, but also to define and explain the rules that dictate the making of those composites of the Bavli that serve a different purpose from Mishnah commentary, I had best begin with the norms of the document, and only then to turn to what is different from the normal but also, in its way, governed by reasons we can uncover.

As the remarkably sustained analytical composition presented in Chapter One has shown us, the writers of the Talmud spoke in a single voice. Whatever its writers wished to say, they said in a single way. Viewed as a whole, the Talmud of Babylonia covers thirty-seven of the Mishnah's sixty-three tractates, and, in discussing these thirty-seven Mishnah tractates, the authorship of the Talmud speaks in a single way. A fixed rhetorical pattern and a limited program of logical inquiry governs throughout. Whatever authors wish to say, they say within a severely restricted repertoire of rhetorical choices, and the intellectual initiatives they are free to explore everywhere dictate one set of questions and problems and not any other. The document's "voice," then, comprises that monotonous and repetitious language, which conveys a recurrent and single melody. In the ancient and great centers of learning in which the Talmud of Babylonia is studied today, masters and their disciples – studying out loud and in dialogue with one another and with the text – commonly and correctly say, "the Talmud says...," (Yiddish: *zogt die gemara*; Hebrew: *hattalmud omeret*), meaning, the anonymous, uniform, ubiquitous voice of the document, speaking in the name of no one in particular and within an indeterminate context of space and time, makes a given statement or point. Through years of encounter with the document, within the conventions of centuries of study in continuing circles of learning, by reference to "the Talmud says," the masters express the result of innumerable observations of coherence, uniformity, and cogency. I represent their usage when I speak of "the Talmud's one voice."

Why do I claim that the document may be read as a single coherent statement? The reason is that the document as a whole is cogent, doing some few things over and over again; it conforms to a few simple rules of rhetoric, including choice of languages for discrete purposes,[1] and that fact attests to the coherent viewpoint of the authorship at the end – the people who put it all together as we have it – because it speaks, over all, in a single way, in a uniform voice. It is not merely an encyclopaedia of information, but a sustained, remarkably protracted, uniform inquiry into the logical traits of passages of the Mishnah or of Scripture. Most of the Talmud deals with the exegesis and amplification of the Mishnah's rules or of passages of Scripture. Wherever we turn, that labor of exegesis and amplification, without differentiation in topics or tractates, conforms to a few simple rules in inquiry, repeatedly phrased, implicitly or explicitly, in a few simple rhetorical forms or patterns.

The Bavli's one voice governs throughout, about a considerably repertoire of topics speaking within a single restricted rhetorical vocabulary. In the pages of *The Bavli's One Voice: Types and Forms of Analytical Discourse and their Fixed Order of Appearance*,[2] that vocabulary – the limited repertoire of speech – is set forth through an inductive process, hence "the Bavli's one voice" refers to a remarkably limited set of intellectual initiatives, only this and that, initiatives that moreover

---

[1]I refer to *Language as Taxonomy. The Rules for Using Hebrew and Aramaic in the Babylonian Talmud* (Atlanta, 1990: Scholars Press for South Florida Studies in the History of Judaism). This work is made possible by my translation, which distinguishes between Hebrew and Aramaic by the use of plain and italic type. Then, quite graphically, how each language serves its own distinct, taxonomic purpose, that is, identifying the status and purpose of what is said in that language, is easily portrayed.

[2]Atlanta, 1991: Scholars Press for South Florida Studies in the History of Judaism.

always adhere to a single sequence or order: this first, then that – but never the other thing. I can identify the Bavli's authorships' rules of composition. These are not many. Not only so, but the order of types of compositions (written in accord with a determinate set of rules) itself follows a fixed pattern, so that a composition written in obedience to a given rule as to form will always appear in the same point in a sequence of compositions that are written in obedience to two or more rules: type A first, type B next, in fixed sequence. The Talmud's one voice then represents the outcome of the work of the following:

1. An author preparing a composition for inclusion in the Bavli would conform to one of a very few rules of thought and expression; and, more to the point,
2. a framer of a cogent composite, often encompassing a set of compositions, for presentation as the Bavli would follow a fixed order in selecting and arranging the types of consequential forms that authors had made available for his use.[3]

With a clear and specific account of the facts yielding that anticipated result, I shall be well justified in asking about the message of the rhetorical and logical method of the Bavli. The Talmud of Babylonia is made up of large-scale composites – completed units of discourse, with a beginning, middle, and end, which supply all of the data a reader (or listener) requires to understand the point that the framer of that composite wishes to make. A composite commonly draws upon available information, made available in part by prior and completed composites, for example, Scripture, the Mishnah, the Tosefta, and in part by compositions worked out entirely within their own limits, which we might compare with a paragraph of a chapter; or a free-standing composition of a few lines. By "rules of composition" I mean the laws that dictated to the framers of a cogent and coherent composites – such as I allege comprise the whole of the Talmud of Babylonia – precisely how to put together whatever they wished to say, together with the supporting evidence as well as argument, in the composition that they proposed to write. Here, then, "rules of composition" govern how

---

[3]The distinction between composition and composite, which is fundamental to all that follows, is explained in *The Rules of Composition of the Talmud of Babylonia. The Cogency of the Bavli's Composite* (Atlanta, 1991: Scholars Press for South Florida Studies in the History of Judaism). And that distinction begins with my development of an analytical reference system, which makes possible the division of columns of undifferentiated words into much more than sentences, paragraphs, chapters, the analytical re-presentation of undifferentiated words into their functional components: principal and subordinate. Here again, it would serve no useful purpose to go over familiar results.

people formed composites that comprise the Bavli: how they are classified, how they are ordered.

Now to set forth the results of the analysis of eleven tractates systematically treated in *The Bavli's One Voice*. It is the simple fact that the Bavli throughout speaks in a single and singular voice. It is single because it is a voice that expresses the same limited set of notes everywhere. It is singular because these notes are arranged in one and the same way throughout. The Bavli's one voice, sounding through all tractates, is the voice of exegetes of the Mishnah. The document is organized around the Mishnah, and that is not a merely formal, but a substantive order. At every point, if the framers have chosen a passage of Mishnah exegesis, that passage will stand at the head of all further discussion. Every turning point brings the editors back to the Mishnah, always read in its own order and sequence. So the Bavli speaks in a single way about some few things, and that is the upshot of my sustained inquiry. It follows that well-crafted and orderly rules governed the character of the sustained discourse that the writing in the Bavli sets forth. All framers of composites and editors of sequences of composites found guidance in the same limited repertoire of rules of analytical rhetoric: some few questions or procedures, directed always toward one and the same prior writing. Not only so, but a fixed order of discourse dictated that a composition of one sort, A, always come prior to a composite of another type, B. A simple logic instructed framers of composites, who sometimes also were authors of compositions, and who sometimes drew upon available compositions in the making of their cogent composites. So we have now to see the Bavli as entirely of a piece, cogent and coherent, made up of well-composed large-scale constructions. It is coherent not only in its rules of the use of Hebrew and Aramaic, it is even more coherent in its rhetorical laws.

The Bavli's one voice utilizes only a few, well-modulated tones: a scale of not many notes. When we classify more than three thousand composites, spread over eleven tractates, we find that nearly 90 percent of the whole comprises Mishnah commentary of various kinds; not only so, but the variety of the types of Mishnah commentary is limited, as a review of the representation of Temurah in detail, and of the ten tractates of our sample in brief characterization, has shown. Cogent composites are further devoted to Scripture or to topics of a moral or theological character not closely tied to the exegesis of verses of Scripture; these form in the aggregate approximately 10 percent of the whole number of composites, but, of tractates to begin with not concerned with scriptural or theological topics (in our sample these are Sanhedrin and Berakhot), they make up scarcely 3 percent of the whole. So the Bavli has one voice, and it is the voice of a person or persons who propose to speak about one document and to do so in some few ways. Let me spell out precisely what I mean. The results of the survey of eleven tractates and classification of all of the composites of each one of them yields firm and one-sided results.

First, we are able to classify all composites in three principal categories: [1] exegesis and amplification of the law of the Mishnah; [2] exegesis and exposition of verses of, or topics in, Scripture; [3] free-standing composites devoted to topics other than those defined by the Mishnah or Scripture. That means that my initial proposal of a taxonomic system left no lacunae.

Second, with the classification in place, we see that much more than four-fifths of all composites of the Bavli address the Mishnah and systematically expound that document. These composites are subject to subclassification in two ways: Mishnah exegesis and speculation and abstract theorizing about the implications of the Mishnah's statements. The former type of composite, further, is to be classified in a few and simple taxa, for example, composites organized around [1] clarification of the statements of the Mishnah; [2] identification of the authority behind an anonymous statement in the Mishnah, [3] scriptural foundation for the Mishnah's rules; [4] citation and not seldom systematic exposition of the Tosefta's amplification of the Mishnah. That means that most of the Bavli is a systematic exposition of the Mishnah.

Third, the other fifth (or less) of a given tractate will comprise composites that take shape around [1] Scripture or [2] themes or topics of a generally theological or moral character. Distinguishing the latter from the former, of course, is merely formal; very often a scriptural topic will be set forth in a theological or moral framework, and very seldom does a composite on a topic omit all reference to the amplification of a verse or topic of Scripture. The proportion of a given tractate devoted to other than Mishnah exegesis and amplification is generally not more than 10 percent. My figure, as we shall note presently, is distorted by the special problems of tractates Sanhedrin and Berakhot, and, in the former, Chapter Eleven in particular.[4]

These two tractates prove anomalous for the categories I have invented, because both of them contain important components that are devoted to begin with to scriptural or theological topics. And it is these anomalies that called my attention to the necessity of a closer look at what I here call "miscellanies." To take the cases before us in particular, Tractate Sanhedrin Chapter Eleven, lists various scriptural figures in catalogues of those who do, or do not, inherit the world to come; it

---

[4]It obviously was this result that told me to select the two tractates for examination in this monograph.

further specifies certain doctrines that define the norms of the community of Israel that inherits the world to come. It will therefore prove quite natural that numerous composites will attend to scriptural or theological topics. Tractate Berakhot addresses matters of prayer and other forms of virtue, with the same consequence. In the analysis that follows, therefore, I calculate the averages of proportions of various types of composites both with and without these anomalous tractates. The upshot is that a rather inconsequential proportion of most tractates, and a small proportion of the whole, of the Bavli, is devoted to the systematic exposition of either verses of Scripture or topics of a theological or moral character. But even though the miscellanies prove anomalous within the Bavli, we are going to see that, in their own setting, viewed in relationship to one another, there are quite clear rules that govern throughout. Someone who had in hand a variety of compositions that were candidates for a composite of a miscellaneous character knew precisely what to choose for his work and exactly how to string together these composites. The one thing that he knew to begin with is that these composites would not serve the purpose of Mishnah commentary. I cannot point to a single miscellaneous composite that intersects with the Mishnah's propositions in any detailed way, and where the composite shares a topic with the Mishnah, the topical congruence plays no role in the framing of said composite. So, up front, we must recognize that the miscellany addresses a problem other than the exegesis and amplification of the Mishnah. The people who made it up then obeyed one rule that is clear at the outset: their "miscellany" would not address the Mishnah in any way at all. But then, if that rule of formation is sound, the miscellanies look considerably less miscellaneous than they did at the outset. Let us now consider in detail the eleven tractates' proportions of types of composites, to see the foundation for these generalizations.

TEMURAH

		NUMBER	PERCENT
1.	Exegesis of the Mishnah	58	75%
2.	Exegesis of Mishnah law	8	10%
3.	Speculation and Abstract Thought on Law	8	10%
4.	Scripture	3	4%
5.	Free-standing Composites	Not calculated	
6.	Miscellanies	0	–
		77	

SUKKAH

		NUMBER	PERCENT
1.	Exegesis of the Mishnah	141	89%
2.	Exegesis of the Mishnah's Law	8	5%
3.	Speculation and Abstract Thought on Law	4	2%
4.	Scripture	1	–
5.	Free-standing Composites	0	–
6.	Miscellanies	5	3%
		159	

KERITOT

		NUMBER	PERCENT
1.	Exegesis of the Mishnah	80	94%
2.	Exegesis of the Mishnah's Law	4	4%
3.	Speculation and Abstract Thought on Law	0	–
4.	Scripture	1	1%
5.	Free-standing Composites	0	–
6.	Miscellanies	0	–
		85	

ARAKHIN

		NUMBER	PERCENT
1.	Exegesis of the Mishnah	127	91%
2.	Exegesis of the Mishnah's Law	8	6%
3.	Speculation and Abstract Thought on Law	2	1.5%
4.	Scripture	0	–
5.	Free-standing Composites	2	1.5%
6.	Miscellanies	0	–
		139	

The importance of the free-standing composites is not reflected by the count, since both items are enormous and the first of the two serves as the prologue to the tractate as a whole.

NIDDAH

		NUMBER	PERCENT
1.	Exegesis of the Mishnah	290	97%
2.	Exegesis of the Mishnah's Law	6	2%
3.	Speculation and Abstract Thought on Law	0	–
4.	Scripture	0	–
5.	Free-standing Composites	3	1%
6.	Miscellanies	0	–
		299	

ABODAH ZARAH

		NUMBER	PERCENT
1.	Exegesis of the Mishnah	244	85%
2.	Exegesis of the Mishnah's Law	3	1%
3.	Speculation and Abstract Thought on Law	0	–
4.	Scripture	28	10%
5.	Free-standing Composites	12	4%
6.	Miscellanies	0	–
		287	

SOTAH

		NUMBER	PERCENT
1.	Exegesis of the Mishnah	193	91%
2.	Exegesis of the Mishnah's Law	0	–
3.	Speculation and Abstract Thought on Law	0	–
4.	Scripture	10	5%
5.	Free-standing Composites	8	4%
6.	Miscellanies	1	0.5%
		212	

BABA MESIA

		NUMBER	PERCENT
1.	Exegesis of the Mishnah	334	86%
2.	Exegesis of the Mishnah's Law	42	11%
3.	Speculation and Abstract Thought on Law	0	–
4.	Scripture	2	0.5%
5.	Free-standing Composites	10	3%
6.	Miscellanies	0	–
		388	

BEKHOROT

	NUMBER	PERCENT
1. Exegesis of the Mishnah	281	98%
2. Exegesis of the Mishnah's Law	2	1%
3. Speculation and Abstract Thought on Law	–	–
4. Scripture	–	–
5. Free-standing Composites	2	1%
6. Miscellanies	–	–
	285	

BERAKHOT

	NUMBER	PERCENT
1. Exegesis of the Mishnah	330	59%
2. Exegesis of the Mishnah's Law	3	0.5%
3. Speculation and Abstract Thought on Law	0	–
4. Scripture	34	6%
5. Free-standing Composites	187	34%
6. Miscellanies	2	0.4%
	556	

SANHEDRIN

	NUMBER	PERCENT
1. Exegesis of the Mishnah	313	45%
2. Exegesis of the Mishnah's Law	6	0.8%
3. Speculation and Abstract Thought on Law	6	0.8%
4. Scripture	163	23%
5. Free-standing Composites	214	30%
6. Miscellanies	0	–
	702	

Seen in the aggregate, the proportions of the eleven tractates devoted solely to Mishnah exegesis average 83 percent. If we omit reference to the two clearly anomalous tractates, Berakhot and Sanhedrin, the proportion of Mishnah exegesis rises to 89.5 percent. If, then, we combine exegesis of the Mishnah and exegesis of the broader implications of the Mishnah's law – and in the process of classification, it was not always easy to keep these items apart in a consistent way – we see a still more striking result. More than 86 percent of the whole of our tractates is devoted to the exegesis of the Mishnah and the amplification of the implications of its law; without the anomalous tractates, the proportion is close to 94 to 95 percent.

We dismiss as a taxon that did not serve any useful purpose the one that was supposed to identify "speculation and abstract thought on law." As a matter of fact, nearly all speculative or abstract thought on law, measured by the number of composites devoted to that purpose, treats the Mishnah's concrete laws; nearly all speculation is precipitated by an inquiry into the premises of those laws. There is virtually no abstract thought on law that does not aim at the clarification of the Mishnah's laws in particular. That result is as stunning as the foregoing.

Composites devoted to Scripture, not the Mishnah, are calculated in two ways. In the first nine tractates, I counted each composite as one entry, just as, overall, I counted each composite devoted to the Mishnah as one entry. On the surface such a mode of counting understated the proportions of the anomalous tractates that are devoted to Scripture exegesis, or to topics drawn from Scripture. Overall, we should expect to find something on the order of 4 percent of a given tractate made up of Scripture composites. If we eliminate the two anomalous tractates, the anticipated proportion would be 2 percent. Free-standing composites, formed in general around themes, rather than passages of the Mishnah or sequences of verses of Scripture or topics provided by Scripture, average 10 percent for eight tractates (omitted: Temurah, Sukkah, Keritot, where I found none), and, without the anomalous ones, 1.5 to 3 percent. The latter figure seems to me more probable than the former.

So I have demonstrated beyond any reasonable doubt that the Talmud speaks through one voice, that voice of logic that with vast assurance reaches into our own minds and by asking the logical and urgent next question tells us what we should be thinking. Fixing our attention upon the Mishnah, the Talmud's rhetoric seduces us into joining its analytical inquiry, always raising precisely the question that should trouble us (and that would trouble us if we knew all of the pertinent details as well as the Talmud does). The Bavli speaks about the Mishnah in essentially a single voice, about fundamentally few things. Its mode of speech as much as of thought is uniform throughout. Diverse topics produce slight differentiation in modes of analysis. The same sorts of questions phrased in the same rhetoric – a moving, or dialectical, argument, composed of questions and answers – turn out to pertain equally well to every subject and problem. The Talmud's discourse forms a closed system, in which people say the same thing about everything. The fact that the Talmud speaks in a single voice supplies striking evidence [1] that the Talmud does speak in particular for the age in which its units of discourse took shape, and [2] that that work was done toward the end of that long period of Mishnah reception that began at the end of the second century and came to an end at the conclusion of the sixth century.

When I speak of the Bavli's one voice, as now is clear, I mean to say it everywhere speaks uniformly, consistently, and predictably. The voice is the voice of a book. The message is one deriving from a community, the collectivity of sages for whom and to whom the book speaks. The document seems, in the main, to intend to provide notes, an abbreviated script which anyone may use to reconstruct and reenact formal discussions of problems: about this, one says that. Curt and often arcane, these notes can be translated only with immense bodies of inserted explanation. All of this script of information is public and undifferentiated, not individual and idiosyncratic. We must assume people took for granted that, out of the signs of speech, it would be possible for anyone to reconstruct speech, doing so in accurate and fully conventional ways. So the literary traits of the document presuppose a uniform code of communication: a single voice.

So it is time to ask the purpose of that composition: what the authors, authorships, or framers of the document wished to say through the writing that they have given us. If there is a single governing method, then what can we expect to learn about the single, repeated message? The evidence before us indicates that the purpose of the Talmud is to clarify and amplify selected passages of the Mishnah. We may say very simply that the Mishnah is about life, and the Talmud is about the Mishnah. That is to say, while the Mishnah records rules governing the conduct of the holy life of Israel, the holy people, the Talmud concerns itself with the details of the Mishnah. The one is descriptive and free-standing, the other analytical and contingent. Were there no Mishnah, there would be no Talmud. But what is the message of the method, which is to insist upon the Mishnah's near monopoly over serious discourse? To begin with, the very character of the Talmud tells us the sages' view of the Mishnah. The Mishnah presented itself to them as constitutive, the text of ultimate concern. So, in our instance, the Mishnah speaks of a quarrel over a coat, the Talmud, of the Mishnah's provision of an oath as a means of settling the quarrel in a fair way: substance transformed into process. What the framers of the Bavli wished to say about the Mishnah will guide us toward the definition of the message of their method, but it will not tell us what that message was, or why it was important. A long process of close study of texts is required to guide us toward the center of matters. The upshot is simple. We may speak about "the Talmud," its voice, its purposes, its mode of constructing a view of the Israelite world. The reason is that, when we claim "the Talmud" speaks, we replicate both the main lines of chronology and the literary character of the document. These point toward the formation of the bulk of materials – its units of discourse – in a process lasting (to take a guess) about half a century, prior to the ultimate arrangement of these units of discourse around passages of the Mishnah and the closure and redaction of the whole into the document we now know. What comes next? Well, now that we know that the Bavli is a document of remarkable integrity, repeatedly insisting upon the harmony of the parts within a whole and unitary structure of belief and behavior, we want to know what the Bavli says: the one thing that is repeated in regard to many things. Dismantling ("deconstructing") its components and identifying them, perhaps even describing the kinds of compilations that the authors of those components can have had in mind in writing their compositions – these activities of literary criticism yield no insight into the religious system that guided the document's framers. But the Talmud of Babylonia recapitulates, in grand and acute detail, a religious system, and the generative problematic of that writing directs our attention not to the aesthetics of writing as literature, but to the religion of writing as a document of faith in the formation of the social order.

Recognizing the orderly character of the Bavli, we may now turn to the agglutinative composites that do not conform to the norms of rhetorical form and logical cogency that impart to the Bavli its wonderful cogency. Forthwith, let us turn to a sample of what I characterize as a miscellany. It is given in Bavli Baba Batra Chapter Five, starting at 73A, with the further folio numbers signified in the text.

IV.2   A.   *Our rabbis have taught on Tannaite authority:*

      B.   He who sells a ship has sold the wooden implements and the water tank on it.

      C.   R. Nathan says, "He who sells a ship has sold its rowboat."

      D.   Sumkhos says, "He who has sold a ship has sold its lighter" [T. B.B. 4:1A-C].

IV.3   A   *Said Raba, "The rowboat and the lighter are pretty much the same thing. But R. Nathan, who was a Babylonian, uses the word familiar to him, as people use that word in Babylonia when referring to the rowboat that is used at the shallows, and Sumkhos, who was from the Land of Israel, used the word that is familiar to him, as people say in the verse, 'And your residue shall be taken away in lighters' (Amos 4:2)."*

IV.4   A   *Said Rabbah, "Sailors told me, 'The wave that sinks a ship appears with a white froth of fire at the crest, and when stricken with clubs on which is incised, "I am that I am, Yah, the Lord of Hosts, Amen, Amen, Selah," it will subside [and not sink the ship].'"*

IV.5   A   *Said Rabbah, "Sailors told me, 'Between one wave and another there is a distance of three hundred parasangs, and the height of the wave is the same three hundred parasangs. Once, when we were on a voyage, a wave lifted us up so high that we could see the resting place of the smallest star, and there was a flash, as if one shot forty arrows of iron; and if it had lifted us* up any higher, we would have been burned by the heat. And one wave called to the next, "Friend, have you left anything in the world that you did not wash away? I'll go and wipe it out." And the other said, "Go see the power of the master, by whose command I must not pass the sand of the shore by even so much as the breadth of a thread: 'Fear you not me? says the Lord? Will you not tremble at my presence, who have placed the sand for the bound of the sea, an everlasting ordinance, which it cannot pass' (Jer. 5:22).'"

IV.6 A Said Rabbah, "I personally saw Hormin, son of Lilith, running on the parapet of the wall of Mahoza, and a rider, galloping below on horseback, could not catch up with him. Once they put a saddle for him on two mules, which [73 B] stood on two bridges of the Rognag, and he jumped from one to the other, backward and forward, holding two cups of wine in his hands, pouring from one to the other without spilling a drop on the ground. It was a stormy day: 'they that go down to the sea in ships mounted up to heaven, they went down to the deeps' (Ps. 107:27). Now when the state heard about this, they killed him."

IV.7 A Said Rabbah bar bar Hannah, "I personally saw a day-old antelope as big as Mount Tabor. How big is Mount Tabor? Four parasangs. Its neck was three parasangs long, and his head rested on a spot a parasang and a half. Its ball of shit blocked up the Jordan River."

IV.8 A And said Rabbah bar bar Hannah, "I personally saw a frog as big as the Fort of Hagronia – how big is that? sixty houses! – and a snake came along and swallowed the frog; a raven came along and swallowed the snake; and perched on a tree. So you can just imagine how strong was the tree."

B. Said R. Pappa bar Samuel "If I weren't there on the spot, I would never have believed it!"

IV.9 A And said Rabbah bar bar Hannah, "Once we were traveling on a ship, and we saw a fish [whale] in the nostrils of which a mud eater had entered. The water cast up the fish and threw it on the shore. Sixty towns were destroyed by it, sixty towns got their food from it, and sixty towns salted the remnants, and from one of its eyeballs three hundred kegs of oil were filled. Coming back twelve months later, we saw that they were cutting rafters from the skeleton and rebuilding the towns."

IV.10 A And said Rabbah bar bar Hannah, "Once we were traveling on a ship, and we saw a fish the back of which was covered with sand out of which grass was growing. We thought it was dry land so we went up and baked and cooked on the back of the fish. When the back got hot, it rolled over, and if the ship hadn't been nearby, we would have drowned."

IV.11 A And said Rabbah bar bar Hannah, "Once we were traveling on a ship, and the ship sailed between one fin of a fish and the other for three days and three nights; the fish was swimming upwards and we were floating downwards [with the wind]."

B. Now, should you suppose that the ship did not sail fast enough, when R. Dimi came, he said, "It covered sixty parasangs in the time that it takes to heat a kettle of water. And when a cavalryman shot an arrow, the ship outstripped the arrow."

C. R. Ashi said, "That was one of the small sea monsters, the ones that have only two fins."

IV.12 A And said Rabbah bar bar Hannah, "Once we were traveling on a ship, and we saw a bird standing in the water only up to its ankles, with its head *touching the sky. So we thought the water wasn't very deep, and we thought of going down to cool ourselves, but an echo called out, 'Don't go down into the water here, for a carpenter's axe dropped into this water seven years ago, and it hasn't yet reached the bottom.' And it was not only deep but also rapidly flowing."*

B. *Said R. Ashi, "The bird was the wild cock, for it is written, 'And the wild cock is with me [with God in heaven]' (Ps 50:11)."*

IV.13 A. *And said Rabbah bar bar Hannah, "Once we were traveling in the desert, and we saw geese whose feathers fell out because they were so fat, and streams of fat flowed under them. I said to them, 'May we have a share of your meat in the world to come?' One of them lifted a wing, the other a leg [showing me what my portion would be]. When I came before R. Eleazar, he said to me, 'Israel will be called to account on account of these geese.'"* [Slotki: The protracted suffering of the geese caused by their growing fatness is due to Israel's sins, which delay the coming of the Messiah.]

IV.14 A. *And said Rabbah bar bar Hannah, "Once we were traveling in the desert, and a Tai-Arab joined us, who could pick up sand and smell it and tell us which was the road to one place and which to another. We said to him, 'How far are we from water?' He said to us, 'Give me sand.' We gave him some, and he said to us, 'Eight parasangs.' When we gave him some sand later, he told us that we were three parasangs off. I had changed the sand, but I was not able to confuse him.*

B. *"He said to me, 'Come on, and I'll show you the dead of the wilderness (Num. 14:32ff.). I went with him and saw them. They looked as though they were exhilarated. [74A] They slept on their backs and the knee of one of them was raised. The Arab merchant passed under the knee, riding on a camel with a spear on high and did not touch it. I cut off one corner of the purple-blue cloak of one of them, but we could not move away. He said to me, 'If you've taken something from them, return it, for we have a tradition that if anybody takes something from them, he cannot move away.' I went and returned it and then we could move away.*

C. *"When I came before rabbis, they said to me, 'Every Abba is an ass, and every son of Bar Hana is an idiot. What did you do that for? Was it to find out whether the law accords with the House of Shammai or the House of Hillel? You could have counted the threads and the joints [to find out the answer to your question].'*

D. *"He said to me, 'Come and I will show you Mount Sinai.' I went and saw scorpions surrounding it, and they stood like white asses. I heard an echo saying, 'Woe is me that I have taken an oath, and now that I have taken the oath, who will release me from it?' When I came before rabbis, they said to me, 'Every Abba is an ass, and every son of Bar Hana is an idiot.' You should have said, 'It is released for you.' But I was thinking that perhaps it was an oath in connection with the flood [which favored humanity]."*

E. *And rabbis?*

F. If so, what need is there for the language, "woe is me"?

G. *"He said to me, 'Come and I will show you those who were associated with Korah who were swallowed up (Num. 16:32ff.). I saw two cracks that emitted smoke. I took a piece of clipped wool and soaked it in water, put it on the point of a spear, and pushed it in there. When I took it out, it was singed. He said to me, 'Listen closely to what you will hear,' and I heard them say, 'Moses and his Torah are truth, and we are liars.' He said to me, 'Every thirty days Gehenna causes them to turn over as one rotates meat in a pot, and this is what they say: "Moses and his Torah are truth and we are liars."'"*

H   *"He said to me, 'Come and I will show you where heaven and earth meet.' I took my basket it and put it in a window of heaven. When I finished saying my prayers, I looked for it but did not find it. I said to him, 'Are there thieves here?' He said to me, 'It is the result of the wheel of heaven turning, wait here until tomorrow, and you will find it.'"*

IV.15 A   *R. Yohanan told this story: "Once we were traveling along on a ship, and we saw a fish that raised its head from the sea. Its eyes were like two moons, and water streamed from its nostrils like the two rivers of Sura."*

IV.16 A   *R. Safra told this story: "Once we were traveling along on a ship, and we saw a fish that raised its head from the sea. It had horns on which was engraven: 'I am a lesser creature of the sea. I am three hundred parasangs long, and I am going into the mouth of Leviathan.'"*

B.   *Said R. Ashi, "That was a sea goat that searches for food, and has horns."*

IV.17 A   *R. Yohanan told this story: "Once we were traveling along on a ship, and we saw a chest in which were set jewels and pearls, surrounded by a kind of fish called a Karisa-fish. A diver went down [74B] to bring up the chest, but the fish realized it and was about to wrench his thigh. He poured on it a bottle of vinegar, and it sank. An echo came forth, saying to us, 'What in the world have you got to do with the chest of the wife of R. Hanina b. Dosa, who is going to store in it the purple-blue for the righteous in the world to come.'"*

IV.18 A   *R. Judah the Hindu told this story: "Once we were traveling along on a ship, and we saw a jewel with a snake wrapped around it. A diver went down to bring up the jewel. The snake drew near, to swallow the ship. A raven came and bit off its head. The waters turned to blood. Another snake and took the head of the snake and attached it to the body again, and it revived. The snake again came to swallow the ship. A bird again came and cut off its head. The diver seized the jewel and threw it into the ship. We had salted birds. We put the stone on them, and they took it up and flew away with it."*

IV.19 A.   *Our rabbis have taught on Tannaite authority:*

B.   There was the case involving R. Eliezer and R. Joshua, who were traveling on a ship. R. Eliezer was sleeping, and R. Joshua was awake. R. Joshua shuddered and R. Eliezer woke up. He said to him, "What's wrong, Joshua? How come you trembled?"

C.   He said to him, "I saw a great light on the sea."

D.   He said to him, "It might have been the eye of Leviathan that you saw, for it is written, 'His eyes are like the eyelids of the morning' (Isa. 27:1)."

IV.20 A   *Said R. Ashi, "Said to me Huna bar Nathan, 'Once we were traveling in the desert, and we had taken with us a leg of meat. We cut it open, picked out [what we are not allowed to eat] and put it on the grass. While we were going to get some wood, the leg returned to its original form, and we roasted it. When we came back after twelve months, we saw the coals still glowing. When I presented the matter to Amemar, he said to me, "The* grass was an herb that can unite severed parts, and the coals were broom *[which burns a long time inside, while the surface is extinguished]."'"*

IV.21 A.   "And God created the great sea monsters" (Gen. 1:21):

B.   *Here this is interpreted, "the sea gazelles."*

C.   R. Yohanan said, "This refers to Leviathan [Slotki:] the slant serpent, and Leviathan the tortuous serpent: 'In that day the Lord with his sore and great and strong sword will punish Leviathan the slant serpent and Leviathan the tortuous serpent' (Isa. 27:1)."

IV.22 A   Said R. Judah said Rab, "Whatever the Holy One, blessed be He, created in his world did he create male and female, and so, too, Leviathan the slant serpent and Leviathan the tortuous serpent he created male and female, and if they had mated with one another, they would have destroyed the whole world.

B.   "What did the Holy One, blessed be He, do? He castrated the male and killed the female and salted it for the righteous in the world to come: 'And he will slay the dragon that is in the sea' (Isa. 27:1).

C.   "And also Behemoth on a thousand hills (Ps. 50:10) he created male and female, and if they had mated with one another, they would have destroyed the whole world.

D.   "What did the Holy One, blessed be He, do? He castrated the male and quick-froze the female and preserved her for the righteous in the world to come: 'Lo, now his strength is in his loins' (Job 40:16) speaks of the male, 'and his force is in the stays of his body' (Job 40:16) speaks of the female."

E.   *In that other case, too, while castrating the male, why did he not simply quick-freeze the female [instead of killing it]?*

F.   *Fish is dissolute [and cooling would not have sufficed].*

G.   *Why not do it in reverse order?*

H.   *If you wish, I shall say that the female fish preserved in salt tastes better, and if you wish, I shall say, "Because it is written, 'There is Leviathan whom you have formed to sport with' (Ps. 104:26), and with the female that would not be seemly.*

I.   Here, too, in the case of the Behemoth, why not preserve the female in salt?

J.   *Salted fish tastes good, salted meat doesn't.*

IV.23 A   And said R. Judah said Rab, "When the Holy One, blessed be He, proposed to create the world, he said to the prince of the sea, 'Open your mouth, and swallow all the water in the world.'

B.   "He said to him, 'Lord of the world, it is enough that I stay in my own territory.'

C.   "So on the spot he hit him with his foot and killed him: 'He stirs up the sea with his power and by his understanding he smites through Rahab' (Job 26:12)."

D.   *Said R. Isaac, "That bears the implication that the name of the prince of the sea is Rahab."*

E.   [Rab continues,] "And had the waters not covered him over, no creature could stand because of his stench: 'They shall not hurt nor destroy in all my holy mountain...as the waters cover the sea' (Isa. 11:9). Do not read 'they cover the sea' but 'they cover the angel of the sea.'"

IV.24 A. And said R. Judah said Rab, "The Jordan issues from the cave of Paneas."

B. *So, too, it has been taught on Tannaite authority:*

C. The Jordan issues from the cave of Paneas.

D. And it goes through the Lake of Sibkay and the Lake of Tiberias and rolls down into the great sea, and from there it rolls onward until it rushes into the mouth of Leviathan: "He is confident because the Jordan rushes forth to his mouth" (Job 40:23).

E. *Objected Raba bar Ulla, "This verse speaks of* Behemoth on a thousand hills."

F. Rather, said Raba bar Ulla, "When is Behemoth on a thousand years confident? When the Jordan rushes into the mouth of Leviathan." [Slotki: So long as Leviathan is alive, Behemoth also is safe.]

IV.25 A. *When R. Dimi came, he said R. Yohanan said, "What is the meaning of the verse,* 'For he has founded it upon the seas and established it upon the floods' (Ps. 24:2)? This refers to the seven seas and four rivers that surround the land of Israel. And what are the seven seas? The sea of Tiberias, the sea of Sodom, the sea of Helath, the sea of Hiltha, the sea of Sibkay, the sea of Aspamia, and the Great sea. And what are the four rivers? The Jordan, the Yarmuk, the Keramyhon, and the Pigah."

IV.26 A. *When R. Dimi came, he said R. Yohanan said,* "Gabriel is destined to organize a hunt [75A] for Leviathan: 'Can you draw out Leviathan with a fish hook, or press down his tongue with a cord' (Job 40:25). And if the Holy One, blessed be He, does not help him, he will never be able to prevail over him: 'He only that made him can make his sword approach him' (Job 40:19)."

IV.27 A. *When R. Dimi came, he said R. Yohanan said,* "When Leviathan is hungry, he sends out fiery breath from his mouth and boils all the waters of the deep: 'He makes the deep to boil like a pot' (Job 41:23). And if he did not put his head into the Garden of Eden, no creature could endure his stench: 'he makes the sea like a spiced broth' (Job 41:23). And when he is thirsty, he makes the sea into furrows: 'He makes a path to shine after him' (Job 41:24)."

B. Said R. Aha bar Jacob, "The great deep does not recover its strength for seventy years: 'One thinks the deep to be hoary' (Job 41:24), and hoary old age takes seventy years."

IV.28 A. Rabbah said R. Yohanan said, "The Holy One, blessed be He, is destined to make a banquet for the righteous out of the meat of Leviathan: 'Companions will make a banquet of it' (Job 40:30). The meaning of 'banquet' derives from the usage of the same word in the verse, 'And he prepared for them a great banquet and they ate and drank' (2 Kgs. 6:23)."

B. "'Companions' can refer only to disciples of sages, in line with this usage: 'You that dwells in the gardens, the companions hearken for your voice, cause me to hear it' (Song 8:13). The rest of the creature will be cut up and sold in the markets of Jerusalem: 'They will part him among the Canaanites' (Job 40:30), and 'Canaanites' must be merchants, in line with this usage: 'As for the Canaanite, the balances of deceit are in his hand, he loves to oppress' (Hos. 12:8).

If you prefer: 'Whose merchants are princes, whose traffickers are the honorable of the earth' (Isa. 23:8)."

IV.29 A   Rabbah said R. Yohanan said, "The Holy One, blessed be He, is destined to make a tabernacle for the righteous out of the hide of Leviathan: 'Can you fill tabernacles with his skin' (Job 40:31). If someone has sufficient merit, a tabernacle is made for him; if he does not have sufficient merit, a mere shade is made for him: 'And his head with a fish covering' (Job 40:31). If someone has sufficient merit, a shade is made for him, if not, then a mere necklace is made for him: 'And necklaces about your neck' (Prov. 1:9). If someone has sufficient merit, a necklace is made for him; if not, then an amulet: 'And you will bind him for your maidens' (Job 40:29).

B.   "And the rest of the beast will the Holy One, blessed be He, spread over the walls of Jerusalem, and the glow will illuminate the world from one end to the other: 'And nations shall walk at your light, and kings at the brightness of your rising' (Isa. 60:3)."

IV.30 A.   "And I will make your pinnacles of rubies" (Isa. 54:12):

B.   *Said R. Samuel bar Nahmani, "There is a dispute between two angels in the firmament, Gabriel and Michael, and some say, two Amoraim in the West, and who might they be? Judah and Hezekiah, sons of R. Hiyya.*

C.   *"One said, 'The word translated rubies means onyx....'*

D.   *"The other said, 'It means jasper.'*

E.   *"Said to them the Holy One, blessed be He, 'Let it be in accord with both this opinion and that opinion.'"*

IV.31 A.   "And your gates of carbuncles" (Isa. 60:3):

B.   *That is in line with what what said when R. Yohanan went into session and expounded as follows: "The Holy One, blessed be He, is destined to bring jewels and pearls that are thirty cubits by thirty and will cut out openings from them ten cubits by twenty, setting them up at the gates of Jerusalem."*

C.   A certain disciple ridiculed him, *"Well, jewels even the size of the egg of a dove are not available, so will jewels of such dimensions be found?"*

D.   *After a while his ship went out to sea. He saw ministering angels engaged in cutting up jewels and pearls thirty cubits by thirty, on which were engravings ten by twenty. He said to him, "For whom are these?"*

E.   *They said to him, "The Holy One, blessed be He, is destined to set them up at the gates of Jerusalem."*

F.   *The man came before R. Yohanan. He said to him, "Give your exposition, my lord. It is truly fitting for you to give an exposition. For just as you said, so I myself have seen."*

G.   He said to him, "Empty-headed idiot! If you had not seen, you would not have believed! So you ridicule the teachings of sages." He set his eye on him and the student turned into a heap of bones.

IV.32 A.   *An objection was raised:*

B.   "And I will lead you upright" (Lev. 26:13) –

C.   [Since the word for "upright" can be read to mean, at twice the normal height], R. Meir says, "That means, two hundred cubits, twice the height of the First Man."

D.   R. Judah says, "A hundred cubits, the height of the temple and its walls: 'We whose sons are as plants grown up in their youth, whose daughters are as corner pillars carved after the fashion of the temple' (Ps. 144:12)." [Slotki: How then in view of their increase to a hundred cubits in height, requiring correspondingly high gates, can Yohanan say that the gates were only twenty cubits in height?]

E. *When R. Yohanan made that statement, it was with reference only to [Slotki:] ventilation windows.*

IV.33 A. And said Rabbah said R. Yohanan, "The Holy One, blessed be He, is destined to make seven canopies for every righteous person: 'And the Lord will create over the whole habitation of Mount Zion and over her assemblies a cloud of smoke by day and the shining of a flaming fire by night, for over all the glory shall be a canopy' (Isa. 4:5). This teaches that for every one will the Holy One create a canopy in accord with the honor that is due him."

B. Why is smoke needed for the canopy?

C. Said R. Hanina, "It is because everyone who treats disciples of sages in a niggardly way in this world will have his eyes filled with smoke in the world to come."

D. Why is fire needed in a canopy?

E. Said R. Hanina, "This teaches that each one will be burned by [envy for] the canopy of the other. Woe for the shame, woe for the reproach!"

IV.34 A. Along these same lines you may say: "And you shall put some of your honor upon him" (Num. 27:20) – but not of your honor.

B. The elders of that generation said, "The face of Moses glows like the face of the sun, the face of Joshua like the face of the moon.

C. "Woe for the shame, woe for the reproach!"

IV.35 A. Said R. Hama bar Hanina, "Ten canopies did the Holy One, blessed be He, make for the First Man in the garden of Eden: 'You were in Eden, the garden of God; every precious stone was your covering, the cornelian, the topaz, the emerald, the beryl, the onyx, the jasper, the sapphire, the carbuncle, and the emerald and gold' (Ezek. 28:13)."

B. Mar Zutra said, "Eleven: 'every precious stone.'"

C. Said R. Yohanan, "The least of them all was gold, *since it was mentioned last.*"

IV.36 A. *What is the meaning of* "by the work of your timbrels and holes" (Ezek. 28:13)?

B. Said R. Judah said Rab, "Said the Holy One, blessed be He, to Hiram, king of Tyre, 'I looked at you [for your arrogance] when I created the excretory holes of human beings."

C. *And some say that this is what he said to him,* "I looked at you [75B] when I decreed the death penalty against the first Man."

IV.37 A. *What is the meaning of* "and over her assemblies" (Isa. 4:5)?

B. Said Rabbah said R. Yohanan, "Jerusalem in the age to come will not be like Jerusalem in this age. To Jerusalem in this age anyone who wants to go up may go up. But to Jerusalem in the age to come only those who are deemed worthy of coming will go up."

IV.38 A. And said Rabbah said R. Yohanan, "The righteous are destined to be called by the name of the Holy One, blessed be He: 'Every one that is called by my name, and whom I have created for my glory, I have formed him, yes, I have made him' (Isa. 43:7)."

IV.39 A   Said R. Samuel bar Nahmani said R. Yohanan, "There are three who
           are called by the name of the Holy One, blessed be He, and these
           are they: the righteous, the Messiah, and Jerusalem.

    B.   "The righteous, as we have just said.

    C.   "The Messiah: 'And this is the name whereby he shall be called, the
           Lord is our righteousness' (Jer. 23:6).

    D.   "Jerusalem: 'It shall be eighteen thousand reeds round about, and
           the name of the city from that day shall be, "the Lord is there"
           (Ezek. 48:35). Do not read 'there' but 'its name.'"

IV.40 A   Said R. Eleazar, "The time will come when 'holy' will be said before
           the name of the righteous as it is said before the name of the Holy
           One, blessed be He: 'And it shall come to pass that he that is left in
           Zion and he that remains in Jerusalem shall be called holy' (Isa.
           4:3)."

IV.41 A   And said Rabbah said R. Yohanan, "The Holy One, blessed be He, is
           destined to lift up Jerusalem to a height of three parasangs: 'And
           she shall be lifted up and be settled in her place' (Isa. 4:3). '...In her
           place' means 'like her place' [Slotki: Jerusalem will be lifted up to a
           height equal to the extent of the space it occupies]."

IV.42 A   *So how do we know that the place that Jerusalem occupied was three
           parasangs?*

    B.   Said Rabbah, "Said to me a certain elder, 'I myself saw the original
           Jerusalem, and it filled up three parasangs.'"

IV.43 A   And lest you suppose that there will be pain in the ascension,
           Scripture states, "Who are these that fly as a cloud and as the doves
           to their cotes" (Isa. 60:8).

    B.   *Said R. Pappa, "You may derive from that statement the fact that a cloud
           rises to a height of three parasangs."*

IV.44 A   Said R. Hanina bar Pappa, "The Holy One, blessed be He, wanted
           to give Jerusalem a fixed size: 'Then said I, Whither do you go?
           And he said to me, To measure Jerusalem, to see what is its breadth
           and what is its length' (Zech. 2:6).

    B.   "Said the ministering angels before the Holy One, blessed be He,
           'Lord of the world, you have created in your world any number of
           cities for the nations of the earth, and you did not fix the
           measurements of their length or breadth. So are you going to fix
           measurements for Jerusalem, in the midst of which are your name,
           sanctuary, and the righteous?'"

    C.   "Then: 'An angel said to him, Run, speak to this young man, saying,
           Jerusalem shall be inhabited without walls, for the multitude of
           men and cattle therein' (Zech. 2:8)."

IV.45 A   Said R. Simeon b. Laqish, "The Holy One, blessed be He, is destined
           to add to Jerusalem [Slotki:] a thousand gardens, a thousand
           towers, a thousand palaces, a thousand mansions. And each one of
           these will be as vast as Sepphoris in its hour of prosperity."

IV.46 A.   *It has been taught on Tannaite authority:*

    B.   Said R. Yosé, "I saw Sepphoris in its hour of prosperity, and in it
           were one hundred and eighty thousand markets for those who sold
           pudding [alone]."

IV.47 A   "And the side chambers were one over another, three and thirty
           times" (Ezek. 41:6):

B.   *What is the meaning of* three and thirty times?
C.   Said R. Pappi in the name of R. Joshua of Sikni, "If there will be three Jerusalems, each building will contain thirty dwellings piled up on top of one another; if there will be thirty Jerusalems, then each building will contain three apartments on top of one another."

From the viewpoint of the Bavli overall, the anomalous traits of the conglomerate are clear: once we have left behind us the Tannaite complement to the Mishnah, there is no clear purpose or point established in what follows, No. 3 provides a talmud to No. 2, that is to say, a well-crafted expansion, in this instance explaining the word choices of the prior item. But then we have a sequence of units that have only the most tenuous connection to the foregoing. Nos. 2-3 have spoken of ships, and No. 4 speaks of a ship. No. 4 does not continue No. 3 (nor does any following unit); it is parachuted down because of a shared subject, that alone. But even the subject is not a substantial point in common, since No. 4 wants to talk about ships that sink and how God participates in the matter, and nothing could be further from the frame of reference of No. 3.

What, then, are the units that do coalesce in the conglomerate that follows? Clearly, Nos. 4, 5 talk about the supernatural in connection with ships that founder at sea. No. 6 runs along the same lines, but its connection to No. 5 is not much tighter than that of No. 4 to No. 3. No. 7, however, is another matter; it shares the "I personally saw" formula, and not only so, but what the master personally saw is a quite extraordinary thing. So we can see how the compositions at Nos. 6, 7, 8 were formed into a piece; obviously, there is no explanation for why one is prior, another later, in the sequence, but there is a tight connection among the three items. Another such set begins at No. 9: "once we were traveling and...," which is the recurrent formula through Nos. 10-18+19. Now why have Nos. 9-18+19 been linked to Nos. 6-8? No. 8 speaks of "I personally saw a frog as big as...," and the next, "Once we were traveling and we saw a fish...as big as...." So the shift is from one rhetorical formula to another, but the subject matter remains the same. That strikes me as rather deft composite making indeed. The following items, Nos. 10-12, conform to the same pattern, talking about wonders of nature that a sage saw. No. 13 then marks another shift, however, since while the wonders of nature go forward, the fat geese are not really of the same order as the amazingly huge fish; and the lesson is a different once, namely, "Israel will be called to account...." That this is the commencement of a new topic, joined with the prior form, is shown at No. 14. Here we retain the "once we were traveling" formula; but we drop the sustaining theme, big fish and the like, and instead, we pick up the new motif, which is, God's judgment of Israel, now: the dead raised by Ezekiel, No. 14; and the same

story repeats the new motif, now the theme of God's judgment of Israel
in connection with the oath of Sinai. What follows at No. 15 is yet
another formula: "X told this story; once we were traveling...," and now
we revert to the theme of the wonders of nature. Have we really lost the
immediately prior theme? Not at all, for now our natural wonders turn
out to concern Leviathan, and, later on, that theme is explicitly joined to
the judgment of Israel: the righteous will get invited to the banquet at
which Leviathan will form the main course. So Nos. 15-17 (and much
that follows) turn out to link the two distinct themes that have been
joined, and, we see, the movement is quite deft. We have a rhetorical
device to link a variety of compositions on a given subject, we retain that
rhetorical device but shift the subject, then we shift the rhetorical device
but retain the same subject, and, finally, we join the two distinct subjects.
The theme of Leviathan holds together Nos. 21-22+23. No. 24 is tacked
on because Leviathan plays a role, and the same is to be said for Nos. 30.
The general interest in the restoration of Israel moves from the messianic
meal to Jerusalem, Nos. 31-45+46, 47. So there is a clear topical program,
and while we have a variety of subunits, these are put together in a way
that we can explain without stretching.

Abbreviating appropriately, let me now repeat the entire composite,
this time clearly distinguishing not the rhetorical but the topical (even
propositional) components. I simply set forth in a single column
everything I take to form a single large-scale composite, distinct from
everything fore and aft thereof.

IV.4   A   *Said Rabbah, "Sailors told me, 'The wave
            that sinks a ship appears with a white
            froth of fire at the crest, and when stricken
            with clubs on which is incised, "I am that
            I am, Yah, the Lord of Hosts, Amen,
            Amen, Selah," it will subside [and not
            sink the ship].'"*

IV.5   A   *Said Rabbah, "Sailors told me, 'Between
            one wave and another there is a distance of
            three hundred parasangs, and the height of
            the wave is the same three hundred
            parasangs. Once, when we were on a
            voyage, a wave lifted us up so high that
            we could see the resting place of the
            smallest star, and there was a flash, as if
            one shot forty arrows of iron; and if it had
            lifted us up any higher, we would have
            been burned by the heat. And one wave
            called to the next, "Friend, have you left
            anything in the world that you did not
            wash away? I'll go and wipe it out." And*

the other said, "Go see the power of the master, by whose command I must not pass the sand of the shore by even so much as the breadth of a thread: 'Fear you not me? says the Lord? Will you not tremble at my presence, who have placed the sand for the bound of the sea, an everlasting ordinance, which it cannot pass' (Jer. 5:22).""

IV.6 A Said Rabbah, "I personally saw Hormin, son of Lilith, running on the parapet of the wall of Mahoza, and a rider, galloping below on horseback, could not catch up with him. Once they put a saddle for him on two mules, which [73B] stood on two bridges of the Rognag, and he jumped from one to the other, backward and forward, holding two cups of wine in his hands, pouring from one to the other without spilling a drop on the ground. It was a stormy day: 'they that go down to the sea in ships mounted up to heaven, they went down to the deeps' (Ps. 107:27). Now when the state heard about this, they killed him."

IV.7 A Said Rabbah bar bar Hannah, "I personally saw a day-old antelope as big as Mount Tabor. How big is Mount Tabor? Four parasangs. Its neck was three parasangs long, and his head rested on a spot a parasang and a half. Its ball of shit blocked up the Jordan River."

IV.8 A And said Rabbah bar bar Hannah, "I personally saw a frog as big as the Fort of Hagronia – how big is that? sixty houses! – and a snake came along and swallowed the frog; a raven came along and swallowed the snake; and perched on a tree. So you can just imagine how strong was the tree."

IV.9 A And said Rabbah bar bar Hannah, "Once we were traveling on a ship, and we saw a fish [whale] in the nostrils of which a mud eater had entered. The water cast up the fish and threw it on the shore. Sixty towns were destroyed by it, sixty towns got their food from it, and sixty towns salted the remnants, and from one of its eyeballs three hundred kegs of oil were filled. Coming back twelve months later,

we saw that they were cutting rafters from
the skeleton and rebuilding the towns."

IV.10 A   *And said Rabbah bar bar Hannah, "Once
we were traveling on a ship, and we saw a
fish the back of which was covered with
sand out of which grass was growing. We
thought it was dry land so we went up
and baked and cooked on the back of the
fish. When the back got hot, it rolled over,
and if the ship hadn't been nearby, we
would have drowned."*

IV.11 A   *And said Rabbah bar bar Hannah, "Once
we were traveling on a ship, and the ship
sailed between one fin of a fish and the
other for three days and three nights; the
fish was swimming upwards and we were
floating downwards [with the wind]."*

IV.12 A   *And said Rabbah bar bar Hannah, "Once
we were traveling on a ship, and we saw a
bird standing in the water only up to its
ankles, with its head touching the sky. So
we thought the water wasn't very deep,
and we thought of going down to cool
ourselves, but an echo called out, 'Don't
go down into the water here, for a
carpenter's axe dropped into this water
seven years ago, and it hasn't yet reached
the bottom.' And it was not only deep but
also rapidly flowing."*

IV.13 A   *And said Rabbah bar bar Hannah, "Once
we were traveling in the desert, and we
saw geese whose feathers fell out because
they were so fat, and streams of fat flowed
under them. I said to them, 'May we have
a share of your meat in the world to
come?' One of them lifted a wing, the
other a leg [showing me what my portion
would be]. When I came before R.
Eleazar, he said to me, 'Israel will be
called to account on account of these
geese.'"* [Slotki: The protracted
suffering of the geese caused by their
growing fatness is due to Israel's sins,
which delay the coming of the
Messiah.]

IV.14 A   *And said Rabbah bar bar Hannah, "Once
we were traveling in the desert, and a Tai-
Arab joined us, who could pick up sand
and smell it and tell us which was the
road to one place and which to another.
We said to him, 'How far are we from*

water?' He said to us, 'Give me sand.'
We gave him some, and he said to us,
'Eight parasangs.' When we gave him
some sand later, he told us that we were
three parasangs off. I had changed the
sand, but I was not able to confuse him."

IV.15 A   R. Yohanan told this story: "Once we
were traveling along on a ship, and we
saw a fish that raised its head from the sea.
Its eyes were like two moons, and water
streamed from its nostrils like the two
rivers of Sura."

IV.16 A   R. Safra told this story: "Once we were
traveling along on a ship, and we saw a
fish that raised its head from the sea. It
had horns on which was engraven: 'I am a
lesser creature of the sea. I am three
hundred parasangs long, and I am going
into the mouth of Leviathan.'"

IV.17 A   R. Yohanan told this story: "Once we
were traveling along on a ship, and we
saw a chest in which were set jewels and
pearls, surrounded by a kind of fish called
a Karisa-fish. A diver went down [74B]
to bring up the chest, but the fish realized
it and was about to wrench his thigh. He
poured on it a bottle of vinegar, and it
sank. An echo came forth, saying to us,
'What in the world have you got to do
with the best of the wife of R. Hanina b.
Dosa, who is going to store in it the
purple-blue for the righteous in the world
to come.'"

IV.18 A   R. Judah the Hindu told this story: "Once
we were traveling along on a ship, and we
saw a jewel with a snake wrapped around
it. A diver went down to bring up the
jewel. The snake drew near, to swallow
the ship. A raven came and bit off its
head. The waters turned to blood.
Another snake and took the head of the
snake and attached it to the body again,
and it revived. The snake again came to
swallow the ship. A bird again came and
cut off its head. The diver seized the jewel
and threw it into the ship. We had salted
birds. We put the stone on them, and they
took it up and flew away with it."

IV.19 A   Our rabbis have taught on Tannaite
authority:

B.   There was the case involving R. Eliezer and R. Joshua, who were traveling on a ship. R. Eliezer was sleeping, and R. Joshua was awake. R. Joshua shuddered and R. Eliezer woke up. He said to him, "What's wrong, Joshua? How come you trembled?"

IV.20 A   *Said R. Ashi, "Said to me Huna bar Nathan, 'Once we were traveling in the desert, and we had taken with us a leg of meat. We cut it open, picked out [what we are not allowed to eat] and put it on the grass. While we were going to get some wood, the leg returned to its original form, and we roasted it. When we came back after twelve months, we saw the coals still glowing. When I presented the matter to Amemar, he said to me, "The grass was an herb that can unite severed parts, and the coals were broom [which burns a long time inside, while the surface is extinguished].""*

IV.21 A   "And God created the great sea monsters" (Gen. 1:21): R. Yohanan said, "This refers to Leviathan [Slotki:] the slant serpent, and Leviathan the tortuous serpent: 'In that day the Lord with his sore and great and strong sword will punish Leviathan the slant serpent and Leviathan the tortuous serpent' (Isa. 27:1)."

IV.22 A   Said R. Judah said Rab, "Whatever the Holy One, blessed be He, created in his world did he create male and female, and so, too, Leviathan the slant serpent and Leviathan the tortuous serpent he created male and female, and if they had mated with one another, they would have destroyed the whole world."

IV.23 A   And said R. Judah said Rab, "When the Holy One, blessed be He, proposed to create the world, he said to the prince of the sea, 'Open your mouth, and swallow all the water in the world.'"

IV.24 A   And said R. Judah said Rab, "The Jordan issues from the cave of Paneas."

IV.25 A   *When R. Dimi came, he said R. Yohanan said, "What is the meaning of the verse,*

'For he has founded it upon the seas and established it upon the floods' (Ps. 24:2)? This refers to the seven seas and four rivers that surround the land of Israel. And what are the seven seas? The sea of Tiberias, the sea of Sodom, the sea of Helath, the sea of Hiltha, the sea of Sibkay, the sea of Aspamia, and the Great sea. And what are the four rivers? The Jordan, the Yarmuk, the Keramyhon, and the Pigah."

IV.26 A *When R. Dimi came, he said R. Yohanan said,* "Gabriel is destined to organize a hunt [75A] for Leviathan: 'Can you draw out Leviathan with a fish hook, or press down his tongue with a cord' (Job 40:25). And if the Holy One, blessed be He, does not help him, he will never be able to prevail over him: 'He only that made him can make his sword approach him' (Job 40:19)."

IV.27 A *When R. Dimi came, he said R. Yohanan said,* "When Leviathan is hungry, he sends out fiery breath from his mouth and boils all the waters of the deep: 'He makes the deep to boil like a pot' (Job 41:23). And if he did not put his head into the Garden of Eden, no creature could endure his stench: 'he makes the sea like a spiced broth' (Job 41:23). And when he is thirsty, he makes the sea into furrows: 'He makes a path to shine after him' (Job 41:24)."

IV.28 A Rabbah said R. Yohanan said, "The Holy One, blessed be He, is destined to make a banquet for the righteous out of the meat of Leviathan: 'Companions will make a banquet of it' (Job 40:30). The meaning of 'banquet' derives from the usage of the same word in the verse, 'And he prepared for them a great banquet and they ate and drank' (2 Kgs. 6:23)."

IV.29 A Rabbah said R. Yohanan said, "The Holy One, blessed be He, is destined to make a tabernacle for the righteous out of the hide of Leviathan: 'Can you fill tabernacles with his skin' (Job 40:31). If someone has sufficient merit, a tabernacle is made for him; if

he does not have sufficient merit, a
mere shade is made for him: 'And his
head with a fish covering' (Job 40:31).
If someone has sufficient merit, a
shade is made for him, if not, then a
mere necklace is made for him: 'And
necklaces about your neck' (Prov. 1:9).
If someone has sufficient merit, a
necklace is made for him; if not, then
an amulet: 'And you will bind him for
your maidens' (Job 40:29)."

IV.30 A.   "And I will make your pinnacles of
            rubies" (Isa. 54:12):

B.   *Said R. Samuel bar Nahmani, "There is a
            dispute between two angels in the
            firmament, Gabriel and Michael, and some
            say, two Amoraim in the West, and who
            might they be? Judah and Hezekiah, sons of
            R. Hiyya.*

C.   *"One said, 'The word translated rubies
            means onyx....'*

D.   *"The other said, 'It means jasper.'*

E.   *"Said to them the Holy One, blessed be He,
            'Let it be in accord with both this opinion
            and that opinion.'"*

IV.31 A.   "And your gates of carbuncles" (Isa.
            60:3):

B.   *That is in line with what what said when R.
            Yohanan went into session and expounded
            as follows:* "The Holy One, blessed be He,
            is destined to bring jewels and pearls
            that are thirty cubits by thirty and will
            cut out openings from them ten cubits
            by twenty, setting them up at the gates
            of Jerusalem."

IV.32 A.   *An objection was raised:*

B.   "And I will lead you upright" (Lev.
            26:13) –

C.   [Since the word for "upright" can be
            read to mean, at twice the normal
            height], R. Meir says, "That means, two
            hundred cubits, twice the height of the
            First Man."

IV.33 A.   And said Rabbah said R. Yohanan, "The
            Holy One, blessed be He, is destined to
            make seven canopies for every righteous
            person: 'And the Lord will create over
            the whole habitation of Mount Zion and
            over her assemblies a cloud of smoke by
            day and the shining of a flaming fire by
            night, for over all the glory shall be a

canopy' (Isa. 4:5). This teaches that for every one will the Holy One create a canopy in accord with the honor that is due him."

IV.34 A. Along these same lines you may say: "And you shall put some of your honor upon him" (Num. 27:20) – but not of your honor.

B. The elders of that generation said, "The face of Moses glows like the face of the sun, the face of Joshua like the face of the moon."

IV.35 A. Said R. Hama bar Hanina, "Ten canopies did the Holy One, blessed be He, make for the First Man in the garden of Eden: 'You were in Eden, the garden of God; every precious stone was your covering, the cornelian, the topaz, the emerald, the beryl, the onyx, the jasper, the sapphire, the carbuncle, and the emerald and gold' (Ezek. 28:13)."

IV.36 A. *What is the meaning of* "by the work of your timbrels and holes" (Ezek. 28:13)?

B. Said R. Judah said Rab, "Said the Holy One, blessed be He, to Hiram, king of Tyre, 'I looked at you [for your arrogance] when I created the excretory holes of human beings."

C. *And some say that this is what he said to him*, "I looked at you [75B] when I decreed the death penalty against the first Man."

IV.37 A. *What is the meaning of* "and over her assemblies" (Isa. 4:5)?

B. Said Rabbah said R. Yohanan, "Jerusalem in the age to come will not be like Jerusalem in this age. To Jerusalem in this age anyone who wants to go up may go up. But to Jerusalem in the age to come only those who are deemed worthy of coming will go up."

IV.38 A. And said Rabbah said R. Yohanan, "The righteous are destined to be called by the name of the Holy One, blessed be He: 'Every one that is called by my name, and whom I have created for my glory, I have formed him, yes, I have made him' (Isa. 43:7)."

IV.39 A. Said R. Samuel bar Nahmani said R. Yohanan, "There are three who are called by the name of the Holy One,

B.

C.

D.

IV.40 A.

IV.41 A.

IV.42 A.

B.

IV.43 A.

IV.44 A.

B.

blessed be He, and these are they: the righteous, the Messiah, and Jerusalem.

"The righteous, as we have just said.

"The Messiah: 'And this is the name whereby he shall be called, the Lord is our righteousness' (Jer. 23:6).

"Jerusalem: 'It shall be eighteen thousand reeds round about, and the name of the city from that day shall be, "the Lord is there" (Ezek. 48:35). Do not read 'there' but 'its name.'"

Said R. Eleazar, "The time will come when 'holy' will be said before the name of the righteous as it is said before the name of the Holy One, blessed be He: 'And it shall come to pass that he that is left in Zion and he that remains in Jerusalem shall be called holy' (Isa. 4:3)."

And said Rabbah said R. Yohanan, "The Holy One, blessed be He, is destined to lift up Jerusalem to a height of three parasangs: 'And she shall be lifted up and be settled in her place' (Isa. 4:3). '...In her place' means 'like her place' [Slotki: Jerusalem will be lifted up to a height equal to the extent of the space it occupies]."

So how do we know that the place that Jerusalem occupied was three parasangs?

Said Rabbah, "Said to me a certain elder, 'I myself saw the original Jerusalem, and it filled up three parasangs.'"

And lest you suppose that there will be pain in the ascension, Scripture states, "Who are these that fly as a cloud and as the doves to their cotes" (Isa. 60:8).

Said R. Hanina bar Pappa, "The Holy One, blessed be He, wanted to give Jerusalem a fixed size: 'Then said I, Whither do you go? And he said to me, To measure Jerusalem, to see what is its breadth and what is its length' (Zech. 2:6).

"Said the ministering angels before the Holy One, blessed be He, 'Lord of the world, you have created in your world any number of cities for the nations of the earth, and you did not fix the measurements of their length or breadth. So are you going to fix measurements for Jerusalem, in the midst of which are your name, sanctuary, and the righteous?'"

IV.45 A. Said R. Simeon b. Laqish, "The Holy One, blessed be He, is destined to add to Jerusalem [Slotki:] a thousand gardens, a thousand towers, a thousand palaces, a thousand mansions. And each one of these will be as vast as Sepphoris in its hour of prosperity."

IV.46 A. *It has been taught on Tannaite authority:*

B. Said R. Yosé, "I saw Sepphoris in its hour of prosperity, and in it were one hundred and eighty thousand markets for those who sold pudding [alone]."

IV.47 A. "And the side chambers were one over another, three and thirty times" (Ezek. 41:6):

B. *What is the meaning of* three and thirty times?

C. Said R. Pappi in the name of R. Joshua of Sikni, "If there will be three Jerusalems, each building will contain thirty dwellings piled up on top of one another; if there will be thirty Jerusalems, then each building will contain three apartments on top of one another."

There is a very clear and simple topical program before us. We treat three subjects, and the order in which they are treated is the only possible order. By that I mean, had we dealt with the third topic first, it would have had no context nor would it have supplied a context to the first and second. The same is to be said with respect to the second; if it came first, then the first sequence would have made no sense at all. So the first sequence prepares the way for the second, the second, for the third. Within each set of compositions, there are some clear points of connection and not mere intersection, let alone formal coherence through a shared topic. Obviously, the triptych can be represented as propositional in only the most general terms. But, equally obviously, we have much more than just this, that, and the other thing, all thrown together: a miscellany. What we have, rather, is a different mode of agglutination of compositions into composites, and small composites into big composites, from the mode that is familiar to us throughout approximately 85 to 90 percent of the Bavli. Our task in the next three chapters is to find out [1] just what principles do explain how one thing is joined to the next, [2] why many things are joined all together, and [3] what all this has to do with the Mishnah.

At this preliminary stage in my argument, however, I do think I have validated these conclusions:

1.   In the miscellany before us, do we identify the first-class, cogent exposition of a proposition?   Not at all.   Is there the sustained consideration of a given problem? No again.

2.   But is it a mere miscellany – disorganized, pointless, a scrap book of one thing and another? Hardly.

Well, then, if not exactly a miscellany, but also not a composite of the kind the predominates in the Bavli in its exposition of the Mishnah, then what do we have? This brief account has raised more questions than it has settled.   The main point must not be lost.   The Bavli contains important composites that differ in their redactional, rhetorical, topical, and logical traits from its paramount composites. Compared to the dominant type of composite, the one that serves as Mishnah commentary and amplification, these other composites exhibit a miscellaneous quality. The real issue is whether or not before us are anomalies, and for that purpose, we shall have to ask not only whether we deal with miscellanies, viewed in their own terms, but whether or not we confront anomalies, viewed in the context of the chapters that contain them. So let us examine three important composites and see [1] how they hold together, and [2] what place they make for themselves in the context of the chapters in which they occur, and [3] how, if at all, the composites or miscellaneous type of composite proposes to expand our understanding of the Mishnah.   Three chapters suffice, two that we already have identified in the context of their tractates, Berakhot and Sanhedrin, respectively, and one chosen more or less at random.

3

Three Massive Miscellanies: [1] Bavli Abodah Zarah Chapter One

In the context of this long and important chapter, we have a variety of miscellanies. We shall address the chapter as a whole, first of all asking in context of the individual entries [1] how they hold together, and second, forming a theory, in the setting of the entire chapter, concerning [2] what place the miscellanies make for themselves in the context of the chapters in which they occur. I shall restrict my comments to the issue of how the miscellanies cohere, what principle has guided the compiler of discrete compositions in linking one with another, in the order before us and not in some other. A full exposition of the chapter as a whole is in my *The Talmud of Babylonia. An American Translation* (Atlanta, 1991: Scholars Press for Brown Judaic Studies). XXV.A. *Tractate Abodah Zarah. Chapters One and Two.* To highlight the composites that I regard as miscellanies, I indent those entries at both margins, leaving at the normal margins both the Mishnah and the portion of the Talmud devoted to the exposition of the Mishnah and its principles. I further indent what I regard as footnotes or appendices to principal components of the Bavli's composite. This further clarifies the character of the document before us.

1:1

A. [2A] Before the festivals of gentiles for three days it is forbidden to do business with them.

B. (1) to lend anything to them or to borrow anything from them.

C. (2) to lend money to them or to borrow money from them.

D. (3) to repay them or to be repaid by them.

E. R. Judah says, "They accept repayment from them, because it is distressing to him."

F. They said to him, "Even though it is distressing to him now, he will be happy about it later."

I.1　A.　[2A] Rab and Samuel [in dealing with the reading of the key word of the Mishnah, translated festival, the letters of which are 'aleph daled, rather than 'ayin daled, which means, calamity]:

B.　*One repeated the formulation of the Mishnah as, "their festivals."*

C.　*And the other repeated the formulation of the Mishnah as "their calamities."*

D.　*The one who repeated the formulation of the Mishnah as "their festivals" made no mistake, and the one who repeated the formulation of the Mishnah as "their calamities" made no mistake.*

E.　*For it is written, "For the day of their calamity is at hand" (Deut. 32:15).*

F.　*The one who repeated the formulation of the Mishnah as "their festivals" made no mistake, for it is written, "Let them bring their testimonies that they may be justified" (Isa. 43:9).*

G.　*And as to the position of him who repeats the formulation of the Mishnah as "their festivals," on what account does he not repeat the formulation of the Mishnah to yield, "their calamities"?*

H.　*He will say to you, "'Calamity' is preferable [as the word choice when speaking of idolatry]."*

I.　*And as to the position of him who repeats the formulation of the Mishnah as "their calamities," on what account does he not repeat the formulation of the Mishnah to yield "their festivals"?*

J.　*He will say to you, "What causes the calamity that befalls them if not their testimony, so testimony is preferable!"*

K.　*And as to the verse, "Let them bring their testimonies that they may be justified" (Isa. 43:9), is this written with reference to gentiles? Lo, it is written in regard to Israel.*

L.　For said R. Joshua b. Levi, "All of the religious duties that Israelites carry out in this world come and give testimony in their behalf in the world to come: 'Let them bring their witnesses that they may be justified' (Isa. 43:9), that is, Israel; 'and let them hear and say, It is truth' (Isa. 43:9) – this refers to gentiles."

M.　Rather, said R. Huna b. R. Joshua, "He who formulates the Mishnah to refer to their calamities derives the reading from this verse: 'They that fashion a graven image are all of them vanity, and their delectable things shall not profit, and their own witnesses see not nor know' (Isa. 44:9)."

The composite begins with a very long, but coherent exposition of a single theme, which is, God's judgment of the nations. No. 2 holds together rather well, once we realize that it is heavily footnoted. I further intend the footnoted materials of that glossed composition.

I.2　A.　R. Hanina bar Pappa, and some say, R. Simlai, gave the following exposition [of the verse,"They that fashion a graven image are all of them vanity, and their delectable things shall not profit, and their own witnesses see not nor know" (Isa. 44:9)]: "In the age to come the Holy One, blessed be He, will bring a scroll of the Torah and hold it in his bosom and say, 'Let him who has kept himself busy with it come and take his reward.' Then all the gentiles will crowd together: 'All of the nations are gathered together' (Isa. 43:9). The Holy One, blessed be He, will say to them, 'Do not crowd together before me in a mob. But let each nation enter together with [2B] its scribes, and let the peoples be gathered together' (Isa. 43:9), and the word 'people' means 'kingdom': 'and one kingdom shall be stronger than the other' (Gen. 25:23)."

B.   *But can there be a mob scene before the Holy One, blessed be He? Rather, it is so that from their perspective they not form a mob, so that they will be able to hear what he says to them.*

C.   [Resuming the narrative of A:] "The kingdom of Rome comes in first."

D.   *How come? Because they are the most important. How do we know on the basis of Scripture they are the most important? Because it is written,* "And he shall devour the whole earth and shall tread it down and break it into pieces" (Gen. 25:23), and said R. Yohanan, "This Rome is answerable, for its definition [of matters] has gone forth to the entire world [Mishcon: 'this refers to Rome, whose power is known to the whole world']."

E.   *And how do we know that the one who is most important comes in first? It is in accord with that which R. Hisda said.*

F.   For said R. Hisda, "When the king and the community [await judgment], the king enters in first for judgment: 'That he maintain the case of his servant [Solomon] and [then] the cause of his people Israel' (1 Kgs. 8:59)."

G.   *And how come? If you wish, I shall say it is not appropriate to keep the king sitting outside. And if you wish, I shall say that [the king is allowed to plea his case] before the anger of the Holy One is aroused."*

H.   [Resuming the narrative of C:] "The Holy One, blessed be He, will say to them, 'How have you defined your chief occupation?'

I.   "They will say before him, 'Lord of the world, a vast number of marketplaces have we set up, a vast number of bathhouses we have made, a vast amount of silver and gold have we accumulated. And all of these things we have done only in behalf of Israel, so that they may define as their chief occupation the study of the Torah.'

J.   "The Holy One, blessed be He, will say to them, 'You complete idiots! Whatever you have done has been for your own convenience. You have set up a vast number of marketplaces to be sure, but that was so as to set up whorehouses in them. The bathhouses were for your own pleasure. Silver and gold belong to me anyhow: "Mine is the silver and mine is the gold, says the Lord of hosts" (Hag. 2:8). Are there any among you who have been telling of "this," and "this" is only the Torah: "And this is the Torah that Moses set before the children of Israel' (Deut. 4:44)." So they will make their exit, humiliated.

K.   "When the kingdom of Rome has made its exit, the kingdom of Persia enters afterward."

L.   *How come? Because they are second in importance. And how*
        do we know it on the basis of Scripture? Because it is written,
        "And behold, another beast, a second, like a bear" (Dan.
        7:5), *and in this connection R. Joseph repeated as a Tannaite*
        formulation, "This refers to the Persians, who eat and drink
        like a bear, are obese like a bear, are shaggy like a bear,
        and are restless like a bear."

M.   "The Holy One, blessed be He, will say to them, 'How have
        you defined your chief occupation?'

N.   "They will say before him, 'Lord of the world, We have thrown
        up a vast number of bridges, we have conquered a vast number
        of towns, we have made a vast number of wars, and all of them
        we did only for Israel, so that they may define as their chief
        occupation the study of the Torah.'

O.   "The Holy One, blessed be He, will say to them, 'Whatever you
        have done has been for your own convenience. You have
        thrown up a vast number of bridges, to collect tolls, you have
        conquered a vast number of towns, to collect the corvée, and,
        as to making a vast number of wars, I am the one who makes
        wars: "The Lord is a man of war" (Ex. 19:17). Are there any
        among you who have been telling of "this," and "this" is only
        the Torah: "And this is the Torah that Moses set before the
        children of Israel" (Deut. 4:44).' So they will make their exit,
        humiliated.

P.   *But if the kingdom of Persia has seen that such a claim issued by*
        the kingdom of Rome did no good whatsoever, how come they go
        in at all?

Q.   *They will say to themselves,* "These are the ones who destroyed
        the house of the sanctuary, but we are the ones who built it."

R.   "And so it will go with each and every nation."

S.   *But if each one of them has seen that such a claim issued by the*
        others did no good whatsoever, how come they go in at all?

T.   *They will say to themselves,* "Those two subjugated Israel, but
        we never subjugated Israel."

U.   *And how come the two conquering nations are singled out as*
        important and the others are not?

V.   *It is because the rule of these will continue until the Messiah*
        comes.

W.   "They will say to him, 'Lord of the world, in point of fact, did
        you actually give it to us and we did not accept it?'"

X.   *But how can they present such an argument, since it is written,*
        "The Lord came from Sinai and rose from Seir to them, he
        shined forth from Mount Paran" (Deut. 33:2), *and further,*
        "God comes from Teman" (Hab. 3:3). *Now what in the*
        world did he want in Seir, and what was he looking for in
        Paran? Said R. Yohanan, "This teaches that the Holy One,
        blessed be He, made the rounds of each and every nation
        and language and none accepted it, until he came to Israel,
        and they accepted it."

Y.   *Rather, this is what they say,* "Did we accept it but then not
        carry it out?"

Z.   *But to this the rejoinder must be, "Why did you not accept it anyhow!"*

AA.   Rather, "This is what they say before him, 'Lord of the world, did you hold a mountain over us like a cask and then we refused to accept it as you did to Israel, as it is written, "And they stood beneath the mountain" (Ex. 19:17).'"

BB.   And [in connection with the verse, "And they stood beneath the mountain" (Ex. 19:17),] said R. Dimi bar Hama, "This teaches that the Holy One, blessed be He, held the mountain over Israel like a cask and said to them, 'If you accept the Torah, well and good, and if not, then there is where your grave will be.'"

CC.   "Then the Holy One, blessed be He, will say to them, 'Let us make known what happened first: "Let them announce to us former things" (Isa. 43:9). As to the seven religious duties that you did accept, where have you actually carried them out?'"

DD.   *And how do we know on the basis of Scripture that they did not carry them out? R. Joseph formulated as a Tannaite statement,* "'He stands and shakes the earth, he sees and makes the nations tremble' (Hab. 3:6): what did he see? He saw the seven religious duties that the children of Noah accepted upon themselves as obligations but never actually carried them out. Since they did not carry out those obligations, he went and remitted their obligation."

EE.   *But then they benefited – so it pays to sin!*

FF.   Said Mar b. Rabina, [3A] "What this really proves is that even when they carry out those religious duties, they get no reward on that account."

GG.   *And they don't, don't they? But has it not been taught on Tannaite authority:* R. Meir would say, "How on the basis of Scripture do we know that, even if it is a gentile, if he goes and takes up the study of the Torah as his occupation, he is equivalent to the high priest? Scripture states, 'You shall therefore keep my statutes and my ordinances, which, if a human being does them, one shall gain life through them' (Lev. 18:5). What is written is not 'priests' or 'Levites' or 'Israelites,' but rather, 'a human being.' So you have learned the fact that, even if it is a gentile, if he goes and takes up the study of the Torah as his occupation, he is equivalent to the high priest."

HH.   Rather, what you learn from this [DD] is that they will not receive that reward that is coming to those who are commanded to do them and who carry them out, but rather, the reward that they receive will be like that coming to the one who is not commanded to do them and who carries them out anyhow.

II.   For said R. Hanina, "Greater is the one who is commanded and who carries out the religious obligations than the one who is not commanded but nonetheless carries out religious obligations."

JJ.   [Reverting to AA:] "This is what the gentiles say before him, 'Lord of the world, Israel, who accepted it – where in the world have they actually carried it out?'

KK.   "The Holy One, blessed be He, will say to them, 'I shall bear witness concerning them, that they have carried out the whole of the Torah!'

LL.   "They will say before him, 'Lord of the world, is there a father who is permitted to give testimony concerning his son? For it is written, "Israel is my son, my firstborn" (Ex. 4:22).'

MM.   "The Holy One, blessed be He, will say to them, 'The Heaven and the earth will give testimony in their behalf that they have carried out the entirety of the Torah.'

NN.   "They will say before him, 'Lord of the world, the Heaven and earth have a selfish interest in the testimony that they give: 'If not for my covenant with day and with night, I should not have appointed the ordinances of Heaven and earth' (Jer. 33:25)."

OO.   *For said R. Simeon b. Laqish, "What is the meaning of the verse of Scripture,* 'And there was evening, and there was morning, the sixth day' (Gen. 1:31)? This teaches that the Holy One, blessed be He, made a stipulation with all of the works of creation, saying to them, 'If Israel accepts my Torah, well and good, but if not, I shall return you to chaos and void.' *That is in line with what is written:* 'You did cause sentence to be heard from Heaven, the earth trembled and was still' (Ps. 76:9). If 'trembling,' then where is the stillness, and if 'stillness,' then where is the trembling? Rather, to begin with, trembling, but at the end, stillness."

PP.   [Reverting to MM-NN:] "The Holy One, blessed be He, will say to them, 'Some of them may well come and give testimony concerning Israel that they have observed the entirety of the Torah. Let Nimrod come and give testimony in behalf of Abraham that he never worshipped idols. Let Laban come and give testimony in behalf of Jacob, that he never was suspect of thievery. Let the wife of Potiphar come and give testimony in behalf of Joseph, that he was never suspect of "sin." Let Nebuchadnezzar come and give testimony in behalf of Hananiah, Mishael, and Azariah, that they never bowed down to the idol. Let Darius come and give testimony in behalf of Daniel, that he did not neglect even the optional prayers. Let Bildad the Shuhite and Zophar the Naamatite and Eliphaz the Temanite and Elihu son of Barachel the Buzite come and testify in behalf of Israel that they have observed the entirety of the Torah: "Let the nations bring their own witnesses, that they may be justified" (Isa. 43:9).'

QQ.   "They will say before him, 'Lord of the world, give it to us to begin with, and let us carry it out.'

RR.   "The Holy One, blessed be He, will say to them, 'World-class idiots! He who took the trouble to prepare on the eve of the Sabbath [Friday] will eat on the Sabbath, but he who took no trouble on the even of the Sabbath – what in the world is he going to eat on the Sabbath! Still, [I'll give you another chance.] I have a rather simple religious duty, which is called "the tabernacle." Go and do that one.'"

SS. *But can you say any such thing? Lo, R. Joshua b. Levi has said, "What is the meaning of the verse of Scripture, 'The ordinances that I command you this day to do them' (Deut. 7:11)? Today is the day to do them, but not tomorrow; they are not to be done tomorrow; today is the day to do them, but not the day on which to receive a reward for doing them."*

TT. Rather, it is that the Holy One, blessed be He, does not exercise tyranny over his creatures.

UU. *And why does he refer to it as a simple religious duty? Because it does not involve enormous expense [to carry out that religious duty].*

VV. "Forthwith every one of them will take up the task and go and make a tabernacle on his roof. But then the Holy, One, blessed be He, will come and make the sun blaze over them as at the summer solstice, and every one of them will knock down his tabernacle and go his way: 'Let us break their bands asunder and cast away their cords from us' (Ps. 23:3)."

WW. But lo, you have just said, "it is that the Holy One, blessed be He, does not exercise tyranny over his creatures"!

XX. *It is because the Israelites, too – sometimes* [3B] *the summer solstice goes on to the festival of Tabernacles, and therefore they are bothered by the heat!*

YY. But has not Raba stated, "One who is bothered [by the heat] is exempt from the obligation of dwelling in the tabernacle"?

ZZ. *Granting that one may be exempt from the duty, is he going to go and tear the thing down?*

AAA. [Continuing from VV:] "Then the Holy One, blessed be He, goes into session and laughs at them: 'He who sits in Heaven laughs' (Ps. 2:4)."

BBB. Said R. Isaac, "Laughter before the Holy One, blessed be He, takes place only on that day alone."

CCC. *There are those who repeat as a Tannaite version this statement of R. Isaac in respect to that which has been taught on Tannaite authority:*

DDD. R. Yosé says, "In the coming age gentiles will come and convert."

EEE. *But will they be accepted? Has it not been taught on Tannaite authority: Converts will not be accepted in the days of the Messiah, just as they did not accept proselytes either in the time of David or in the time of Solomon?*

FFF. Rather, "they will make themselves converts, and they will put on phylacteries on their heads and arms and fringes on their garments and a mezuzah on their doors. But when they witness the war of Gog and Magog, he will say to them, 'How come you have come?' They will say,

'"Against the Lord and against his Messiah."' For so it is said, 'Why are the nations in an uproar and why do the peoples mutter in vain' (Ps. 2:1). Then each one of them will rid himself of his religious duty and go his way: 'Let us break their bands asunder' (Ps. 2:3). Then the Holy One, blessed be He, goes into session and laughs at them: 'He who sits in Heaven laughs' (Ps. 2:4)."

GGG.   Said R. Isaac, "Laughter before the Holy One, blessed be He, takes place only on that day alone."

HHH.   But is this really so? And has not R. Judah said Rab said, "The day is made up of twelve hours. In the first three the Holy One, blessed be He, goes into session and engages in study of the Torah; in the second he goes into session and judges the entire world. When he realizes that the world is liable to annihilation, he arises from the throne of justice and takes up a seat on the throne of mercy. In the third period he goes into session and nourishes the whole world from the horned buffalo to the brood of vermin. During the fourth quarter he laughs [and plays] with leviathan: 'There is leviathan, whom you have formed to play with' (Ps. 104:26)." [This proves that God does laugh more than on that one day alone.]

III.   Said R. Nahman bar Isaac, "With his creatures he laughs [every day], but at his creatures he laughs only on that day alone."

I.3   A   Said R. Aha to R. Nahman bar Isaac, "From the day on which the house of the sanctuary, the Holy One blessed be He has had no laughter.

B.   *"And how on the basis of Scripture do we know that he has had none? If we say that it is because it is written,* 'And on that day did the Lord, the God of hosts, call to weeping and lamentation' (Isa. 22:12), *that verse refers to that day in particular. Shall we then say that that fact derives from the verse,* 'If I forget you, Jerusalem, let my right hand forget her cunning, let my tongue cleave to the roof of my mouth if I do not remember you' (Ps. 137:5-6)? *That refers to forgetfulness, not laughter. Rather, the fact derives from this verse:* 'I have long held my peace, I have been still, I have kept in, now I will cry' (Isa. 42:14)."

I.4   A   [Referring to the statement that during the fourth quarter he laughs [and plays] with leviathan,] *[nowadays] what does he do in the fourth quarter of the day?*

B.   He sits and teaches Torah to kindergarten students: "Whom shall one teach knowledge, and whom shall one make understand the message? Those who are weaned from the milk?" (Isa. 28:19).

C.   *And to begin with [prior to the destruction of the Temple, which ended his spending his time playing with leviathan], who taught them?*

D.   *If you wish, I shall say it was Metatron, and if you wish, I shall say that he did both [but now does only one].*

E.   And at night what does he do?

F.   *If you wish, I shall say that it is the sort of thing he does by day;*

G.   *and if you wish, I shall say,* he rides his light cherub and floats through eighteen thousand worlds: "The chariots of God are myriads, even thousands and thousands [*shinan*] (Ps. 68:17). Read the letters translated as thousands, *shinan*, as though they were written, *she-enan*, meaning, that are not [thus: the chariots are twice ten thousand less two thousand, eighteen thousand (Mishcon)]."

H   *And if you wish, I shall say,* he sits and listens to the song of the Living Creatures [*hayyot*]: "By the day the Lord will command his loving kindness and in the night his song shall be with me" (Ps. 42:9).

If we regard the deeply indented materials as footnotes and appendices, attached for thematic reasons, then we can see Nos. 1-4 as an entirely coherent statement, a composite to be sure, but in no way a miscellany. Having examined that set and seen the clear connections between one composition and the next, on the one side, and the coherent character of the whole (with its footnotes and appendix), on the other, we are now ready to look at the miscellany that follows and to ask ourselves how each entry is linked to what is juxtaposed to it, fore and aft. If I had to find a rational explanation for putting No. 5 in at all, it is because it addresses the theme of study of Torah, to which No. 4 has made reference.

I.5   A.   Said R. Levi, "To whoever stops studying the words of the Torah and instead takes up words of mere chatter they feed glowing coals of juniper: 'They pluck salt-wort with wormwood and the roots of juniper are their food' (Job 30:4)."

     B.   Said R. Simeon b. Laqish, "For whoever engages in study of the Torah by night – the Holy One, blessed be He, draws out the thread of grace by day: 'By day the Lord will command his loving kindness, and in the night his song shall be with me' (Ps. 42:9). Why is it that 'By day the Lord will command his loving kindness'? Because 'in the night his song shall be with me.'"

     C.   *Some say,* said R. Simeon b. Laqish, "For whoever engages in study of the Torah in this world, which is like the night, – the Holy One, blessed be He, draws out the thread of grace in the world to come, which is like the day: 'By day the Lord will command his loving kindness, and in the night his song shall be with me' (Ps. 42:9). [Supply: Why is it that 'By day the Lord will command his loving kindness'? Because 'in the night his song shall be with me.']"

The sustaining character of study of the Torah, No. 5, explains the relevance of the composition of No. 6.

I.6   A   Said R. Judah said Samuel, "*What is the meaning of the verse of Scripture,* 'And you make man as the fish of the sea and as the creeping things, that have no ruler over them' (Hab. 1:14)? Why are human beings compared to fish of the sea? To tell you, just as fish in the sea, when they come up on dry land, forthwith begin to die, so with human beings, when they take their leave of teachings of the Torah and religious deeds, forthwith they begin to die.

       B   "Another matter: just as the fish of the sea, as soon as dried by the sun, die, so human beings, when struck by the sun, die."

       C   *If you want, this refers to this world, and if you want, this refers to the world to come.*

       D   *If you want, this refers to this world, in line with that which R. Hanina [said],* for said R. Hanina, "Everything is in the hands of Heaven except cold and heat: 'colds and heat boils are in the way of the froward, he who keeps his soul holds himself far from them' (Prov. 22:5)."

       E   *And if you want, this refers to the world to come, in accord with that which was stated by R. Simeon b. Laqish.* For said R. Simeon b. Laqish, "In the world to come, there is no Gehenna, but rather, the Holy One, blessed be He, brings the sun out of its sheathe and he heats the wicked but heals the righteous through it. The wicked are brought to judgment by [4A] it: 'For behold, the day comes, it burns as a furnace, and all the proud and all who do wicked things shall be stubble, and the day that comes shall set them ablaze, says the Lord of hosts, that it shall leave them neither root nor branch' (Mal. 3:19).

       F   "'It shall leave them neither root' – in this world; 'nor branch' – in the world to come.

       G   "'but heals the righteous through it': 'But to you that fear my name shall the sun of righteousness arise with healing in its wings' (Mal. 3:19). They will revel in it: 'And you shall go forth and gambol as calves of the stall' (Mal. 3:20)."

       H   [Continuing C, above:] "Another matter: just as with the fish of the sea, whoever is bigger than his fellow swallows his fellow, so in the case of human beings, were it not for fear of the government, whoever is bigger than his fellow would swallow his fellow."

       I   *That is in line with what we have learned in the Mishnah:* R. Hananiah, Prefect of the Priests, says, "Pray for the welfare of the government. For if it were not for fear of it, one man would swallow his fellow alive" [M. Abot 3:2A-B].

The foregoing has mentioned the theme of Gehenna and the world to come, and we shall now pursue that theme, now the contrast between Gehenna and the world to come, the gentiles and Israel, God's anger and God's grace. No. 7 contrasts the time of judgment and the time of God's war against his enemies; No. 8 then deals with the anger of God with the gentiles; Nos. 9, 10 with God's destruction.

I.7 A R. *Hinena bar Pappa contrasted verses of Scripture:* "It is written, 'As to the almighty, we do not find him exercising plenteous power' (Job 37:23), but by contrast, 'Great is our Lord and of abundant power' (Ps. 147:5), and further, 'Your right hand, Lord, is glorious in power' (Ex. 15:6).

     B "But there is no contradiction between the first and second and third statements, for the former speaks of the time of judgment [when justice is tempered with mercy, so God does not do what he could] and the latter two statements refer to a time of war [of God against his enemies]."

I.8 A R. *Hama bar Hanina contrasted verses of Scripture:* "It is written, 'Fury is not in me' (Isa. 27:4) but also 'The Lord revenges and is furious' (Nah. 1:2).

     B *"But there is no contradiction between the first and second statements,* for the former speaks of Israel, the latter of the gentiles."

     C R. Hinena bar Pappa said, "'Fury is not in me' (Isa. 27:4), for I have already taken an oath: 'would that I had not so vowed, then as the briars and thorns in flame would I with one step burn it altogether.'"

I.9 A *That is in line with what R. Alexandri said,* "What is the meaning of the verse, 'And it shall come to pass on that day that I will seek to destroy all the nations' (Zech. 12:9) –

     B "'Seek' – seek permission from whom?

     C "Said the Holy One, blessed be He, 'I shall seek in the records that deal with them, to see whether there is a cause of merit, on account of which I shall redeem them, but if not, I shall destroy them.'"

I.10 A *That is in line with what Raba said,* "What is the meaning of the verse, 'Howbeit he will not stretch out a hand for a ruinous heap though they cry in his destruction' (Job 30:24)?

     B "Said the Holy One, blessed be He, to Israel, 'When I judge Israel, I shall not judge them as I do the gentiles, for it is written, "I will overturn, overturn, overturn it" (Ezek. 21:32), rather, I shall exact punishment from them as a hen pecks.'

     C "Another matter: 'Even if the Israelites do not carry out a religious duty before me more than a hen pecking at a rubbish heap, I shall join together [all the little pecks] into a great sum: "although they pick little they are saved" (Job 30:24) [following Mishcon's rendering].'

     D "Another matter: 'As a reward for their crying out to me, I shall help them' (Job 30:24) [following Mishcon's rendering]."

The sequence of compositions on the same theme, God's judgment, this world and the world to come, suffering in this world so as to enjoy the world to come, Israel's suffering in this world and its enjoyment of the world to come, goes on through Nos. 11, 12, 13, 14. Then there is a set on

God's anger. The movement is imperceptible, since No. 15 simply refers to God's anger in the context of judgment. But forthwith, at No. 16, we move into the theme of divine anger, and that sets us off in a slightly different direction from the one that we have followed up to now.

I.11 A *That is in line with what R. Abba said, "What is the meaning of the verse, 'Though I would redeem them, yet they have spoken lies against me' (Hos. 7:23)? 'I said that I would redeem them through [inflicting a penalty] on their property in this world, so that they might have the merit of enjoying the world to come, "yet they have spoken lies against me" (Hos. 7:23).'"*

I.12 A *That is in line with what R. Pappi in the name of Raba said, "What is the meaning of the verse, 'Though I have trained [and] strengthened their arms, yet they imagine mischief against me' (Hos. 7:15)?*

    B. *Said the Holy One, blessed be He, I thought that I would punish them with suffering in this world, so that their arm might be strengthened in the world to come, "yet they have spoken lies against me" (Hos. 7:23).'"*

I.13 A *R. Abbahu praised R. Safra to the minim [in context: Christian authorities of Caesarea], saying that he was a highly accomplished authority. They therefore remitted his taxes for thirteen years.*

    B. *One day they came upon him and said to him, "It is written, 'You only have I known among all the families of the earth; therefore I will visit upon you all your iniquities' (Amos 3:2). If one is angry, does he vent it on someone he loves?"*

    C. *He fell silent and said nothing at all. They wrapped a scarf around his neck and tortured him. R. Abbahu came along and found them. He said to them, "Why are you torturing him?"*

    D. *They said to him, "Didn't you tell us that he is a highly accomplished authority, but he does not know how to explain this verse!"*

    E. *He said to them, "True enough, I told you that he was a master of Tannaite statements, but did I say anything at all to you about his knowledge of Scripture?"*

    F. *They said to him, "So how come you know?"*

    G. *He said to them, "Since we, for our part, spend a lot of time with you, we have taken the task of studying it thoroughly, while others [in Babylonia, Safra's place of origin] do not study [Scripture] that carefully."*

    H. *They said to him, "So tell us."*

    I. *He said to them, "I shall tell you a parable. To what is the matter comparable? To the case of a man who lent money to two people, one a friend, the other an enemy. From the friend he collects the money little by little, from the enemy he collects all at once."*

I.14 A *Said R. Abba bar Kahana, "What is the meaning of the following verse of Scripture: 'Far be it from you to do after this manner, to slay the righteous with the wicked' (Gen. 18:25).*

B.   "Said Abraham before the Holy One, blessed be He, 'Lord of the world! It is a profanation to act in such a way [a play on the Hebrew letters, shared by the words 'far be it' and 'profanation'], 'to slay the righteous with the wicked' (Gen. 18:25)."

C.   But is it not [so that God might do just that]? And is it not written, "And I will cut off from you the righteous and the wicked" (Ezek. 21:8)?

D.   That speaks of one who is not completely righteous, but not of one who is completely righteous.

E.   And will he not do so to one who is completely righteous? And is it not written, "And begin the slaughter with my sanctuary" (Ezek. 9:6), in which connection R. Joseph repeated as a Tannaite version, "Read not 'with my sanctuary' but rather, 'with those who are holy to me,' namely, the ones who carried out the Torah beginning to end."

F.   *There, too,* since they had the power to protest against the wickedness of the others and did not do so, they were not regarded as completely righteous at all.

I.15   A.   *R. Pappa contrasted verses of Scripture: "It is written, 'God is angry every day' (Ps. 7:12) but also 'who could stand before his anger' (Nah. 1:6).*

B.   *"But there is no contradiction between the first and second statements,* for the former speaks of the individual, the latter of the community."

The reference to God's anger, No. 16, marks an imperceptible movement to a new theme, namely Balaam, the prophet of the gentiles. Balaam then forms the unifying theme for Nos. 17-19. Because I regard these as footnote entries, I indent them.

I.16   A.   *Our rabbis have taught on Tannaite authority:*

B.   "God is angry every day" (Ps. 7:12), and how long is his anger? It is for a moment. And how long is a moment? The portion 1/53,848th of an hour is a moment.

C.   And no creature can determine that moment, except for Balaam that wicked man, of whom it is written, [4B] "who knew the knowledge of the Most High" (Num. 24:16).

D.   How can it be that a man who did not know the mind of his animal could have known the mind of the Most High?

I.17   A.   *And what is the meaning of the statement that he did not know the mind of his animal?*

B.   *When they saw him riding on his ass, they said to him, "How come you're not riding on a horse?"*

C.   *He said to them, "I sent it to the meadow."*

D.   Forthwith: "The ass said, Am I not your ass" (Num. 22:30).

E.   *He said to it, "Just as a beast of burden in general."*

F.   *She said to him, "Upon whom you have ridden" (Num. 22:30).*

G.   *He said to it, "Only from time to time."*

	H	*She said to him,* "ever since I was yours (Num. 22:30). And not only so, but I serve you for riding by day and fucking by night."
	I	For here the word "I was wont" is used, and the same letters bear the meaning of bed-mate: "...and she served him as a bed-mate" (1 Kgs. 1:2).
I.18	A	*And what is the meaning of the statement that* he could have known the mind of the Most High?
	B.	For he knew precisely that moment at which the Holy One, blessed be He, was angry.
	C.	*That is in line with what the prophet had said to them,* "O my people, remember now what Balak king of Moab consulted and what Balaam son of Beor answered him from Shittim to Gilgal, that you may know the righteousness of the Lord" (Mic. 6:5).
I.19	A.	["O my people, remember now what Balak king of Moab consulted and what Balaam son of Beor answered him from Shittim to Gilgal, that you may know the righteousness of the Lord" (Mic. 6:5)]:
	B.	Said R. Eleazar, "Said R. Eleazar, "Said the Holy One, blessed be He, to Israel, 'My people, see how many acts of righteousness I carried out with you, for I did not grow angry with you during all those [perilous] days, for if I had grown angry with you, there would not have remained from Israel a remnant or a survivor.'
	C.	"And that is in line with what Balaam says: 'How can I curse seeing that God does not curse, and how can I be wrathful, seeing that the Lord has not been wrathful' (Num. 23:8)."

We now realize that Nos. 17-19 form a protracted footnote to No.16, for No. 20 will return us to the theme broken off at No. 16, namely, God's anger. The composite that follows, Nos. 20-23, is held together by that theme.

I.20	A	And how long is his wrath? It is for a moment. And how long is a moment? The portion 1/53,848th of an hour is a moment.
	B.	And how long is a moment?
	C.	Said Amemar – others say, Rabina – "So long as it takes to say the word 'moment.'"
	D.	*And how on the basis of Scripture do we know that his wrath lasts for only a moment?*
	E.	*As it is written,* "For his anger is for a moment, his favor is for a lifetime" (Ps. 30:6).
	F.	*If you prefer:* "Hide yourself for a brief moment, until the wrath be past" (Isa. 26:20).
I.21	A.	*When is he angry?*
	B.	*Said Abbayye,* "In the first three hours of the day, when the comb of the cock is white."
	C.	*Isn't it white all the rest of the day?*
	D.	*At other times it has red streaks, but then it has none.*

I.22	A.	*R. Joshua b. Levi – a certain Min would bother him about verses of Scripture. Once he took a chicken and put it between the legs of the bed and watched it. He reasoned, "When that hour comes, I shall curse him."*
	B.	*But when that hour came, he was dozing. He said, "What you learn from this experience is that it is not correct to act in such a way: 'His tender mercies are over all his works' (Ps. 145:9), 'Neither is it good for the righteous to inflict punishment' (Prov. 17:26)."*
I.23	A.	*It was taught as a Tannaite version in the name of R. Meir, "[That time at which God gets angry comes] when the kings put on their crowns on their heads and prostrate themselves to the sun. Forthwith the Holy One, blessed be He, grows angry."*

Once again we are at a borderline between one set and another, and once more, the movement is subtle. We have just now referred to times at which God is angry, and times at which he is merciful. God is particularly angry, No. 23, when the kings put their crowns on their heads and worship the sun; No. 24 completes this composite, a different but related distinction between the time to pray and the time not to pray.

I.24	A.	*Said R. Joseph, "A person should not recite the Prayer of the Additional Service for the first day of the New Year [the Day of Judgment] during the first three hours of the day or in private, lest, since that is the time of judgment, his deeds may be examined, and his prayer rejected."*
	B.	*If so, then the prayer of the community also should not be recited at that time?*
	C.	*The merit [accruing to the community as a whole] is greater.*
	D.	*If so, then that of the Morning Service also should not be recited in private?*
	E.	*Since at that time the community also will be engaged in reciting the Morning Prayer, the individual's recitation of the Prayer will not be rejected.*
	F.	*But have you not said, "In the first three the Holy One, blessed be He, goes into session and engages in study of the Torah; in the second he goes into session and judges the entire world"?*
	G.	*Reverse the order.*
	H	*Or, if you prefer, actually do not reverse the order.* For when God is occupied with study of the Torah, called by Scripture "truth" as in "buy the truth and do not sell it" (Prov. 23:23), the Holy One, blessed be He, in any event will not violate the strict rule of justice. But when engaged in judgment, which is not called "truth" by Scripture, the Holy One, blessed be He, may step across the line of strict justice [towards mercy].

No. 25 is going to direct our attention way back to 2.RR. What we have, then, is a massive appendix to that reference, once that was formed in its own terms and is coherent around its own theme. That theme is the religious deeds and duties carried out by Israel, and how these will be rewarded not now but in the world to come. No. 26 introduces David's sin in the context of this discussion, explicitly referring back to No. 25. Then, Nos. 26-27, we pursue a composite devoted to David.

I.25	A.	Reverting to the body of the prior text:
	B.	*R. Joshua b. Levi has said, "What is the meaning of the verse of Scripture, 'The ordinances that I command you this day to do them' (Deut. 7:11)? Today is the day to do them, but not tomorrow; they are not to be done tomorrow; today is the day to do them, but today is not the day on which to receive a reward for doing them":*
	C.	Said R. Joshua b. Levi, "All the religious duties that Israelites do in this world come and give evidence in their behalf in the world to come: 'Let them bring their witnesses that they may be justified, let them hear and say it is truth."
	D.	"Let them bring their witnesses that they may be justified": this is Israel.
	E.	"Let them hear and say it is truth": this refers to the gentiles.
	F.	And said R. Joshua b. Levi, "All the religious duties that Israelites do in this world come and flap about the faces of gentiles in the world to come: 'Keep them and do them, for this, your wisdom and understanding, will be in the eyes of the peoples' (Deut. 4:6).
	G.	"What is stated here is not 'in the presence of the peoples' but 'in the eyes of the peoples,' which teaches you that they will come and flap about the faces of gentiles in the world to come."
	H.	And said R. Joshua b. Levi, "The Israelites made the golden calf only to give an opening to penitents: 'O that they had such a heart as this always, to fear me and keep my commandments' (Deut. 5:26)."
I.26	A.	That is in line with what R. Yohanan said in the name of R. Simeon b. Yohai: "David was really not so unfit as to do such a deed [as he did with Beth Sheva]: 'My heart is slain within me' (Ps. 109:22) [Mishcon: David's inclinations had been completely conquered by himself]. And the Israelites were hardly the kind of people to commit such an act: "O that they had such a heart as this always, to fear me and keep my commandments' (Deut. 5:26). So why did they do it?
	B.	"[5A] It was to show you that if an individual has sinned, they say to him, 'Go to the individual [such as David, and follow his example], and if the community as a whole has sinned, they say to them, 'Go to the community [such as Israel].'
	C.	*And it was necessary to give both examples. For had we been given the rule governing the individual, that might have been supposed to be because his personal sins were not broadly known, but in the case of the community, the sins of which will be broadly known, I might have said that that is not the case.*
	D.	*And if we had been given the rule governing the community, that might have been supposed to be the case because they enjoy greater mercy, but an individual, who has not got such powerful zekhut, might have been thought not subject to the rule.*
	E.	*So both cases had to be made explicit.*

I.27   A   *That is in line with what R. Samuel bar Nahmani said R. Jonathan said, "What is the meaning of the verse of Scripture, 'The saying of David, son of Jesse, and the saying of the man raised on high'* (2 Sam. 23:1)?

       B.   "It means, 'The saying of David, son of Jesse, the man who raised up the yoke of repentance.'"

No. 28 brings us back to the general theme of doing a good deed in this world and enjoying the result in the world to come. That theme spills over into No. 29.

I.28   A   Said R. Samuel bar Nahmani said R. Jonathan, "Whoever does a religious duty in this world – that deed goes before him to the world to come, as it is said, 'And your righteousness shall go before you' (Isa. 58:8).

       B.   "And whoever commits a transgression in this world – that act turns aside from him and goes before him on the Day of Judgment, as it is said, 'The paths of their way are turned aside, they go up into the waste and perish' (Job 6:18)."

       C.   R. Eliezer says, "It attaches to him like a dog, as it is said, 'He did not listen to her to lie by her or to be with her' (Gen. 39:10).

       D.   "'To lie by her' in this world.

       E.   "'Or to be with her' in the world to come."

I.29   A   Said R. Simeon b. Laqish, "Come and let us express our gratitude to our ancestors, for if it were not for their having sinned, we for our part should never have been able to come into the world: 'I said you are gods and all of you sons of the Most High' (Ps. 82:6). Now that you have ruined things by what you have done, 'you shall indeed die like mortals' (Ps. 82:6)."

       B.   *Does that statement then bear the implication, therefore, that if they had not sinned, they would not have propagated? But has it not been written,* "And you, be fruitful and multiply" (Gen. 9:7)?

       C.   *That applies up to Sinai.*

       D.   *But in connection with Sinai it also is written,* "Go say to them, Go back to your tents" (Ex. 19:15), *meaning, to marital relationships. And is it not also written,* "that it might be well with them and with their children" (Deut. 5:26)?

       E   That speaks only to those who were actually present at Mount Sinai.

       F.   *But has not R. Simeon b. Laqish stated, "What is the meaning of that which is written:* 'This is the book of the generations of Adam' (Gen. 5:1)? Now did the first Adam have a book? The statement, rather, teaches that the Holy One, blessed be He, showed to the first Adam each generation and its authoritative expositors, each generation and its sages, each generation and those that administered its affairs. When he came to the generation of R. Aqiba, he rejoiced in the master's Torah but he was saddened by the master's death.

       G   "He said, 'How precious are your thoughts to me, O God' (Ps. 139:17)."

H   And said R. Yosé, "The son of David will come only when all of
     the souls that are stored up in the body will be used up: 'For I
     will not contend for ever, neither will I be always angry, for the
     spirit should fall before me and the spirits which I have made'
     (Isa. 57:16)." [Mishcon: In the face of the foregoing teachings,
     how could it be stated that had it not been for the sin of the
     golden calf, we should not have come into the world?]

I   *Do not, therefore, imagine that the sense of the statement is,* we
     should have not come into the world [if our ancestors had not
     sinned], *but rather,* it would have been as though we had not
     come into the world.

J.   *Does that then bear the implication that, if they had not sinned, they
     would never have died? But have not the passages been written that
     deal with the deceased childless brother's widow and the chapters
     about inheritances [which take for granted that people die]?*

K   These passages are written conditionally [meaning, if people
     sin and so die, then the rules take effect, but it is not necessary
     that they take effect unless that stipulation is fulfilled].

L   *And are there then any verses of Scripture that are stated
     conditionally?*

M   *Indeed so, for said R. Simeon b. Laqish, "What is the meaning of that
     which has been written, 'And it was evening and it was morning,
     the sixth day' (Gen. 1:31)? This teaches that the Holy One,
     blessed be He, made a stipulation with the works of creation
     and said, 'If the Israelites accept the Torah, well and good, but
     if not, I shall send you back to the condition of formlessness
     and void."*

N   *An objection was raised:* "O that they had such a heart as this
     always, to fear me and keep my commandments, that it may be
     well with them and their children" (Deut. 5:26): it is not
     possible to maintain that the meaning here is that he would
     take away the angel of death from them, for the decree had
     already been made. It means that the Israelites accepted the
     Torah only so that no nation or tongue would rule over them:
     "that it might be well with them and their children after them."
     [Mishcon: How could R. Simeon b. Laqish hold that but for the
     golden calf worship Israel would have enjoyed physical
     deathlessness?]

Q   *[R. Simeon b. Laqish] made his statement in accord with the position
     of this Tannaite authority, for it has been taught on Tannaite
     authority:*

P.   R. Yosé says, "The Israelites accepted the Torah only so that the
     angel of death should not have power over them: 'I said you
     are gods and all of you are sons of the Most High. Now that
     you have ruined things by what you have done 'you shall
     indeed die like mortals' (Ps. 82:6)."

Q   *But to R. Yosé also must be addressed the question, has it not been
     written,* "O that they had such a heart as this always, to fear me
     and keep my commandments, that it may be well with them
     and their children" (Deut. 5:26)? *Goodness is what is promised,
     but there still will be death!*

R.   *R. Yosé will say to you, "If there is no death, what greater goodness can there ever be?"*

S.   *And the other Tannaite authority – how does he read the phrase, "You shall indeed die"?*

T.   *The sense of "death" here is "poverty,"* for a master has said, "Four classifications of persons are equivalent to corpses, and these are they: the poor man, the blind man, the person afflicted with the skin disease [of Lev. 13], and the person who has no children.

U.   "The poor man, as it is written: 'for all the men are dead who sought your life' (Ex. 4:19). *Now who were they? This refers to Dathan and Abiram, and they were certainly not then dead,* they had only lost all their money.

V.   "The blind man, as it is written: 'He has made me dwell in darkness as those that have been long dead' (Lam. 3:6).

W.   "The person afflicted with the skin disease, as it is written: 'Let her, I pray you, not be as one who is dead' (Num. 12:12).

X.   "And the person who has no children, as it is written: 'Give me children or else I die' (Gen. 30:1)."

A new composite of compositions now commences. No. 30 begins with reference to Israel's sin. The connection to No. 29, so far as I can see, is simple. We have dealt with Israel's good deeds in this world, which yield the world to come. No. 29 also has referred to the penalties for sin, and how these are appropriate. Now we turn to Israel's bad deeds. The composite on Israel's sins will continue through Nos. 30-33.

I.30   A.   *Our rabbis have taught on Tannaite authority:*

      B.   "If you walk in my statutes" (Lev. 26:3) – the word "if" is used in the sense of supplication, as in the verse, O that my people would hearken to me, that Israel would walk in my ways...I should soon subdue their enemies" (Ps. 81:14-15); "O that you had listened to my commandments, then my peace would have been as a river, your seed also would have been as the sand" (Isa. 48:18).

I.31   A.   *Our rabbis have taught on Tannaite authority:*

      B.   "O that they had such a heart as this always, to fear me and keep my commandments, that it may be well with them and their children" (Deut. 5:26).

      C.   Said Moses to the Israelites, "You are a bunch of ingrates, children of ingrates. When the Holy One, blessed be He, said to you, 'O that they had such a heart as this always, to fear me and keep my commandments, that it may be well with them and their children' (Deut. 5:26), they should have said, 'You give it.'

      D.   "They were ingrates, since it is written, 'Our soul loathes [5B] this light bread' (Num. 21:5).

      E.   "...the children of ingrates: 'The woman whom you gave to be with me, she gave me of the fruit of the tree and I ate it' (Gen. 3:12).

F. "So our rabbi, Moses, gave an indication of that fact to the Israelites only after forty years: 'And I have led you forty years in the wilderness...but the Lord has not give you a heart to know and eyes to see and ears to hear unto this day' (Deut. 29:3, 4)."

I.32 A. ["And I have led you forty years in the wilderness...but the Lord has not given you a heart to know and eyes to see and ears to hear unto this day" (Deut. 29:3, 4):]

B. Said Raba, "This proves that a person will fully grasp the mind of his master only after forty years have passed."

I.33 A. *Said R. Yohanan in the name of R. Benaah, "What is the meaning of the verse of Scripture,* 'Happy are you who sow beside all waters, that send forth the feet of the ox and the ass' (Isa. 32:20)? 'Happy are you, O Israel, when you are devoted to the Torah and to doing deeds of grace, then their inclination to do evil is handed over to them, and they are not handed over into the power of their inclination to do evil.

B. "For it is said, 'Happy are you who sow beside all waters.' For what does the word 'sowing' mean, if not 'doing deeds of grace,' in line with the use of the word in this verse: 'Sow for yourselves in righteousness, reap according to mercy' (Hos. 10:12), and what is the meaning of 'water' if not Torah: 'Oh you who are thirsty, come to the water' (Isa. 55:1)."

C. As to the phrase, "that send forth the feet of the ox and the ass":

D. it has been taught by the Tannaite authority of the household of Elijah:

E. "A person should always place upon himself the work of studying the Torah as an ox accepts the yoke, and as an ass, its burden."

That completes the miscellany. It certainly plays no role in Mishnah exegesis. It also sets forth no proposition, in a way in which compositions of Mishnah exegesis, and even composites thereof, commonly do. Rather, we have a set of compositions of a rather diverse quality, which are grouped by common themes; the points that they make jointly are at best commonplaces. The grouping of the compositions into subcomposites is fairly easy to explain, and their further agglutination into the large-scale composite before us lays within the range of reasonable explanation. We have something more than a random scrapbook of this-and-that. The survey just now concluded leaves us with an impression somewhat different from what we expected at the outset. First of all, identifying the supplementary entries – footnotes, appendices – shows us that a fair amount of the miscellany in fact is made up of secondary expansions of a quite coherent text. Within the technical limitations of our authorship, who, after all, had no way of signifying footnotes and appendices, the framers of the whole had no choice but to gloss. Second, the rather sizable sequence of free-standing compositions in the aggregate is made up of conglomerates, the cogency of which we are able to explain. Third, the order of the conglomerates is not entirely beyond reason, since if we were to state the propositions not proved but illustrated by what is before us, we would have these simple statements:

1. Study of the Torah on the part of a human being elicits in God a counterpart response, one of grace.
2. Israel lives through study of the Torah.
3. God favors Israel, by reason of Israel's study of the Torah, and is angry with the gentiles.
4. Israel's good deeds in this world will be rewarded not now but in the world to come.

We then end with what is labelled as an appendix to materials introduced earlier. Now while we can hardly claim that the enormous composite made up of No. 2 through 33 is a sustained and well-crafted whole, we also cannot settle for the characterization of the set as a mere miscellany. It is made up of clearly identifiable composites, each of them comprising already made up compositions. Where there is a movement from one to the next, there is ordinarily a clear connection, for example, a reference to a subtheme now given principal place as a main theme; an allusion to a person, now formed into the focus of a set of compositions. What holds the parts together, one to the next, is a connection of a formal, generally a thematic character. What holds the whole together is a sequence of unfolding themes. It would claim far too much to allege that we have a demonstration of a single proposition, for example, God hates and is angry with idolators and loves and rewards Israel. But it would be obtuse not to observe that that theme, remarkably coherent with the Mishnah tractate overall and with the opening paragraph of the Mishnah in particular, is present and is treated.

Let me now summarize the whole. I.1 begins with a systematic inquiry into the correct reading of the Mishnah's word choices. The dispute is fully articulated in balance, beginning to end. No. 2 then forms a footnote to No. 1. No. 3 then provides a footnote to the leitmotif of No. 2, the conception of God's not laughing. and No. 4 returns us to the exposition of No. 2, at HHH. Nos. 5, 6 are tacked on – a Torah study anthology – because they continue the general theme of Torah study every day, which formed the main motif of No. 2 – the gentiles did not accept the Torah, study it, or carry it out. So that theme accounts for the accumulation of sayings on Torah study in general, a kind of appendix on the theme. Then – so far as I can see, because of the reference to God's power – No. 7 begins with a complement to 6.I. The compositions, Nos. 7, 8, then are strung together because of a point that is deemed to link each to its predecessor. No. 7 is linked to the foregoing because of the theme of God's power; but it also intersects with 2.HHH and complements that reference; the entire sequence beyond No. 2 then in one way or another relates to either No. 2, theme or proposition, or to an item that is tacked on to No. 2 as a complement. Thus No. 8 is joined to No. 7 because of the shared method of contrasting verses. Then No. 9 is tacked on because it continues the proposition of No. 8. No. 10 continues the foregoing. No. 11 is tacked on to No. 10 for the reason made explicit: it continues what has gone before. The same is so for No. 12. No. 13 continues the theme, but not the form or the proposition, of the prior compositions, namely, punishment little by little, for example, in this world, in exchange for a great reward later on. The established theme then is divine punishment and how it is inflicted: gently to Israel, harshly to the gentiles; the preferred form is the contrast among two verses. That overall principle of conglomeration – form and theme – explains the inclusion of Nos. 14, 15+16, which is tacked on to 15. But then the introduction of Balaam, taken as the prototype for the min, accounts for the inclusion of a variety of further sayings on the same theme, specifically, No. 17, a gloss on the foregoing; No. 18, a continuation of the foregoing process of glossing, No. 19, an amplification on the now-dominant theme; No. 20, a reversion to No. 16; No. 21, a story on the theme of how difficult it is to define precisely the matter dealt with in the foregoing. No. 21, 22, 23 complete the discussion of that particular time at which God is angry, a brief moment but one that is marked by a just cause. No. 23 then introduces the theme of choosing the right time – that is not the moment of divine wrath – for prayer. This seems to me a rather miscellaneous item, and it marks the conclusion of the systematic expansion begun much earlier. That that is the fact is shown by the character of No. 24, which cites 2.HHH, and by No. 25, which explicitly reverts to 2.SS, which justifies my insistence that the entire corpus of materials that follow No. 2 simply amplify and augment No. 2, and that is done in a very systematic way. Some of the sets, as we have seen, were formed into conglomerates prior to insertion here, but once we recognize that all of the sets serve the single task at hand, we see the coherent of what on the surface appears to be run on and miscellaneous. In my *Rules of Composition*, Chapter Two, I show in a graphic way how these materials serve No. 2, some as footnotes, some as appendices, and some as footnotes or appendices to footnotes or appendices. No. 26 is a fine case in point. It complements 25.H, and is tacked on for that reason. Then No. 27 complements No. 26's statements concerning David. Bearing a formal tie to No. 27, with the same authority, No. 28 fits in also because it reverts to the theme of No. 25, the power of the religious duties that one carries out. No. 29 continues the theme of No. 28, that is, death and the day of judgment. Simeon's statement defines the center of gravity of the passage, which obviously was complete prior to its inclusion here. The reason it has been added is its general congruence to the discussions of sin, penitence, death and forgiveness. No. 30 is attached to No. 31, and No. 31 is tacked on because it refers to the prooftext in the prior composition. No. 32 takes up the prooftext of No. 31. No. 33 writes a solid conclusion to the whole, addressing as it does the basic theme that Israel's actions define their fate, and that study of the Torah is what determines everything else. That is a thematic conclusion to a composite largely devoted, one way or another, to that one theme.

What then leads us to see Nos. 2 through 33 as a miscellany? It is the contrast between that composite and the amazingly coherent character of the Talmud's Mishnah commentary. And since the Talmud is made up mostly of Mishnah commentary, what holds together its thematic sets, and what accounts for their relationship to the Mishnah, are considerations that are easy to miss. But in the case of what is before us, we can readily see both what holds the several composites together, what links one composite to the next, and what defines the relationship of the entire group of composites to the Mishnah paragraph that stands at the head. The upshot may be easily stated. The miscellanies really are not at all miscellaneous. They form an integral part of the Talmud's program of Mishnah commentary. But they are made up of materials that, on their own, do not address the language or propositions of the Mishnah, only its (implicit) themes. As a result, they do not exhibit the literary cogency that makes the bulk of the Talmud so remarkably coherent. Viewed in their own terms, however, the materials we have examined answer the question the Mishnah paragraph raises and respond to its topical program: gentiles observe holy days in the service of idols. Israel should have nothing to do with such things. God loves Israel, who study the Torah, forgives their sins, and in the world to come will give them their lasting, and just reward. In light of the propositions of the Mishnah, we can hardly have asked for a more appropriate set of compositions than those selected and arranged in the massive "miscellany" at hand. Now to the more difficult problem of the two "anomalous" chapters I identified in Chapter One.

4

Three Massive Miscellanies: [2] Bavli Berakhot Chapter One

The first sample has given us a different picture of the character of the miscellaneous composite from the one with which we began. What we observed is that the miscellany is anything but random. A set of discrete compositions is not just thrown together. The lot is put together into composites that adhere in accord with a readily discerned principle of agglutination, so that groups of compositions form cogent composites because of shared topics and even propositions. We were able to explain what joined one entry to another, fore and aft, and we could furthermore identify sizable blocks of coherent compositions. It follows that we may characterize the composites as different from those that serve as Mishnah exegesis and amplification, but as composites nonetheless. What makes them different is that while composites addressed to the Mishnah and its law prove sustainedly analytical and not uncommonly proposition, those that do not speak to the Mishnah hold together because they treat a shared theme, or because they are attributed to the same authority, in descending order of frequency. So – in the complex document before us – agglutinative discourse gains coherence in a different way from analytical discourse, but, nonetheless, we must regard it as cogent. That hypothesis represents a considerable step away from our starting point. It remains to be tested against the two massive miscellanies to which my analysis of the *Bavli's One Voice* drew attention, those of Berakhot, in the present chapter, and in Sanhedrin, in the next.

1:1

A. From what time do they recite the Shema in the evening?

B. From the hour that the priests [who had immersed after uncleanness and awaited sunset to complete the process of purification] enter [a state of cleanness, the sun having set, so as] to eat their heave-offering –

C. "Until the end of the first watch," the words of R. Eliezer.

D. And sages say, "Until midnight."

E. Rabban Gamaliel says, "Until the rise of dawn."

F. M'SH S: His sons came from the banquet hall.

G. They said to him, "We do not recite the Shema."

H   He said to them, "If the morning star has not yet risen, you are obligated to recite [the Shema]."

I. And not only [in] this [case], rather, all [commandments] which sages said [may be performed] until midnight, their religious duty to do them applies until the rise of the morning star.

J. [For example], as to the offering of the fats and entrails – the religious duty to do them applies until the rise of the morning star.

K   All [sacrifices] which are eaten for one day, their religious duty to do them applies until the rise of the morning star.

L. If so why did sages say [that these actions may be performed only] until midnight?

M. In order to keep a man far from sin.

I.

A   On what basis does the Tannaite authority stand when he begins by teaching the rule, "From what time...," [in the assumption that the religious duty to recite the *Shema* has somewhere been established? In point of fact, it has not been established that people have to recite the *Shema* at all.]

B. Furthermore, on what account does he teach the rule concerning the evening at the beginning? Why not start with the morning?

C. The Tannaite authority stands upon the authority of Scripture, [both in requiring the recitation of the *Shema* and in beginning with the evening], for it is written, "When you lie down and when you rise up" (Deut. 6:7).

D. And this is the sense of the passage: When is the time for the recitation of the *Shema* when one lies down? It is *from the hour that the priests enter [a state of cleanness so as] to eat their heave-offering [M. 1:1B].*

E. And if you prefer, I may propose that the usage derives from the order of the description of creation, for it is said, "And there was evening, and there was morning, one day" (Gen. 1:5).

F. If that were the principal consideration, then let us take note of the formulation of the rules that occurs later on: *In the morning one says two blessings before reciting the Shema and one afterward, and in the evening, one says two blessings beforehand and two afterward [M. 1:4].* [The formulation therefore ignores the order of the description of creation.]

G   [By the reasoning just now proposed,] should not the Tannaite authority speak first of evening?

H   The Tannaite authority at hand began by discussing matters pertaining to the *Shema* recited in the evening, and then he proceeded to take up matters having to do with reciting the *Shema* at dawn. While dealing with the matters having to do with the dawn, he proceeded to spell out other rules on the same matter, and then, only at the end, he went on to spell out other matters having to do with the evening.

II.

A.	A master stated: *From the hour that the priests [who had immersed after uncleanness and awaited sunset to complete the process of purification] enter [a state of cleanness, the sun having set, so as] to eat their heave-offering [M. 1:1B].*

B.	In point of fact, when is it that the priest actually eats food in the status of heave-offering [having completed the process of purification]? Is it not when the stars come out? So let the frame of the passage say simply, "From when the stars come out."

C.	His intent was to inform about a quite distinct matter *en passant*, namely, when in fact do priests eat heave-offering [once the process of purification has been completed]? It is from the time that the stars come out.

D.	And lo, what he further tells us is that the rite of atonement for having been unclean [an element of the rite of purification] is not essential [to the matter of eating food in the status of heave-offering].

E.	For it has been taught on Tannaite authority:

F.	"And when the sun sets and the day is clear [for eating heave-offering]" (Lev. 22:7).

G.	The sense is that the setting of the sun is what is essential in permitting the priest to eat food in the status of heave-offering, and the completion of the purification rite through an atonement sacrifice is not essential in permitting the priest to eat food in the status of heave-offering.

H.	How do we know that the sense of the words is, "And the sun sets so that the day is clear"?

I.	[2B] Perhaps the sense is, "When the sun comes [up the next day], *then* the man will be clean"?

J.	Said Rabbah bar R. Shila, "If that were the case, Scripture would have had to say, 'And he *will be* clean.' What is the sense of 'and it is clear'? The meaning is that the day clears out, as people say, 'The sun has set and the day has cleared out.'"

K.	In the West [in the Land of Israel] this statement of Rabbah b. R. Shila was not available, so they framed the matter in this way: "Does the expression, 'And the sun sets,' refer to the setting of the sun? And what is the sense of 'will be clean'? Does it mean that the day is clear, or perhaps that the appearance of the sun is such that the man becomes clean?"

L.	They went and solved the problem by reference to a Tannaite teaching, for it has been taught in a Tannaite teaching:

M.	**A mnemonic for the matter consists in the appearance of the stars [T. Ber. 1:1D].**

N.	That mnemonic then bears the implication that the reference is to sunset, with the sense of "will be clean" that the day will be clear.

III.

A   A master has said: *From the hour that the priests [who had immersed after uncleanness and awaited sunset to complete the process of purification] enter [a state of cleanness, the sun having set, so as] to eat their heave-offering [M. 1:1B]:*

B.   An objection was raised on the basis of the following statement:

C   From what time do people recite the *Shema* in the evening? From when a poor man goes in to eat his bread and salt, until he stands up to leave his meal.

D.   The second clause [limiting the time for reading the *Shema* to a brief interval] assuredly contradicts the Mishnah passage before us.

E.   But as to the former passage, may we say that there is a disagreement between the cited version and the Mishnah passage at hand?

F.   No, not necessarily so. Since the poor man and the priest are subject to the same specification of the appropriate time for eating the meal, [namely, at sunset, the two statements simply refer to the same hour in different ways].

IV.

A   An objection was raised [from a different version of the rule at hand:]

B.   **From what time does one recite the Shema in the evening [M. Ber. 1:1A]?**

C   **"From the time that people go to eat their meal on the eve of the Sabbath," the words of R. Meir.**

D.   **And sages say, "From the time that the priests are permitted to eat their heave-offering [M. Ber. 1:1B].**

E.   **"A mnemonic for the matter [which designates the proper time] is the emergence of the stars."**

F.   **Even though there is no [explicit scriptural] proof for the matter, there is an allusion to the matter [in the verse,] so we labored at the work and half of them held the spears from the break of dawn till the stars came out (Neh. 4:15 [= RSV 4:21]) [T. Ber. 1:1A-E].**

G   And Scripture further states, "That in the night they may be a guard for us and may labor in the day" (Neh. 4:16).

H.   What is the sense of this further prooftext?

I   It is this: Should you ask, "Now the night indeed begins with sunset, but they, for their part, got up and left early and, furthermore, came home early as well," [I prove my case with the verse, to which] you should pay heed: "That in the night they may be a guard for us and may labor in the day" (Neh. 4:16).

J.   [Reverting to the point at which we began:] Now you presumably maintain that the poor person and ordinary folk are subject to the same specification of time for supper. [Hence we take for granted that the poor man of unit III and the people of the cited passage of Tosefta eat at the same time.]

K   But if you maintain that the poor man and the priest are subject to the same specification of time [as unit III has said], then we find that sages and R. Meir say the same thing. [That is impossible, since the point of the passage at hand is that they are in disagreement.]

L.   That surely proves that a poor man is subject to one specification of time, and a priest to a different specification of time.

M.   No, not necessarily so. A poor man and a priest are subject to a single specification of time, but a poor man and ordinary folk are not subject to the same specification of time.

N.   Is it then the case that the poor man and the priest really accord with the same specification of time [at which they eat supper]?

O.   An objection was raised from the following:

P.   "From what time do people start to recite the *Shema* in the evening? From the moment at which, on the eve of the Sabbath, the day is sanctified [by sunset]," the words of R. Eliezer.

Q.   R. Joshua says, "From the time that priests have attained cleanness so as to eat their heave-offering."

R.   R. Meir says, "From the time that priests immerse so as to be able to eat heave-offering."

S.   Said R. Judah to him, "But do not the priests immerse while it is day?"

T.   R. Hanina says, "From the time that a poor man goes in to eat his bread and salt."

U.   R. Ahai, and some say, R. Aha, says, "From the time that most people go in to recline [at their meal]."

V.   Now if you maintain that the poor man and the priest are subject to a single specification of time, then R. Hanina and R. Joshua are saying the same thing.

W.   Does it not follow, then, that the specification of time for reciting the *Shema* for a poor man is different from the specification of time for the priest?

X.   It does indeed follow.

Y.   Which of the specified times comes later?

Z.   It is reasonable to assume that that of the poor man comes later.

AA.   For if you maintain that that of the poor man comes earlier [than that of the priest], it follows that R. Hanina is saying the same thing as R. Eliezer.

BB.   Does it not then follow that the time for the poor man to recite the *Shema* is later than the time for the priest?

CC.   It does indeed follow.

V.

A.   A master has said: "Said to him R. Judah, 'But do not the priests immerse while it is still day?'"

B.   R. Judah's reply to R. Meir is a good one.

C.   This is what R. Meir can reply to him, "Do you suppose that I make reference to twilight as you define it? I make reference to twilight as R. Yosé defines it."

D.   R. Yosé has said, "Twilight lasts for as long as the blinking of an eye. As soon as the one [night] comes in, the other [day] goes out. It is not possible to fix it exactly. [Simon, p. 5, n. 6: And consequently the priests may bathe at twilight as defined by R. Yosé since it is still day, and one may also recite the *Shema* at that time since it is practically night]."

E.   [3A] The views of R. Meir appear to contradict one another [since he says people recite the *Shema* when they come home for supper on the Sabbath night, and that is after twilight, but he also sets a time that is prior to twilight].

F. What we have in hand are the versions of two different Tannaite authorities concerning the opinion of R. Meir.

G. The views of R. Eliezer appear to contradict one another [as before].

H What we have in hand are the versions of two different Tannaite authorities concerning the opinion of R. Eliezer.

I. Or, if you prefer, I shall propose that the first of the two opinions does not belong to R. Eliezer at all.

VI.

A. *"Until the end of the first watch," the words of R. Eliezer [M. 1:1C].*

B. What is R. Eliezer's view [about the division of the night watches]?

C. If he takes the view that the night is divided into three watches, let him say, "Until four hours [have passed in the night]."

D. If he takes the view that the night is divided into four watches, let him say, "Until three hours [have passed in the night]."

E. In point of fact he takes the view that the night is divided into three watches. And by phrasing matters as he does, he informs us that there are watches in the firmament and watches on earth, [and these correspond].

F. For it has been taught on Tannaite authority:

G. R. Eliezer says, "The night is divided into three watches, and [in heaven] over each watch the Holy One, blessed be He, sits and roars like a lion,

H "as it is said, 'The Lord roars from on high and raises his voice from his holy habitation, roaring he does roar because of his fold' (Jer. 25:30).

I. "The indication of each watch is as follows: At the first watch, an ass brays, at the second, dogs yelp, at the third, an infant sucks at its mother's breast or a woman whispers to her husband."

J. What is R. Eliezer's reckoning?

K. If he is reckoning from the beginning of the several watches, then what need is there to give a sign for the beginning of the first watch? It is twilight.

L. If he is reckoning from the end of the several watches, then what need is there to give a sign for the end of the third watch? It is marked by the coming of the day.

M But he is reckoning at the end of the first watch, beginning of the last, and the middle of the middle watch, and that is what the specified signs indicate.

N Or, if you prefer, I shall propose that in all cases he reckons from the end of the watches. And, as to your question, why is it necessary to specify the end of the third watch, for what difference would it make?

O. The answer is this: It is important for the recitation of the *Shema* in the case of someone who sleeps in a darkened room and does not know when it is time for reciting the *Shema:* When a woman whispers to her husband or an infant sucks from the breast of its mother, it is time for him to get up and to recite the *Shema.*

VII.

A Said R. Isaac bar Samuel in the name of Rab, "The night is divided into three watches, and over each watch, the Holy One, blessed be He, sits and roars like a lion.

B. "He says, 'Woe to the children, on account of whose sins I have wiped out my house and burned my palace, and whom I have exiled among the nations of the world.'"

VIII.

A. It has been taught on Tannaite authority:

B. Said R. Yosé, "Once I was going along the way, and I went into one of the ruins of Jerusalem to pray. Elijah, of blessed memory, came and watched over me at the door until I had finished my prayer. After I had finished my prayer, he said to me, 'Peace be to you, my lord.'

C. "And I said to him, 'Peace be to you, my lord and teacher.'

D. "And he said to me, 'My son, on what account did you go into this ruin?'

E. "And I said to him, 'To pray.'

F. "And he said to me, 'You would have done better to pray on the road.'

G. "And I said to him, 'I was afraid lest some bypassers interrupt me.'

H "He said to me, 'You would have been better off to say an abbreviated form of the prayer.'

I. "Thus I learned three lessons from him. I learned that people should not go into ruins, I learned that people may say a prayer on the road, and I learned that if one is praying on the road, he should say an abbreviated version of the prayer.

J. "And he said to me, 'My son, what sound did you hear in this ruin?'

K. "I said to him, 'I heard the sound of an echo moaning like a pigeon and saying, "Woe to the children, on account of whose sins I have wiped out my house and burned my palace and whom I have exiled among the nations of the world."'

L. "He said to me, 'By your life and the life of your head, it is not only at this moment that the echo speaks in such a way, but three times daily, it says the same thing.

M "'And not only so, but when Israelites go into synagogues and schoolhouses and respond, "May the great name be blessed," the Holy One shakes his head and says, "Happy is the king, whom they praise in his house in such a way! What does a father have, who has exiled his children? And woe to the children who are exiled from their father's table!"'"

IX.

A. Our rabbis have taught on Tannaite authority:

B. For three reasons people should not go into a ruin, because of suspicion [of an assignation there], because of the danger of collapse, and because of demons."

C. [Why mention all three reasons?] "Because of suspicion" is not needed, since it would be sufficient to give the reason of danger of a collapse.

D. [3B] That would not apply to a new ruin.

E.   Then offer as the sole reason "on account of demons."

F.   We deal with a case in which two people go in [and demons do not bother two people].

G.   If there are two people, then there is no consideration of suspicion of an assignation.

H.   It might be two people who are known as licentious.

I.   "Because of the danger of collapse" – but why not merely because of suspicion and demons? You might have two people who are honorable [in which case the other considerations do not apply].

J.   "Because of demons" – and why not suffice with the considerations of suspicion or collapse?

K.   You might have the case of a new ruin, and two people who are honorable.

L.   If there are two people, then what consideration of demons is at hand?

M.   In a place which demons inhabit, there is danger [even to two].

N.   If you prefer, I shall propose that we deal only with one person and with a new ruin located in the fields. In such a case there is no consideration of suspicion of an assignation, for women do not go out by themselves to the fields. But there is surely a consideration of demons.

X.

A.   Our rabbis have taught on Tannaite authority:

B.   **"The night has four watches," the words of Rabbi.**

C.   **Rabbi Nathan says, "Three."**

D.   **What is the scriptural basis for the view of R. Nathan?**

E.   **As it is written, "So Gideon and the hundred men that were with him came into the outermost part of the camp in the beginning of the middle watch" (Judg. 7:19).**

F.   **A Tannaite authority stated, "There can be a middle watch only if there is one before it and one after it" [hence, three] [T. Ber. 1:1G-L].**

G.   And, so far as Rabbi is concerned, what is the meaning of, "...middle..."? [How does he explain it?]

H.   The sense of the passage is, one of *two* middle ones.

I.   But R. Nathan may respond: Is "one of the middle ones" written? What is written is, "the middle *one*" [of three].

J.   What is the scriptural basis for the view of Rabbi?

K.   Said R. Zeriqa said R. Ammi said R. Joshua b. Levi, "One verse of Scripture says, 'At midnight I rise to give thanks to you because of your righteous ordinances' (Ps. 119:62).

L.   "And another verse of Scripture says, 'My eyes open before the watches' (Ps. 119:148).

M   "How so [Simon, p. 8, n. 5: that somebody may rise at midnight and still have two watches before him, the minimum of the plural watches being two]?

N.   "The night is divided into four watches."

O.   And R. Nathan accords with the view of R. Joshua.

P.   For we have learned in the Mishnah:

Q   *R. Joshua says, "Until the third hour, for it is the practice of royalty to rise at the third hour" [M. Ber. 1:2E-F].*

R. Six hours of the night and two of the day add up to two watches. [Simon, p. 8, n. 7: Since the day for royal personages begins at eight a.m., that is with the third hour when they rise. David by rising at midnight forestalled them by eight hours, i.e., two watches, each have four hours.]

S. R. Ashi said, "A watch and a half may also be called 'watches.'"

XI.

A. And [continuing X.K] R. Zeriqa said R. Ammi said R. Joshua b. Levi said, "In the presence of a corpse people may speak only about matters having to do with the deceased."

B. Said R. Abba bar Kahana, "That rule applies only to speaking about words of Torah, but as to commonplace matters, we have no objection."

C. And there are those who say, said R. Abba bar Kahana, "That rule applies even to words of Torah, and all the more so to commonplace matters."

XII.

A. [Reverting to the statement at K that David got up at midnight:] Did David get up at midnight? He got up at dusk of the evening.

B. For it is written, "I got up with the *neshef* and cried" (Ps. 119:147).

C. And this word *neshef* speaks of the evening, for it is written, "In the *neshef*, in the evening of the day, in the blackness of the night and the darkness" (Prov. 7:9).

D. Said R. Oshaiah said R. Aha, "This is the sense of the passage: 'Half the night never passed for me in sleep' [and that is the meaning of Ps. 119:162]."

E. R. Zira said, "Up to midnight he would doze like a horse, from that point he would regain full energy like a lion."

F. R. Ashi said, "Up to midnight he would deal with teachings of Torah. From that point he would engage in songs and praises."

G. But does the word *neshef* refer to dusk? Surely the word refers to the morning light, for it is written, "And David slew them from the *neshef* to the evening of the next day" (1 Sam. 30:17), with the sense "from the morning to evening."

H. No, that is not the sense. Rather, it is from dusk, to dusk on the next day.

I. If that were the case, the passage should read, "From dusk to dusk" or "from evening to evening."

J. Rather, said Raba, "The word *neshef* has two meanings. One refers to the dawn of day, when the evening disappears and the morning comes, and the other to when the day disappears and the evening comes [and *neshef* in this instance refers to dusk]."

XIII.

A. Did David really know exactly when it was midnight?

B. Now Moses, our master, did not know, for it is written, "At about midnight I will go out into the midst of Egypt" (Ex. 11:4).

C. What is the sense of "at about midnight" cited in the preceding verse?

D. If I should say that that is language which the Holy One, blessed be He, said to him, that is, "At about midnight," is it possible that before Heaven there is such a doubt [as to the exact time of night? That is impossible.]

E.   Rather, [God] said to him, "At midnight," but Moses is the one who came along and said, "At about midnight."

F.   It follows that he was in doubt as to exactly when it was midnight. Could David then have known exactly when it was?

G.   David had a device for telling when it was.

H   For R. Aha bar Bizna said R. Simeon the Pious said, "David had a harp suspended over his bed, and when midnight came, the north wind would come and blow on the strings, and the harp would play on its own. David immediately got up and undertook Torah study until dawn.

I.   "When it was dawn, the sages of Israel came in to him. They said to him, 'Our lord, O king, your people Israel needs sustenance.'

J.   "He said to them, 'Let them go and make a living from one another.'

K.   "They said to him, 'A handful [of food] cannot satisfy a lion, and a hole in the ground cannot be filled up from its own clods.'

L.   "He said to them, 'Go and organize marauders.'

M   "They forthwith took counsel with Ahitophel and sought the advice of the sanhedrin and addressed a question to the Urim and Thumim."

N   Said R. Joseph, "What verse indicates this? 'And after Ahithophel was Jehoiada, son of Benaiah, and Abiathar, and the captain of the king's host was Joab' (1 Chr. 27:34).

O.   "'Ahithophel was counsellor,' and so it is said, 'Now the counsel of Ahithophel, which he counselled in those days, was as if a man inquired of the word of God' (2 Sam. 16:23).

P.   [4A] "'Benaiah, son of Jehoiada' refers to the sanhedrin.

Q   "'And Abiathar' refers to the Urim and Thumim. And so it says, 'And Benaiah, son of Jehoiada, was in charge of the Kerethi and Pelethi' (2 Sam. 20:23).

R.   "Why were the Urim and Thumim so called? They were called 'Kerethi' because their words are decisive *[korethim]*, and 'Pelethi' because they are distinguished *(muflaim)* through what they say.

S.   "And then comes 'the captain of the king's host, Joab.'"

T.   Said R. Isaac bar Ada, and some say R. Isaac, son of R. Idid, said, "What is the verse of Scripture that makes this point? 'Awake, my glory, awake, psaltery and harp, I will awake the dawn' (Ps. 57:9)."

U.   [Reverting to A-B, F] R. Zira said, "Moses most certainly knew when it was midnight, and so did David.

V.   "But since David knew, what did he need a harp for? It was to wake him up from his sleep.

W.   "And since Moses also knew, why did he say, 'at *about* midnight'?

X.   "Moses thought that the astrologers of Pharoah might make a mistake and then claim that Moses was a charlatan [should the event not take place exactly when Moses predicted, if he made too close a statement for their powers of calculation]."

Y.   For a master has said, 'Teach your tongue to say, 'I don't know,' lest you turn out to lie.'"

Z. R. Ashi said, "[The matter of Ex. 11:4] took place at midnight on the night of the thirteenth toward dawn of the fourteenth.

AA. "And this is what Moses said to Israel: 'The Holy One, blessed be He, has said, "Tomorrow at about midnight, at around this time, I shall go forth into the midst of Egypt."'"

XIV.

A. "A prayer of David: Keep my soul, for I am pious" (Ps. 86:1-2).

B. Levi and R. Isaac.

C. One of them said, "This is what David said before the Holy One, blessed be He, 'Lord of the world, am I not pious? For all kings, east and west, sleep to the third hour, but as for me: "At midnight, I rise to give thanks to you" (Ps. 119:62).'"

D. The other said, "This is what David said before the Holy One, blessed be He, 'Lord of the world, am I not pious? For all kings, east and west, sit in all their glory with their retinues, but as for me, my hands are sloppy with menstrual blood and the blood of the foetus and placenta, which I examine so as to declare a woman clean for sexual relations with her husband.

E. "'And not only so, but, further, in whatever I do, I take counsel with Mephibosheth, my master, and I say to him, "Rabbi Mephibosheth, did I do right in the judgment I gave? Did I do right in acquitting? Did I do right in awarding an advantage? Did I do right in declaring something clean? Did I do right in declaring something unclean?" and in no way have I been ashamed [to depend on his judgment].'"

F. Said R. Joshua, son of R. Idi, "What verse of Scripture supports that view of David? 'And I recite your testimonies before kings and am not ashamed' (Ps. 119:46)."

XV.

A. A Tannaite authority stated: His name was not Mephibosheth but Ishbosheth. But why did he bear that name? Because he shamed David in criticizing his legal decisions. Therefore David gained merit so that Kileab (2 Sam. 3:3) should come forth from him."

B. And R. Yohanan said, "His name was not Kileab but rather Daniel. Why, then, was he called Kileab? Because he shamed Mephibosheth in criticizing his legal decisions.

C. "And concerning him said Solomon in his sagacity, 'My son, if your heart is wise, my heart will be glad, even mine' (Prov. 23:15).

D. "And he further said, 'My son, be wise and make my heart glad, that I may answer him who taunts me' (Prov. 27:11)."

XVI.

A. Now did David really call himself "pious"?

B. And has it not been written, "I am not sure to see the good reward of the Lord in the land of the living" (Ps. 27:13). [How could David have been unsure, if he knew he was pious?]

C. A Tannaite authority taught in this connection in the name of R. Yosé, "Why are there dots over the word for 'not sure'?

D. "Said David before the Holy One, blessed be He, 'Lord of the world, I am confident you pay a good reward to the righteous in the coming future, but I do not know if I shall have a share among them or not. Perhaps sin will cause [punishment for me instead of reward].'"

E.   That accords with what R. Jacob bar Idi said, for R. Jacob bar Idi contrasted two verses of Scripture, as follows: "It is written, 'And behold, I am with you and will keep you wherever you go' (Gen. 28:15), and another verse states, 'Then Jacob was greatly afraid' (Gen. 32:8).

F.   "[Why the contrast between God's promise and Jacob's fear?] [Jacob thought to himself,] 'Sin which I have done may cause [punishment for me instead].'"

G.   That accords with what has been taught on Tannaite authority:

H   "Till your people pass over, O Lord, till your people pass over, that you have acquired" (Ex. 15:16).

I.   "Till your people pass over" refers to the first entry into the land [in Joshua's time].

J.   "Till your people pass over, that you have acquired" refers to the second entry into the land [in the time of Ezra and Nehemiah. Thus a miracle was promised not only on the first occasion, but also on the second. But it did not happen the second time around. Why not?]

K.   On the basis of this statement, sages have said, "The Israelites were worthy of having a miracle performed for them in the time of Ezra also, just as it had been performed for them in the time of Joshua b. Nun, but sin caused [the miracle to be withheld]."

XVII.

A.   *And sages say, "Until midnight" [M. 1:1D]:*

B.   [Since Eliezer holds that the time of "lying down" is when one goes to bed, on which account Eliezer has the *Shema* recited only until the end of the first watch, and since Gamaliel allows the *Shema* to be recited until dawn, understanding "lying down" to refer to the entire period of sleep, we ask:] Which view did sages adopt?

C.   If they take the view of R. Eliezer [that "lying down" refers to going to bed], then let them state, "... in accord with R. Eliezer."

D.   [4B] If they take the view of Rabban Gamaliel [that "lying down" refers to the time in which people sleep], then let them state, "... in accord with Rabban Gamaliel."

E.   In point of fact sages accord with the view of Rabban Gamaliel, but the reason that *they have said, "until midnight" is in order to keep a man far from sin [M. 1:1M-N].*

F.   This accords with that which has been taught on Tannaite authority:

G.   The sages have established a fence for their rulings.

H   It is so that a person may not come in from the field in the evening and say, "I shall go to my house, eat a bit, drink a bit, sleep a bit, and afterward I shall recite the *Shema* and say the Prayer." But then sleep may overtake him, and he will end up sleeping all night long.

I.   Rather a person should come in from the field in the evening and go directly into the synagogue. If he is in the habit of reciting Scripture, then let him recite Scripture, and if he is in the habit of repeating Mishnah sayings, then let him repeat Mishnah sayings, and then let him recite the *Shema* and say the Prayer. Only then should he eat his bread and say the blessing [and sleep].

J.   And whoever violates the teachings of sages is liable to death.

K.   Now why is it that in all other passages the Tannaite formulation does not include the statement that one may be liable to death, while in the present case the Tannaite formulation includes the words, "And he is liable to death"?

L.   If you wish, I shall propose that there is the consideration that sleep might come inadvertently [so ordinarily there would be no penalty, but here there is a penalty even in a case of inadvertence.]

M.   And if you wish, I shall propose that the reason is that the formulation serves, as an additional teaching, to exclude the view of him who says, "The recitation of the Prayer in the evening is an optional matter."

N.   In phrasing matters in this way, we are informed that it is obligatory.

XVIII.

A.   A Master has said, "He recites the *Shema* and says the Prayer."

B.   This supports the view of R. Yohanan.

C.   For R. Yohanan has said, "Who belongs to the world to come? It is one who places the recitation of the blessing for the redemption from Egypt right next to the recitation of the Prayer in the evening [and thus recites the *Shema* and the Prayer in sequence]."

D.   And R. Joshua b. Levi says, "The [sages] ordained that the Prayers should be said in the middle [between the two recitations of the *Shema*, morning and night. Thus there will be the *Shema*, one Prayer, then, at dark the next Prayer and then the final *Shema*]."

E.   What is the point at issue?

F.   If you wish, I may propose that at issue is the exegesis of a verse of Scripture, and if you wish, I shall propose that it is a point of reasoning.

G.   If you wish I shall propose that it is a point of reasoning:

H.   R. Yohanan takes the view that while the redemption from Egypt took place in the full light of day, there was an act of redemption by night as well, [on which account the blessing for the redemption from Egypt must be stated at night in sequence with the recitation of the Prayer, which, after all, includes prayers for personal and national redemption].

I.   And R. Joshua b. Levi takes the view that since the full redemption took place only by day, the redemption by night was not really of like order [with the equivalent, opposite consequence].

J.   If you wish, I shall propose that at issue is the exegesis of a verse of Scripture. In fact, both authorities interpret a single verse.

K.   It is written, "When you lie down and when you rise up" (Deut. 6:7).

L.   R. Yohanan takes the theory that Scripture therefore establishes an analogy between lying down and rising up. Just as, when one gets up, he recites the *Shema* and afterward says the Prayer, so when he lies down, he also says the *Shema* and afterward says the Prayer.

M.   R. Joshua b. Levi theorizes that the analogy serves to compare lying down to rising up. Just as when one gets up, the recitation of the *Shema* is accomplished close to the point at which he gets out of bed, so when he lies down, the recitation of the *Shema* should be close to the point at which he goes to bed.

N   To the theory at hand Mar, son of Rabina, objected, "*In the evening one recites two blessings before it and two blessings after it [M. Ber. 1:4].* Now if you maintain that one has to set one thing near the other, lo, in this case a person does not set the blessing for redemption next to the Prayer, for lo, he has to say the prayer beginning, 'Cause us to lie down in peace...' [so the reasoning of Joshua b. Levi does not work]."

O   One may reply as follows: Since rabbis are the ones who ordained that one should recite, "Cause us to lie down...," it is a kind of protracted prayer concerning redemption.

P.   If you do not maintain that thesis, then in the prayer at dawn, how can one place the one prayer next to the other?

Q   For lo, R. Yohanan has said, "At the beginning of the Prayer, one says, 'O Lord, open my lips...' (Ps. 51:17). [Here, too, there is an interruption between the one and the other, that is, between the blessing for redemption and the recitation of the Prayer.] And at the end, one should recite, 'Let the words of my mouth be acceptable' (Ps. 19:15)."

R.   But in the case at hand, since the rabbis are the ones who ordained that one must say, "O Lord, open my lips," it is regarded as a protracted recitation of the Prayer. Here, too, since rabbis have ordained that one must recite, "Cause us to lie down in peace," it falls into the category of a protracted blessing for redemption.

XIX.

A   Said R. Eleazar bar Abina, "Whoever says the Psalm, 'Praise of David' (Ps. 145) three times a day may be assured that he belongs to the world to come."

B.   What is the scriptural basis for that view?

C   If you should say that it is because the Psalm follows the order of the alphabet, there also is the Psalm, "Happy are they that are upright in the way" (Ps. 119) which goes through the alphabet eight times [and should be a preferred choice on that account].

D.   Rather, it is because [in Ps. 145] there is the sentence, "You open your hand and satisfy every living thing with favor" (Ps. 145:16).

E.   If that is the case, then in the Great Hallel (Ps. 136), we find the phrase, "Who gives food to all flesh" (Ps. 136:25), which one would do better to recite.

F.   Rather, it is because [in Ps. 145] there are both considerations [namely, the entire alphabet and the statement that God provides].

XX.

A   [Referring to Ps. 145], said R. Yohanan, "On what account is there no verse beginning with an N is Psalm 145?

B.   "It is because the N starts the verse referring to the fall of [the enemies of] Israel.

C   "For it is written, 'Fallen (NPLH), no more to rise, is the virgin of Israel' (Amos 5:2)."

D.   In the West [the Land of Israel] the verse at hand is laid out in this way: "Fallen, and no more to fall, the virgin of Israel will arise."

    E.   Said R. Nahman bar Isaac, "Even so, David went and by the Holy Spirit brought together the N with the following letter of the alphabet, S: 'The Lord upholds (SMK) all those who fall (NPL) (Ps. 145:14)."

XXI.

    A.   Said Eleazar bar Abina, "What is said about Michael is greater than what is said about Gabriel.

    B.   "In regard to Michael, it is written, 'Then one of the seraphim flew to me' (Isa. 6:6), while in respect to Gabriel, it is written, 'The man Gabriel whom I had seen in the vision at the beginning, being cause to fly in a flight' (Dan. 9:21)."

    C.   How do we know that this "one" refers in particular to Michael?

    D.   Said R. Yohanan, "We draw an analogy to other references to 'one.' Here it is written, 'Then one of the seraphim flew to me' (Isa. 6:6). And there it is written, 'And behold, Michael, one of the chief princes, came to help me' (Dan. 10:13)."

    E.   It was taught on Tannaite authority:

    F.   Michael [reaches his destination] in one [leap], Gabriel in two, Elijah in four, and the angel of death in eight, but during a time of plague, it is in one.

XXII.

    A.   Said R. Joshua b. Levi, "Even though a person has recited the *Shema* in the synagogue, it is a religious duty to recite it in bed."

    B.   Said R. Yosé, "What verse of Scripture indicates it? 'Tremble and do not sin, commune with your own heart upon your bed and be still, selah' (Ps. 4:5)."

    C.   Said R. Nahman, "[5A] If he is a disciple of a sage, he does not have to do so."

    D.   Said Abbayye, "Even a disciple of a sage has [in bed] to recite one verse, to plead for mercy, for example, 'Into your hand I commit my spirit, you have redeemed me, O Lord, you God of truth' (Ps. 31:6)."

XXIII.

    A.   Said R. Levi bar Hama said R. Simeon b. Laqish, "A person should always provoke his impulse to do good against his impulse to do evil,

    B.   "as it is said, 'Provoke and do not sin' (Ps. 4:5).

    C.   "If [the good impulse] wins, well and good. If not, let him take up Torah study,

    D.   "as it is said, 'Commune with your own heart' (Ps. 4:5).

    E.   "If [the good impulse] wins, well and good. If not, let him recite the *Shema*,

    F.   "as it is said, '...upon your bed' (Ps. 4:5).

    G.   "If [the good impulse] wins, well and good. If not, let him remember the day of death,

    H.   "as it is said, 'And keep silent. Sela' (Ps. 4:5)."

    I.   And R. Levi bar Hama said R. Simeon b. Laqish said, "What is the meaning of the verse of Scripture, 'And I will give you the tables of stone, the law and the commandment, which I have written, that you may teach them' (Ex. 24:12)?

    J.   "'The tables' refers to the Ten Commandments.

    K.   "'Torah' refers to Scripture.

L.   "'Commandment' refers to Mishnah.

M.   "'Which I have written' refers to the Prophets and the Writings.

N.   "'That you may teach them' refers to the *Gemara*.

O.   "'This teaches that all of them were given to Moses from Sinai.'"

XXIV.

A.   Said R. Isaac, "Whoever recites the *Shema* on his bed is as if he holds a two-edged sword in his hand [to fight against demons],

B.   "as it is said, 'Let the high praises of God be in their mouth, and a two-edged sword in their hand' (Ps. 149:6)."

C.   What is the proof [from that verse]?

D.   Said Mar Zutra, and some say, R. Ashi, "It derives from the opening part of the same passage,

E.   "for it is written, 'Let the saints exult in glory, let them sing for joy upon their beds' (Ps. 149:5), and then it is written, 'Let the high praises of God be in their mouth, and a two-edged sword in their hand.'"

F.   And R. Isaac said, "From whoever recites the *Shema* on his bed demons stay away.

G.   "For it is said, 'And the sons of *reshef* [sparks] fly upward' (Job 5:7).

H.   "The word used for 'fly' speaks only of the Torah, as it is written, 'Will you cause your eyes to close [using the same root] upon it? It is gone' (Prov. 23:5)."

I.   "And the word *reshef* refers solely to demons, as it is said, 'The wasting of hunger and the devouring of the *reshef* and bitter destruction' (Deut. 32:24)."

J.   Said R. Simeon b. Laqish, "From whoever takes up the study of Torah suffering stays away,

K.   "as it is said, 'And the sons of *reshef* fly upward' (Job 5:7).

L.   "The word used for 'fly' speaks only of the Torah, as it is written, 'Will you cause your eyes to close upon it? It is gone' (Prov. 23:5).

M.   "And the word *reshef* refers solely to suffering, as it is said, 'The wasting of hunger, and the devouring of the *reshef*...' (Deut. 32:24)."

N.   Said R. Yohanan to him, "Lo, even children in kindergarten know that, for it is written, 'And he said, If you will diligently hearken to the voice of the Lord your God and will do that which is right in his eyes and will give ear to his commandments and keep all his statutes, I will put none of the diseases upon you which I have put upon the Egyptians, for I am the Lord who heals you' (Ex. 15:26).

O.   "Rather, [phrase the matter in this way:] 'Upon whoever has the possibility of taking up the study of Torah and does not do so, the Holy One, blessed be He, brings ugly and troubling suffering, as it is said, "I was dumb with silence, I kept silence from the good thing, and so my pain was stirred up" (Ps. 39:3).

P.   "'The good thing' speaks only of the Torah, as it is said, 'For I give you a good doctrine, do not forsake my teaching' (Prov. 4:2)."

XXV.

A.   Said R. Zira, and some say, R. Hanina bar Papa, "Take note that the trait of the Holy One, blessed be He, is not like the trait of mortals."

B.   "When a mortal sells something to his fellow, the seller is sad and the buyer happy. But the Holy One, blessed be He, is not that way. He gave the Torah to Israel and was happy about it.

C. "For it is said, 'For I give you a good doctrine, do not forsake my teaching' (Prov. 4:2)."

XXVI.

A. Said Raba, and some say, R. Hisda, "If a person sees that sufferings afflict him, let him examine his deeds.

B. "For it is said, 'Let us search and try our ways and return to the Lord' (Lam. 3:40).

C. "If he examined his ways and found no cause [for his suffering], let him blame the matter on his wasting [time better spent in studying] the Torah.

D. "For it is said, 'Happy is the man whom you chastise, O Lord, and teach out of your Torah' (Ps. 94:12).

E. "If he blamed it on something and found [after correcting the fault] that that had not, in fact, been the cause at all, he may be sure that he suffers the afflictions that come from God's love.

F. "For it is said, 'For the one whom the Lord loves he corrects' (Prov. 3:12)."

G. Said Raba said R. Sehorah said R. Huna [said], "Whomever the Holy One, blessed be He, prefers he crushes with suffering.

H. "For it is said, 'The Lord was pleased with him, hence he crushed him with disease' (Isa. 53:10).

I. "Is it possible that even if the victim did not accept the suffering with love, the same is so?

J. "Scripture states, 'To see if his soul would offer itself in restitution' (Isa. 53:10).

K. "Just as the offering must be offered with the knowledge and consent [of the sacrificer], so sufferings must be accepted with knowledge and consent.

L. "If one accepted them in that way, what is his reward?

M. "'He will see his seed, prolong his days' (Isa. 53:10).

N. "Not only so, but his learning will remain with him, as it is said, 'The purpose of the Lord will prosper in his hand' (Isa. 53:10)."

XXVII.

A. R. Jacob bar Idi and R. Aha bar Hanina differed. One of them said, "What are sufferings brought on by God's love? They are any form of suffering which does not involve one's having to give up studying Torah.

B. "For it is said, 'Happy is the man whom you chasten, O Lord, and yet teach out of your Torah' (Ps. 94:12)."

C. The other said, "What are sufferings brought on by God's love? They are any form of suffering which does not involve having to give up praying.

D. "For it is said, 'Blessed be God, who has not turned away my prayer nor his mercy from me' (Ps. 66:20)."

E. Said to them R. Abba, son of R. Hiyya bar Abba, "This is what R. Hiyya bar Abba said R. Yohanan said, 'Both constitute forms of suffering brought on by God's love.

F. "'For it is said, "For him whom the Lord loves he corrects" (Prov. 3:12).

G   "'What is the sense of the Scripture's statement, "And you teach him out of your Torah"? Do not read it as "You teach him," but "You teach us."

H   "'This matter you teach us out of your law, namely, the argument [concerning the meaning of the suffering brought on by God's love] a fortiori resting on the traits of the tooth and the eye:

I   "'Now if, on account of an injury done to the slave's tooth or eye, which are only one of a person's limbs, a slave goes forth to freedom, sufferings, which drain away the whole of a person's body, how much the more so [should a person find true freedom on their account].'"

J. This furthermore accords with what R. Simeon b. Laqish said.

K   For R. Simeon b. Laqish said, "A 'covenant' is stated in respect to salt, and a covenant is mentioned with respect to suffering.

L   "With respect to a covenant with salt: 'Neither shall you allow the salt of the covenant of your God to be lacking' (Lev. 2:13).

M   "With respect to a covenant with suffering: 'These are the words of the covenant' (Deut. 28:69) [followed by discourse on Israel's suffering].

N   "Just as the covenant noted with salt indicates that salt sweetens meat, so the covenant noted with suffering indicates that suffering wipes away all of a person's sins."

XXVIII.

A. It has been taught on Tannaite authority:

B. R. Simeon b. Yohai says, "Three good gifts did the Holy One, blessed be He, give to Israel, and all of them he gave only through suffering.

C. "These are they: Torah, the Land of Israel, and the world to come.

D. "How do we know that that is the case for Torah? As it is said, 'Happy is the man whom you chasten, O Lord, and teach out of your Torah' (Ps. 94:12).

E. "The Land of Israel? 'As a man chastens his son, so the Lord your God chastens you,' (Deut. 8:5), after which it is said, 'For the Lord your God brings you into a good land' (Deut. 8:7).

F. "The world to come? 'For the commandment is a lamp and the teaching is light, and reproofs of sufferings are the way of life' (Prov. 6:23)."

XXIX.

A   A Tannaite authority repeated the following statement before R. Yohanan: "Whoever devotes himself to study of the Torah or acts of loving kindness, [5B] or who buries his children, is forgiven all his sins."

B. Said to him R. Yohanan, "Now there is no issue with regard to study of the Torah or practice of deeds of loving kindness, for it is written, 'By mercy and truth iniquity is expiated' (Prov. 16:6).

C   "'Mercy' refers to acts of loving kindness, for it is said, 'He who follows after righteousness and mercy finds life, prosperity, and honor' (Prov. 21:21).

D. "'Truth' of course refers to Torah, for it is said, 'Buy the truth and do not sell it' (Prov. 23:23).

E. "But how do we know that that is the case for one who buries his children?"

F. An elder repeated for him on Tannaite authority the following statement in the name of R. Simeon b. Yohai, "We draw an analogy to the sense of the word 'sin' used in several passages.

G. "Here it is written, 'By mercy and truth iniquity is expiated' (Prov. 16:6), and elsewhere, 'And who repays the iniquity of the fathers into the bosom of their children' (Jer. 32:18)."

XXX.

A. Said R. Yohanan, "The suffering brought by skin ailments [such as are listed at Lev. 13-14] and by the burial of one's children are not sufferings that are brought by God's love."

B. Is it really the case that the sufferings brought by the skin ailments are not [sufferings of love]?

C. And has it not been taught on Tannaite authority:

D. "Whoever has any one of the four skin traits that indicate the presence of the skin ailment may know that these serve solely as an altar for atonement [of his sins]"?

E. To be sure, they serve as an altar for atonement, but they are not sufferings that come on account of God's love.

F. If you prefer, I shall explain that the one teaching belongs to us [in Babylonia], the other to them [in the Land of Israel].

G. If you wish, I shall propose that the one teaching [that they are sufferings brought on by God's love] applies when the skin ailment appears on hidden places of the body, the other, when it appears on parts of the body that people see.

H. And with respect to burying one's children is it not [a sign of suffering brought on by God's love]?

I. Now what sort of case can be in hand? If I say that one actually had the children but they died,

J. did not R. Yohanan say, "This is the bone of my tenth son [whom I buried]"? [Yohanan then regarded the death of the child as suffering brought on by God's love.]

K. Rather, the one case involves someone who never had any children at all, the other, to someone who had children who died.

XXXI.

A. R. Hiyya bar Abba got sick. R. Yohanan came to him. He said to him, "Are these sufferings precious to you?"

B. He said to him, "I don't want them, I don't want their reward."

C. He said to him, "Give me your hand."

D. He gave him his hand, and [Yohanan] raised him up [out of his sickness].

E. R. Yohanan got sick. R. Hanina came to him. He said to him, "Are these sufferings precious to you?"

F. He said to him, "I don't want them. I don't want their reward."

G. He said to him, "Give me your hand."

H. He gave him his hand and [Hanina] raised him up [out of his sickness].

I. Why so? R. Yohanan should have raised himself up?

J. They say, "A prisoner cannot get himself out of jail."

XXXII.

A. R. Eliezer got sick. R. Yohanan came to see him and found him lying in a dark room. [The dying man] uncovered his arm, and light fell [through the room]. [Yohanan] saw that R. Eliezer was weeping. He said to him, "Why are you crying? Is it because of the Torah that you did not learn sufficiently? We have learned: 'All the same are the ones who do much and do little, so long as each person will do it for the sake of heaven.'

B. "If it is because of insufficient income? Not everyone has the merit of seeing two tables [Torah and riches, as you have. You have been a master of Torah and also have enjoyed wealth].

C. "Is it because of children? Here is the bone of my tenth son [whom I buried, so it was no great loss not to have children, since you might have had to bury them]."

D. He said to him, "I am crying because of this beauty of mine which will be rotting in the ground."

E. He said to him, "For that it certainly is worth crying," and the two of them wept together.

F. He said to him, "Are these sufferings precious to you?"

G. He said to him, "I don't want them, I don't want their reward."

H. He said to him, "Give me your hand."

I. He gave him his hand, and [Yohanan] raised him up [out of his sickness].

XXXIII.

A. Four hundred barrels of wine turned sour on R. Huna. R. Judah, brother of R. Sala the Pious, and rabbis came to see him (and some say it was R. Ada bar Ahba and rabbis). They said to him, "The master should take a good look at his deeds."

B. He said to them, "And am I suspect in your eyes?"

C. They said to him, "And is the Holy One, blessed be He, suspect of inflicting a penalty without justice?"

D. He said to them, "Has anybody heard anything bad about me? Let him say it."

E. They said to him, "This is what we have heard: the master does not give to his hired hand [the latter's share of] vine twigs [which are his right]."

F. He said to them, "Does he leave me any! He steals all of them to begin with."

G. They said to him, "This is in line with what people say: 'Go steal from a thief but taste theft too!' [Simon: If you steal from a thief, you also have a taste of it.]"

H. He said to them, "I pledge that I'll give them to him."

I. Some say that the vinegar turned back into wine, and some say that the price of vinegar went up so he sold it off at the price of wine.

XXXIV.

A. It has been taught on Tannaite authority:

B. Abba Benjamin says, "I have been particularly attentive to two matters for my entire life, first, that my prayer should be said before my bed, second, that my bed should be placed on a north-south axis."

C. "That my prayer should be said before my bed" – what is the meaning of that statement?

D. Can it be literally in front of my bed? And has not R. Judah said Rab said, (and some say R. Joshua b. Levi said it), "How do we know that there should be nothing that intervenes between one who says a prayer and the wall? As it is said, 'Then Hezekiah turned his face to the wall and prayed' (Isa. 38:2)? [So prayer before the bed would be contrary to Hezekiah's practice.]

E. Do not, therefore, maintain that it is "before my bed" but rather "near my bed."

F. "That my bed should be placed on a north-south axis" [– what is the meaning of that statement]?

G. This is in line with that which R. Hama b. R. Hanina said R. Isaac said, "Whoever sets his bed on a north-south axis will have male children.

H. "For it is said, 'And whose belly you fill at the north [lit.: with your treasure], who has sons in plenty' (Ps. 17:14)."

I. R. Nahman bar Isaac said, "Also, his wife will not have miscarriages. It is written here, 'And whose belly you fill with your treasure' (Ps. 17:14). And elsewhere: 'And when her days to be delivered were fulfilled, behold, there were twins in her womb' (Gen. 25:24)."

XXXV.

A. It has been taught on Tannaite authority:

B. Abba Benjamin says, "If two people go in to say a prayer, and one of them finished saying a prayer sooner than the other and did not wait for his fellow but left, [in Heaven the angels] tear up his prayer in his very presence [and it is rejected].

C. "For it is written, 'You tear yourself in your anger, shall the earth be forsaken for you' (Job 18:4).

D. "Not only so, but he makes the Presence of God abandon Israel, for it is said, 'Or shall the rock be removed out of its place' (Job 18:4).

E. "And the word 'rock' refers only to the Holy One, blessed be He, as it is said, 'Of the rock that begot you you were not mindful' (Deut. 32:18)."

F. And if one does wait, what is his reward?

G. [6A] Said R. Yosé b. R. Hanina, "He has the merit of receiving the blessings specified in the following verse: 'Oh that you would listen to my commandments! Then your peace would be as a river, and your righteousness as the waves of the sea, your seed also would be as the sand, and the offspring of your body like the grains of the sand' (Isa. 48:18-19)."

XXXVI.

A. It has been taught on Tannaite authority:

B. Abba Benjamin says, "If the eye had the power to see them, no creature could withstand the demons."

C. Said Abbayye, "They are more numerous than we and stand around us like a ridge around a field."

D. Said R. Huna, "At the left hand of each one of us is a thousand of them, and at the right hand, ten thousand."

E.   Said Raba, "The crowding at the public lectures comes from them, the fact that the clothing of rabbis wears out from rubbing comes on account of them, the bruising of the feet comes from them.

F.   "If someone wants to know that they are there, take ashes and sprinkle them around the bed, and in the morning, he will see something like footprints of a cock.

G.   "If someone wants actually to see them, take the afterbirth of a black she-cat, offspring of the same, firstborn of a firstborn. Roast it in fire and grind it to powder. Put the ash into his eye. He will see them.

H.   "Let him pour it into an iron tube and seal it with an iron signet [Simon:] so that they will not grab it from him.

I.   "Let him keep his mouth closed, lest they harm him."

J.   R. Bibi bar Abbayye did this. He saw them but was injured. Rabbis prayed for mercy for him and he was healed.

XXXVII.

A.   It has been taught on Tannaite authority:

B.   Abba Benjamin says, "A prayer of a person is heard only if it is said in the synagogue.

C.   "For it is said, 'To hearken unto the song and to the prayer' (1 Kgs. 8:28).

D.   "Where there is song, there should the prayer take place."

E.   Said Rabin bar R. Ada said R. Isaac, "How do we know on the basis of Scripture that the Holy One, blessed be He, is found in the synagogue? As it is said, 'God stands in the congregation of God' (Ps. 82:1).

F.   "And how do we know that when ten are praying, the Presence of God is with them? As it is said, 'God stands in the congregation of God [which is ten]' (Ps. 82:1).

G.   "And how do we know that where three are sitting in judgment the Presence of God is with them? As it is said, 'In the midst of the judges he judges' (Ps. 82:1).

H.   "And how do we know that where two are sitting and studying the Torah, the Presence of God is with them? As it is said, 'Then they that feared the Lord spoke one with another, and the Lord hearkened and heard, and a book of remembrance was written before him, for them that feared the Lord and that thought upon his name' (Mal. 3:16)."

I.   What is the meaning of "Who thought upon his name"?

J.   Said R. Ashi, "If a person gave thought to doing a religious deed but perforce was not able to do it, Scripture credits it to him as if he had actually done it."

K.   [Continuing Isaac's statement,] "And how do we know that even if one person alone is sitting and studying the Torah, the Presence of God is with him? As it is said, 'In every place where I cause my name to be mentioned I will come to you and bless you' (Ex. 20:21)."

L.   Now since it is the case that even if one is studying by himself [the Presence is with him], why was it necessary to make the statement concerning two?

M   The words of two are written down in the book of remembrances, while the words of one are not written down in the book of remembrances.

N   And since it is the case that even if two are studying [the Presence is with them], why was it necessary to make the statement concerning three?

Q   What might you have said? Judging cases serves only for the purpose of making peace in this world, and the Presence of God would not come on that account. So we are informed that that is not the case, for judging a case also is an act of Torah.

P.   And since it is the case that even when three [are studying Torah, the Presence is with them], what need was there to speak of ten?

Q   In the case of ten, the Presence of God comes first, while in the case of three, the Presence comes only when the people actually go into session.

XXXVIII.

A.   Said R. Abin bar Ada said R. Isaac, "How do we know on the basis of Scripture that the Holy One, blessed be He, puts on phylacteries? As it is said, 'The Lord has sworn by his right hand, and by the arm of his strength' (Isa. 62:8).

B.   "'By his right hand' refers to Torah, as it is said, 'At his right hand was a fiery law for them' (Deut. 33:2).

C.   "'And by the arm of his strength' refers to phylacteries, as it is said, 'The Lord will give strength to his people' (Ps. 29:11).

D.   "And how do we know that phylacteries are a strength for Israel? For it is written, 'And all the peoples of the earth shall see that you are called by the name of the Lord and they shall be afraid of you' (Deut. 28:10)."

E.   And it has been taught on Tannaite authority:

F.   R. Eliezer the Great says, "This (Deut. 28:10) refers to the phylacteries that are put on the head."

XXXIX.

A.   Said R. Nahman bar Isaac to R. Hiyya bar Abin, "As to the phylacteries of the Lord of the world, what is written in them?"

B.   He said to him, "'And who is like your people Israel, a singular nation on earth' (1 Chr. 17:21)."

C.   "And does the Holy One, blessed be He, sing praises for Israel?"

D.   "Yes, for it is written, 'You have avouched the Lord this day...and the Lord has avouched you this day' (Deut. 26:17, 18).

E.   "Said the Holy One, blessed be He, to Israel, 'You have made me a singular entity in the world, and I shall make you a singular entity in the world.

F.   "'You have made me a singular entity in the world,' as it is said, 'Hear O Israel, the Lord, our God, the Lord is one' (Deut. 6:4).

G.   "'And I shall make you a singular entity in the world,' as it is said, 'And who is like your people, Israel, a singular nation in the earth' (1 Chr. 17:21)."

H.   Said R. Aha, son of Raba to R. Ashi, "That takes care of one of the four subdivisions of the phylactery. What is written in the others?"

I.   He said to him, "'For what great nation is there....And what great nation is there...' (Deut. 4:7, 8), 'Happy are you, O Israel...' (Deut.

33:29), 'Or has God tried...,' (Deut. 4:34). And 'To make you high above all nations' (Deut. 26:19)."

J. "If so, there are too many boxes!

K. "But the verses, 'For what great nation is there' and 'And what great nation is there,' which are equivalent, are in one box, and 'Happy are you, O Israel' and 'Who is like your people Israel' are in one box, and 'Or has God tried...,' in one box, and 'To make you high' in one box.

L. [6B] "And all of them are written in the phylactery that is on the arm."

XL.

A. Said Rabin bar R. Ada said R. Isaac, "About anyone who regularly comes to the synagogue, but does not come one day, the Holy One, blessed be He, inquires.

B. "For it is said, 'Who is among you who fears the Lord, who obeys the voice of his servant, and now walks in darkness and has no light' (Isa. 50:10).

C. "If it was on account of a matter of religious duty that the person has gone away [from regular synagogue attendance], he nonetheless 'will have light.'

D. "But if it was on account of an optional matter that he did so, he 'has no light.'

E. "'Let him trust in the name of the Lord' (Isa. 50:10).

F. "Why so? Because he should have trusted in the name of the Lord but did not."

XLI.

A. Said R. Yohanan, "When the Holy One, blessed be He, comes to a synagogue and does not find ten present, he forthwith becomes angry.

B. "For it is said, 'Why when I came was there no one there? When I called, there was no answer' (Isa. 50:2)."

XLII.

A. Said R. Helbo said R. Huna, "For whoever arranges a regular place for praying, the God of Abraham is a help, and when he dies, they say for him, 'Woe for the humble man, woe for the pious man, one of the disciples of Abraham, our father.'

B. "And how do we know in the case of Abraham, our father, that he arranged a regular place for praying?

C. "For it is written, 'And Abraham got up early in the morning on the place where he had stood' (Gen. 19:27).

D. "'Standing' refers only to praying, for it is said, 'Then Phinehas stood up and prayed' (Ps. 106:30)."

E. Said R. Helbo to R. Huna, "He who leaves the synagogue should not take large steps."

F. Said Abbayye, "That statement applies only when one leaves, but when he enters, it is a religious duty to run [to the synagogue].

G. "For it is said, 'Let us run to know the Lord' (Hos. 6:3)."

H. Said R. Zira, "When in the beginning I saw rabbis running to the lesson on the Sabbath, I thought that the rabbis were profaning the Sabbath. But now that I have heard what R. Tanhum said R. Joshua b. Levi said,

    I.   "namely, 'A person should always run to take up a matter of law, and even on the Sabbath, as it is said, "They shall walk after the Lord who shall roar like a lion [for he shall roar, and the children shall come hurrying]" (Hos. 11:10),'

    J.   "I, too, run."

XLIII.

    A.   Said R. Zira, "The reward for attending the lesson is on account of running [to hear the lesson, not necessarily on account of what one has learned]."

    B.   Said Abbayye, "The reward for attending the periodic public assembly [of rabbis] is on account of the crowding together."

    C.   Said Raba [to the contrary], "The reward for repeating what one has heard is in reasoning about it."

    D.   Said R. Papa, "The reward for attending a house of mourning is on account of one's preserving silence there."

    E.   Said Mar Zutra, "The reward for observing a fast day lies in the acts of charity one performs on that day."

    F.   Said R. Sheshet, "The reward for delivering a eulogy lies in raising the voice."

    G.   Said R. Ashi, "The reward for attending a wedding lies in the words [of compliment paid to the bride and groom]."

XLIV.

    A.   Said R. Huna, "Whoever prays behind the synagogue is called wicked,

    B.   "as it is said, 'The wicked walk round about' (Ps. 12:9)."

    C.   Said Abbayye, "That statement applies only in the case of one who does not turn his face toward the synagogue, but if he turns his face toward the synagogue, we have no objection."

    D.   There was a certain man who would say his prayers behind the synagogue and did not turn his face toward the synagogue. Elijah came by and saw him. He appeared to him in the guise of a Tai-Arab.

    E.   He said to him, "Are you now standing with your back toward your master?" He drew his sword and killed him.

    F.   One of the rabbis asked R. Bibi bar Abbayye, and some say, R. Bibi asked R. Nahman bar Isaac, "What is the meaning of the verse, 'When vileness is exalted among the sons of men' (Ps. 12:9)?"

    G.   He said to him, "This refers to matters that are exalted, which people treat with contempt."

    H.   R. Yohanan and R. Eleazar both say, "When a person falls into need of the help of other people, his face changes color like the *kerum*, for it is said, 'As the *kerum* is to be reviled among the sons of men' (Ps. 12:9)."

    I.   What is the meaning of *kerum*?

    J.   When R. Dimi came, he said, "There is a certain bird among the coast towns, called the *kerum*. When the sun shines, it turns many colors."

    K.   R. Ammi and R. Assi both say, "[When a person turns to others for support], it is as if he is judged to suffer the penalties of both fire and water.

L.   "For it is said, 'When you caused men to ride over our heads, we went through fire and through water' (Ps. 66:12)."

XLV.

A.   And R. Helbo said R. Huna said, "A person should always be attentive at the afternoon prayer.

B.   "For lo, Elijah was answered only at the afternoon prayer.

C.   "For it is said, 'And it came to pass at the time of the offering of the late afternoon offering, that Elijah the prophet came near and said, "Hear me, O Lord, hear me"' (1 Kgs. 18:36-37)."

D.   "Hear me" so fire will come down from heaven.

E.   "Hear me" that people not say it is merely witchcraft.

F.   R. Yohanan said, "[A person should also be attentive about] the evening prayer.

G.   "For it is said, 'Let my prayer be set forth as incense before you, the lifting up of my hands as the evening sacrifice' (Ps. 141:2)."

H.   R. Nahman bar Isaac said, "[A person should also be attentive about] the morning prayer.

I.   "For it is said, 'O Lord, in the morning you shall hear my voice, in the morning I shall order my prayer to you, and will look forward' (Ps. 5:4)."

XLVI.

A.   And R. Helbo said R. Huna said, "Whoever enjoys a marriage banquet and does not felicitate the bridal couple violates five 'voices.'

B.   "For it is said, 'The voice of joy and the voice of gladness, the voice of the bridegroom and the voice of the bride, the voice of those who say, "Give thanks to the Lord of hosts"' (Jer. 33:11)."

C.   And if he does felicitate the couple, what reward does he get?

D.   Said R. Joshua b. Levi, "He acquires the merit of the Torah, which was handed down with five voices.

E.   "For it is said, 'And it came to pass on the third day, when it was morning, that there were voices [thus two], and lightnings, and a thick cloud upon the mount, and the voice of a horn, and when the voice of the horn waxed louder... Moses spoke and God answered him by a voice...' (Ex. 19:16, 19) [thus five voices in all]."

F.   Is it so [that there were only five voices]?

G.   And lo, it is written, "And all the people saw the voices" (Ex. 20:15). [So this would make seven voices.]

H.   These voices came before the giving of the Torah [and do not count].

I.   R. Abbahu said, "It is as if the one [who felicitated the bridal couple] offered a thanksgiving-offering.

J.   "For it is said, 'Even of them that bring thanksgiving-offerings into the house of the Lord' (Jer. 33:11)."

K.   R. Nahman bar Isaac said, "It is as if he rebuilt one of the ruins of Jerusalem.

L.   "For it is said, 'For I will cause the captivity of the land to return as at the first, says the Lord' (Jer. 33:11)."

XLVII.

A.   And R. Helbo said R. Huna said, "The words of any person in whom is fear of Heaven are heard.

B. "For it is said, 'The end of the matter, all having been heard: Fear God and keep his commandments, for this is the whole duty of man' (Qoh. 12:13)."

C. What is the meaning of the phrase, "For this is the whole duty of man" (Qoh. 12:13)?

D. Said R. Eleazar, "Said the Holy One, blessed be He, 'The entire world has been created only on account of this one.'"

E. R. Abba bar Kahana said, "This one is worth the whole world."

F. Simeon b. Zoma says, "The entire world was created only to accompany this one."

XLVIII.

A. And R. Helbo said R. Huna said, "Whoever knows that his fellow regularly greets him should greet the other first.

B. "For it is said, 'Seek peace and pursue it' (Ps. 34:15).

C. "If he greeted him and the other did not reply, the latter is called a thief.

D. "For it is said, 'It is you who have eaten up the vineyard, the spoil of the poor is in your houses' (Isa. 3:14)."

XLIX.

A. [7A] Said R. Yohanan in the name of R. Yosé, "How do we know that the Holy One, blessed be He, says prayers?

B. "Since it is said, 'Even them will I bring to my holy mountain and make them joyful in my house of prayer' (Isa. 56:7).

C. "'Their house of prayer' is not stated, but rather, 'my house of prayer.'

D. "On the basis of that usage we see that the Holy One, blessed be He, says prayers."

E. What prayers does he say?

F. Said R. Zutra bar Tobiah said Rab, "'May it be my will that my mercy overcome my anger, and that my mercy prevail over my attributes, so that I may treat my children in accord with the trait of mercy and in their regard go beyond the strict measure of the law.'"

L.

A. It has been taught on Tannaite authority:

B. Said R. Ishmael b. Elisha, "One time I went in to offer up incense on the innermost altar, and I saw the Crown of the Lord, enthroned on the highest throne, and he said to me, 'Ishmael, my son, bless me.'

C. "I said to him, 'May it be your will that your mercy overcome your anger, and that your mercy prevail over your attributes, so that you treat your children in accord with the trait of mercy and in their regard go beyond the strict measure of the law.'

D. "And he nodded his head to me."

E. And from that story we learn that the blessing of a common son should not be negligible in your view.

LI.

A. And said R. Yohanan in the name of R. Yosé, "How do we know that one should not placate a person when he is angry?

B. "It is in line with the following verse of Scripture: 'My face will go and then I will give you rest' (Ex. 33:14).

C. "Said the Holy One, blessed be He, to Moses, 'Wait until my angry countenance passes, and then I shall give you rest.'"

D. But does the Holy One, blessed be He, get angry?

E. Indeed so.

F. For it has been taught on Tannaite authority:

G. "A God that is angry every day" (Ps. 7:12).

H. And how long is this anger going to last?

I. A moment.

J. And how long is a moment?

K. It is one fifty-eight thousand eight hundred and eighty-eighth part of an hour.

L. And no creature except for the wicked Balaam has ever been able to fix the moment exactly.

M. For concerning him it has been written, "He knows the knowledge of the Most High" (Num. 24:16).

N. Now if Balaam did not even know what his beast was thinking, was he likely to know what the Most High is thinking?

O. But this teaches that he knew exactly how to reckon the very moment that the Holy One, blessed be He, would be angry.

P. That is in line with what the prophet said to Israel, "O my people, remember now what Balak, king of Moab, devised, and what Balaam, son of Beor, answered him...that you may know the righteous acts of the Lord" (Mic. 6:5).

Q. Said R. Eleazar, "The Holy One, blessed be He, said to Israel, 'Know that I did any number of acts of righteousness with you, for I did not get angry in the time of the wicked Balaam. For had I gotten angry, not one of (the enemies of) Israel would have survived, not a remnant.'

R. "That is in line with what Balaam said to Balak, 'How shall I curse whom God has not cursed, and how shall I execrate whom the Lord has not execrated?' (Num. 23:8).

S. "This teaches that for that entire time [God] did not get mad."

T. And how long is God's anger?

U. It is a moment.

V. And how long is a moment?

W. Said R. Abin, and some say, R. Abina, "A moment lasts as long as it takes to say 'a moment.'"

X. And how do we know that a moment is how long God is angry?

Y. For it is said, "For his anger is but for a moment, his favor is for a lifetime" (Ps. 30:6).

Z. If you like, you may derive the lesson from the following: "Hide yourself for a little while until the anger be past" (Isa. 26:20).

AA. And when is God angry?

BB. Said Abbayye, "It is during the first three hours of the day, when the comb of the cock is white, and it stands on one foot."

CC. But it stands on one foot every hour.

DD. To be sure, it stands on its foot every hour, but in all the others it has red streaks, and in the moment at hand there are no red streaks [in the comb of the cock].

LII.

A. A certain Sadducean who lived in R. Joshua b. Levi's neighborhood would give him plenty of trouble by citing verses of Scripture. One day [Joshua] took a cock and put it between the legs of his bed and watched it. He thought, "When that very moment comes [that the comb is unstreaked], I shall curse him."

B. When that very moment came, [Joshua] was dozing. He said to him, "That fact implies that it is not proper to do things this way."

C. "'And his tender mercies are over all his works' (Ps. 155:9), and it is written, 'Neither is it good for the righteous to punish' (Prov. 17:26)."

LIII.

A. It has been taught on Tannaite authority in the name of R. Meir, "When the sun comes up, and all kings, east and west, put their crowns on their heads and bow down to the sun, forthwith the Holy One, blessed be He, grows angry."

LIV.

A. And R. Yohanan said in the name of R. Yosé, "Better is one self-reproach that a person sets in his own heart [on account of what he has done] than a great many scourgings.

B. "For it is said, 'And she shall run after her lovers... then shall she say [in her heart], I shall go and return to my first husband, for then it was better for me than now' (Hos. 2:9)."

C. And R. Simeon b. Laqish said, "It is better than a hundred scourgings,

D. "as it is said, 'A rebuke enters deeper into a man of understanding than a hundred stripes into a fool' (Prov. 17:10)."

LV.

A. And R. Yohanan said in the name of R. Yosé, "There were three things that Moses sought from the Holy One, blessed be He, and he gave them to him.

B. "He asked that the Presence of God should come to rest on Israel, and he gave him his request, as it is said, 'Is it not in that you go with us...' (Ex. 33:16).

C. "He asked that the Presence of God not come to rest on idolators, and he gave him his request, as it is said, 'So we are distinguished, I and your people' (Ex. 33:16).

D. "He asked that he teach him the ways of the Holy One, blessed be He, and he gave him his request, as it is said, 'Show me now your ways' (Ex. 33:13).

E. "He said before him, 'Lord of the world, on what account can there be a righteous man who has it good, a righteous man who has it bad, a wicked man who has it good, and a wicked man who has it bad?'

F. "He said to him, 'Moses, in the case of a righteous man who has it good, it is a righteous man, son of a righteous man, a righteous man who has it bad is a righteous man, son of a wicked man, a wicked man who has it good is a wicked man, son of a righteous man, and a wicked man who has it bad is a wicked man, son of a wicked man.'"

G. A master has said, "A righteous man who has it good is a righteous man, son of a righteous man, a righteous man who has it bad is a righteous man, son of a wicked man."

H   But is this so? And lo, it is written, "Visiting the wickedness of the fathers upon the children" (Ex. 34:7), and it also is written, "Neither shall the children be put to death for the fathers" (Deut. 24:16).

I   These two verses were set into contrast with one another, and we learned, "It is not a contradiction. The one verse speaks of a case in which the sons take hold of the deeds of the fathers and do them, and the other speaks of a case in which the sons do not take hold of the deeds of the fathers and do them."

J.   Rather, this is what he said to him, "A righteous man who has it good is a totally righteous man. A righteous man who has it bad is a righteous man who is not totally righteous. A wicked man who has it good is a wicked man who is not totally wicked. A wicked man who has it bad is a totally wicked man."

K.   What R. Yohanan has said differs from what R. Meir said.

L   For R. Meir said, "Two [of the three] requests were granted to him, and one was not.

M   "For it is said, 'For I shall be gracious to whom I shall be gracious' (Ex. 33:19), even though he may not be worthy of it, 'And I will show mercy on whom I will show mercy' (Ex. 33:19), even though he may not be worthy of it."

LVI.

A.   "And he said, 'You cannot see my face' (Ex. 33:20)."

B.   It was taught on Tannaite authority in the name of R. Joshua b. Qorha, "This is what the Holy One, blessed be He, said to Moses:

C.   "'When I wanted [you to see my face], you did not want to, now that you want to see my face, I do not want you to.'"

D.   This differs from what R. Samuel bar Nahmani said R. Jonathan said.

E.   For R. Samuel bar Nahmani said R. Jonathan said, "As a reward for three things he received the merit of three things.

F.   "As a reward for: 'And Moses hid his face,' (Ex. 3:6), he had the merit of having a glistening face.

G.   "As a reward for: 'Because he was afraid to' (Ex. 3:6), he had the merit that 'They were afraid to come near him' (Ex. 34:30).

H   "As a reward for: 'To look upon God' (Ex. 3:6), he had the merit: 'The similitude of the Lord does he behold' (Num. 12:8)."

LVII.

A   "And I shall remove my hand and you shall see my back" (Ex. 33:23).

B.   Said R. Hana bar Bizna said R. Simeon the Pious, "This teaches that the Holy One, blessed be He, showed Moses [how to tie] the knot of the phylacteries."

LVIII.

A   And R. Yohanan said in the name of R. Yosé, "Every word containing a blessing that came forth from the Mouth of the Holy One, blessed be He, even if stated conditionally, was never retracted.

B.   "How do we know it? It is from Moses, our master.

C.   "For it is said, 'Let me alone, that I may destroy them and blot out their name from under heaven, and I will make of you a nation mightier and greater than they' (Deut. 9:14).

    D.   "Even though Moses prayed for mercy, so that the matter was nullified, even so, [the blessing] was carried out in his seed.

    E.   "For it is said, 'The sons of Moses, Gershom and Eliezer...and the sons of Eliezer were Rehabiah the chief...and the sons of Rehabiah were very many' (1 Chr. 23:15-17)."

    F.   And in this regard R. Joseph stated on Tannaite authority, "They were more than sixty myriads."

    G.   "This is to be derived from an analogy between two uses of the word 'many.'

    H.   "Here it is written, 'They were very many' (1 Chr. 23:17).

    I.   "And elsewhere it is written, 'And the children of Israel were very fruitful and increased abundantly and became very many' (Ex. 1:7). [At that time they were sixty myriads.]"

LIX.

    A.   [7B] Said R. Yohanan in the name of R. Simeon b. Yohai, "From the day on which the Holy One, blessed be He, created the world, there was no man who called the Holy One, blessed be He, 'Lord,' until Abraham came along and called him Lord.

    B.   "For it is said, 'And he said, O Lord, God, whereby shall I know that I shall inherit it' (Gen. 15:8)."

    C.   Said Rab, "Daniel, too, was answered only on account of Abraham.

    D.   "For it is said, 'Now therefore, O our God, hearken to the prayer of your servant and to his supplications and cause your face to shine upon your sanctuary that is desolate, for the Lord's sake' (Dan. 9:17).

    E.   "'For your sake' is what he should have said, but the sense is, 'For the sake of Abraham, who called you 'Lord.'"

LX.

    A.   And R. Yohanan said in the name of R. Simeon b. Yohai, "How do we know that people should not seek to appease someone when he is mad?

    B.   "As it is said, 'My face will go and then I will give you rest' (Ex. 33:14)."

LXI.

    A.   And R. Yohanan said in the name of R. Simeon b. Yohai, "From the day on which the Holy One, blessed be He, created his world, there was no one who praised the Holy One, blessed be He, until Leah came along and praised him.

    B.   "For it is said, 'This time I will praise the Lord' (Gen. 29:35)."

    C.   As to Reuben, said R. Eleazar, "Leah said, 'See what is the difference [the name of Reuben yielding *reu*, see, and *ben*, between] between my son and the son of my father-in-law.

    D.   "The son of my father-in-law, even knowingly, sold off his birthright, for it is written, 'And he sold his birthright to Jacob' (Gen. 25:33).

    E.   "See what is written concerning him: 'And Esau hated Jacob' (Gen. 27:41), and it is written, 'And he said, is not he rightly named Jacob? for he has supplanted me these two times' (Gen. 27:36).

    F.   "My son, by contrast, even though Jacob forcibly took away his birthright, as it is written, 'But for as much as he defiled his father's couch, his birthright was given to the sons of Joseph' (1 Chr. 5:1), did not become jealous of him, for it is written, 'And Reuben heard it and delivered him out of their hand' (Gen. 37:21)."

G. As to the meaning of the name of Ruth, said R. Yohanan, "It was because she had the merit that David would come forth from her, who saturated [RWH] the Holy One, blessed be He, with songs and praises."

H. How do we know that a person's name affects [his life]?

I. Said R. Eleazar, "It is in line with the verse of Scripture: 'Come, behold the works of the Lord, who has made desolations in the earth' (Ps. 46:9).

J. "Do not read 'desolations' but 'names' [which the same root yields]."

LXII.

A. And R. Yohanan said in the name of R. Simeon b. Yohai, "Bringing a child up badly is worse in a person's house than the war of Gog and Magog.

B. "For it is said, 'A Psalm of David, when he fled from Absalom, his son' (Ps. 3:1), after which it is written, 'Lord how many are my adversaries become, many are they that rise up against me' (Ps. 3:2).

C. "By contrast, in regard to the war of Gog and Magog it is written, 'Why are the nations in an uproar? And why do the peoples mutter in vain' (Ps. 2:1).

D. "But it is not written in that connection, 'How many are my adversaries become.'"

E. "A Psalm of David, when he fled from Absalom, his son" (Ps. 3:1):

F. "A Psalm of David"? It should be, "A lamentation of David"!

G. Said R. Simeon b. Abishalom, "The matter may be compared to the case of a man, against whom an outstanding bond was issued. Before he had paid it, he was sad. After he had paid it, he was glad.

H. "So, too, with David, when he the Holy One had said to him, 'Behold, I will raise up evil against you out of your own house,' (2 Sam. 2:11), he was sad.

I. "He thought to himself, 'Perhaps it will be a slave or a bastard child, who will not have pity on me.'

J. "When he saw that it was Absalom, he was happy. On that account, he said a psalm."

LXIII.

A. And R. Yohanan said in the name of R. Simeon b. Yohai, "It is permitted to contend with the wicked in this world,

B. for it is said, 'Those who forsake the Torah praise the wicked, but those who keep the Torah contend with them' (Prov. 28:4)."

C. It has been taught on Tannaite authority along these same lines:

D. R. Dosetai bar Matun says, "It is permitted to contend with the wicked in this world, for it is said, 'Those who forsake the Torah praise the wicked, but those who keep the Torah contend with them' (Prov. 28:4)."

E. And if someone should whisper to you, "But is it not written, 'Do not contend with evildoers, nor be envious against those who work unrighteousness' (Ps. 37:1)," say to him, "Someone whose conscience bothers him thinks so.

F.   "In fact, 'Do not contend with evildoers' means, do not be like them, 'nor be envious against those who work unrighteousness,' means, do not be like them.

G.   "And so it is said, 'Let your heart not envy sinners, but fear the Lord all day' (Prov. 23:17)."

H.   Is this the case? And lo, R. Isaac has said, "If you see a wicked person for whom the hour seems to shine, do not contend with him, for it is said, 'His ways prosper at all times' (Ps. 10:5).

I.   "Not only so, but he wins in court, as it is said, 'Your judgments are far above, out of his sight' (Ps. 10:5).

J.   "Not only so, but he overcomes his enemies, for it is said, 'As for all his enemies, he farts at them' (Ps. 10:5)."

K.   There is no contradiction. The one [Isaac] addresses one's own private matters [in which case one should not contend with the wicked], but the other speaks of matters having to do with heaven [in which case one should contend with them].

L.   And if you wish, I shall propose that both parties speak of matters having to do with Heaven. There is, nonetheless, no contradiction. The one [Isaac] speaks of a wicked person on whom the hour shines, the other of a wicked person on whom the hour does not shine.

M.   And if you wish, I shall propose that both parties speak of a wicked person on whom the hour shines, and there still is no contradiction. The one [Yohanan, who says the righteous may contend with the wicked] speaks of a completely righteous person, the other [Isaac] speaks of someone who is not completely righteous.

O.   For R. Huna said, "What is the meaning of this verse of Scripture: 'Why do you look, when they deal treacherously, and hold your peace, when the wicked swallows up the man that is more righteous than he' (Hab. 1:13)?

P.   "Now can a wicked person swallow up a righteous one?

Q.   "And lo, it is written, 'The Lord will not leave him in his hand' (Ps. 37:33). And it is further written, 'No mischief shall befall the righteous' (Prov. 12:21).

R.   "The fact therefore is that he may swallow up someone who is more righteous than he, but he cannot swallow up a completely righteous man."

S.   And if you wish, I shall propose that, when the hour shines for him, the situation is different.

LXIV.

A.   And R. Yohanan said in the name of R. Simeon b. Yohai, "Beneath anyone who establishes a regular place for praying do that person's enemies fall.

B.   "For it is said, 'And I will appoint a place for my people Israel, and I will plant them, that they may dwell in their own place and be disquieted no more, neither shall the children of wickedness afflict them any more as at the first' (2 Sam. 7:10)."

C.   R. Huna pointed to a contradiction between two verses of Scripture: "It is written, 'To afflict them,' and elsewhere, 'To exterminate them' (1 Chr. 17:9).

D. "To begin with, merely to afflict them, but, at the end, to exterminate them."

LXV.

A. And R. Yohanan said in the name of R. Simeon b. Yohai, "Greater is personal service to Torah than learning in Torah, [so doing favors for a sage is of greater value than studying with him].

B. "For it is said, 'Here is Elisha, the son of Shaphat, who poured water on the hands of Elijah' (2 Kgs. 3:11).

C. "It is not said, 'who learned' but 'who poured water.'

D. "This teaches that greater is service to Torah than learning in Torah."

LXVI.

A. Said R. Isaac to R. Nahman, "What is the reason that the master did not come to the synagogue to say his prayers?"

B. He said to him, "I could not do it."

C. He said to him, "Let the master gather ten to say prayers [at home]."

D. He said to him, "It was too much trouble for me."

E. "And let the master ask the agent of the community to let him know when the congregation prays [so he could do so at the same time]?"

F. He said to him, "Why all this bother?"

G. He said to him, "For R. Yohanan said in the name of R. Simeon b. Yohai, [8A], 'What is the meaning of that which is written, "But as for me, let my prayer be made to you, O Lord, in an acceptable time" (Ps. 69:14)? When is an acceptable time? It is the time that the community is saying its prayers.'"

H. R. Yosé b. R. Hanina said, "The proof of the same principle derives from here: 'Thus says the Lord, in an acceptable time I have answered you' (Isa. 49:8)."

I. R. Aha b. R. Hanina said, "From here: 'Behold, God does not despise the mighty' (Job 36:5). And it is written, 'He has redeemed my soul in peace so that none came near me, for they were many with me' (Ps. 55:19) [showing that when many pray together, they are listened to]."

J. It has been taught along these same lines on Tannaite authority:

K. R. Nathan says, "How do we know that the Holy One, blessed be He, does not reject the prayer of the community?

L. "As it is said, 'Behold, God does not despise the mighty' (Job 36:5), and it is further said, 'He has redeemed my soul in peace so that none came near me, for they were many with me' (Ps. 55:19).

M. "Said the Holy One, blessed be He, 'Whoever is occupied with study of the Torah and with the doing of deeds of loving kindness and who prays with the community do I regard as though he had redeemed me and my children from among the nations of the world.'"

LXVII.

A. Said R. Simeon b. Laqish, "Whoever has a synagogue in his town and does not go in there to pray is called a bad neighbor.

B. "For it is said, 'Thus says the Lord, as for all my evil neighbors, who touch the inheritance that I have caused my people Israel to inherit' (Jer. 12:14).

C. "Not only so, but he causes himself and his children to go into exile, as it is said, 'Behold, I will pluck them up from off their land and will pluck up the house of Judah from among them' (Jer. 12:14)."

LXVIII.

A. They told R. Yohanan that there are old men in Babylonia. He was amazed. He said, "'That your days may be multiplied, and the days of your children, upon the land' (Deut. 11:21) – and not outside the land."

B. When they told him that the people came early and left late so as to attend upon synagogue worship, he said, "This is what gives them the advantage [that permits them to live a long time]."

C. That accords with what R. Joshua b. Levi said to his children, "Come up early and go home late so as to attend upon synagogue worship, so that you will live for a long time."

D. Said R. Aha b. R. Hanina, "What proves the same point? 'Happy is the man who hearkens to me, watching daily at my gates, waiting at the posts of my doors' (Prov. 8:34), followed by, 'For whoever finds me finds life' (Prov. 8:35)."

E. Said R. Hisda, "A person should always enter two doors to the synagogue."

F. "Two doors" is what you think?

G. Rather, I should say, "A distance of two doors, and afterward he should say his prayer."

LXIX.

A. "For this let every one who is pious pray to you in the time of finding' (Ps. 32:6).

B. Said R. Hanina, "'The time of finding' refers to a wife, as it is said, 'Who has found a wife has found a great good' (Prov. 18:22)."

C. In the West when a man married a woman, they would say this to him: "'Found' or 'find'?"

D. "Found" as it is written, "Who has found a wife has found a great good" (Prov. 18:22).

E. "Find" as it is written, "And I find more bitter than death the woman" (Qoh. 7:26).

F. R. Nathan says, "'The time of finding' refers to Torah, as it is said, 'For who finds me finds life' (Prov. 8:35)."

G. R. Nahman bar Isaac said, "'The time of finding' refers to death, as it is said, 'The findings of death' (Ps. 68:22)."

H. It has been taught along these same lines on Tannaite authority:

I. Nine hundred and three sorts of death were created in the world, as it is said, "The findings of death" (Ps. 68:22), and the numerical value of the letters in the word for findings is nine hundred three.

J. The most difficult death of all is croup, and the easiest, a kiss.

K. Croup is like [Simon:] a thorn in a ball of wool pulled out backwards.

L. Some say, "It is like [pulling] a rope through the loopholes of a ship."

M. The kind by a kiss is like drawing a hair out of milk.

N. R. Yohanan said, "'The time of finding' refers to burial."

O. Said R. Hanina, "What is the prooftext for that proposition? 'Who rejoice unto exultation and are glad when they can find the grave' (Job 3:22)."

P. Said Rabbah bar R. Shila, "That is in line with what people say: 'People should pray for peace even as the last clod of earth [is thrown upon the grave].'"

Q. Mar Zutra said, "'The time of finding' refers to finding a toilet."

R. In the West they say, "This statement of Mar Zutra is the best of the lot."

LXX.

A. Said Raba to Rafram bar Papa, "Let the master tell us some of those excellent sayings having to do with the synagogue which were said in the name of R. Hisda."

B. He said to him, "This is what R. Hisda said: 'What is the meaning of the verse of Scripture, "The Lord loves the gates of Zion [SYN] more than all the dwellings of Jacob" (Ps. 87:2)? The Lord loves the gates that are distinguished [SYN] in law more than synagogues and schoolhouses.'"

C. That is in line with what R. Hiyya bar Ami said in the name of Ulla, "From the day on which the house of the sanctuary was destroyed, the Holy One, blessed be He, has had in his world only the four cubits of the law alone."

D. And Abbayye said, "To begin with I would study at home and pray in the synagogue. Once I heard this statement that R. Hiyya bar Ammi stated in the name of Ulla, 'From the day on which the house of the sanctuary was destroyed, the Holy One, blessed be He, has had in his world only the four cubits of the law alone,' I have had the practice of saying my prayers only in the place in which I study."

E. Even though they had thirteen synagogues in Tiberias, R. Ammi and R. Assi would pray only among the columns [of the basilica] where they were studying.

LXXI.

A. And R. Hiyya bar Ammi said in the name of Ulla, "Greater is the status of one who derives benefit from his own labor than one who fears heaven.

B. "For with regard to one who fears heaven, it is written, 'Happy is the man who fears the Lord' (Ps. 112:1).

C. "With regard to the one who derives benefit from his own labor, by contrast, it is written, 'When you eat the work of your hands, happy you shall be, and it shall be well with you' (Ps. 128:2).

D. "'Happy are you' in this world and 'it shall be well with you' in the world to come.

E. "With respect to the one who fears heaven, 'And it shall be well with you' is not written."

LXXII.

A. And R. Hiyya bar Ami said in the name of Ulla, "A person should always live in the place in which his master lives.

B. "For so long as Shimei, son of Gera, was alive, Solomon did not marry the daughter of Pharaoh."

C. But has it not been taught on Tannaite authority: One should not dwell [where his master does]?

D. There is no contradiction. The one [saying one should live near the master] speaks of a disciple who is submissive, the other of one who is not.

LXXIII.

A. Said R. Huna bar Judah said R. Menahem said R. Ammi, "What is the meaning of the verse that follows: 'And they who forsake the Lord shall be consumed' (Isa. 1:28)?

B. "This refers to one who leaves the scroll of the Torah [when it is read] and goes out [of the synagogue]."

C. R. Abbahu would go out [at the breaks in the lections] between the reading of one person and the next.

D. R. Pappa asked about the law governing leaving the synagogue between the reading of one verse and the next.

E. The question stands.

F. R. Sheshet would turn his face away and study [his legal traditions during the reading of the Torah lection].

G. He said, "We with our [Torah], they with theirs."

LXXIV.

A. Said R. Huna bar Judah said R. Ammi, "A person should always complete the reading of his passage of Scripture along with the congregation [studying the same lection from the Pentateuch as is read in the synagogue], following the practice of repeating the verse of Scripture two times, with one reading from the translation of the same verse into Aramaic.

B. [8B] "And that is the case even with 'Ataroth and Digon' (Num. 32:3). [Simon, p. 42, n. 5: Even strings of names which are left untranslated in the Targum should be recited in Hebrew and in the Aramaic version.]"

C. "For whoever completes the reading of his passage of Scripture along with the congregation is given long days and a lengthy life."

D. R. Bibi bar Abbayye considered completing his recitation of the entire scriptural lections for the year on the eve of the Day of Atonement.

E. Hiyya b. Rab of Difti recited to him on Tannaite authority: "It is written, 'And you shall afflict your souls, on the ninth day of the month at evening' (Lev. 23:32). Now do people fast on the ninth of the month? Do they not fast on the tenth of the month? But the passage serves to tell you the following:

F. "Whoever eats and drinks on the ninth of the month is regarded by Scripture as if he had fasted on the ninth and the tenth."

G. He thereupon considered completing them still sooner. A certain elder said to him, "It has been taught on Tannaite authority: 'However, he should not recite [the verses of the lections] either before or after [the congregation does]."

H. This accords with what R. Joshua b. Levi said to his children, "Complete your lections with the congregation, reading each verse twice as written in Scripture and once as written in the Aramaic translation.

I.   "And be careful to deal with the jugular veins [in slaughtering a beast] in accord with the teaching of R. Judah, for we have learned in the Mishnah: *R. Judah says, '[An act of slaughter is valid] only if one cuts through the jugular veins' [M. Hul. 2:1].*

J.   "And be attentive to an old man who has forgotten his learning on account of some untoward condition [through no fault of his own].

K.   "For we say: 'The tablets [of the law] as well as the broken sherds of the tablets were put away in the ark.'"

LXXV.

A.   Said Raba to his children, "When you cut meat, do not cut it while holding it in your hand."

B.   Some say it is because of the danger of injury, and some say it is because of ruining the food for the meal.

C.   [Raba continues,] "And do not sit on the bed of an Aramean woman, and do not pass behind a synagogue when the community is saying its prayers."

D.   "Do not sit on the bed of an Aramean woman": Some say his meaning was not to go to bed without saying the *Shema*; some say his meaning was not to marry a female proselyte; and some say he referred to an actual Aramean woman, on account of the story involving R. Papa.

E.   For R. Papa went to visit an Aramean woman. She brought out a bed for him, saying to him, "Sit."

F.   He said to her, "I shall not sit down until you raise up the bed [so that I can see what is underneath it]."

G.   She raised up the bed and they found a dead child there.

H.   On the basis of that incident, sages said, "It is forbidden to sit on the bed of an Aramean woman."

I.   "Do not pass behind a synagogue when the community is saying its prayers":

J.   That statement supports the view of R. Joshua b. Levi.

K.   For R. Joshua b. Levi said, "It is forbidden for someone to pass behind a synagogue when the community is saying its prayers."

L.   Said Abbayye, "But that statement has been made only where there is no other entry. But if there is another entry, there is no objection to doing so.

M.   "And that objection applies when there is no other synagogue, but if there is another synagogue, there is no objection to doing so.

N.   "And that objection applies, finally, when one is not carrying a burden, not running, or not wearing phylacteries. But if one of these conditions applies, there is no objection to doing so."

LXXVI.

A.   It has been taught on Tannaite authority:

B.   Said R. Aqiba, "On three counts I admire the Medes:

C.   "When they cut meat, they cut it only on a table.

D.   "When they kiss, they kiss only on the hand.

E.   "When they take counsel, they take counsel only in a field."

F.   Said R. Ada bar Ahba, "What verse of Scripture [proves E]? 'And Jacob sent and called Rachel and Leah to the field, to his flock' (Gen. 31:4)."

G.   It has been taught on Tannaite authority:

H. Said Rabban Gamaliel, "On three counts I admire the Persians:

I. "They are modest when they eat.

J. "They are modest in the privy.

K. "They are modest in conducting another matter [sexual relations]."

L. [By contrast to the foregoing:] "I have commanded my consecrated ones" (Isa. 13:3):

M. R. Joseph repeated on Tannaite authority, "This refers to the Persians, who are consecrated and designated for Gehenna."

LXXVII.

A. *Rabban Gamaliel says, etc. [M. Ber. 1:1E]:*

B. Said R. Judah said Samuel, "The law accords with the view of Rabban Gamaliel."

LXXVIII.

A. It has been taught on Tannaite authority:

B. R. Simeon b. Yohai says, "There are occasions on which a person recites the *Shema* twice in a single night, once before dawn, the other time afterward, and thereby carries out his obligation for both day and night."

C. The statement as formulated contains a contradiction, for you have said, "There are occasions on which a person recites the *Shema* twice in a single night," which bears the implication that after the morning star rises, it is still night.

D. And then the cited passage continues, "...and thereby carries out his obligation for both day and night," which bears the implication that it then is day.

E. Indeed, there is no real contradiction. It is really night, and the reason that one may call it "day" is that there are people who get up at that time.

F. Said R. Aha bar Hanina said R. Joshua b. Levi, "The decided law accords with the view of R. Simeon b. Yohai."

G. There are some who repeat that statement of R. Aha bar Hanina in regard to the following, which has been taught on Tannaite authority:

H R. Simeon b. Yohai says in the name of R. Aqiba, "There are occasions on which a person may recite the *Shema* twice by day, once before sunrise, once after sunrise, and he thereby carries out his obligation for both day and night."

I. Lo, there is a contradiction in the framing of that statement:

J. You have said, "There are occasions on which a person may recite the *Shema* twice by day," which bears the implication that the time prior to sunrise is regarded as day.

K Then the passage proceeds to state, "...and thereby carries out his obligation for both day and night," which bears the implication that it is night.

L. [9A] No, there is no real contradiction. It really is day, and the reason that it is called "night" is that there are people who are in bed at that time.

M Said R. Aha bar Hanina said R. Joshua b. Levi, "The decided law is in accord with what R. Simeon has said in the name of R. Aqiba."

N   Said R. Zira, "And that is the case so long as the person does not recite the prayer, 'Cause us to lie down in peace....'" [That prayer is said only by night.]

Q   When R. Isaac bar Judah came, he said, "The statement of R. Aha bar Hanina that R. Joshua b. Levi said was not made explicitly but rather made on the basis of inference.

P.   "For there was a pair of scholars who got drunk at the wedding banquet of R. Joshua b. Levi's son. They came before R. Joshua b. Levi. He ruled, 'R. Simeon is sufficiently reliable for an emergency [but under ordinary circumstances, one cannot recite the *Shema* two times, once before, once after sunrise, and so carry out his obligation for night and day].'"

LXXIX.

A.   *M'SH S: His sons came [M. 1:1F]:*

B.   And up to that point had they never heard that statement from Rabban Gamaliel?!

C.   This is what they had to say to him, "Rabbis differ from you, and in the case where there is an individual view against that of the majority, the decided law follows the majority.

D.   "But is it possible that rabbis really concur with you, and the reason that they say, *Up to midnight* is only *to keep a man far from sin* [and that is the question they addressed to him]?"

E.   He said to them, "Rabbis concur with me, and you are liable [to recite the *Shema*].

F.   "And the reason that they say, *Up to midnight* is only *to keep a man far from sin.*"

LXXX.

A.   *And not only in this case [M. 1:11]:*

B.   [Inquiring into the formulation of the matter at hand, we ask:] Has Rabban Gamaliel stated, "To midnight," that he should then add, "*And not only in this case have they stated matters...*"? [The cited clause is not connected to Gamaliel's lemma.]

C.   This is the sense of what Rabban Gamaliel said to his sons, "Even in accord with rabbis, who take the view that the recitation is to take place before midnight, the religious duty pertaining to the recitation applies until dawn.

D.   "And the reason that they have said, *Until midnight* is *in order to keep a man far from sin.*"

LXXXI.

A.   *The offering of the fats [M. 1:1K]:*

B.   Now we note that the framer of the Mishnah does not make mention of the rule governing the eating of the Passover sacrifices [which by inference may not be done up to dawn but must be completed before midnight].

C.   The following then was adduced as an objection to the inference yielded by the present formulation.

D.   The religious duty governing the recitation of the *Shema* at night, the recitation of *Hallel* on Passover night, and the eating of the Passover sacrifice, applies until dawn. [So there is a clear contradiction between the framing of the Mishnah passage and the cited Tannaite teaching.]

E.   Said R. Joseph, "There is no contradiction. The one represents the
      view of R. Eleazar b. Azariah, the other, of R. Aqiba."
F.   For it has been taught on Tannaite authority:
G.   "And they shall eat the meat in that night" (Ex. 12:8).
H   R. Eleazar b. Azariah says, "Here it is stated, 'In that night,' and
      later on it is stated, 'For I shall pass through the land of Egypt in
      that night' (Ex. 12:12).
I.   "Just as, in the latter usage, the reference is to the period up to
      midnight, so here the reference is to the period up to midnight."
J.   Said to him R. Aqiba, "And has it not already been stated, 'You
      shall eat it in haste' (Ex. 12:11)? The meaning is, 'until the time of
      haste' [which was dawn, at which point they scurried out of Egypt].
K.   "Why then does Scripture say, 'By night'? One might suppose that
      the Passover sacrifice may be eaten by day, as is the case with Holy
      Things. Accordingly, Scripture says, 'By night,' meaning, 'It is by
      night that the Passover sacrifice is eaten, and not by day.'"
L.   Now with respect to the view of R. Eleazar b. Azariah, who argues
      by constructing an analogy [between the references to "night,"] it
      was necessary for Scripture to make explicit references to "that"
      [night]. But how does R. Aqiba deal with the reference to "that"?
M.   He regards it as important to exclude reference to another night.
N   [How so?] I might have thought that, since the Passover sacrifice
      falls into the category of Lesser Holy Things, and peace-offerings
      fall into the category of Lesser Holy Things,
O   just as peace-offerings may be eaten over a span of two days and
      the intervening night [from the time that they are slaughtered], so a
      Passover-offering may be eaten [not for one night only] but over a
      space of two nights as the counterpart to the two days, so that it
      may be eaten for two nights and the intervening day.
P.   Accordingly, we are informed that it must be eaten "in that night,"
      that is, in that night it must be eaten, and it may not be eaten on yet
      another night [following].
Q   And R. Eleazar b. Azariah? He derives the same lesson from the
      explicit statement, "You shall not leave any of it over until the
      morning" (Ex. 12:10).
R.   And R. Aqiba? If it were necessary to derive the lesson from that
      statement, I might have argued, What is the sense of "morning"? It
      is the second morning [after slaughter].
S.   And R. Eleazar would say to you, "Whenever reference is made to
      'morning,' it means the first morning only [after the event that has
      taken place, not the second morning. So the meaning imputed by
      Aqiba is impossible anyhow.]"
T.   The dispute among the Tannaite authorities just now cited follows
      the same lines as the dispute among these Tannaite authorities:
U.   "There you shall sacrifice the Passover-offering in the evening, at
      the going down of the sun, at the season that you came forth out of
      Egypt" (Deut. 16:6).
V.   R. Eliezer says, "'At evening' [in the afternoon] you make the
      sacrifice, 'at sunset' you eat the meat, and 'at the season that you
      came forth from Egypt' [midnight] you must burn what is left
      over."

W.   R. Joshua says, "'At evening' you make the sacrifice, 'at sunset' you eat the meat, and until how long may you continue eating? Until 'the season that you came forth from Egypt' [midnight]."

X.   Said R. Abba, "All concur that when the Israelites were redeemed from Egypt, they were redeemed only in the evening.

Y.   "For it is said, 'The Lord your God brought you forth out of Egypt by night' (Deut. 16:1).

Z.   "And when they came forth, they came forth only by day, as it is said, 'On the morrow after the Passover the children of Israel went out with a high hand' (Num. 33:3).

AA.   "Concerning what point is there a disagreement?

BB.   "They disagree concerning the 'time of haste.'

CC.   "R. Eleazar b. Azariah takes the view that the sense of 'haste' pertains [not to the Israelites but] to the Egyptians, and R. Aqiba supposes that the sense of 'haste' pertains to the Israelites. [At midnight the Egyptians hastened to go out. That is the basis for the disagreement on the time in which it is permitted to eat the Passover-sacrifice, so Simon, p. 47, ns. 7-9.]"

DD.   It has been taught along these same lines on Tannaite authority:

EE.   "The Lord your God brought you forth out of Egypt by night" (Deut. 16:1):

FF.   Now did they go forth by night? And was it not by day that they went forth, as it is said, "On the morrow after the Passover the children of Israel went out with a high hand" (Num. 33:3)?

GG.   But the passage teaches that the redemption began for them by night.

LXXXIII.

A.   "Speak now in the ears of the people" (Ex. 11:2).

B.   In the house of R. Yannai they say, "The word for 'now' bears the implication of a request ['by your leave'].

C.   "Said the Holy One, blessed be He, to Moses, 'By your leave, go and say to the Israelites,' [and] 'By your leave, ask of the Egyptians utensils of silver and gold.'

D.   "[God continues,] 'It is so that that righteous man [Abraham] may not say [9B], "The promise, 'And they shall serve them and they shall afflict them' (Gen. 15:14) he indeed carried out, but the promise, 'And afterward they shall come out with great wealth' (Gen. 15:14) he did not carry out for them."'

E.   "They said to [Moses], 'Would that we can get out with our very lives.'"

F.   The case may be compared to that of a man who was imprisoned, and they said to him, "People are coming tomorrow to take you out from prison and they are going to give you a great deal of money."

G.   He will answer them, "By your leave, just get me out of here today, and I won't ask for anything else."

LXXXIV.

A.   "And they let them have what they asked" (Ex. 12:36):

B.   Said R. Ammi, "This teaches that they handed over [property] to them against their wills."

C.   There are those who say that it was against the will of the Egyptians.

D. And there are those who say that it was against the will of the Israelites.

E. He who says that it was against the will of the Egyptians points to what is written, "And she who tarries at home divides the spoil" (Ps. 68:13).

F. And he who says that it was against the will of the Israelites explains that it was on account of the burden of carrying the spoil [that the Israelites did not want it].

G. "And they spoiled Egypt" (Ex. 12:36):

H R. Ammi said, "This teaches that they made it like a snare without grain [to trap birds]."

I. R. Simeon b. Laqish said, "They made it like a pond without fish."

LXXXV.

A. "I am that I am" (Ex. 3:14):

B. Said the Holy One, blessed be He, to Moses, "Go, say to the Israelites: 'I was with you in this subjugation, and I shall be with you when you are subjugated to the [pagan] kingdoms.'"

C. He said to him, "Lord of the world, sufficient for the hour is the trouble [in its own time. Why mention other troubles that are coming?]"

D. Said the Holy One, blessed be He, to him, "Go, say to them, '"I am" has sent me to you' (Ex. 3:14)."

LXXXVI.

A. "Hear me, O Lord, hear me" (1 Kgs. 18:37):

B. Said R. Abbahu, "Why did Elijah say, 'Hear me,' two times?

C. "It teaches that Elijah said before the Holy One, blessed be He, 'Lord of the universe, answer me, so that fire may come down from heaven and eat what is on the altar.

D. "'And answer me that you may divert them so that they will not say that it was mere enchantment.'

E. "For it is said, 'You did turn their heart backward' (1 Kgs. 18:37)."

To understand how the redactors have arranged this vast array of materials, let us divide matters up among Mishnah sentences, to see the points at which the units of discourse take up the exegesis or amplification of the Mishnah:

M. 1:1A-B: *From what time....From the hour that the priest....*
   I-V

M. 1:1C: *Until the end of the first watch, so Eliezer.*
   VI

M. 1:1D: *Sages say, "Until midnight."*
   XVII-XVIII

M. 1:1E-N: *Gamaliel, "Until dawn."*
   LXXVII-LXXXI

Clearly, several very large blocks of materials have been collected and inserted without regard to the requirements of either close exegesis or secondary amplification of the Mishnah passage at hand. These are three: VII-XVI, XIX-LXXVI, and LXXXIII-LXXXVI.

If we begin with the shortest set, we see that the attached constructions deal with the redemption from Egypt, to which the immediately preceding unit of discourse is addressed. So it is a thematic amplification. Why the passage on Abbahu is tacked on (since it has already occurred) I cannot say.

Moving then to the second shortest, VII-XVI, we find the following topics:

VII: The night has three watches, ending, "Woe to the children."
VIII: Do not pray in a ruin, ending, "Woe to the children."
IX: Do not go into a ruin.
X: The night has three watches or four watches.
XI: Continues X.K.
XII: Continues X.K.
XIII: Continues established theme, David, study at midnight.
XIV: David's prayer. Mephibosheth.
XV: Mephibosheth.
XVI: Continues foregoing.

Accordingly, what we have is really an effort to complement materials directly relevant to the Mishnah passage. Secondary continuation of discussion of the materials introduced for Mishnah expansion is added. Thus VII-XVI have in common the single theme of the watches of the night (VIII is tacked on because of sharing the key phrase, and IX then complements VIII), and, finally, the issue of David's conduct during the night and secondary amplifications of that theme. The person who gathered and organized these materials followed a rather simple plan: explain the Mishnah passage, expand upon it, then expand upon the expansions, in sequence and very systematically.

This brings us to the much more complicated mass of material, XIX-LXXVI, an amazingly protracted discussion of many things. Can we account for this unit, which would form about the third of the volume of a small Talmud tractate? Let us begin by outlining the topics, then see how we may group the topics into a set of large thematic constructions:

XIX: Ps. 145.
XX: Ps. 145.
   Who belongs to the world to come, including one who recites Ps. 145.
XXI: Michael and Gabriel.
   No clear connection.

XXII: Reciting the Shema in bed.

    Yohanan at XVIII has insisted one should say the Shema in the evening. Now we stress that it must be done, in addition, in bed. Prooftext: Ps. 4:5.

XXIII: Ps. 4:5.

    Continues discourse on prooftext.

XXIV: Reciting the Shema in bed.

    Continues XXII. Prooftext: Ps. 4:2. Keeps demons away.

XXV: Ps. 4:2.

    Continues discourse on prooftext.

XXVI: Causes of suffering.

    XXIV has referred to the suffering of someone who could study Torah but does not do so. This leads to the notion that study of Torah keeps one from suffering.

XXVII: Suffering brought on by various causes.

    Continues foregoing theme, God's love.

XXVIII: God gave Israel gifts.

    Continues foregoing theme through suffering.

XXIX: He who studies Torah or does acts of loving kindness or buries his children is forgiven all his sins.

    Continues foregoing theme.

XXX: Suffering brought on by skin ailments is a sign of God's love.

    Continues foregoing theme.

XXXI: Stories of sick rabbis.

    Continues foregoing theme.

XXXII: Stories of sick rabbis.

    Continues foregoing theme.

XXXIII: Stories of rabbi's loss of property.

    Continues foregoing theme.

XXXIV: Say a prayer before one's bed.

    Now begins a new theme: rules on where bed, place bed on north-south axis and how to say prayers. Abba Benjamin.

XXXV: If two people pray together, they should stay together until both have finished.

    Rules on praying. Abba Benjamin.

XXXVI: Demons are numerous. Abba Benjamin.

    Same authority, new topic.

XXXVII: Prayer of a person is heard only in the synagogue.

    Rules on praying. Abba Benjamin.

XXXVIII: Rules on phylacteries. God puts them on.

    Rules on phylacteries. Abin bar Ada/Isaac.

XXXIX: Rules on phylacteries.

Nahman bar Isaac to Hiyya bar Abin on what is in God's phylacteries? Theme of phylacteries.

XL: Importance of praying in synagogue.

Rules on praying. Rabin bar Ada/Isaac.

XLI: God is angry when he finds fewer than ten in a synagogue.

Continues the foregoing.

XLII: Set up a regular place in which to pray.

Rules on praying. Helbo, Huna.

XLIII: Reward for attending a discourse on law.

This continues the immediately preceding item, on running to hear a lesson, etc.

XLIV: Not praying behind a synagogue.

Rules on praying, Huna.

XLV: Attentive at afternoon prayer.

Helbo, Huna.

XLVI: Felicitate bridal couple.

Helbo, Huna. Same authority, new topic.

XLVII: Heaven hears words of one who fears heaven.

Rules on praying. Helbo, Huna.

XLVIII: One should greet his friend without waiting to be greeted.

Helbo, Huna. Same authority, new topic.

XLIX: God says prayers.

New topic, related to the theme of praying. Now we speak of God saying prayers. Yohanan/Yosé. Continues foregoing.

L: God's prayer.

Continues foregoing.

LI: God's anger.

Continues theme begun at XLIX.

LII: Importance of mercy.

Continues foregoing.

LIII: God's anger.

Continues foregoing.

LIV: Person should reproach himself.

New theme, same authorities, Yohanan/Yosé.

LV: God gave Moses three things that he asked for.

New theme, same authorities, Yohanan/Yosé.

LVI: Expansion on one of the things Moses asked for, with reference to Ex. 33:20.

Continues foregoing theme.

LVII: Expansion on the theme of Moses' requests.

Continues foregoing theme.

LVIII: God never retracted a conditional promise to do good for Israel.

New theme, same authorities, Yohanan/Yosé.

LIX: Abraham was the first to call God "Lord."

New theme, same authority, now Yohanan/Simeon b. Yohai.

LX: How do we know not to appease someone when he is angry?

New theme, same authority, now Yohanan/Simeon b. Yohai.

LXI: Leah was the first to praise God.

Same theme as LIX, same authorities, Yohanan/Simeon b. Yohai.

LXII: Bringing up a child badly is worse than war of Gog and Magog.

New theme, same authorities, Yohanan/Simeon b. Yohai.

LXIII: One may contend with the wicked in this world.

New theme, same authorities, Yohanan/Simeon b. Yohai.

LXIV: Anyone who has a regular place for praying vanquishes his enemies.

New theme, same authorities, Yohanan/Simeon b. Yohai.

LXV: Personal service to a sage more important than studying with him.

New theme, same authorities, Yohanan/Simeon b. Yohai.

LXVI: Importance of saying prayers with the community, not by self.

New theme: rules for saying prayers with the community.

LXVII: One who does not say prayers with the community is a bad neighbor.

Rules for saying prayers with the community.

LXVIII: People live long who say prayers with the community.

As above.

LXIX: Praying at the right time.

Meaning of "the right time." But this "right time" is now interpreted as having to do with something other than praying. It stands at the head of a series on what is more important than praying.

LXX: God loves study of law more than praying.

Continues established theme.

LXXI: Greater is one who works for his own living than one who fears heaven.

No clear relationship to foregoing. Saying of Hiyya bar Ami/Ulla.

LXXII: Person should live where his master does.

No clear relationship to foregoing. Saying of Hiyya bar Ami/Ulla.

LXXIII: One should not leave synagogue when Torah is being read.
New topic: importance of reading the Torah along with the community.

LXXIV: One should read the same Scripture at home that the community is reading in the synagogue.
Continues established topic. Ends with Joshua b. Levi's advice to his children.

LXXV: Raba's advice to his children.
I take it the connection is that Raba accords with a statement that Joshua b. Levi has made. But it is not the same statement that occurs at LXXIV.

LXXVI: Reasons for admiring Medes, Persians.
I see no connection to the foregoing.

If we now seek to group the foregoing, we find the following principles of conglomeration and organization:

1. *Common theme, spelled out over a number of distinct units of discourse on aspects of the one theme:* 21.

    XIX-XX; XXI-XXXIII; LXVI-LXX; LXXIII

2. *Common authorities behind a number of statements on discrete topics:* 37.

    Abba Benjamin: XXXIV-XXXVII; Abin bar Ada/Isaac: XXXVIII-XLI; Helbo-Huna, XLII-XLVIII; Yohanan/Yosé, XLIX-LVIII; Yohanan/Simeon b. Yohai, LIX-LXV; Hiyya bar Ami/Ulla, LXX-LXXII; Joshua b. Levi, LXXIV-LXXV

3. *No clear explanation:* 2.

    XXI; LXXVI

The upshot is that there were two principles for the redaction of large conglomerates of materials, the one, thematic, the other, the name of the authority and tradent (X says Y says). In this second principle, the tradent's name will predominate, thus Yohanan/Yosé and Yohanan/Simeon b. Yohai materials are grouped, XLIX-LXIX, 21 units of discourse, to which we should attach Ulla's set, added because Ulla's name occurs in the foregoing composite. Can we then rigidly differentiate thematic or topical compositions, for example, rules on public prayer or on praying in synagogues, from tradental compositions, for instance, sayings in the name of a given tradent and authority? Yes and no. What all topical compositions have in common, of course, is focus on a given topic. But some tradental compositions are arranged around a single topic, and in most a given subject will predominate, even though tangentially or not at all related topics will enter. So while we may say that all topical compositions as a group differ from all tradental ones, we may not rigidly distinguish tradental compositions from topical ones. What we have to recognize as the distinctive trait of the tradental composition is the predominance of a given tradent's name, which will explain the insertion of a thematically irrelevant (or, at best, neutral) item. It follows that the Talmud of Babylonia is made up, so far as our protracted sample is concerned, of four types of material: Mishnah exegesis, expansion of Mishnah exegesis, topical compositions in some way relevant to the largest themes of the Mishnah tractate, or the Mishnah paragraph, at hand, and tradental compositions possibly relevant in the same way, possibly not. What proportion of the chapter is occupied by the materials before us? The entire chapter covers approximately 189,000 bytes; the miscellanies run approximately 86,000, thus approximately 45 percent of the entirety of the chapter.

Thus far we have seen two principles of agglutination in play, common theme, common attribution. There is a third principle of agglutination, which yields sustained composites, and that is, agglutination of treatments of a succession of verses of Scripture. As it happens, the same chapter, Bavli Berakhot Chapter One, provides us with a fine example of this principle in action.

1:2

A.	From what time do they recite the Shema in the morning?
B.	From the hour that one can distinguish between blue and white.
C.	R. Eliezer says, "Between blue and green."
D.	And one completes it by sunrise.
E.	R. Joshua says, "By the third hour.
F.	"For it is the practice of royalty to rise [at] the third hour."
G.	One who recites the Shema from then on has not lost [the merit of the act entirely, since he is] like one who recites from the Torah.

I.

A.	What is the meaning of "between blue and white"?
B.	If I should propose that it means the difference between a white piece of wool and a blue piece of wool, that difference can be discerned by night [as much as by day].
C.	Rather, [the sense is to distinguish] between the blue and the white [threads in the same piece of wool].

II.

A.	It has been taught on Tannaite authority:
B.	R. Meir says, "Once one can tell the difference between a wolf and a dog."
C.	R. Aqiba says, "...between an ass and a wild ass."
D.	Others say, "Once one can see his fellow four cubits away and recognize who it is" [T. Ber. 1:2B].
E.	Said R. Huna, "The decided law accords with the position of 'others.'"

F. Said Abbayye, "The law as to the phylacteries accords with the view of 'others,' while the law on reciting the *Shema* accords with the view of the oldtimers."

G. For R. Yohanan said, "The oldtimers would complete the recitation of the *Shema* by dawn."

III.

A. It has been taught on Tannaite authority along these same lines:

B. The oldtimers would complete the recitation of *Shema* exactly at dawn so as to place the prayer for redemption [with which the *Shema* closes] right next to the Prayer [of supplication], and one will turn out to say the Prayer in daylight.

C. Said R. Zira, "What verse of Scripture supports this practice? 'They shall fear you with the sun and so long as the moon throughout all generations' (Ps. 82:5)."

D. R. Yosé b. Eliaqim gave testimony in behalf of the holy community of Jerusalem, "Whoever recites the prayer for Redemption immediately prior to the Prayer [of supplication] will not suffer injury that entire day."

E. Said R. Zira, "Is that so? But lo, I joined the two but I still was injured that day."

F. He said to him, "What went wrong with you? Was it that you had to carry a myrtle branch into the royal palace? In that case that was no injury at all, because you should have had to pay a fee to have the right to see the face of the king! [It was no injury at all to have to pay the *corvee* under such circumstances.]"

G. For R. Yohanan said, "A person should always try to run to meet the kings of Israel, and not the kings of Israel alone, but even the kings of the idolators,

H. "so that if one should have the merit, he may know the difference between the kings of Israel and the kings of the idolators [living so long as to see the restoration of the Israelite monarchy]."

IV.

A. Said R. Ila to Ulla, "When you go up there, greet my brother, R. Berona, in the presence of the entire community [of scholars], for he is a great man and takes great joy in carrying out religious duties.

B. "Once he managed to join the recitation of the prayer for redemption to the Prayer [of supplication], and he did not stop smiling the whole day."

V.

A. But how is it possible to join the two prayers without interruption?

B. For R. Yohanan said, "At the beginning [of the Prayer], a person has to recite, 'O Lord, open my lips' (Ps. 51:17), and at the end, 'Let the words of my mouth be acceptable' (Ps. 19:15). [So at the beginning there is a prayer that intervenes between the blessing for redemption and the Prayer itself.]"

C. Said R. Eleazar, "The inclusion of the cited verses must be only at the Prayer said in the evening."

D. But did not R. Yohanan say, "Who belongs to the category of the world to come? It is a person who joins the prayer for redemption said at night to the Prayer that is recited at night."

E. Rather, said R. Eleazar, "The added verses should come in the Prayer when it is recited in the late afternoon."

F. R. Ashi said, "You may take the position that the additional verses of Scripture belong in the Prayer when it is said throughout the day [morning, afternoon, night]. For since rabbis have ordained that these verses should be added to the Prayer, it is as if the Prayer itself has simply been protracted.

G. "For if you do not take this position, how in the Prayer said at night can we join the prayer for redemption to the Prayer. For in any event a person has in the middle to recite, 'Cause us to lie down....'

H. "Rather, the operative principle is that, since rabbis have ordained that we say, 'Cause us to lie down....,' it is in the category of a protracted prayer for Redemption.

I. "Here, too, since rabbis have ordained the inclusion of the verses of Psalms in the Prayer, it is as if the Prayer had been lengthened."

VI.

A. Since the verse, "May the words of my mouth be acceptable" (Ps. 19:15) would serve equally well at the end of the Prayer as much as at the beginning, why did rabbis ordain that it was to be said at the end of the Eighteen Blessings [the Prayer]? Why not say it at the beginning?

B. Said R. Judah, son of R. Simeon b. Pazzi, "Since David said that verse only at the end of eighteen chapters [of Psalms, namely, at the end of Psalm 19], rabbis on that account ordained that it should come at the end of the Eighteen Blessings."

C. But the eighteen Psalms [to which reference has just been made] in fact are nineteen!

D. "Happy is the man" and "Why are the nations in an uproar" (Ps. 1:1, 2:1) constitute a single chapter.

E. For R. Judah, son of R. Simeon b. Pazzi said, "David recited 103 Psalms, and he never said 'Halleluyah' until he had witnessed the downfall of the wicked.

F. "For it has been said, 'Let sinners cease out of the earth, and let the wicked be no more. Bless the Lord, O my soul. Halleluyah' (Ps. 104:35)."

G. These 103 Psalms in fact are 104 Psalms.

H. That then yields the inference that "Happy is the man" and "Why are the nations in an uproar" (Ps. 1:1, 2:1) constitute a single chapter.

I. For R. Samuel bar Nahmani said R. Yohanan said, [10A] "Every chapter that was particularly beloved for David did he open by saying 'Happy' and close by saying 'Happy.'

J. "He began with 'Happy,' as Scriptures states, 'Happy is the man' (Ps. 1:1) and he closed with 'Happy,' as Scriptures states, 'Happy are all who trust in him' (Ps. 2:11)."

VII.

A. There were some thugs in R. Meir's neighborhood, who gave him a lot of trouble. R. Meir prayed for mercy for himself so that they would die. His wife, Beruriah, said to him, "What is on your mind? [Do you pray that they should die] because it is written [at Ps.

104:35], 'Let sins die'? Is it written 'sinners'? What is written is 'sins.'

B.   "And at the end of the verse, moreover, it is written, 'And let wicked men be no more' (Ps. 104:35).

C.   "Since my sins will stop, there will be no more wicked men.

D.   "Rather, pray for mercy concerning them that they will revert in repentance and not be wicked any more."

E.   He prayed for mercy concerning them, and they did revert in repentance.

VIII.

A.   A certain *min* said to Beruriah, "It is written, 'Sing, O barren woman, who has not born...' (Isa. 54:1).

B.   "Because the woman is barren, should she rejoice?"

C.   She said to him, "Idiot, look at the end of the same verse of Scripture, for it is written, 'For the children of the desolate shall be more than the children of the married woman, says the Lord' (Isa. 54:1).

D.   "What then is the sense of, 'Barren woman, who has not born'?

E.   "Rejoice, O congregation of Israel, which is like a barren woman [that is,] who has not born children destined for Gehenna such as yourself."

IX.

A.   A certain *min* said to R. Abbahu, "It is written, 'A Psalm of David when he fled from Absalom, his son' (Ps. 3:1). And it is written, 'A *mihtam* of David, when he fled from Saul in the cave' (Ps. 57:1).

B.   "Which incident took place first? Since it was the incident with Saul, it should have been written first."

C.   He said to him, "You, who do not execute an exegesis of Scripture based on the juxtaposition of passages, find the issue a problem. We, who execute exegeses based on the juxtaposition of verses, do not find the matter a problem."

D.   For R. Yohanan said, "The principle of the exegesis of passages based on juxtapositions derives from the Torah itself.

E.   "Whence do we know that fact? As it is written, "They are joined together forever and ever they are done in truth and uprightness" (Ps. 111:8).

F.   [Reverting to Abbahu:] "Why is the passage concerning Absalom placed in juxtaposition with the passage dealing with Gog and Magog [that is, Ps. 2]? For if someone should say to you, 'Is there such a thing as a slave that rebels against his master,' you may say to him, 'Is there such a thing as a son who rebels against his father?' But just as the one thing happened so did the other."

X.

A.   Said R. Yohanan in the name of R. Simeon b. Yohai, "What is the meaning of the Scripture, 'She opens her mouth with wisdom, and the Torah of kindness is on her tongue' (Prov. 31:26)?

B.   "With regard to whom did Solomon say this verse? He said it only with reference to his father, David, who dwelled in five worlds and said a song [in each].

C.   "He dwelled in the belly of his mother and said a song, as it is said, 'Bless the Lord, O my soul, and all my inwards bless his holy name' (Ps. 103:1).

D.   "He came forth into the world and looked at the stars and planets and said a song, as it is said, 'Bless the Lord, you angels of his, you mighty in strength that fulfill his word, hearkening to the voice of his word. Bless the Lord, all you his hosts' (Ps. 103:20, 21).

E.   "He sucked at the tit of his mother and looked at her breasts and said a song, as it is said, 'Bless the Lord, O my soul, and forget not all his benefits' (Ps. 103:2)."

F.   What is the meaning of "all his benefits"?

G.   Said R. Abbahu, "That God put the breasts at the place of understanding [the heart]."

H.   What is the reason?

I.   Said R. Judah, "So that one should not gaze upon the woman's sexual parts."

J.   R. Mattena said, "So that one should not suck from a smelly place."

K.   [Resuming Simeon b. Yohai's statement:] "He saw the catastrophe that came upon the wicked and said a song, as it is said, 'Let sinners cease out of the earth and let the wicked be no more. Bless the Lord, O my soul, Halleluyah' (Ps. 104:35).

L.   "He looked upon the day of death and said a song, as it is said, 'Bless the Lord, O my soul. O Lord my God, you are very great, you are clothed with glory and majesty' (Ps. 104:1)."

M.   How do we know that the cited verse refers to the day of death?

N.   Said Rabbah bar R. Shila, "We derive that information from the latter part of the same clause: 'You hide your face, they vanish, you withdraw their breath, they perish' (Ps. 104:29)."

XI.

A.   R. Shimi bar Uqba, and some say, Mar Uqba, often was in session before R. Simeon b. Pazzi, who had laid forth exegeses before R. Joshua b. Levi. He said to him, "What is the meaning of the verse of Scripture, 'Bless the Lord, O my soul, and all that is within me bless his holy name' (Ps. 103:1)?"

B.   He said to him, "Come and take note of the fact that the trait of the Holy One, blessed be He, is not like the trait of mortals.

C.   "If a mortal makes a drawing on the wall, he cannot put into it spirit and breath, bowels and intestines. But the Holy One, blessed be He, is, is not that way. He can make a drawing within a drawing and put into it spirit and breath, bowels and intestines.

D.   "And that is in line with what Hannah said, 'There is none holy as the Lord, for this is none beside you, neither is there any form [SR] like our God' (1 Sam. 2:2).

E.   "What is the sense of, 'neither is there any form like our God'?

F.   "There is no artist [SYR] like our God."

G.   What is the meaning of, "For there is none beside you" (Ps. 1, Sam. 2:2)?

H.   Said R. Judah bar Menassia, "Do not read it as if it says, 'There is none beside you,' but rather, 'There is none to outlive you.'

I.   "For the trait of the Holy One, blessed be He, is not like the trait of mortals.

J.   "The trait of mortals is that what mortals create outlives them.

K.   "But the Holy One, blessed be He, outlives his own creations."

L.   He said to him, 'This is what I meant to say to you: As to these five references to 'Bless the Lord, O my soul' [which David said], to whom did David allude when he said them?

M.   "He alluded only to the Holy One blessed be He, and to the soul.

N   "Just as the Holy One, blessed be He, fills the whole world, so the soul fills the whole body.

O.   "Just as the Holy One, blessed be He, sees but is not seen, so the soul sees but is not seen.

P.   "Just as the Holy One, blessed be He, sustains the whole world, so the soul sustains the whole body.

Q.   "Just as the Holy One, blessed be He, is pure, so the soul is pure.

R.   "Just as the Holy One, blessed be He, sits in the innermost chambers, so the soul dwells in the innermost chambers.

S.   "Let that which bears all these five traits come and give praise to the One in whom are all these five traits."

XII.

A.   Said R. Hamnuna, "What is the meaning of the verse of Scripture, 'Who is as the wise man? And who knows the interpretation of a matter?' (Qoh. 8:1)?

B.   "Who is like the Holy One, blessed be He, who knows how to accomplish a mediating interpretation of the claims of two righteous men, Hezekiah and Isaiah.

C.   "Hezekiah said, 'Let Isaiah come to me, for we find in the case of Elijah that he came to Ahab.'

D.   "Isaiah said, 'Let Hezekiah come to me, for we find in the case of Jehoram, son of Ahab, that he came to Elisha.'

E.   "What did the Holy One, blessed be He, do? He brought suffering upon Hezekiah and said to Isaiah, 'Go and pay a call on the sick man.'

F.   "For it is said, 'In those days Hezekiah was sick unto death. And Isaiah the prophet, son of Amoz, came to him and said to him, Thus says the Lord, Set your house in order, for you will die and not live' (Isa. 38:1)."

G.   What is the meaning of, "You shall die and not live"?

H   "You shall die" in this world "and shall not live" in the world to come.

I   [Resuming the interrupted narrative:] "He said to him, 'Why all this?'

J.   "He said to him, 'Because you did not engage in carrying out the religious duty to be fruitful and multiply.'

K.   "He said to him, 'It was because I saw by the Holy Spirit that from me would go forth sons who were not worthy.'

L.   "He said to him, 'What business is it of yours to get involved with the secrets of the All-Merciful? What you are commanded to do is what you have to do, and what pleases the Holy One, blessed be He, he will do.'

M.   "He said to him, 'Then give me your daughter. Perhaps the merit that has accrued to me and the merit that has accrued to you will serve so that out of me worthy sons will come forth.'

N. "He said to him, 'The decree has already been made against you.'

Q. "He said to him, 'Ben Amoz, finish your prophecy and leave. Thus have I received as a tradition from the house of the father of my father: "Even if a sharp sword is lying on a man's neck, he should not refrain from praying for mercy."'"

P. It has been stated on Amoraic authority along these same lines:

Q. R. Yohanan and R. Eleazar both say, "Even if a sharp sword is resting on a man's neck, he should not refrain from praying for mercy,

R. "For it is said, 'Though he slay me, yet I will trust in him' (Job 13:15)."

S. [10B] Said R. Hanan, "Even if the master of dreams says to a man that he will die tomorrow, he should not refrain from praying for mercy.

T. "For it is said, 'For in the multitude of dreams are vanities, and also many words, but fear you God' (Qoh. 5:6)."

U. [Resuming the interrupted narrative:] "Forthwith, 'Hezekiah turned his face to the wall and prayed to the Lord' (Isa. 38:2)."

V. What is the sense of "wall"?

W. Said R. Simeon b. Laqish, "[He prayed] from the innermost walls of his heart, as it is said, 'My bowels, my bowels, I writhe in pain. The walls of my heart...' (Jer. 4:19)."

X. R. Levi said, "He prayed concerning matters having to do with a wall. He said before him, 'Lord of the world, now if for the Shunamit woman, who only made a small wall[ed hut], you brought her son back to life, for father's father, who covered the entire house with silver and gold, all the more so [should you restore me to life].'"

Y. "'Remember now, O Lord, I beseech you, how I have walked before you in truth and with a whole heart and have done that which is good in your sight" (Isa. 38:3).

Z. What is the meaning of, "I have done that which is good in your sight"?

AA. Said R. Judah said Rab, "What he did was to juxtapose the prayer for redemption to the Prayer."

BB. R. Levi said, "He hid away the scroll containing cures."

XIII.

A. Our rabbis have taught on Tannaite authority:

B. King Hezekiah did six things. On account of three of them [sages] praised him, and on account of three they did not praise him.

C. On account of three they praised him:

D. He hid away the book of cures and they praised him.

E. He pulverized the copper snake and they praised him.

F. He dragged the bones of his father on a bed of ropes and they praised him.

G. On account of three they did not praise him.

H. He shut off the waters of Gihon, and they did not praise him.

I. He cut off the gold from the doors of the Temple and sent it to the king of Assyria, and they did not praise him.

J. He intercalated the month of Nisan during the month of Nisan itself and they did not praise him.

K.   But did Hezekiah not concur with the law, "'This month shall be unto you the beginning of months' (Ex. 12:2), which means that this month is Nisan, and no other month can be declared Nisan [so that one may not intercalate a month into the year and call it Nisan]"?

L.   But he erred with respect to the matter that is framed in the teaching of Samuel.

M.   For Samuel said, "People may not intercalate the year on the thirtieth day of Adar, since that day may belong to Nisan" [Simon, p. 57, n. 1: if the new moon is observed on it].

N.   He said, "We do not invoke the possibility that it might belong [to Nisan], [so he intercalated a second Adar in that year, doing so on the thirtieth day of the first Adar]."

XIV.

A.   R. Yohanan said in the name of R. Yosé b. Zimra, "Whoever relies [in his petition to Heaven] on his own merit is made to depend upon the merit of others, and whoever relies on the merit of others is made to depend upon his own merit.

B.   "Moses depended upon the merit of others, as it is said, 'Remember Abraham, Isaac, and Israel, your servants' (Ex. 32:13), so the matter was made to depend upon his own merit, as it is said, 'Therefore he said that he would destroy them, had not Moses his chosen stood before him in the breach to turn back his wrath, lest he should destroy them' (Ps. 106:23).

C.   "Hezekiah depended upon his own merit, as it is said, 'Remember, now O Lord, I beseech you, how I have walked before you' (Isa. 38:3). So he was made to depend upon the merit of others, for it says, 'I will defend this city to save it, for my own sake and for my servant David's sake' (Isa. 37:35)."

D.   That is in line with what R. Joshua b. Levi said.

E.   For R. Joshua b. Levi said, "What is the meaning of the following verse of Scripture: 'Behold for my peace I had great bitterness' (Isa. 38:17)?

F.   "Even when the Holy One, blessed be He, sent him peace, it was bitter to him [Simon, p. 57, n. 8: because it was not made to depend on his own merit]."

XV.

A.   "Let us make, I pray you, a little walled chamber on the roof" (2 Kgs. 4:10):

B.   Rab and Samuel:

C.   One said, "There was an upper chamber there, and they made a roof for it."

D.   The other said, "There was a large veranda, and they divided it into two."

E.   Now in the view of him who said there was a veranda, that is why it is written, "...wall...," [which is to say, they added another wall].

F.   But in the view of him who says that it was a chamber, why does it say "...wall...[QYR]"?

G.   For they roofed [QYR] it.

H.   Now in the view of him who says there was an upper chamber ['LH], that is why it is written "chamber ['LH]."

I.   But in the view of him who says it was a veranda, why does it say "chamber"?

J.   It was the best ['LH] of all the rooms.

K.   "And let us set a bed for him there, a table, stool, and candlestick" (2 Kgs. 4:10):

L.   Said Abbayye, and some say, R. Isaac, "He who wants to derive benefit [from hospitality] should do so as did Elisha, and he who does not wish to derive benefit should not do so, in the model of Samuel of Ramah.

M.   "For it is said, 'And his return was to Ramah, for there was his house' (1 Sam. 7:17).'"

N.   And R. Yohanan said, "Wherever he went, there his house was with him."

O.   "And she said to her husband, Behold now, I perceive that he is a holy man of God" (2 Kgs. 4:9):

P.   Said R. Yosé bar Hanina, "This proves that a woman recognizes the character of guests more accurately than does her husband."

Q.   "A holy man" (2 Kgs. 4:9):

R.   How did she know?

S.   Rab and Samuel:

T.   One said, "Because she never saw a fly passing the table on which he [ate]."

U.   And the other said, "Because she spread a linen sheet on his bed, and she did not see a drop of semen on it."

V.   "He is holy" (2 Kgs. 4:9):

W.   Said R. Yosé b. R. Hanina, "He is holy, but his servant is not holy.

X.   "For it is said, 'And Gehazi came near to thrust her away' (2 Kgs. 4:27).

Y.   R. Yosé b. R. Hanina said, "He grabbed her by the breast."

Z.   "He passes by us all the time" (2 Kgs. 4:9):

AA.   Said R. Yosé b. R. Hanina in the name of R. Eliezer b. Jacob, "Whoever provides hospitality in his own home for a disciple of a sage and provides for him from his prosperity is regarded by Scripture as though he had offered daily whole-offerings."

XVI.

A.   And R. Yosé b. R. Hanina said in the name of R. Eliezer b. Jacob, "A person should not stand in a high place and say his prayer, but he should stand in a low place and say his prayer.

B.   "For it is said, 'Out of the depths I have called to you, O Lord' (Ps. 130:1)."

C.   It has been taught on Tannaite authority along the same lines:

D.   A person should not stand either on a chair or on a stool or on a high place and say his prayers, but he should stand on a low place and say his prayers.

E.   For there is no such thing as elevation before the Omnipresent.

F.   For it is said, "Out of the depths I have called to you, O Lord" (Ps. 130:1).

G.   And it is written, "A prayer of the afflicted, when he faints" (Ps. 102:1).

H.   And R. Yosé b. R. Hanina said in the name of R. Eliezer b. Jacob, "He who says the Prayer has to line up his feet [side by side],

I.   "as it is said, 'And their feet were straight' (Ezek. 1:7)."

J.   And R. Yosé b. R. Hanina said in the name of R. Eliezer b. Jacob, "What is the meaning of this verse of Scripture: 'You shall not eat with the blood' (Lev. 19:26)?

K.   "Do not eat before you have said your prayer concerning your own blood [so pray as to save your own life]."

L.   And R. Isaac said R. Yohanan said R. Yosé b. R. Hanina said in the name of R. Eliezer b. Jacob, "Whoever eats, drinks, and only then says his prayers is regarded by Scripture as follows: 'And me have you cast beyond your back' (1 Kgs. 14:9).

M.   "Do not read the letters as though they say 'your back' but rather, 'your pride.'

N.   "Said the Holy One, blessed be He, 'After this one has taken pride in himself, only then has he accepted the dominion of heaven!'"

XVII.

A.   *Said R. Joshua, "By the third hour" [M. 1:2E]:*

B.   Said R. Judah said Samuel, "The decided law accords with the position of R. Joshua."

XVIII.

A.   *One who recites the Shema from then on has not lost...[M. 1:2G]:*

B.   Said R. Hisda said Mar Uqba, "But that is on condition that one not say the blessing, '...who forms the light.'"

C.   An objection was raised from the following statement: *He who recites the Shema from then on has not lost [the merit of the act entirely, since he is] like one who recites from the Torah.* But he has to say two blessings [including 'who forms light'] before reciting the *Shema* and one afterward.

D.   Is this not a refutation of R. Hisda's view?

E.   It is an explicit refutation.

F.   Some report the matter as follows:

G.   Said R. Hisda said Mar Uqba, "What is the sense of '...he has not lost...'? That he has not lost the blessings [recited prior to, and following, the recitation of the *Shema*]."

H.   It has been taught along these same lines on Tannaite authority:

I.   *He who recites the Shema from then on has not lost [the merit of the act entirely, since he is] like one who recites from the Torah.* But he has to say two blessings before reciting the *Shema* and one afterward.

XIX.

A.   Said R. Mani, "Greater is the merit according to him who recites the *Shema* at its proper time than that accruing to one who takes up study of the Torah.

B.   "Since the Mishnah states, '*He who recites the Shema from then on has not lost the merit of the act entirely, since he is like one who recites from the Torah,* there is the implication that the one who recites it in its proper time is still better off.

The sizable portion at hand includes materials brought together to serve as exegesis of the Mishnah, others worked out on a single theme and proposition, and still others conglomerated around the name of a single authority and tradent. Units I, II, complemented by III, serve the opening phrase of the Mishnah. Units IV, V take up a detail of unit III, juxtaposition of the Shema to the Prayer. Since unit V has referred to Ps. 19:15, unit VI proceeds to develop ideas on that verse. Since unit VI has included a reference to Ps. 104:35, unit VII tells a story in which that verse figures. Since unit VII refers to Beruriah, unit VIII tells another story about Beruriah. Since unit VIII's story refers to a Min, unit IX introduces another story about a Min. I am not entirely sure why unit X is introduced. It does not seem to me that including Yohanan at IX.D accounts for introducing a sizable unit of discourse of his. My best guess is that what we have is another instance of building an exegesis based on the juxtaposition of verses. The appearance, at X.C, of Ps. 103:1, however, certainly explains the introduction of unit XI. Unit XII does strike me as a random insertion. I see no connection whatever to what has gone before, nor any to what will follow after the completion of unit XI in units XII, XIII, XIV – more on Hezekiah. Unit XV is introduced because of XII V-X, that is, the reference to the word 'wall,' on the one side, and the Shunamit woman, on the other. Now we have a rather elaborate treatment of that and subsequent verses. Because we end with Yosé b. R. Hanina's citation of Eliezer, we are given the entire construction of which XV X is the opening line, that is, unit XVI, a tradental construction. We end, XVII-XIX, with a reversion to Mishnah commentary.

My sense of the purpose of inserting everything between III and XVI is that the redactor simply gathered together masses of connected materials and placed them where he did as a way of providing them with a home. Why were the materials connected to begin with? Once more we see that entire sets were assembled around sequential verses of Scripture, on the one side, or around the name of a tradent and authority, on the other. A dominant theme, third, will account for the gathering of yet other materials. It seems to me the set at hand is more clearly meant to form a continuous – if somewhat meandering – discourse than the foregoing. So these are the principles of agglutination: [1] common authority; [2] common theme; [3] common passage of Scripture, sequentially expounded. In the next chapter we shall discern precisely the same principles of agglutination, the most important being a common theme, less important, common authority, least important, common passage of Scripture (except where a given theme is treated, for example, a scriptural personality). Not only so, but the themes will be supplied by the Mishnah, so, as a matter of fact, the order of the themes too. It will then be transparent that the miscellany serves as Mishnah commentary, but not the same kind of Mishnah commentary as the propositional, analytical, and syllogistic one that predominates, as I explained in Chapter Two, throughout most of the Bavli.

5

Three Massive Miscellanies: [3] Bavli Sanhedrin Chapter Ten

We proceed directly to a still more sizable miscellany, one that, on the face of it, in no way can be described as coherent. In fact, a simple outline, given at the end, will show that this massive miscellany serves a simple purpose as Mishnah commentary, pure and simple. True, it is not an propositional or analytical or syllogistic kind of commentary. But then, the Mishnah that is commented upon does not provoke analysis, only exemplification. And that is what is given.

11:1

A. All Israelites have a share in the world to come,

B. as it is said, "your people also shall be all righteous, they shall inherit the land forever; the branch of my planting, the work of my hands, that I may be glorified" (Isa. 60:21).

C. And these are the ones who have no portion in the world to come:

D. He who says, the resurrection of the dead is a teaching which does not derive from the Torah, and the Torah does not come from Heaven; and an Epicurean.

E. R. Aqiba says, "Also: He who reads in heretical books,

F. "and he who whispers over a wound and says, 'I will put none of the diseases upon you which I have put on the Egyptians, for I am the Lord who heals you' (Ex. 15:26)."

G. Abba Saul says, "Also: He who pronounces the Divine Name as it is spelled out."

11:2

A. Three kings and four ordinary folk have no portion in the world to come.

B. Three kings: Jeroboam, Ahab, and Manasseh.

C. R. Judah says, "Manasseh has a portion in the world to come,

D. "since it is said, 'And he prayed to him and he was entreated of him and heard his supplication and brought him again to Jerusalem into his kingdom' (2 Chr. 33:13)."

E. They said to him, "To his kingdom he brought him back, but to the life of the world to come he did not bring him back."

F. Four ordinary folk: Balaam, Doeg, Ahitophel, and Gehazi.

I.

A. Why all this [that is, why deny the world to come to those listed]?

B. On Tannaite authority [it was stated], "Such a one denied the resurrection of the dead, therefore he will not have a portion in the resurrection of the dead.

C. "For all the measures [meted out by] the Holy One, blessed be He, are in accord with the principle of measure for measure."

D. For R. Samuel bar Nahmani said R. Jonathan said, "How do we know that all the measures [meted out by] the Holy One, blessed be He, accord with the principle of measure for measure?

E. "As it is written, 'Then Elisha said, Hear you the word of the Lord. Thus says the Lord, Tomorrow about this time shall a measure of fine flour be sold for a sheqel, and two measures of barley for a sheqel in the gates of Samaria' (2 Kgs. 7:1).

F. "And it is written, 'Then a lord on whose hand the king leaned answered the man of God and said, Behold, if the Lord made windows in heaven, might this thing be? And he said, Behold, you shall see it with your eyes, but shall not eat thereof' (2 Kgs. 7:2).

G. [90B] "And it is written, 'And so it fell unto him; for the people trod him in the gate and he died' (2 Kgs. 7:20).

H. But perhaps it was Elisha's curse that made it happen to him, for R. Judah said Rab said, "The curse of a sage, even for nothing, will come about"?

I. If so, Scripture should have said, "They trod upon him and he died." Why say, "They trod upon him in the gate"?

J. It was that on account of matters pertaining to [the sale of wheat and barley at] the gate [which he had denied, that he died].

II.

A. How, on the basis of the Torah, do we know about the resurrection of the dead?

B. As it is said, "And you shall give thereof the Lord's heave-offering to Aaron the priest" (Num. 18:28).

C. And will Aaron live forever? And is it not the case that he did not even get to enter the Land of Israel, from the produce of which heave-offering is given?

D. Rather, this teaches that he is destined once more to live, and the Israelites will give him heave-offering.

E. On the basis of this verse, therefore, we see that the resurrection of the dead is a teaching of the Torah.

III.

A. A Tannaite authority of the house of R. Ishmael [taught], "'...to Aaron...,' 'like Aaron.' [That is to say,] just as Aaron was in the status of an associate [who ate his produce in a state of cultic cleanness even when not in the Temple], so his sons must be in the status of associates."

B. Said R. Samuel bar Nahmani said R. Jonathan, "How on the basis of Scripture do we know that people do not give heave-offering to a priest who is in the status of an ordinary person [and not an associate]?

C. "As it is said, 'Moreover he commanded the people who lived in Jerusalem to give the portion of the Levites, that they might hold fast to the Torah of the Lord' (2 Chr. 31:4).

D. "Whoever holds fast to the Torah of the Lord has a portion, and whoever does not hold fast to the Torah of the Lord has no portion:

E. Said R. Aha bar Ada said R. Judah, "Whoever hands over heave-offering to a priest who is in the status of an ordinary person is as if he throws it in front of a lion.

F. "Just as, in the case of a lion, it is a matter of doubt whether he will tear at the prey and eat it or not do so,

G. "so in the case of a priest who is in the status of an ordinary person, it is a matter of doubt whether he will eat it in a condition of cultic cleanness or eat it in a condition of cultic uncleanness."

H. R. Yohanan said, "[if one gives it to an improper priest], he also causes him to die, for it is said, 'And...die therefore if they profane it' (Lev. 22:9).

I. The Tannaite authority of the house of R. Eliezer B. Jacob [taught], "One also gets him involved in the sin of guilt [of various kinds], for it is written, 'Or suffer them to bear the iniquity of trespass when they eat their holy things' (Lev. 22:16)."

IV.

A. It has been taught on Tannaite authority:

B. R. Simai says, "How on the basis of the Torah do we know about the resurrection of the dead?

C. "As it is said, 'And I also have established my covenant with [the patriarchs] to give them the land of Canaan' (Ex. 6:4).

D. "'With you' is not stated, but rather, 'with them,' indicating on the basis of the Torah that there is the resurrection of the dead."

V.

A. *Minim* asked Rabban Gamaliel, "How do we know that the Holy One, blessed be He, will resurrect the dead?'

B. He said to them, "It is proved from the Torah, from the Prophets, and from the Writings." But they did not accept his proofs.

C. "From the Torah: For it is written, 'And the Lord said to Moses, Behold, you shall sleep with your fathers and rise up' (Deut. 31:16)."

D. They said to him, "But perhaps the sense of the passage is, 'And the people will rise up' (Deut. 31:16)?"

E. "From the Prophets: As it is written, 'Thy dead men shall live, together with my dead body they shall arise. Awake and sing, you that live in the dust, for your dew is as the dew of herbs, and the earth shall cast out its dead' (Isa. 26:19)."

F. "But perhaps that refers to the dead whom Ezekiel raised up."

G.   "From the Writings: As it is written, 'And the roof of your mouth, like the best wine of my beloved, that goes down sweetly, causing the lips of those who are asleep to speak' (Song 7:9)."

H.   "But perhaps this means that the dead will move their lips?"

I.   That would accord with the view of R. Yohanan.

J.   For R. Yohanan said in the name of R. Simeon b. Yehosedeq, "Any authority in whose name a law is stated in this world moves his lips in the grave,

K.   "as it is said, 'Causing the lips of those that are asleep to speak.'"

L.   [The *minim* would not concur in Gamaliel's view] until he cited for them the following verse: "'Which the Lord swore to your fathers to give to them' (Deut. 11:21) – to them and not to you, so proving from the Torah that the dead will live."

M.   And there are those who say that it was the following verse that he cited to them: "'But you who cleaved to the Lord your God are alive, everyone of you this day' (Deut. 4:4). Just as on this day all of you are alive, so in the world to come all of you will live."

VI.

A.   Romans asked R. Joshua b. Hananiah, "How do we know that the Holy One will bring the dead to life and also that he knows what is going to happen in the future?"

B.   He said to them, "Both propositions derive from the following verse of Scripture:

C.   "As it is said, 'And the Lord said to Moses, Behold you shall sleep with you fathers and rise up again, and this people shall go awhoring...' (Deut. 31:16).

D.   "But perhaps the sense is, '[the people] will rise up and go awhoring.'"

E.   He said to them, "Then you have gained half of the matter, that God knows what is going to happen in the future."

VII.

A.   It has also been stated on Amoraic authority:

B.   Said R. Yohanan in the name of R. Simeon b. Yohai, "How do we know that the Holy One, blessed be He, will bring the dead to life and knows what is going to happen in the future?

C.   "As it is said, 'Behold, you shall sleep with you fathers, and...rise again...(Deut. 31:16)."

VIII.

A.   It has been taught on Tannaite authority:

B.   Said R. Eliezer b. R. Yosé, "In this matter I proved false the books of the *minim*.

C.   "For they would say, 'The principle of the resurrection of the dead does not derive from the Torah.'

D.   "I said to them, 'You have forged your Torah and have gained nothing on that account.

E.   "'For you say, "The principle of the resurrection of the dead does not derive from the Torah."

F.   "'Lo, Scripture says, "[Because he has despised the word of the Lord...] that soul shall be cut off completely, his iniquity shall be upon him" (Num. 15:31).

G. ""…shall be utterly cut off…," in this world, in which case, at what point will "…his iniquity be upon him…"?

H. "'Will it not be in the world to come?'"

I. Said R. Pappa to Abbayye, "And might one not have replied to them that the words 'utterly…' '…cut off…,' signify the two worlds [this and the next]?"

J. [He said to him,] "They would have answered, 'The Torah speaks in human language [and the doubling of the verb carries no meaning beyond its normal sense].'"

IX.

A. This accords with the following Tannaite dispute:

B. "'That soul shall be utterly cut off' – 'shall be cut off' – in this world, 'utterly' – in the world to come," the words of R. Aqiba.

C. Said R. Ishmael to him, "And has it not been said, 'He reproaches the Lord, and that soul shall be cut off' (Num. 15:31). Does this mean that there are three worlds?

D. "Rather: '…it will be cut off…,' in this world, '…utterly…,' in the world to come, and 'utterly cut off…,' indicates that the Torah speaks in ordinary human language."

E. Whether from the view of R. Ishmael or of R. Aqiba, what is the meaning of the phrase, "His iniquity shall be upon him"?

F. It accords with that which has been taught on Tannaite authority:

G. Is it possible that that is the case even if he repented?

H. Scripture states, "His iniquity shall be upon him."

I. I have made the statement at hand only for a case in which "his iniquity is yet upon him" [but not if he repented].

X.

A. Queen Cleopatra asked R. Meir, saying, "I know that the dead will live, for it is written, 'And [the righteous] shall blossom forth out of your city like the grass of the earth' (Ps. 72:16).

B. "But when they rise, will they rise naked or in their clothing?"

C. He said to her, "It is an argument a fortiori based on the grain of wheat.

D. "Now if a grain of wheat, which is buried naked, comes forth in many garments, the righteous, who are buried in their garments, all the more so [will rise in many garments]!"

XI.

A. Caesar said to Rabban Gamaliel, "You maintain that the dead will live. But they are dust, and can the dust live?"

B. [91A] His daughter said to him, "Allow me to answer him.

C. "There are two potters in our town, one who works with water, the other who works with clay. Which is the more impressive?"

D. He said to her, "The one who works with water."

E. She said to him, "If he works with water, will he not create even more out of clay?"

XII.

A. A Tannaite authority of the house of R. Ishmael [taught], "[Resurrection] is a matter of an argument a fortiori based on the case of a glass utensil.

B. "Now if glassware, which is the work of the breath of a mortal man, when broken, can be repaired,

C.   "A mortal man, who is made by the breath of the Holy One, blessed be He, how much the more so [that he can be repaired, in the resurrection of the dead]."

XIII.

A.   A *min* said to R. Ammi, "You say that the dead will live. But they are dust, and will the dust live?"

B.   He said to him, "I shall draw a parable for you. To what may the matter be compared?

C.   "It may be compared to the case of a mortal king, who said to his staff, 'Go and build a great palace for me, in a place in which there is no water or dirt [for bricks].

D.   "They went and built it, but after a while it collapsed.

E.   "He said to them, 'Go and rebuild it in a place in which there are dirt and water [for bricks].'

F.   "They said to him, 'We cannot do so.'

G.   "He became angry with them and said to them, 'In a place in which there is neither water nor dirt you were able to build, and now in a place in which there are water and dirt, how much the more so [should you be able to build it]!'

H.   "And if you [the *min*] do not believe it, go to a valley and look at a rat, which today is half flesh and half dirt and tomorrow will turn into a creeping thing, made all of flesh. Will you say that it takes much time? Then go up to a mountain and see that today there is only one snail, but tomorrow it will rain and the whole of it will be filled with snails."

XIV.

A.   A *min* said to Gebiha, son of Pesisa, [a hunchback,] "Woe for you! You are guilty! For you say that the dead will live. Those who are alive die, and will those who are dead live?"

B.   He said to him, "Woe for you! You are guilty! For you say that the dead will not live. [Now if we] who were not [alive before birth] now live, will not those who do live all the more so [live again]?"

C.   He said to him, "Have you then called me guilty? If I stood up, I could kick you and straighten out your hump."

D.   He said to him, "If you could do that, you would be a physician, a specialist who collects enormous fees."

XV.

A.   Our rabbis have taught on Tannaite authority:

B.   On the twenty-fourth of Nisan the tax farmers were dismissed from Judea and Jerusalem.

C.   When the Africans came to trial with Israel before Alexander of Macedonia, they said to him, 'The land of Canaan belongs to us, for it is written, 'The land of Canaan, with the coasts thereof' (Num. 34:2), and Canaan was the father of these men."

D.   Said Gebiha, son of Pesisa, to sages, "Give me permission, and I shall go and defend the case with them before Alexander of Macedonia. If they should win out over me, say, 'You won over a perfectly common person of our group,' and if I should win out over them, say to them, 'It is the Torah of Moses that overcame you.'"

E.   They gave him permission, and he went and engaged in debate with them. He said to them, "From whence do you bring proof?"

F.   They said to him, "From the Torah."

G.   He said to them, "I, too, shall bring you proof only from the Torah, for it is said, 'And he said, Cursed be Canaan, a servant of servants shall he be to his brothers' (Gen. 9:25).

H.   "Now if a slave acquires property, for whom does he acquire it? And to whom is the property assigned?

I.   "And not only so, but it is quite a number of years since you have served us."

J.   Said King Alexander to them, "Give him an answer."

K.   They said to him, "Give us a span of three days time." He gave them time.

L.   They searched and did not find an answer. They forthwith fled, leaving their fields fully sown and their vineyards laden with fruit, and that year was the Sabbatical Year. [So the Israelites could enjoy the produce in a time in which they most needed it.]

XVI.

A.   There was another time, [and] the Egyptians came to lay claim against Israel before Alexander of Macedonia. They said to him, "Lo, Scripture says, 'And the Lord gave the people favor in the sight of the Egyptians, and they lent them gold and precious stones' (Ex. 12:36). Give us back the silver and gold that you took from us."

B.   Said Gebiha, son of Pesisa, to sages, "Give me permission, and I shall go and defend the case with them before Alexander of Macedonia. If they should win out over me, say, 'You won over a perfectly common person of our group,' and if I should win out over them, say to them, 'It is the Torah of Moses, our master, that overcame you.'"

C.   They gave him permission, and he went and engaged in debate with them. He said to them, "From whence do you bring proof?"

D.   They said to him, "From the Torah."

E.   He said to them, "I, too, shall bring you proof only from the Torah, for it is said, 'Now the sojourning of the children of Israel, who dwelt in Egypt, was four hundred and thirty years' (Ex. 12:40).

F.   "Now pay us the salary of six hundred thousand people whom you enslaved in Egypt for four hundred and thirty years."

G.   Said Alexander of Macedonia to them, "Give him an answer."

H.   They said to him, "Give us time, a span of three days."

I.   He gave them time. They searched and found no answer. They forthwith fled, leaving their fields sown and their vineyards laden with fruit, and that year was the Sabbatical Year.

XVII.

A.   There was another time, [and] the children of Ishmael and the children of Keturah came to trial with the Israelites before Alexander of Macedonia. They said to him, "The land of Canaan belongs to us as well as to you, for it is written, 'Now these are the generations of Ishmael, son of Abraham' (Gen. 25:12), and it is written, 'And these are the generations of Isaac, Abraham's son' (Gen. 25:19). [Both Ishmael and Isaac have an equal claim on the land, hence so, too, their descendants]."

B. Said Gebiha, son of Pesisa, to sages, "Give me permission, and I shall go and defend the case with them before Alexander of Macedonia. If they should win out over me, say, 'You won over a perfectly common person of our group,' and if I should win out over them, say to them, 'It is the Torah of Moses, our master, that overcame you.'"

C. They gave him permission, and he went and engaged in debate with them. He said to them, "From whence do you bring proof?'

D. They said to him, "From the Torah."

E. He said to them, "I, too, shall bring you proof only from the Torah, for it is said, 'And Abraham gave all that he had to Isaac. But to the sons of the concubines which Abraham had Abraham gave gifts' (Gen. 25:5-6).

F. "In the case of a father who gave a bequest to his sons while he was yet alive and sent them away from one another, does any one of them have a claim on the other? [Certainly not.]"

G. What were the gifts [that he gave]?

H   Said R. Jeremiah bar Abba, "This teaches that he gave them [the power of utilizing the Divine] Name [for] unclean [purposes]."

XVIII.

A. Antoninus said to Rabbi, "The body and the soul both can exempt themselves from judgment.

B. "How so? The body will say, 'The soul is the one that has sinned, for from the day that it left me, lo, I am left like a silent stone in the grave.'

C. "And the soul will say, 'The body is the one that sinned. For from the day that I left it, lo, I have been flying about in the air like a bird.'"

D. He said to him, "I shall draw a parable for you. To what may the matter be likened? To the case of a mortal king who had a lovely orchard, and in it were [91B] luscious figs. He set in it two watchmen, one crippled and one blind.

E. "Said the cripple to the blind man, 'There are luscious figs that I see in the orchard. Come and carry me, and let us get some to eat. The cripple rode on the blind man and they got the figs and ate them. After a while the king said to them, 'Where are the luscious figs?'

F. "Said the cripple, 'Do I have feet to go to them?'

G. "Said the blind man, 'Do I have eyes to see?'

H   "What did the king do? He had the cripple climb onto the blind man, and he inflicted judgment on them as one.

I. "So the Holy One, blessed be He, brings the soul and places it back in the body and judges them as one, as it is said, 'He shall call to the heavens from above and to the earth, that he may judge his people' (Ps. 50:4).

J. "'He shall to call to the heavens from above' – this is the soul.

K. "'And to the earth, that he may judge his people' – this is the body."

XIX.

A. Said Antoninus to Rabbi, "Why does the sun rise in the east and set in the west?"

B. He said to him, "If thing were opposite, you would still ask me the same thing!"

C.   He said to him, "This is what I meant to ask you: Why does it set in the west?"

D.   He said, "To give a greeting to its maker, as it is written, 'And the host of the heavens make obeisance to you' (Neh. 9:6)...."

E.   He said to him, "Then let it go halfway through the firmament, pay its respects, and then ascend from there [eastward]."

F.   "It is because of workers and wayfarers [who need to know when the day is over]."

XX.

A.   Said Antoninus to Rabbi, "At what point is the soul placed in man? Is it at the moment that it is decreed [that the person shall be born] or when the embryo is formed?"

B.   He said to him, "From the moment when it is formed."

C.   He said to him, "Is it possible that a piece of flesh should keep for three days if it is not salted and not become rotten?

D.   "Rather, it should be from the time at which it is decreed [that the person should come into being."

E.   Said Rabbi, "This is something that Antoninus taught me, and a verse of Scripture supports his view, for it is said, 'And your decree has preserved my soul' (Job 10:12)."

XXI.

A.   And Antoninus said to Rabbi, "At what point does the impulse to do evil take hold of a man? Is it from the moment of creation or from the moment of parturition?"

B.   He said to him, "It is from the moment of creation."

C.   He said to him, "If so, the fetus will kick its mother's womb and escape. Rather, it is from the moment of parturition."

D.   Said Rabbi, "This is something that Antoninus taught me, and a verse of Scripture supports his view, for it is said, 'At the door [of the womb] sin lies in wait' (Gen. 4:7)."

XXII.

A.   R. Simeon b. Laqish contrasted [these two verses]: "It is written, 'I will gather them...with the blind and the lame, the woman with child and her that travails with child together' (Jer. 31:8), and it is written, 'Then shall the lame man leap as a hart and the tongue of the dumb sing, for in the wilderness shall waters break out and streams in the desert' (Isa. 35:6). How so [will the dead both retain their defects and also be healed]?

B.   "They will rise [from the grave] bearing their defects and then be healed."

XXIII.

A.   Ulla contrasted [these two verses]: "It is written, 'He will destroy death forever and the Lord God will wipe away tears from all faces' (Isa. 25:9), and it is written, 'For the child shall die a hundred years old...there shall no more die thence an infant of days' (Isa. 65:20).

B.   "There is no contradiction. The one speaks of Israel, the other of idolators."

C.   But what do idolators want there [Freedman, p. 612, n. 9: in the reestablished state after the resurrection]?

D. It is to those concerning whom it is written, "And strangers shall stand and feed your flocks, and the sons of the alien shall be your plowmen and your vinedressers" (Isa. 61:5).

XXIV.

A. R. Hisda contrasted [these two verses]: "It is written, 'Then the moon shall be confounded and the sun ashamed, when the Lord of hosts shall reign' (Isa. 24:23), and it is written, 'Moreover the light of the moon shall be as the light of seven days' (Isa. 30:26).

B. "There is no contradiction. The one refers to the days of the Messiah, the other to the world to come."

C. And in the view of Samuel, who has said, "There is no difference between the world to come and the days of the Messiah, except the end of the subjugation of the exilic communities of Israel"?

D. There still is no contradiction. The one speaks of the camp of the righteous, the other the camp of the Presence of God.

XXV.

A. Raba contrasted [these two verses]: "It is written, 'I kill and I make alive' (Deut. 32:39) and it is written, 'I wound and I heal' (Deut. 32:39). [Freedman, p. 613, n. 4, 5: The former implies that one is resurrected just as he was at death, thus with blemishes, and the other implies that at the resurrection all wounds are healed].

B. "Said the Holy One, blessed be He, 'What I kill I bring to life,' and then, 'What I have wounded I heal.'"

XXVI.

A. Our rabbis have taught on Tannaite authority: "I kill and I make alive" (Deut. 32:39).

B. Is it possible to suppose that there is death for one person and life for the other, just as the world is accustomed [now]?

C. Scripture says, "I wound and I heal" (Deut. 32:39).

D. Just as wounding and healing happen to one person, so death and then resurrection happen to one person.

E. From this fact we derive an answer to those who say, "There is no evidence of the resurrection of the dead based on the teachings of the Torah."

XXVII.

A. It has been taught on Tannaite authority:

B. R. Meir says, "How on the basis of the Torah do we know about the resurrection of the dead?

C. "As it is said, 'Then shall Moses and the children of Israel sing this song to the Lord' (Ex. 15:1).

D. "What is said is not 'sang' but 'will sing,' on the basis of which there is proof from the Torah of the resurrection of the dead.

E. "Along these same lines: 'Then shall Joshua build an altar to the Lord God of Israel' (Josh. 8:30).

F. "What is said is not 'built' but 'will build,' on the basis of which there is proof from the Torah of the resurrection of the dead.

G. Then what about this verse: 'Then will Solomon build a high place for Chemosh, abomination of Moab" (1 Kgs. 11:7)? Does it mean that he will build it? Rather, the Scripture treats him as though he had built it [even though he had merely thought about doing so].

XXVIII.

A.   Said R. Joshua b. Levi, "How on the basis of Scripture may we prove the resurrection of the dead?

B.   "As it is said, 'Blessed are those who dwell in your house, they shall ever praise you, *selah*' (Ps. 84:5).

C.   "What is said is not 'praised you' but 'shall praise you,' on the basis of which there is proof from the Torah of the resurrection of the dead."

D.   And R. Joshua b. Levi said, "Whoever recites the song [of praise] in this world will have the merit of saying it in the world to come,

E.   "as it is said, 'Happy are those who dwell in you house, they shall ever praise you, *selah*' (Ps. 84:5)."

F.   Said R. Hiyya b. Abba said R. Yohanan, "On what basis do we know about the resurrection of the dead from Scripture?"

G.   "As it says, 'Your watchman shall lift up the voice, with the voice together they shall sing (Isa. 52:8).'"

H.   What is said is not 'sang' but 'will sing' on the basis of which there is proof from the Torah of the resurrection of the dead.

I.   Said R. Yohanan, "In the future all the prophets will sing in unison, as it is written, 'Your watchman shall lift up the voice, with the voice together they shall sing (Isa. 57:8).'"

XXX.

A.   Said R. Judah said Rab, "Whoever withholds a teaching of law from a disciple is as if he steals the inheritance of his fathers from him,

B.   "for it is said, 'Moses commanded us Torah, even the inheritance of the congregation of Jacob' (Deut. 33:4).

C.   "It is an inheritance destined for all Israel from the six days of creation."

D.   Said R. Hana bar Bizna said R. Simeon the Pious, "Whoever withholds a teaching of law from a disciple is cursed even by the fetuses in their mothers' wombs, as it is said, 'He who withholds grain [92A] will be cursed by the embryo' (Prov. 11:26), for the word at hand can only mean 'embryo,' as it is written, 'And one embryo shall be stronger than the other people' (Gen. 25:23) [referring to Jacob and Esau in the womb].

E.   "And the cited word can only mean 'cursing,' as it is written, 'How shall I curse whom God has not cursed?' (Num. 23:8).

F.   "And the word for grain speaks only of 'the Torah,' as it is written, 'Nourish yourselves with grain lest he be angry' (Ps. 2:12)."

G.   Ulla bar Ishmael says, "They pierce him like a sieve, for here it is written, 'The people will pierce him,' (Prov. 11:26), and the word means pierce in the verse, 'And he pierced a hole in the lid of it' (2 Kgs. 12:10)."

H.   And Abbayye said, "He will be like a fuller's trough [so perforated as a drainage plank]."

I.   An if he does teach a law, what is his reward?

J.   Said Raba said R. Sheshet, "He will merit blessings like those that came to Joseph, as it is said, 'But blessing shall be upon the head of the one who sells' (Prov. 11:26).

K.   "And the one who sells speaks only of Joseph, as it is said, 'And Joseph was the governor over the land, and he was the one who sells to all the people of the land' (Gen. 47:6)."

XXXI.

A.   Said R. Sheshet, "Whoever teaches Torah in this world will have the merit of teaching it in the world to come,

B.   "as it is said, 'And he who waters shall water again, too' (Prov. 11:25)."

XXXII.

A.   Said Raba, "How on the basis of the Torah do we find evidence for the resurrection of the dead?

B.   "As it is said, 'Let Reuben live and not die' (Deut. 33:6).

C.   "'Let Reuben live' in this world, and 'not die,' in the world to come."

D.   Rabina said, "Proof derives from here: 'And many of them that sleep in the dust of the earth shall awake, some to everlasting life, and some to shame and everlasting contempt' (Dan. 12:2)."

E.   R. Ashi said, "Proof derives from here: 'But go your way till the end be, for you shall rest and stand in your lot at the end of days' (Dan. 12:13)."

XXXIII.

A.   Said R. Eleazar, "Every authority who leads the community serenely will have the merit of leading them in the world to come, as it is said, 'For he who has mercy on them shall lead them, even by springs of water shall he guide them' (Isa. 49:10)."

B.   And said R. Eleazar, "Great is knowledge, for it is set between two names [lit. letters] [of God], as it is written, 'For a God of knowledge is the Lord' (1 Sam. 2:3)."

C.   And said R. Eleazar, "Great is the sanctuary, for it is set between two names [of God], as it is written, 'You have made for yourself, O Lord, a sanctuary, O Lord, your hands have established it' (Ex. 15:17)."

D.   To this view R. Ada Qarhinaah objected, "Then how about the following: Great is vengeance, for it is set between two names [of God], as it is written, 'O God of vengeance, O Lord, O God of Vengeance, appear' (Ps. 94:1)."

E.   He said to him, "In context, that is quite so, in line with what Ulla said."

F.   For Ulla said, "What purpose is served by these two references to 'appear'? One speaks of the measure of good, the other, the measure of punishment."

G.   And said R. Eleazar, "In the case of any man who has knowledge it is as if the house of the sanctuary had been built in his own time, for this [knowledge] is set between two names of [God], and that [the Temple] likewise is set between two names of [God]."

H.   And said R. Eleazar, "Any man in whom there is knowledge in the end will be rich, for it is said, 'And by knowledge shall the chambers be filled with all precious and pleasant riches' (Prov. 24:4)."

I.   And said R. Eleazar, "It is forbidden to have pity on any man in whom there is no knowledge, as it is said, 'For it is a people of no understanding; therefore he that made them will not have mercy upon them, and he that formed them will show them no favor' (Isa. 27:11)."

J.   And said R. Eleazar, "Whoever gives his bread to someone who does not have knowledge in the end will be afflicted with sufferings, for it is said, 'They who eat your bread have laid a wound under you, there is no understanding in him' (Obad. 1:7), and the word for 'wound' can mean only suffering, as it is written, 'When Ephraim saw his sickness and Judah his suffering' [using the same word] (Hos. 5:13)."

K.   And said R. Eleazar, "Any man who has no knowledge in the end will go into exile, as it is said, 'Therefore my people have gone into exile, because they have no knowledge' (Isa. 5:13)."

L.   And said R. Eleazar, "Any house in which words of Torah are not heard by night will be eaten up by fire, as it is said, 'All darkness is hid in his secret places; a fire not blown shall consume him; he grudges him that is left in his tabernacle' (Job 20:26).

M.   "The word for 'grudges' means only a disciple of a sage, as it is written, 'And in those left [using the same root] whom the Lord shall call' (Joel 3:5). [Freedman, p. 616, n. 12: The first part of the verse, 'all darkness is hid...,' is interpreted as, his secret places are not illumined by the study of the law; the last part, 'he grudges...,' as, he looks with disfavor upon any student who enters his house for a meal]."

N.   And said R. Eleazar, "Whoever does not give a benefit to disciples of sages from his property will see no blessing ever, as it is said, 'There is none who remains to eat it, therefore shall he not hope for prosperity' (Job 20:21).

O.   "The word for 'remain' refers only to a disciple of a sage, as it is written, 'And in those left whom the Lord shall call' (Joel 3:5)."

P.   And said R. Eleazar, "Anyone who does not leave a piece of bread on his table will never see a sign of blessing, as it is said, 'There be none of his food left, therefore shall he not hope for his prosperity' (Job 20:21)."

Q.   But has not R. Eleazar said, "Whoever leaves pieces of bread on his table is as if he worships an idol, as it is said, 'That prepare a table for God and that furnish the drink-offering to Meni' (Isa. 65:11)"?

R.   There is no contradiction, in the one case [the latter] a complete loaf is left alongside, and in the other case [the former], no complete loaf is left [with the crumbs].

S.   And said R. Eleazar, "Whoever goes back on what he has said is as if he worships an idol.

T.   "Here it is written, 'And I seem to him as a deceiver' (Gen. 27:12), and elsewhere it is written, 'They [idols] are vanity and the work of deceivers' (Jer. 10:15)."

U.   And said R. Eleazar, "Whoever stares at a woman's sexual parts will find that his 'bow' is emptied out, as it is said, 'Shame shall empty you bow [of strength]' (Hab. 3:9)."

V.   And said R. Eleazar, "One should always accept [things] and so endure."

W.   Said R. Zira, "We, too, also have learned on Tannaite authority:

X.   "*As to a room without windows, people are not to open windows for it to examine whether or not it is afflicted with a plague sign [M. Neg. 2:3].* [Thus the possible signs will be missed because of the obscurity of the room. Likewise humility protects one's life.]"

Y.   That makes the case.

XXXIV.

A   Said R. Tabi said R. Josiah, "What is the meaning of this verse of Scripture: 'The grave and the barren womb and the earth that is not filled by water' (Prov. 30:16).

B.   "What has the grave to do with the womb?

C   It is to say to you, just as the womb takes in and gives forth, so Sheol takes in and gives forth.

D.   "And is it not an argument a fortiori? If in the case of the womb, in which they insert [something] in secret, the womb brings forth in loud cries, Sheol, into which [bodies] are placed with loud cries, is it not reasonable to suppose that from the grave people will be brought forth with great cries?

E   "On the basis of this argument there is an answer to those who say that the doctrine of the resurrection of the dead does not derive from the Torah."

XXXV.

A   A Tannaite authority of the house of Elishah [taught], "The righteous whom the Holy One, blessed be He, is going to resurrect will not revert to dust,

B.   "for it is said, 'And it shall come to pass that he that is left in Zion and he that remains in Jerusalem shall be called holy, even everyone that is written among the living in Jerusalem, (Isa. 4:3).

C.   "Just as the Holy One lives forever, so they shall live forever.

D.   [92B] "And if you want to ask, as to those years in which the Holy One, blessed be He, will renew his world, as it is said, 'And the Lord alone shall be exalted in that day' (Isa. 2:11), during that time what will the righteous do?

E   "The answer is that the Holy One, blessed be He, will make them wings like eagles, and they will flutter above the water, as it is said, 'Therefore we will not fear, when the earth be moved and the mountains be carried in the midst of the sea' (Ps. 46:3).

F.   "And if you should say that they will have pain [in all this], Scripture says, 'But those who wait upon the Lord shall renew their strength, they shall mount up with wings as eagles, they shall run and not be weary, they shall walk and not be faint' (Isa. 40:31).

G   And should we derive [the opposite view] from the dead whom Ezekiel resurrected?

H   He accords with the view of him who said that, in truth, it was really a parable.

I.   For it has been taught on Tannaite authority:

J.   R. Eliezer says, "The dead whom Ezekiel resurrected stood on their feet, recited a song, and they died."

K.   What song did they recite?

L.   "The Lord kills in righteousness and revives in mercy" (1 Sam. 2:6).

M   R. Joshua says, "They recited this song, 'The Lord kills and makes live, he brings down to the grave and brings up' (1 Sam. 2:6)."

N.   R. Judah says, "It was true it was a parable."

O.   Said to him R. Nehemiah, "If it was true, then why a parable? And if a parable, why true? But in truth it was a parable."

P.   R. Eliezer, son of R. Yosé the Galilean, says, "The dead whom Ezekiel resurrected went up to the Land of Israel and got married and produced sons and daughters."

Q.   R. Judah b. Betera stood up and said, "I am one of their grandsons, and these are the phylacteries that father's father left me from them."

R.   And who were the dead whom Ezekiel resurrected?

S.   Said Rab, "They were the Ephraimites who reckoned the end of time and erred, as it is said, 'And the sons of Ephraim, Shuthelah and Bared his son and Tahath his son and Eladah his son and Tahath his son. And Zabad his son and Shuthelah his son and Ezzer and Elead, whom the men of Gath that were born in the land slew' (1 Chr. 7:20-21). And it is written, 'And Ephraim their father mourned many days and his brethren came to comfort him' (1 Chr. 7:22)."

T.   And Samuel said, "They were those who denied the resurrection of the dead, as it is said, 'Then he said to me, Son of man, these bones are the whole house of Israel; behold, they say, Our bones are dried and our hope is lost, we are cut off for our parts' (Ezek. 37:11)."

U.   Said R. Jeremiah, 'These were the men who had not a drop of religious duties to their credit, as it is written, 'O you dry bones, hear the word of the Lord' (Ezek. 37:4)."

V.   R. Isaac Nappaha said, "They were the men who had covered the sanctuary entirely with abominations and creeping things, as it is said, 'So I went in and saw, and behold, every form of creeping things and abominable beasts and all the idols of the house of Israel, were portrayed upon the wall round about' (Ezek. 8:10).

W.   "While [in the case of the dry bones] it is written, 'And caused me to pass by them round about' (Ezek. 37:2). [Freedman, p. 620, n. 1: The identification is based on the use of 'round about' in both narratives. In his view even those who in their despair surrender themselves to abominable worship are not excluded from the bliss of resurrection.]"

X.   R. Yohanan said, "They were the dead in the valley of Dura."

Y.   And said R. Yohanan, "From the river Eshel to Rabbath is the valley of Dura. For when Nebuchadnezzar, that wicked man, exiled Israel, there were young men who outshone the sun in their beauty. Chaldean women would see them and reach orgasm [from the mere gaze]. They told their husbands and their husbands told the king. The king ordered them killed. Still, the wives would reach orgasm [merely from laying eyes on the corpses]. The king gave an order and they trampled [the corpses beyond all recognition]."

XXXVI.

A.   Our rabbis have taught on Tannaite authority:

B.   When Nebuchadnezzar, the wicked man, cast Hananiah, Mishael, and Azariah, into the fiery furnace, the Holy One, blessed be He, said to Ezekiel, "Go and raise the dead in the valley of Dura."

C.   When he had raised them, the bones came and smacked that wicked man in his face. He said, "What are these things?"

D.   They said to him, "The friend of these is raising the dead in the valley of Dura."

E.   He then said, "'How great are his signs, and how mighty his wonders. His kingdom is an everlasting kingdom, and his dominion is from generation to generation' (Dan. 3:23)."

F.   Said R. Isaac, "May liquid gold pour into the mouth of that wicked man.

G.   "For had not an angel come and slapped his mouth shut, he would have attempted to shame [by the excellence of his composition] all the songs and praises that David had recited in the book of Psalms."

XXXVII.
A.   Our rabbis have taught on Tannaite authority:

B.   Six miracles were done on that day, and these are they:

C.   The furnace floated, the furnace split open, the foundations crumbled, the image was turned over on its face, the four kings were burned up, and Ezekiel raised the dead in the valley of Dura.

D.   And all of the others were a matter of tradition, but the [miracle of the] four kings is indicated in a verse of Scripture: "Then Nebuchadnezzar the king sent to gather together the princes, the governors, and the captains, the judges, the treasurers, the counselors, the sheriffs, and all the rulers of the provinces [to come to the dedication of the image]" (Dan. 3:2),

E.   and it is written, "There are certain Jews..." (Deut. 3:2),

F.   and also: "And the princes, governors, and captains, and the king's counselors, being gathered together, saw these men, upon whom the fire had no power" (Dan. 3:27).

XXXVIII.
A.   A Tannaite authority of the house of R. Eliezer b. Jacob [taught], "Even in time of danger a person should not pretend that he does not hold his high office,

B.   "For it is said, 'Then these men were bound in their coats, their hose, and their other garments' (Dan. 3:21). [Freedman, p. 621, n. 8: These were garments specially worn by men in their exalted position, and they did not doff them though cast into the furnace.]"

XXXIX.
A.   Said R. Yohanan, [93A] "The righteous are greater than ministering angels.

B.   "For it is said, 'He answered and said, Lo, I see four men loose, walking in the midst of the fire, and they are not hurt, and the form of the fourth is like the son of God' (Dan. 3:25) [Freedman, p. 621, n. 9: Thus the angel is mentioned last, as being least esteemed]."

XL.
A.   Said R. Tanhum bar Hanilai, "When Hananiah, Mishael, and Azariah went out of the fiery furnace, all the nations of the world came and slapped the enemies of Israel [that is, Israel] on their faces.

B.   "They said to them, 'You have a god such as this, and yet you bow down to an idol!'

C.   "Forthwith they said this verse, 'O Lord, righteousness belongs to you, but to us shamefacedness, as at this day' (Dan. 9:7).

XLI.

A.   Said R. Samuel bar Nahmani said R. Jonathan, "What is the meaning of the verse of Scripture, 'I said, I will go up to the palm tree, I will take hold of the boughs thereof' (Song 7:9)?

B.   "'I said I will go up to the palm tree' refers to Israel.

C.   "But now 'I grasped' only one bough, namely, Hananiah, Mishael, and Azariah."

XLII.

A.   And said R. Yohanan, "What is the meaning of the verse of Scripture, 'I saw by night, and behold a man riding upon a red horse, and he stood among the myrtle trees that were in the bottom' (Zech. 1:8)?

B.   What is the meaning of, 'I saw by night'?

C.   "The Holy One blessed be He, sought to turn the entire world into night.

D.   "'And behold, a man riding' – 'man' refers only to the Holy One, blessed be He, as it is said, 'The Lord is a man of war, the Lord is his name' (Ex. 15:3).

E.   "'On a red horse' – the Holy One, blessed be He, sought to turn the entire world to blood.

F.   "When, however, he saw Hananiah, Mishael, and Azariah, he cooled off, as it is said, 'And he stood among the myrtle trees that were in the deep.'

G.   "The word for 'myrtle trees' speaks only of the righteous as it is written, 'And he brought up the myrtle' (Est. 2:7) [another name of Esther].

H.   "And the word for 'deep' speaks only of Babylonia, as it is said, 'That says to the deep, be dry, and I will dry up your rivers' (Isa. 44:27) [Freedman, p. 622, n. 11: To Babylon, situated in a hollow].

I.   "Forthwith, those who were filled with [red] anger turned pale, and those who were red turned white [in serenity]."

J.   Said R. Pappa, "This proves that a white horse in a dream is a good sign."

XLIII.

A.   The rabbis [Hananiah, Mishael, and Azariah] – where did they go?

B.   Said Rab, "They died through the working of the evil eye."

C.   And Samuel said, "They drowned in spit."

D.   And R. Yohanan, said, "They went up to the Land of Israel, got married, and produced sons and daughters."

E.   This accords with a Tannaite dispute on the same issue:

F.   R. Eliezer says, "They died through the working of the evil eye."

G.   R. Joshua says, "They drowned in spit.

H.   And sages say, "They went up to the Land of Israel, got married, and produced sons and daughters, as it is said, 'Hear now, Joshua, the high priest, and your fellows who sit before you, for they are men wondered at' (Zech. 3:8).

I.   "Who are men who are wondered at? One must say, This refers to Hananiah, Mishael, and Azariah."

J.   And where did Daniel go?

K.   Said Rab, "To dig a large well at Tiberias."

L.   And Samuel said, "To buy fodder."

M.   R. Yohanan said, "To buy pigs in Alexandria, Egypt."

N.   Can this be true?

O.   And have we not learned in the Mishnah:

P.   *Todos the physician said, "A cow or a pig does not leave Alexandria, Egypt, out of which they do not cut its womb, so that it will not breed"* [M. San. 4:4].

Q.   He brought little ones, to which they gave no thought.

XLIV.

A.   Our rabbis have taught on Tannaite authority:

B.   There were three who were involved in that scheme [to keep Daniel out of the furnace]: the Holy One, blessed be He, Daniel, and Nebuchadnezzar.

C.   The Holy One, blessed be He, said, "Let Daniel leave here, so that people should not say that they were saved on account of Daniel's merit [and not on their own merit]."

D.   Daniel said, "Let me get out of here, so that through me the verse will not be carried out, 'The graven images of their gods you shall burn with fire' (Dan. 7:25). [They may make a god of me.]"

E.   Nebuchadnezzar said, "Let Daniel get out of here, lest people say that [the king] has burned up his god [Daniel] in fire."

F.   And how do we know that [Nebuchadnezzar] worshiped [Daniel]?

G.   As it is written, "Then the king Nebuchadnezzar fell upon his face and worshiped Daniel" (Dan. 2:46).

XLV.

A.   Thus says the Lord of hosts, the God of Israel, of Ahab, son of Kolaiah, and of Zedekiah, son of Maaseiah, who prophesy a lie to you in my name" (Jer. 29:21).

B.   And it is written, "And of them shall be taken up a curse by all the captivity of Judah who are in Babylonia, saying, The Lord make you like Zedekiah and like Ahab, whom the king of Babylonia roasted in fire" (Jer. 29:22).

C.   What is said is not "whom he burned in fire" but "whom he roasted in fire."

D.   Said R. Yohanan in the name of R. Simeon b. Yohai, "This teaches that he turned them into popcorn."

XLVI.

A.   "Because they have committed villainy in Israel and have committed adultery with their neighbors' wives" (Jer. 29:23):

B.   What did they do?

C.   They went to Nebuchadnezzar's daughter. Ahab said to her, "Thus said the Lord, 'Give yourself to Zedekiah.'"

D.   And Zedekiah said, "Thus said the Lord, 'Give yourself to Ahab.'"

E.   She went and told her father. He said to her, "The god of these men hates lewdness. When they come to you, send them to me."

F.   When they came to her, she sent them to her father. He said to them, "Who said this to you?"

G.   They said, "The Holy One, blessed be He."

H   "But lo, I asked Hananiah, Mishael, and Azariah, and they said to me, 'It is forbidden.'"

I.   They said to him, "We, too, are prophets like them. To them the message was not given, to us [God] gave the message."

J.   He said to him, "I want to test you in the same manner I tested Hananiah, Mishael, and Azariah."

K.   They said to him, "They were three, and we are two."

L.   He said to them, "Choose anyone you like to go with you."

M   They said to him, "Joshua, the high priest." They were thinking, "Joshua, whose merit is great, will protect us."

N   They seized them and tossed them into the fire. They were roasted. As to Joshua, the high priest, his clothing was singed.

O.   For it is said, "And he showed me Joshua, the high priest, standing before the angel of the Lord" (Zech. 3:1), and it is written, "And the Lord said to Satan, the Lord rebuke you, O Satan" (Zech. 3:2).

P.   [Nebuchadnezzar] said to [Joshua], "I know that you are righteous. But what is the reason that the fire had any power whatsoever over you? Over Hananiah, Mishael, and Azariah the fire had no power at all."

Q.   He said to him, "They were three, and I am only one."

R.   He said to him, "Lo, Abraham was only one."

S.   "But there were no wicked men with him, and the fire was not given power to burn him, while in my case, I was joined with wicked men, so the fire had the power to burn me."

T.   This is in line with what people say, "If there are two dry brands and one wet one, the dry ones kindle the wet one."

U.   Why was he punished in this way?

V.   Said R. Pappa, "Because his sons had married wives who were not fit for marriage into the priesthood and he did not object, as it is said, 'Now Joshua was clothed with filthy clothing' (Zech. 3:3).

W.   "Now was it Joshua's way to dress in filthy garments? Rather this teaches that his sons had married women who were not worthy to marry into the priesthood, and he did not object."

XLVII.

A.   Said R. Tanhum, "In Sepphoris, Bar Qappara interpreted the following verse: 'These six [grains] of barley gave he to me' (Ruth 3:17).

B.   "What are the six of barley? If we should say that they were actually six of barley, was it the way of Boaz to give out a gift of only six barley grains?

C.   "[93B] Rather it must have been six *seahs* of barley?

D.   "And is it the way of a woman to carry six *seahs*?

E.   "Rather, this formed an omen to her that six sons are destined to come forth from her, each of whom would receive six blessings, and these are they: David, the Messiah, Daniel, Hananiah, Mishael, and Azariah.

F.   "David, as it is written, 'Then answered one of the servants and said, Behold I have seen the son of Jesse, the Bethlehemite, who is cunning in playing and a mighty, valiant man, and a man of war, and understanding in matters, and a handsome man, and the Lord is with him' (1 Sam. 16:18). [Freedman, p. 626, n. 1: The six epithets, *viz.*, cunning in playing, mighty, valiant, etc., are regarded as blessings applicable to each of the six persons mentioned.]"

G.   And said R. Judah said Rab, "The entire verse was stated by Doeg only as vicious gossip.

H.   "'Cunning in playing' – skillful in asking questions;

I.   "'a mighty valiant man' – skillful in answering them;

J.   "'a man of war' – skillful in the battle of Torah learning;

K.   "'understanding in matters' – understanding in learning one thing from another;

L.   "'and a comely person' – who argues for his position with considerable reasons;

M   "'and the Lord is with him' – the law everywhere follows his opinion.

N.   "And in all regards, he said to him, 'my son Jonathan is his equal.'

O.   "When he said, 'The Lord is with him' – something which did not apply to himself – he was humbled and envied him.

P.   "For of Saul it is written, 'And wherever he turned about, he vexed them' (1 Sam. 14:47), while of David it is written, 'And wherever he turned about he prospered.'"

Q.   How do we know that this was Doeg?

R.   It is written here, "then one of the servants answered," meaning, "one who was distinguished from the other young men," and there it is written, "Now a man of the servants of Saul was there that day, detained before the Lord, and his name was Doeg, an Edomite, head herdmen that belonged to Saul" (1 Sam. 21:8). [Freedman, p. 626, n. 8: Thus "a man" that is, "one distinguished" is the epithet applied to Doeg.]

S.   [Reverting to Bar Qappara's statement:] "The Messiah, as it is written, 'And the spirit of the Lord shall rest upon him, the spirit of wisdom and understanding, the spirit of counsel and might, the spirit of knowledge of the fear of the Lord, and shall make him of quick understanding in the fear of the Lord' (Isa. 11:2-3)."

T.   And R. Alexandri said, "The use of the words 'for quick understanding' indicates that he loaded him down with good deeds and suffering as a mill [which uses the same letters] is loaded down."

U.   [Explaining the same word, now with reference to the formation of the letters of the word to mean "smell,"] said Raba, "[The Messiah] smells and judges, for it is written, 'And he shall judge not after the sight of his eyes nor reprove after the hearing of his ears, yet with righteousness shall he judge the poor' (Ex. 11:3-4)."

V.   Bar Koziba ruled for two and a half years. He said to rabbis, "I am the Messiah."

W.   They said to him, "In the case of the Messiah it is written that he smells a man and judges. Let us see whether you can smell a man and judge."

X.   When they saw that he could not smell a man and judge, they killed him.

Y.   [Reverting again to Bar Qappara's statement:] "Daniel, Hananiah, Mishael, and Azariah, as it is written, 'In whom there was no blemish, but well favored, skillful in all wisdom, and cunning in knowledge, understanding science, and such as had ability in them to stand in the king's palace, and whom they might teach the learning and the tongue of the Chaldeans' (Dan. 1:4)."

Z. What is the meaning of, "In whom there was no blemish" (Dan. 1:4)?

AA. Said R. Hama bar Hanina, "Even the scar made by bleeding was not on them."

BB. What is the meaning of, "And such as had ability in them to stand in the king's palace" (Dan. 1:3)?

CC. Said R. Hama in the name of R. Hanina, "This teaches us that they restrained themselves from laughing and chatting, from sleeping, and they held themselves in when they had to attend to the call of nature, on account of the reverence owing to the king."

XLVIII.

A. "Now among these were of the children of Judah, Daniel, Hananiah, Mishael, and Azariah" (Dan. 1:6):

B. Said R. Eleazar, "All of them came from the children of Judah."

C. And R. Samuel bar Nahmani said, "Daniel came from the children of Judah, but Hananiah, Mishael, and Azariah came from the other tribes."

XLIX.

A. "And of your sons which shall issue from you, which you shall beget, shall they take away, and they shall be eunuchs in the palace of the king of Babylonia" (2 Kgs. 20:18):

B. What are these "eunuchs"?

C. Rab said, "Literally, eunuchs."

D. And R. Hanina said, "The sense is that idolatry was castrated [i.e. made sterile] in their time."

E. In the view of him who has said that idolatry was castrated in their time, that is in line with the verse of Scripture, "And there is no hurt in them" (Dan. 3:25).

F. But in the view of him who says that "eunuch" is in its literal sense, what is the meaning of, "And there is no hurt in them" (Dan. 3:25) [Since they had been castrated]?

G. It is that the fire did them no injury.

H. But has it not been written, "Nor the smell of fire had passed on them" (Dan. 3:27)?

I. There was neither injury nor the smell of fire.

J. In the view of him who has said that idolatry was made a eunuch in their time, that is in line with the following verse: "For thus says the Lord to the eunuchs who keep my Sabbaths" (Isa. 56:4).

K. But in the view of him who says that eunuch is in its literal sense, would Scripture dwell on what is embarrassing to the righteous?

L. Among the group were both sorts [actual eunuchs, as well as those in whose day were idols sterilized].

M. Now there is no difficulty for the view of him who says that they were literally eunuchs in the following verse: "Even to them will I give in my house and within my walls a place and a name better than of sons and of daughters" (Isa. 56:5).

N. But in the view of the one who says that the sense is that in their day idolatry was made a eunuch, what is the sense of the statement, "Better than of sons and of daughters"?

O.   Said R. Nahman bar Isaac, "Better than the sons whom they had already had and who had died."

P.   What is the meaning of the statement, "I shall give them an everlasting name, that shall not be cut off" (Isa. 56:5)?

Q.   Said R. Tanhum, "Bar Qappara interpreted the matter in Sepphoris: This refers to the book of Daniel, which is called by his name."

L.

A.   Now since whatever concerns Ezra was stated by Nehemiah b. Hachlia, what is the reason that the book was not called by his name?

B.   Said R. Jeremiah bar Abba, "It is because he took pride in himself, as it is written, 'Think upon me for good, my God' (Neh. 5:19)."

C.   David also made such a statement, "Remember me, Lord, with the favor that you bear for your people, visit me with your salvation" (Ps. 106:4).

D.   It was supplication that David sought.

E.   R. Joseph said, "It was because [Nehemiah] had spoken disparagingly about his predecessors, as it is said, 'But the former governors who had been before me were chargeable unto the people and had taken of them bread and wine, beside forty sheqels of silver' (Neh. 5:15).

F.   "Furthermore, he spoke in this way even of Daniel, who was greater than he was."

G.   And how do we know that Daniel was greater than he was?

H.   As it is written, "And I Daniel alone saw the vision, for the men that were with me did not see the vision, but a great quaking fell upon them, so that they fled to hide themselves" (Dan. 10:7).

I.   "For the men that were with me did not see the vision" (Dan. 10:7):

J.   Who were they?

K.   R. Jeremiah (some say, R. Hiyya b. Abba) said, "They were Haggai, Zechariah, and Malachi" **[94A]**.

L.   They were greater than he, and he was greater than they.

M.   They were greater than he, for they were prophets, and he was not a prophet.

N.   And he was greater than they, for he saw a vision and they did not see a vision.

O.   And since they did not see it, what is the reason that they were frightened?

P.   Even though they did not see it, their star saw it.

Q.   Said Rabina, "That yields the conclusion that one who is afraid even though he saw nothing is so because his star saw something.

R.   "What is his remedy?

S.   "Let him jump four cubits from where he is standing.

T.   "Or let him recite the *Shema*.

U.   "But if he is standing in an unclean place, let him say, 'The butcher's goat is fatter than I am.'"

LI.

A.   "Of the increase of his government and peace there shall be no end" (Isa. 9:6):

B.   R. Tanhum said, "In Sepphoris, Bar Qappara expounded this verse as follows:

C. "'On what account is every M in the middle of a word open, but the one in the word "increase" is closed?

D. "'The Holy One, blessed be He, proposed to make Hezekiah Messiah, and Sennacherib into Gog and Magog.

E. "'The attribute of justice said before the Holy One, blessed be He, "Lord of the world, Now if David, king of Israel, who recited how many songs and praises before you, you did not make Messiah, Hezekiah, for whom you have done all these miracles, and who did not recite a song before you, surely should not be made Messiah."

F. "On that account the M was closed.

G. "'Forthwith, the earth went and said before him, "Lord of the world, I shall say a song before you in the place of this righteous man, so you make him Messiah."'

H. "'The earth went and said a song before him, as it is said, "From the uttermost part of the earth we have heard songs, even glory to the righteous" (Isa. 24:16).

I. "'Said the prince of the world before him, "Lord of the world, [The earth] has carried out your wish in behalf of this righteous man."

J. "'An echo went forth and said, "It is my secret, it is my secret" (Ps. 24:16).

K. "'Said the prophet, "Woe is me, woe is me" (Isa. 24:16). How long?'

L. "How the treacherous dealt treacherously, yes, the treacherous dealers have dealt very treacherously" (Isa. 24:16).

M. And said Raba, and some say, R. Isaac, "Until spoilers come, and those who spoil spoilers."

LII.

A. "The burden of Dumah. He calls to me out of Seir, Watchman, what of the night? Watchman, what of the night?" (Isa. 21:11).

B. Said R. Yohanan, "That angel who is appointed over the souls is named Dumah. All the souls gathered to Dumah, and said to him, 'Watchman, what of the night? Watchman, what of the night?' (Isa. 21:11).

C. "Said the watchman, 'The morning comes and also the night, if you will inquire, inquire, return, come' (Isa. 21:11)."

LIII.

A. A Tannaite authority in the name of R. Pappias [said], "It was a shame for Hezekiah and his associates that they did not recite a song until the earth opened and said a song, as it is said, 'From the uttermost part of the earth have we heard songs, even glory to the righteous' (Isa. 24:16)."

B. Along these same lines you may say, "And Jethro said, Blessed be the Lord who has delivered you" (Ex. 18:10).

C. A Tannaite authority in the name of R. Pappias said, "It was a shame for Moses and the six hundred thousand, that they did not say, 'Blessed...,' until Jethro came and said, 'Blessed is the Lord.'"

LIV.

A. "And Jethro rejoiced" (Ex. 18:9):

B. Rab and Samuel –

C. Rab said, "It was that he passed a sharp knife across his flesh [circumcising himself]."

D. And Samuel said, "All his flesh became goose pimples [because of the destruction of the Egyptians]."

E. Said Rab, "That is in line with what people say, 'As to a proselyte, up to the tenth generation do not insult an Aramaean [since he retains his former loyalty, as Jethro did to the Egyptians].'"

LV.

A. "Therefore shall the Lord, the Lord of hosts, send among his fat ones leanness" (Isa. 10:16):

B. What is "among his fat ones leanness"?

C. Said the Holy One, blessed be He, "Let Hezekiah come, who has eight names, and exact punishment from Sennacherib, who has eight names."

D. As to Hezekiah, it is written, "For unto us a child is born, unto us a son is given, and the government shall be upon his shoulder, and his name shall be called wonderful, counselor, mighty, judge, everlasting, father, prince, and peace" (Isa. 9:5).

E. And there is yet the name "Hezekiah" too?

F. [Hezekiah] means "Whom God has strengthened."

G. Another matter: It is Hezekiah, for he strengthened Israel for their father in heaven.

H. As to Senacherib, it is written, "Tiglath-pileser" (2 Kgs. 15:29), "Pilneser" (1 Chr. 5:26), "Shalmeneser" (2 Kgs. 17:3), "Pul" (2 Kgs. 15:29), "Sargon" (Isa. 20:1), "Asnapper" (Ezra 4:10), "Rabba" (Ezra 4:10), and "Yaqqira" (Ezra 4:10).

I. And there is yet the name "Sennacherib" too.

J. It bears the sense that his conversation is contentious.

K. Another matter: He talked and babbled against the Most High.

L. [Referring to Ezra 4:10], said R. Yohanan, "On what account did that wicked man have the merit of being called 'the great and noble Asnapper' (Ezra 4:10)?

M. "Because he did not speak critically of the Land of Israel, as it is said, 'Until I come and take you away to a land like your own land' (2 Kgs. 18:32)."

N. Rab and Samuel: One said he was a shrewd king, and the other said he was a foolish king.

O. In the view of him who said that he was a shrewd king, if he had said, "A land that is better than yours," they would have said to him, "You are lying to us."

P. In the view of him who said that he was a foolish king, if [the land to which they would be exiled was no better than their own], then what value was there [in their agreeing to go].

Q. Where did he exile them?

R. Mar Zutra said, "To Africa."

S. R. Hanina said, "To the mountains of Salug."

T. But [for its part], the Israelites spoke critically about the Land of Israel. When they came to Shush, they said, "This is the same as our land."

U. When they got to Elmin, they said, "It is like the house of eternities [Jerusalem]."

V. When they go to Shush Tere, they said, "This is twice as good."

LVI.
- A. "And beneath his glory shall he kindle a burning like the burning of a fire" (Isa. 10:16):
- B. Said R. Yohanan, "Under his glory, but not actually his glory."
- C. That is in line with how R. Yohanan called his clothing "Those who do me honor."
- D. R. Eleazar said, "'Under his glory' literally, just as is the burning of the sons of Aaron.
- E. "Just as in that case it was a burning of the soul while the body endured, so here there is a burning of the soul while the body remained intact."

LVII.
- A. A Tannaite authority in the name of R. Joshua b. Qorhah taught, "Since Pharaoh blasphemed personally, the Holy One, blessed be He, exacted punishment from him personally.
- B. "Since Sennacherib blasphemed **[94B]** through a messenger, the Holy One, blessed be He, exacted punishment from him through a messenger.
- C. "In the case of Pharaoh, it is written, "Who is the Lord, that I should obey his voice' (Ex. 5:2).
- D. "The Holy One, blessed be He, exacted punishment from him personally, as it is written, 'And the Lord overthrew the Egyptians in the midst of the sea' (Ex. 14:27), and it also is written, 'You did walk through the sea with your horses' (Hab. 3:15).
- E. "In the case of Sennacherib, it is written, 'By your messengers you have reproached the Lord' (2 Kgs. 19:23), so the Holy One, blessed be He, exacted punishment from him through a messenger, as it is written, 'And the angel of the Lord went out and smote in the camp of the Assyrians a hundred fourscore and five thousand' (2 Kgs. 19:23)."

LVIII.
- A. R. Hanina b. Pappa contrasted two verses: "It is written, 'I will enter the height of his border' (Isa. 37:24), and it is further written, 'I will enter into the lodgings of his borders' (2 Kgs. 19:23).
- B. "Said that wicked man, 'First I shall destroy the lower dwelling, and afterward I shall destroy the upper dwelling.'"

LIX.
- A. Said R. Joshua b. Levi, "What is the meaning of the verse of Scripture, 'Am I now come up without the Lord against this place to destroy it? The Lord said to me, Go up against this land and destroy it' (2 Kgs. 18:25).
- B. "What is the sense of the passage?
- C. "He had heard the prophet, who had said, 'Since this people refuses the waters of Shiloah that go softly and rejoice in Rezina and Ramaliah's son, [now therefore behold the Lord brings up upon them the waters of the river, strong and many, even the king of Assyria and all his glory, and he shall come up over all his channels and go over all his banks]' (Isa. 8:6). [Freedman, p. 635, n. 3: This was understood by Sennacherib as an order to possess Jerusalem.]"
- D. Said R. Joseph, "Were it not for the following rendering of this verse of Scripture, I should not have understood what it meant:

'Because this people is tired of the rule of the house of David, which rules them mildly, like the waters of Shiloah, which flow gently, and have preferred Razin and the son of Ramaliah.'"

LX.

A. Said R. Yohanan, "What is the meaning of this verse: 'The curse of the Lord is in the house of the wicked, but he blesses the habitation of the just' (Prov. 3:33)?

B. "'The curse of the Lord is in the house of the wicked' refers to Pekah, son of Ramaliah, who would eat forty *seahs* of pigeons for dessert.

C. "'But he blesses the habitation of the just' refers to Hezekiah, king of Judea, who would eat a *litra* of vegetables for a whole meal."

LXI.

A. "Now therefore behold, the Lord brings up upon them the waters of the river, strong and many, even the king of Assyria and all his glory" (Isa. 8:7).

B. And it is written, "And he shall pass through Judea, he shall overflow and go over, he shall reach even to the neck" (Isa. 8:8).

C. Then why was [Sennacherib] punished?

D. The prophet prophesied about the ten tribes, but [Sennacherib] gave mind to the whole of Jerusalem.

E. The prophet came to him and said to him, "'For the wearied is not for the oppressor' (Isa. 8:23)."

F. Said R. Eleazar b. R. Berekhiah, "The people that is weary because of its devotion to Torah study will not be given into the power of the one that oppresses it."

LXII.

A. What is the meaning of this verse: "When aforetime the land of Zebulun and the land of Naphtali lightened its burden, but in later times it was made heavy by the way of the sea, beyond Jordan, in Galilee of the nations" (Isa. 8:23)?

B. It was not like the early generations, who made the yoke of the Torah light for themselves, but the later generations, who made the yoke of the Torah heavy for themselves.

C. And these were worthy that a miracle should be done for them, just as was done for those who passed through the sea and trampled over the Jordan.

D. If Sennacherib should repent, well and good, but if not, I shall make him into dung among the nations [a play on the letters GLL, the word for Galilee and dung].

LXIII.

A. "After these things, and the truth thereof, Sennacherib, king of Assyria, came and entered Judea and encamped against the fortified cities and thought to win them for himself" (2 Chr. 32:1):

B. Such a recompense [to Hezekiah] for such a gift? [Freedman, p. 636, n. 9: The previous verse relates that Hezekiah turned earnestly to the service of God. Was then Sennacherib's invasion his just reward?]

C. What is the sense of, "After these things and the truth thereof" (2 Chr. 32:1)?

D. Said Rabina, "After the Holy One, blessed be He, went and took an oath, saying 'If I say to Hezekiah that I am going to bring Sennacherib and hand him over to you, he will say to me, "I don't want him and I don't want his terror either.""'

E. "So the Holy One, blessed be He, went ahead and took an oath ahead of time that he would bring him, as it is said, 'The Lord of hosts has sworn, saying, Surely as I have thought, so shall it come to pass, and as I have purposed, so shall it stand, that I will break the Assyrian in my land and upon my mountains tread him under foot; then shall his yoke depart from off them, and his burden depart from off their shoulders' (Isa. 14:24-25)."

F. Said R. Yohanan, "Said the Holy One, blessed be He, 'Let Sennacherib and his company come and serve as a crib for Hezekiah and his company.'"

LXIV.

A. "And it shall come to pass in that day that his burden shall be taken away from off your shoulders and his yoke from off your neck, and the yoke shall be destroyed because of the oil" (Isa. 10:27):

B. Said R. Isaac Nappaha, "The yoke of Sennacherib will be destroyed because of the oil of Hezekiah, which he would kindle in the synagogues and schoolhouses.

C. "What did [Hezekiah] do? He affixed a sword at the door of the schoolhouse and said, 'Whoever does not take up study of the Torah will be pierced by this sword.'

D. "They searched from Dan to Beer Sheba and found no ignoramus, from Gabbath to Antipatris and found no boy or girl, no man or woman, not expert in the laws of uncleanness and cleanness.

E. "Concerning that generation Scripture says, 'And it shall come to pass in that day that a man shall nourish a young cow and two sheep' (Isa. 7:21), and it says, 'And it shall come to pass on that day that every place shall be, where there were a thousand vines at a thousand silverlings, it shall even be for briers and thorns' (Isa. 7:23).

F. "Even though 'a thousand vines are worth a thousand pieces of silver,' yet it shall be 'for briers and thorns.'"

LXV.

A. "And your spoil shall be gathered like the gathering of a caterpillar" (Isa. 33:4):

B. Said the prophet to Israel, "Gather your spoil."

C. They said to him, "Is it for individual spoil or for sharing?"

D. He said to them, "'Like the gathering of a caterpillar' (Isa. 33:4): Just as in the gathering of a caterpillar it is each one for himself, so in your spoil it is each one for himself."

E. They said to him, "And is not the money of the ten tribes mixed up with it?"

F. He said to them, "'As the watering of pools does he water it' (Isa. 33:4): Just as pools of water serve to raise up a human being from a state of uncleanness to a state of cleanness, so the money that has belonged to Israelites, once it has fallen into the hands of idolators, forthwith imparts cleanness. [Freedman, p. 638, n. 5: When the

Israelites have abandoned all hope of the return thereof other Jews may take it.]"

LXVI.

A.   Said R. Huna, "That wicked man [Sennacherib] made ten marches that day,

B.   "as it is said, 'He is come to Aiath, he is passed at Migron, at Michmash he has laid up his carriages, they are gone over the passage, they have taken up their lodgings at Geba, Ramah is afraid, Gibeah of Saul is fled, lift up your voice, O daughter of Gallim, cause it to be heard to Laish, O poor Anathoth, Madmenah is removed, the inhabitants of Gebim gather themselves to flee' (Isa. 10:28-31)."

C.   But they are more than [ten]?

D.   [Huna responded,] "Lift up your voice, O daughter of Gallim," was said by the prophet to the congregation of Israel [as follows]:

E.   "'Lift up your voice, O daughter of Gallim' – daughter of Abraham, Isaac, and Jacob, who carried out religious duties like the waves of the ocean [in number].

F.   "'Cause it to be heard to Laish' – from this one do not fear, but fear the wicked Nebuchadnezzar, who is compared to a lion.

G.   "For it is written, 'The lion is come up from his thicket' (Jer. 4:7)."

H.   What is [95A] the sense of "O poor Anathoth" (Isa. 10:31)?

I.   Jeremiah b. Hilkiah is destined to come up from Anathoth and to prophesy, as it is written, "The words of Jeremiah, son of Hilkiah, of the priests who were in Anathoth in the land of Benjamin" (Jer. 1:1).

J.   But is there any parallel? There [Nebuchadnezzar] is called a lion, but what is written here is *laish* [another word for lion].

K.   Said R. Yohanan, "A lion is called six things: *ari* (Jer. 4:7), *kefir* (Gen. 49:9), *labi* (Gen. 39:9), *laish* (Judg. 14:5), *shahal* (Ps. 91:13), and *shahaz* (Job 28:8)."

L.   If so, they are fewer [than ten]?

M.   "They are gone over" [and] "the passage" add up to two [more].

LXVII.

A.   What is the meaning of the statement, "As yet shall he halt at Nob that day" (Isa. 10:32)?

B.   Said R. Huna, "That day alone remained [for the punishment of] the sin committed at Nob [Sam. 22:17-19]. [Freedman, p. 639, n. 9: When the priests of Nob were massacred. God set a term for punishment, of which that day was the last.]

C.   "The Chaldean [soothsayers] said to him, 'If you go now, you will overpower it, and if not, you will not overpower it.'

D.   "A journey that should require ten days required only one day.

E.   "When they got to Jerusalem, they piled up mattresses so that, when he climbed up and took up his position on the top one, he could see Jerusalem. When he saw it, it looked tiny in his eyes. He said, 'Is this really the city of Jerusalem, on account of which I moved all my troops and came up and conquered the entire province? Is it not smaller and weaker than all of the cities of the peoples that by my power I have already conquered?!'

F. "He went and got up and shook his head and waved his hand backward and forward, with contempt, toward the mountain of the house of the sanctuary in Zion and toward the courts of Jerusalem.

G. "They said, 'Let us raise a hand against it right now.'

H "He said to them, 'You are tired. Tomorrow each one of your bring me a stone and we shall stone it [Freedman, following Jastrow].'

I. "Forthwith: 'And it came to pass that night that the angel of the Lord went out and smote in the camp of the Assyrians a hundred fourscore and five thousand, and when they arose early in the morning, behold they were all dead corpses' (2 Kgs. 19:35)."

J. Said R. Pappa, "That is in line with what people say: 'Justice delayed is justice denied.'"

LXVIII.

A "And Ishbi-benob, who was of the sons of the giant, the weight of whose spear weighed three hundred sheqels of brass in weight, being girded with a new sword, thought to have slain David" (2 Sam. 21:16):

B. What is the sense of "Ishbi-benob"?

C. Said R. Judah said Rab, "It was a man [ish] who came on account of the matter of [the sin committed at] Nob.

D. "Said the Holy One, blessed be He, to David, 'How long will the sin committed [against Nob] be concealed in your hand. On your account, Nob was put to death, the city of priests, on your account, Doeg the Edomite was sent into exile; on your account, Saul and his three sons were killed.

E. "'Do you want your descendants to be wiped out, or do you want to be handed over into the power of an enemy?'

F. "He said to him, 'Lord of the world, it is better that I be handed over to an enemy but that my descendents not be wiped out.'"

G. One day, when he went out to Sekhor Bizzae [Freedman, p. 640, n. 7: literally: "your seed to cease"], Satan appeared to him in the form of a deer. He shot an arrow at it, and the arrow did not reach [the deer]. It drew him until he came to the land of the Philistines. When Ishbi-benob saw him, he said, "This is the one who killed Goliath, my brother."

H He bound him, doubled him up, and threw him under an olive press. A miracle was done for [David], in that the earth underneath him became soft. This is in line with the following verse of Scripture: "You have enlarged my steps under me, that my feet did not slip" (Ps. 18:37).

I. That day was the eve of the Sabbath [Friday]. Abishai ben Zeruiah [David's nephew] was washing his head in four casks of water. He saw stains of blood [in the water].

J. Some say a dove came and slapped its wings before him.

K. He said, "The congregation of Israel is compared to a dove, for it is said, 'You are as the wings of a dove covered with silver' (Ps. 68:14). This then bears the inference that David, king of Israel, is in trouble."

L. He came to his house and did not find him. He said, "We have learned in the Mishnah: *People are not to ride on his horse or sit on his throne or hand his sceptre* [M. San. 2:5].

M.   "What is the rule about a time of crisis?"

N   He came and asked at the schoolhouse. They said to him, "In a time of crisis it is all right."

O.   He mounted his mule and rode off and the earth crumbled up [to make the journey quick]. While he was riding along, he saw Orpah, mother of [Ishbi-benob] who was spinning. When she saw him, she broke off the spindle." He threw it at her head and killed her.

P.   When Ishbi-benob saw him, he said, "Now there are two against me, and they will kill me."

Q   He threw David up and stuck his spear [into the ground], saying, "Let him fall on it and be killed."

R.   [Abishai] shouted the Name [of God], so David was suspended between heaven and earth.

S.   But why should David himself not have said it?

T.   Because one who is bound cannot free himself from his chains.

U.   He said to him, "What do you want here?"

V.   He said to him, "This is what the Holy One, blessed be He, has said to me, and this is what I said to him."

W.   He said to him, "Take back your prayer. May your son's son sell wax, but may you not suffer."

X.   He said to him, "If so, help me."

Y.   That is in accord with what is written, "But Abishai, son of Zeruiah, helped him" (2 Sam. 21:17).

Z.   Said R. Judah said Rab, "He helped him in prayer."

AA.   Abishai pronounced the Name and brought [David] down.

BB.   He pursued the two of them. When they came to Kubi, they said, "Let us stand against him."

CC.   When they came to Bethre, they said, "Will two whelps kill a lion?"

DD.   They said to him, "Go find Orpah, your mother, in the grave."

EE.   When they mentioned the name of his mother to him, he grew weak, and they killed him.

FF.   So it is written, "Then the men of David swore to him, saying, You shall no more go out with us to battle, that you not put out the light of Israel" (2 Sam. 21:17).

LXIX.

A.   Our rabbis have taught on Tannaite authority:

B.   For three did the earth fold up [to make their journey quicker]: Eliezer, Abraham's servant, Jacob our father, and Abishai b. Zeruiah.

C.   As to Abishai, son of Zeruiah, it is as we have just said.

D.   As to Eliezer, Abraham's servant, it is written, "And I came this day to the well" (Gen. 24:42), meaning that that very day he had set out.

E.   As to Jacob, our father, [95B] as it is written, "And Jacob went out from Beer Sheba and went to Haran" (Gen. 28:10), and it is said, "And he lighted upon a certain place and tarried there all night, because the sun had set" (Gen. 28:11).

F.   When he got to Haran, he said, "Is it possible that I have passed through a place in which my ancestors have prayed, and I did not say a prayer there?"

G. He wanted to go back. As soon as the thought of going back had entered his mind, the earth folded up for him. Forthwith: "He lighted upon a place" (Gen. 28:11).

H. Another matter: "Lighting upon..." refers only to praying, as it is written, "Therefore do not pray for this people or lift up a cry or prayer for them nor make intercession [using the same root] to me" (Jer. 7:16).

I. "And he tarried there all night, because the sun had set" (Gen. 28:10):

J. After he had prayed, he wanted to go back. Said the Holy One, blessed be He, "This righteous man has come to the house of my dwelling. Should he go forth without spending the night?"

K. Forthwith the sun set. That is in line with what is written, "And as he passed over Penuel, the sun rose for him" (Gen. 32:32).

L. And did it rise only for him? And did it not rise for the entire world?

M. "But," said R. Isaac, "Since the sun had set [too soon] on his account, it also rose on his account."

LXX.

A. And how do we know that the seed of David ceased [cf. LXVIII.E]?

B. As it is written, "And when Athaliah, mother of Ahaziah, saw that her son was dead, she rose and destroyed all the royal seed" (2 Kgs. 11:1).

C. And lo, Joash remained. Also Abiathar remained, for it is written, "And one of the sons of Ahimelech, son of Ahitub, named Abiathar, escaped" (1 Sam. 22:20).

D. Said R. Judah said Rab, "If Abiathar were not left to Ahimelech, son of Ahitub, neither shred nor remnant of the seed of David would have survived."

LXXI.

A. Said R. Judah said Rab, "The wicked Sennacherib came against them with forty-five thousand men, sons of kings seated on golden chariots, with their concubines and whores, and with eighty thousand mighty soldiers, garbed in coats of mail, and sixty thousand swordsmen running before him, and the rest cavalry."

B. And so they came against Abraham, and in the age to come so they will come with Gog and Magog.

C. On Tannaite authority it was taught: The length of his camp was four hundred parasangs, and the breadth of his horses, neck to neck, was forty parasangs, and the total of his army was two million six hundred thousand less one.

D. Abbayye asked, "Does this mean less one myriad or one thousand?"

E. The question stands.

LXXII.

A. It was taught on Tannaite authority:

B. The first ones crossed by swimming, as it is said, "He shall overflow and go over" (Isa. 8:8).

C. The middle ones crossed standing up, as it is said, "He shall reach even to the neck" (Isa. 8:8).

D. The last group brought up the dirt [of the river] with their feet and so found no water in the river to drink, so that they had to bring them water from some other place, which they drank, as it is said, "I dug wells and drank water" (Isa. 37:25).

E. [How could the army have been so large,] for is it not written, "Then the angel of the Lord went forth and smote in the camp of the Assyrians a hundred and fourscore and five thousand, and when they arose early in the morning, behold, they were all dead corpses" (Isa. 37:36)?

F. Said R. Abbahu, "Those were the heads of the troops."

G. Said R. Ashi, "Read the text closely with the same result, for it is written, '[therefore shall the Lord...send] among his fat ones leanness [i.e. the cream of the crop].'"

H. Said Rabina, "Read the text closely with the same result; for it is written, 'And the Lord sent an angel, which cut off all the men of valor, and the leaders and the princes in the camp of the king of Assyria. So he returned with shamefacedness to his own land, and when he entered into the house of his god, they that came forth of his own bowels slew him there with the sword' (2 Chr. 32:21)."

I. This proves [that the reference is only to the leaders (Freedman, p. 644, n. 6)].

LXXIII.

A. How did [the angel] smite [the army]?

B. R. Eliezer says, "He hit them with his hand, as it is said, 'And Israel saw the great hand' (Ex. 14:31), that was destined to exact punishment of Sennacherib."

C. R. Joshua says, "He hit them with a finger, as it is said, 'Then the magicians said to Pharaoh, This is the finger of God' (Ex. 8:14), that finger that was destined to exact punishment of Sennacherib."

D. R. Eleazar, son of R. Yosé the Galilean, says, "Said the Holy One, blessed be He, to Gabriel, 'Is your sickle sharpened?'

E. "He said before him, 'Lord of the world, it has been ready and sharpened since the six days of creation, as it is said, 'For they fled from the swords, from the sharpened sword' (Isa. 21:15)."

F. R. Simeon b. Yohai says, "That season was the time for the ripening of the produce. Said the Holy One, blessed be He, to Gabriel, When you go forth to ripen the produce, attack them, as it is said, 'As he passes, he shall take you, for morning by morning shall he pass by, by day and by night, and it shall be a sheer terror to understand the report' (Isa. 28:19)."

G. Said R. Pappa, "This is in line with what people say: 'As you pass by, reveal yourself to your enemy' [and so take revenge whenever you have the chance]."

H. Others say, "He blew into their noses and they died, as it is said, 'And he shall also blow upon them, and they shall wither' (Isa. 40:24)."

I. R. Jeremiah b. Abba said, "He clapped his hands at them and they died, as it is written, 'I will also smite my hands together and I will cause my fury to rest' (Ezek. 21:22)."

J. R. Isaac Nappaha said, "He opened their eyes for them and they heard a song of the living creatures [of the heaven] and they died, as it is written, 'At your exaltation the people were scattered' (Isa. 33:3)."

LXXIV.

A. How many [of Sennacherib's army] remained?

B. Rab said, "Ten, as it is said, 'And the rest of the trees of his forest shall be few, that a child may write them' (Isa. 10:19).

C. "What is the letter representing a number that a child can write? The one that stands for ten."

D. Samuel said, "Nine, as it is written, 'Yet gleaning grapes shall be left in it, as the shaking of an olive tree, two and three berries in the top of the uppermost bough, four and five in the utmost fruitful branches thereof' (Isa. 17:6)." [Freedman, p. 645, n. 12: This is rendered: "just as after the shaking of an olive tree there may remain two olives here and three there, so shall there be left of the arm army *four* here and *five* there – nine in all."]

E. R. Joshua b. Levi said, "Fourteen, as it is written, 'Two, three..., four, five' (Isa. 17:6)."

F. R. Yohanan said, "Five: Sennacherib, his two sons, Nebuchadnezzar, and Nebuzaradan.

G. "Nebuzaradan['s survival is] a tradition.

H. "Nebuchadnezzar, as it is written, 'And the form of the fourth is like an angel of God' (Dan. 3:25).

I. "If he had not seen [an angel], how would he have known?

J. "Sennacherib and his two sons, as it is written, 'And it came to pass, as he was worshiping in the house of Nisroch his god, that Adrammelech and Sharezer, his sons, smote him with the sword' (2 Kgs. 19:37)."

LXXV.

A. Said R. Abbahu, "Were it not that a verse of Scripture is explicitly spelled out, it would not have been possible to say it:

B. "For it is written, 'In the same day shall the Lord shave with a razor that is hired, namely, by the riverside, by the king of Assyria, the head and the hair of the feet, and it shall consume the beard' (Isa. 7:20.

C. "The Holy One, blessed be He, came and appeared before [Sennacherib] as an old man. He said to him, 'When you go against the kings of east and west, whose sons you brought and saw killed, what will you say to them?'

D. "He said to him, 'This man [I] was also fearful on that account.'

E. "He said to him, 'What should we do?'

F. "He said to him, 'Go [96A] and change your appearance.'

G. "'How shall I change?'

H. "He said to him, 'Go and bring me a razor, and I shall shave you.'

I. "'Where shall I get it?'

J. "He said to him, 'Go to that house and bring it from there.'

K. "He went and found it. Ministering angels came and appeared to him in the form of men, grinding palm nuts.'

L. "He said to them, 'Give me the razor.'

M. "They said to him, 'Grind a cask of palm nuts, and we shall give it to you.'

N. "He ground a cask of palm nuts, and they gave the razor to him.

O "It got dark before he came back. [God] said to [Sennacherib], 'Go and bring fire.'

P. "He went and brought fire. While he was blowing on it, the fire caught his beard, so [God] shaved his head as well as his beard. [Freedman, p. 646, n. 8: Thus he was shaved with a razor hired by his own work, a work which is done 'by the riverside,' 'grinding,' the water providing power for the mill.]"

Q They said, "This is in line with what is written: 'And it shall also consume the beard' (Isa. 7:20)."

R Said R. Pappa, "This is in line with what people say: 'If you are singeing an Aramaean's hair and it suits him, light a fire to his beard, so you will not suffer his mockery.'"

S [Reverting to the tale of Abbahu:] "He went and found a plank from Noah's ark. He said, 'This must be the great god who saved Noah from the flood.'

T. "He said, 'If that man [I] goes and is victorious, he will offer his two sons before you.'

U. "His sons heard and killed him. That is in line with the verse of Scripture, 'And it came to pass, as he was worshiping in the house of Nisroch his god, that Adrammelech and Sharezer his sons smote him with the sword' (2 Kgs. 19:37)."

LXXVI.

A "And he fought against them, he and his servants, by night, and smote them" (Gen. 14:15):

B Said R. Yohanan, "That angel who was assigned to Abraham was named 'Night,' as it is said, '[Let the day perish wherein I was born] and the Night which said, There is a man-child conceived' (Job 3:3). [Freedman, p. 647, n. 4: The verse, Gen. 14:15, is translated, and Night fought on their behalf, he and his....']"

C R. Isaac Nappaha ["the smith"] said, "It did for him the deeds that are done by night, as it is said, 'They fought from heaven, the stars in their courses fought against Sisera' (Judg. 5:20)."

D R. Simeon b. Laqish said, "What the smith [Yohanan] has said is better than what the son of the smith [Isaac] has said."

E. "And he pursued them to Dan" (Gen. 14:14):

F. Said R. Yohanan, "When that righteous man came to Dan, he grew weak. He foresaw that the children of his children were destined to commit acts of idolatry in Dan, as it is said, 'And he set the one in Beth El, and the other he put in Dan' (1 Kgs. 12:29).

G "And also that wicked man [Nebuchadnezzar] did not grow strong until he reached Dan, as it is said, 'From Dan the snorting of his horses was heard' (Jer. 8:16)."

LXXVII.

A Said R. Zira, "Even though R. Judah b. Beterah sent word from Nisibis, 'Pay heed to an elder who has forgotten his learning through no fault of his own and to cut the jugular veins [in slaughtering a beast], in accord with the view of R. Judah,

B "'and take heed of the sons of the ordinary folk, for from them [too] will Torah go forth,'

C "for such a matter as the following we may convey matters to them [and not refrain from teaching this lesson:]

D. "'You are righteous, Lord, when I plead with you, yet let me talk to thee of your judgments, wherefore does the way of the wicked prosper? Wherefore are all they happy who deal very treacherously? You have planted them, yes, they have taken root, they grow, yes, they bring forth fruit' (Jer. 12:1-2).

E. "'What did he answer him? "If you have run with the footmen and they have tired you, then how can you contend with the horses? And if in a land of peace, in which you trust, they have wearied you, how will you do in the prideful swelling of the Jordan?" (Jer. 12:5).

F. "The matter may be compared to the case of a man who said "I can run in a marsh three *parasangs* before horses." He happened upon a man on foot and ran before him for only three *mils* on dry land, and he got tired.

G. "'He said to him, "Now if matters are this way when you run before a man on foot, all the more so [will you be unable to run] before horses! And if matters are this way for three *mils*, how much the more so in three *parasangs*! And if matters are this way in dry land, how much the more so in a marsh!

H. ""'So it is with you. If on account of the reward for taking four steps [explained later, J-Y] that I paid that wicked man, which he took in running on account of my honor, you are amazed, when I pay the reward owing to Abraham, Isaac, and Jacob, who ran before me like horses, how much the more so [will you be amazed]!"'

I. "This is in line with the following verse of Scripture: "My heart within me is broken because of the prophets, all my bones shake, I am like a drunken man, and like a man whose wine has overcome, because of the Lord and because of the words of his holiness" (Jer. 23:9).'"

J. As to the reference to the four steps [taken by the wicked man in honor of God], what is its meaning?

K. It is in accord with that which is written: "At that time Merodach-baladan, son of Baladan, king of Babylonia, sent letters and a present to Hezekiah [for he had heard that he had been sick and recovered]" (Isa. 39:1).

L. And merely because Hezekiah was sick and got better, did he send him letters and a present?!

M. Yes, so as "to inquire of the wonder that was done in the land" (2 Chr. 32:31).

N. For R. Yohanan said, "That day on which Ahaz died was only two hours long, and on the day on which Hezekiah got sick and got better, the Holy One, blessed be He, gave back the other ten hours.

O. "For it is written, 'Behold I will bring again the shadow of the degrees which is gone down in the sun dial of Ahaz, ten degrees backward. So the sun returned ten degrees, by which degrees it was gone down' (Isa. 38:8). [Freedman, p. 649, ns. 5-6: The sun had set ten hours too soon, to allow no time for funeral eulogies. This was in order to make atonement for his sins, for the disgrace of being deprived of the usual funeral honors expiates one's misdeeds. The return of the ten degrees to which Isaiah refers is assumed to mean a prolongation of the day by ten hours, light having healing powers.]

P.   "[Merodach-baladan] said to [his staff], 'What is going on?'

Q.   "They said to him, 'Hezekiah got sick and got better.'

R.   "He said, 'Is there such a great man in the world, and should I not want to greet him?'

S.   "He wrote him, 'Peace to King Hezekiah, peace to the city of Jerusalem, peace to the Great God!'

T.   "Nebuchadnezzar was the scribe of Baladan. At that time he was not there. When he came, he said to him, 'What did you write?'

U.   "They said to him, 'This is what we wrote.'

V.   "He said to him, 'You called him "the great God" and yet you mentioned him last?'

W.   "He said, 'Rather, this is how you should write: "Peace to the great God, peace to the city of Jerusalem, peace to King Hezekiah."'

X.   "They said to him, 'Let the one who has read the letter serve as the messenger.'

Y.   "He ran after [the messenger] [thus in honor of God]. But when he had run four steps, Gabriel came and froze him in place."

Z.   Said R. Yohanan, "Had Gabriel not come and kept him standing in place, there would have been no remedy for (the enemies of) Israel." [Freedman, p. 650, n. 3: The learned children of the ordinary folk should thus be informed that the honor paid to them is due to the slight merit of their fathers, as in this case.]

LXXVIII.

A.   What is the meaning of the fact that [Merodach-] Baladan is called "the son of Baladan"?

B.   They say: Baladan was king, and his appearance changed into that of a dog, so his son sat on the throne.

C.   When he would sign a document, he would write his name and the name of his father, "King Baladan."

D.   This is the sense of that which is written: "A son honors his father, and a servant his master" (Mal. 1:6).

E.   "A son honors his father" (Mal. 1:6) refers to what we have just said.

F.   As to "A servant his master" (Mal. 1:6)?

G.   It is in line with that which is written: "Now in the fifth month, on the tenth day of the month, the nineteenth year of Nebuchadnezzar, king of Babylonia, came Nebuzaradan, captain of the guard, and stood before the king of Babylonia in Jerusalem. And he burned the house of the Lord and the house of the king" (Jer. 52:12-13).

H.   [96B] But did Nebuchadnezzar go up to Jerusalem? Has it not been written, "They carried him up to the King of Babylonia, to Riblah" (Jer. 52:9)? And, said R. Abbahu, "That town is the same as Antioch."

I.   R. Hisda and R. Isaac b. Abodimi: One said, "His picture was engraved on [Nebuzaradan's] chariot."

J.   "The other said, "He was so much in awe of him that it was as though he were standing before him."

LXXIX.

A. Said Raba, "It was bearing three hundred mules loaded with iron axes that could break iron that Nebuchadnezzar sent Nebuzaradan. All of them broke on one gate of Jerusalem, as it is said, 'And now they attack its gate together; with axes and hammers they hit it' (Ps. 74:6).

B. "He wanted to go back. He said, 'I am afraid that they might do to me as they did to Sennacherib.

C. "A voice came forth: 'Leaper son of a leaper, leap, Nebuzaradan! The time has come for the sanctuary to be destroyed and the palace burned.'

D. "Left to him was only a single axe. He went and hit it with its head, and the gate opened, as it is said, 'A man was famous according as he had lifted up axes upon thick trees' (Ps. 74:5).

E. "He continued with the killing until he reached the Temple. He set fire to it. The Temple sought to rise up [to heaven], but from heaven it was pushed down, as it is said, 'The Lord has trodden down the virgin daughter of Judah as in a winepress' (Lam. 1:15).

F. "He was elated, but an echo came and said, 'You have killed a dead people, you have burned a burned Temple, you have crushed already ground corn, as it is said, 'Take the millstones and grind meal, uncover your locks, make the leg bare, uncover the thigh, pass over the rivers' (Isa. 47:2).

G. "What is said is not 'wheat' but 'ground meal.'"

H. [Nebuzaradan] saw the blood of Zechariah boiling. He said to them, "What is this?"

I. They said to him, "It is the blood of the sacrifices, that has been poured out."

J. He said to them, "Come and let us bring [animal blood to make a comparison to see whether they are alike or not alike]." He slaughtered an animal and the blood was not like [that which was boiling].

K. He said to them, "Explain it to me, and if not, I shall comb your flesh with iron combs."

L. They said to him, "This one was a priest and a prophet, and he prophesied to Israel concerning the destruction of Jerusalem, so they killed him."

M. He said to them, "I shall be the one to appease him." He brought rabbis and killed them over him, but [the blood] did not come to rest. He brought school children and killed them over him, but still the blood did not come to rest. He brought the blossoms of the priesthood and killed them over him, and still the blood did not come to rest, until he had killed over him ninety-four myriads, and still his blood did not rest.

N. He drew near [the blood] and said, "Zechariah, Zechariah, I have destroyed the best of them. Do you want me to kill them all?"

O. Forthwith the blood came to rest.

P. He gave thought to repentance, saying, "Now if they, who killed only a single person, were treated in such a way, that man [I] – what will come of him?"

Q   He fled, sent his instructions to his household [giving over his property to his family], and then converted [to Judaism].

LXXX.

A.   Our rabbis have taught on Tannaite authority:

B.   Naaman was a resident proselyte.

C.   Nebuzaradan was a righteous proselyte.

D.   Grandsons of Sisera studied Torah in Jerusalem.

E.   Grandsons of Sennacherib taught Torah in public.

F.   And who were they? Shemaiah and Abtalion.

G.   Grandsons of Haman studied Torah in Bene Beraq.

H   And so, too, grandsons of that wicked man [Nebuchadnezzar] did the Holy One, blessed be He, want to bring under the wings of the Presence of God.

I.   Said the ministering angels before the Holy One, blessed be He, "Lord of the world, will you bring under the wings of your Presence him who destroyed your house and burned your Temple?"

J.   For it is written, "We should have healed Babylonia, but she is not healed" (Jer. 21:9).

K.   Said Ulla, "This speaks of Nebuchadnezzar."

L.   Said R. Samuel b. Nahmani, "This refers to the 'canals of Babylonia' (Ps. 137:1), which flow among the palm trees of Babylonia."

LXXXI.

A.   Said Ulla, "Ammon and Moab were bad neighbors of Jerusalem.

B.   "When they heard the prophets prophesying the destruction of Jerusalem, they sent word to Nebuchadnezzar, 'Go out and come here.'

C.   "He said, 'I am afraid that they will do to me what they did to those who came before me.'

D.   "They sent to him, '"For the man is not at home" (Prov. 7:19), and "man" can refer only to the Holy One, blessed be He, as it is said, "The Lord is a man of war" (Ex. 15:3).'

E.   "He replied, 'He is nearby and he will come.'

F.   "They sent to him, '"He has gone on a far journey" (Prov. 7:19).'

G.   "He sent to them, 'There are righteous men there, who will pray for mercy and bring him back.'

H   "They sent to him, '"He has taken a bag of money with him" (Prov. 7:20), and "money" refers only to the righteous, as it is said, "So I bought her to me for fifteen pieces of silver and for a *homer* of barley and a half-*homer* of barley" (Hos. 3:2).'

I.   "He sent word to them, 'The wicked may repent and pray for mercy and bring him back.'

J.   "They sent to him, '"He has already set a time for them, as it is said, "And he will come home at the day appointed" (Prov. 7:20), and "day appointed" can refer only to time, as it is said, "In the time appointed on our solemn feast day" (Ps. 81:1, 3).'

K.   "He sent word to them, 'It is winter, and I cannot make the trip because of the snow and rain.'

L.   "They sent to him, 'Come through the mountains [if need be]. For it is said, "Send you a messenger to the ruler of the earth [that he may come] by way of the rocks to the wilderness to the mountain of the daughter of Zion" (Isa. 16:1).'

M   "He sent to them, 'If I come, I shall not have a place in which to make camp.'

N   "They sent word to him, 'Their cemeteries are superior to your palaces, as it is written, "At that time, says the Lord, they shall bring out the bones of the king of Judea and the bones of his princes and the bones of the priests and the bones of the prophets and the bones of the inhabitants of Jerusalem, out of their graves. And they shall spread them before the sun and the moon and all the host of heaven, whom they have loved and whom they have served and after whom they have walked" (Jer. 8:1-2).'" [Freedman, p. 654, n. 1: The great burial vaults will be cleared out to give shelter to Nebuchadnezzar's army.]

LXXXII.

A   Said R. Nahman to R. Isaac, "have you heard when the son of 'the fallen one' will come?"

B.   He said to him, "Who is the son of 'the fallen one'?"

C.   He said to him, "It is the Messiah."

D.   "Do you call the Messiah 'the son of the fallen one'?"

E   He said to him, "Yes, for it is written, 'On that day I will raise up [97A] the tabernacle of David, the fallen one' (Amos 9:11)."

F.   He said to him, "This is what R. Yohanan said, 'The generation to which the son of David will come will be one in which disciples of sages grow fewer,

G   "'and, as to the others, their eyes will wear out through suffering and sighing,

H   "'and troubles will be many, and laws harsh, forever renewing themselves so that the new one will hasten onward before the old one has come to an end.'"

LXXXIII.

A.   Our rabbis have taught on Tannaite authority:

B.   The seven-year cycle in which the son of David will come:

C   As to the first one, the following verse of Scripture will be fulfilled: "And I will cause it to rain upon one city and not upon another" (Amos 4:7).

D.   As to the second year, the arrows of famine will be sent forth.

E   As to the third, there will be a great famine, in which men, women, and children will die, pious men and wonder workers alike, and the Torah will be forgotten by those that study it.

F.   As to the fourth year, there will be plenty which is no plenty.

G   As to the fifth year, there will be great prosperity, and people will eat, drink, and rejoice, and the Torah will be restored to those that study it.

H.   As to the sixth year, there will be rumors.

I.   As to the seventh year, there will be wars.

J.   As to the end of the seventh year [the eighth year], the son of David will come.

K   Said R. Joseph, "Lo, how many septennates have passed like that one, and yet he has not come."

L.   Said Abbayye, "Were there rumors in the sixth year and wars in the seventh year?

M.   "And furthermore, did they come in the right order?"

LXXXIV.

A.   It has been taught on Tannaite authority:

B.   R. Judah says, "In the generation in which the son of David will come, *the gathering place will be for prostitution, Galilee will be laid waste, Gablan will be made desolate, and the men of the frontier will go about from town to town, and none will take pity on them; and the wisdom of scribes will putrefy; and those who fear sin will be rejected; and the truth will be herded away [M. Sot. 9:15AA-GG].*

C.   "For it is said, 'And the truth will be herded away' (Isa. 59:15)."

D.   What is the meaning of the statement, "The truth will be herded away" (Isa. 59:15)?

E.   Said members of the house of Rab, "This teaches that it will be divided into herds and herds, each going its way."

F.   What is the meaning [of the concluding passage of the same verse], "And he who departs from evil makes himself a prey" (Isa. 59:15)?

G.   Said members of the house of R. Shila, "Whoever departs from evil will be treated as a fool [using the same letters as those for prey] by other people."

LXXXV.

A.   Said Raba, "To begin with I had supposed that there is no truth in the world. One of the rabbis, R. Tabut by name (and some say, R. Tabyomi by name), who would not go back on his word even though people gave him all the treasures of the world, said to me that one time he happened to come to a place called Truth.

B.   "It was a place in which people would not go back on their word, and in which no person died before his day.

C.   "He took a woman of theirs as wife and had two sons from her.

D.   "One day his wife was sitting and shampooing her hair. Her neighbor came and knocked on the door. Thinking that it would be improper [to say what his wife was doing], he said to her, 'She is not here.'

E.   "His two sons died.

F.   "The people of the place came to him and said to him, 'What is going on?'

G.   "He said to them, 'This is what happened.'

H   "They said to him, 'By your leave, please go away from our place, so as not to encite Satan against these men [us].'"

LXXXVI.

A.   It has been taught on Tannaite authority:

B.   R. Nehorai says, "In the generation in which the son of David will come, *children will shame elders, and elders will stand up before children. 'The daughter rises up against the mother, and the daughter-in-law against her mother-in-law' (Mic. 7:6). The face of the generation is the face of a dog, and a son is not ashamed before his father" [M. Sot. 9:15HH-KK].*

LXXXVII.

A.   It has been taught on Tannaite authority:

B.   R. Nehemiah says, "In the generation in which the son of David will come, *presumption increases, and dearth increases, and the vine gives its fruit and wine at great cost. The government turns to heresy, and there is no reproof"* [M. Sot. 9:15W-Z].

C.   That statement supports the view of R. Isaac.

D.   For R. Isaac said, "The son of David will come only when the entire kingdom has turned to heresy."

E.   Said Raba, "What is the text of Scripture that makes that point?

F.   "'It is all turned white, he is clean' (Lev. 13:13). [Freedman, p. 656, n. 5: When all are heretics, it is a sign that the world is about to be purified by the advent of the Messiah.]"

LXXXVIII.

A.   Our rabbis have taught on Tannaite authority:

B.   "For the Lord shall judge his people and repent himself of his servants, when he sees that their power has gone, and there is none shut up or left" (Deut. 32:36).

C.   The son of David will come only when traitors are many.

D.   Another matter: Only when disciples are few.

E.   Another matter: Only when a penny will not be found in anyone's pocket.

F.   Another matter: Only when people will have given up hope of redemption, as it is said, "There is none shut up or left" (Deut. 32:36), as it were, when there is none [God being absent] who supports and helps Israel.

G.   That accords with the statement of R. Zira, who, when he would find rabbis involved in [figuring out when the Messiah would come], would say to them, 'By your leave, I ask you not to put it off.

H.   "'For we have learned on Tannaite authority: "Three things come on the spur of the moment, and these are they: the Messiah, a lost object, and a scorpion."'"

LXXXIX.

A.   Said R. Qattina, "The world will exist for six thousand years and be destroyed for one thousand,

B.   "as it is said, 'And the Lord alone shall be exalted in that day' (Isa. 2:11)."

C.   Abbayye said, "It will be desolate for two thousand years, as it is said, 'After two days will he revive us, in the third day, he will raise us up and we shall live in his sight' (Hos. 6:2)."

D.   It has been taught on Tannaite authority in accord with the view of R. Qattina:

E.   Just as at the advent of the Sabbatical Year the world will lie fallow for one out of seven years.

F.   So it is with the world. A thousand years will the world lie fallow out of seven thousand years,

G.   as it is said, "And the Lord alone shall be exalted in that day" (Isa. 2:11), and Scripture says, "A Psalm and song for the Sabbath Day" (Ps. 92:1) – a day that is wholly the Sabbath.

H.   And Scripture says, "For a thousand years in your sight are but as yesterday when they are past" (Ps. 90:4). [A day stands for a thousand years.]

XC.

A   A Tannaite authority of the house of Elijah [said], "For six thousand years the world will exist.

B.   "For two thousand it will be desolate, two thousand years [will be the time of] Torah, and two thousand years will be the days of the Messiah.

C.   [97B] but on account of our numerous sins what has been lost [of those years, in which the Messiah should have come but has not come] has been lost.

XCI.

A   Said Elijah to R. Sala the Pious, "The world will last for no fewer than eighty-five Jubilees [of fifty years each], and the son of David will come in the last one."

B.   He said to him, "Will it be in the first or the last year of the last Jubilee?"

C.   He said to him, "I do not know."

D.   "Will it come at the end or not come at the end of the fiftieth year?"

E.   He said to him, "I do not know."

F.   R. Ashi said, "This is what he said to him: 'Up to that time, do not look for his coming, but from that time onward, do look for his coming.'"

XCII.

A   R. Hanan, son of Tahalipa, sent to R. Joseph, "I came across a man who had in hand a scroll, written in Assyrian [block] letters in the holy language.

B.   "I said to him, 'Where did you get this?'

C.   "He said to me, 'I was employed in the Roman armies, and I found it in the Roman archives.'

D.   "In the scroll it is written that after four thousand two hundred ninety-two years from the creation of the world, the world will be an orphan.

E.   "[As to the years to follow] in some there will be wars of the great dragons, and in some, wars of Gog and Magog, and the rest will be the days of the Messiah.

F.   "And the Holy One, blessed be He, will renew his world only after seven thousand years."

G.   R. Aha, son of Raba, said, "'After five thousand years' is what is to be repeated."

XCIII.

A.   It has been taught on Tannaite authority:

B.   R. Nathan says, "This verse of Scripture pierces to the depth:

C.   "'For the vision is yet for an appointed time, but at the end it shall speak and not lie; though he tarry, wait for him; because it will surely come, it will not tarry' (Hab. 2:3)."

D.   This is not in accord with our rabbis, who interpreted, "Until a time and times and the dividing of time" (Dan. 7:25).

E.   Nor does it accord with R. Simlai, who would interpret, "You feed them with the bread of tears and given them tears to drink a third time" (Ps. 80:6).

F. Nor does it accord with R. Aqiba, who would interpret the verse, "Yet once, it is a little while, and I will shake the heavens and the earth" (Hag. 2:6).

G. Rather, the first kingdom will last for seventy years, the second kingdom for fifty-two years, and the kingdom of Ben Koziba will be for two-and-a-half years.

XCIV.

A. What is the meaning of the verse, "But at the end it shall speak and not lie" (Hab. 2:3)?

B. Said R. Samuel bar Nahmani said R. Jonathan, "[Freedman, p. 659, n. 5: Reading the verse as, 'He will blast him who calculates the end,'] blasted be the bones of those who calculate the end [when the Messiah will come].

C. "For they might say, 'Since the end has come and he has not come, he will not come.'

D. "Rather, wait for him, as it is said, 'Though he tarry, wait for him' (Hab. 2:3).

E. "Should you say that we shall wait, but he may not wait, Scripture responds, 'And therefore will the Lord wait, that he may be gracious to you, and therefore will he be exalted, that he may have mercy upon you' (Isa. 30:18).

F. "Then, since we are waiting and he is waiting, what is holding things up?

G. "It is the attribute of justice that is holding things up.

H. "But if the attribute of justice is holding things up, why should we wait?

I. "It is so as to receive the reward for our patience, as it is written, 'Blessed are all those who wait for him' (Isa. 30:9)."

XCV.

A. Said Abbaye, "There are in the world never fewer than thirty-six righteous men, who look upon the face of the Presence of God every day, for it is said, 'Happy are those who wait for him' (Isa. 30:18), and the numerical value of the letters in the word 'for him' is thirty-six."

B. Is this so? And did not Raba say, "The row of the righteous before the Holy One, blessed be He, is made up of eighteen thousand, as it is said, 'There shall be eighteen thousand round about' (Ezek. 48:35)"?

C. There is no contradiction between the two views. The former number refers to those few who see him through a bright mirror, the latter number refers to those many who see him only through a dirty mirror.

D. And are they so numerous?

E. And did not Hezekiah said R. Jeremiah said in the name of R. Simeon b. Yohai, "I have myself seen the inhabitants of the upper world, and they are only a few. If they are a thousand, my son and I are among their number. If they are only a hundred, my son and I are among their number. If they are only two, they are only my son and I."

F.   There is still no contradiction. The larger number speaks of those who go inside only with permission, the smaller number those who go inside even without permission.

XCVI.

A.   Said Rab, "All of the ends have passed, and the matter now depends only on repentance and good deeds."

B.   And Samuel said, "It is sufficient for a mourner to remain firm in his mourning."

C.   This accords with the following dispute among Tannaite authorities:

D.   R. Eliezer says, "If the Israelites repent, they will be redeemed, and if not, they will not be redeemed."

E.   Said R. Joshua to him, "If they do not repent, will they not be redeemed?!

F.   "Rather, the Holy One, blessed be He, will raise up for them a king whose decrees will be as harsh as those of Haman, and the Israelites will repent, and [God] will restore them to a good path]."

G.   A further Tannaite version:

H.   R. Eliezer says, "If the Israelites repent, they will be redeemed, as it is said, 'Return, backsliding children, and I will heal your backslidings' (Jer. 3:22)."

I.   Said to him R. Joshua, "And is it not written, 'You have sold yourselves for nought, and you shall be redeemed without money' (Isa. 52:3)?

J.   "'You have sold yourselves for nought' – for idolatry.

K.   "'But you shall be redeemed without money' – with neither repentance nor doing good deeds."

L.   Said to him R. Eliezer, "But is it not written, 'Return to me and I shall return to you' (Mal. 3:7)?"

M.   Said to him R. Joshua, "But is it not written, 'For I am master over you, and I will take you, one from a city and two from a family and I will bring you to Zion' (Jer. 3:14)?"

N.   Said to him R. Eliezer, "But it is written, 'In returning and rest you shall be saved' (Isa. 30:5)."

O.   Said R. Joshua to R. Eliezer, "But is it not written, 'Thus says the Lord, the redeemer of Israel, and his holy one, to him whom man despises, to him whom the nations abhor, to a servant of rulers, [98A] kings shall see and arise, princes also shall worship' (Isa. 49:7)?"

P.   Said to him R. Eliezer, "But is it not written, 'If you will return, O Israel, says the Lord, return to me' (Jer. 4:1)?"

Q.   Said to him R. Joshua, "But it is written elsewhere, 'And I heard the man clothed in linen, which was upon the waters of the river, when he held up his right hand and his left hand to heaven and swore by him who lives forever that it shall be for a year, two years, and half a year and when he shall have accomplished scattering the power of the holy people, all these things shall be finished' (Dan. 12:7)."

R.   And R. Eliezer shut up.

XCVII.

A.   And said R. Abba, "You have no indication of the end more openly stated than the following, as it is said: 'But you, O mountains of

Israel, shall shoot forth your branches and yield your fruit to my people, Israel, for they are at hand to come' (Ezek. 36:8)."

B. R. Eliezer says, "Also the following, as it is said: 'For before these days there was no hire for man, nor any hire for beast neither was there any peace to him that went out or came in because of the affliction' (Zech. 8:10)."

C. What is the meaning of the phrase, "Neither was there any peace to him that went out or came in because of the affliction"?

D. Rab said, "Even to disciples of sages, concerning whom peace is written in Scripture, as it is written, 'Great peace shall they have who love your Torah' (Ps. 119:165)."

E. "Neither was there any peace...because of the affliction" (Zech. 8:10):

F. And Samuel said, "Until all prices will be equal."

XCVIII.

A. Said R. Hanina, "The son of David will come only when a fish will be sought for a sick person and not be found, as it is said, 'Then I will make their waters deep and cause their rivers to run like oil' (Ezek. 32:14), and it is written, 'In that day I will cause the horn of the house of Israel to sprout forth' (Ezek. 29:21)."

B. Said R. Hama bar Hanina, "The son of David will come only when the rule over Israel by the least of the kingdoms will come to an end, as it is said, 'He shall both cut off the springs with pruning hooks and take away and cut down the branches' (Isa. 18:5), and further: 'In that time shall the present be brought to the Lord of hosts of a people that is scattered and peeled' (Isa. 18:7)."

C. Said Zeiri said R. Hanina, "The son of David will come only when arrogant people will no longer be [found] in Israel, as it is said, 'For then I will take away out of the midst of you those who rejoice in your pride' (Zeph. 8:11), followed by: 'I will also leave in the midst of you an afflicted and poor people, and they shall take refuge in the name of the Lord' (Zeph. 3:12)."

D. Said R. Simlai in the name of R. Eliezer b. R. Simeon, "The son of David will come only when all judges and rulers come to an end in Israel, as it is said, 'And I will turn my hand upon you and purely purge away your dross and take away all your tin, and I will restore your judges as at the first' (Isa. 1:25-26)."

XCIX.

A. Said Ulla, "Jerusalem will be redeemed only through righteousness, as it is written, 'Zion shall be redeemed with judgment and her converts with righteousness' (Isa. 1:27)."

B. Said R. Pappa, "If the arrogant end [in Israel], the Magi will end [in Iran], if the judges end [in Israel], the rulers of thousands will come to an end [in Iran].

C. "If the arrogant end [in Israel], the magi will end [in Iran], as it is written, 'And I will purely purge away your haughty ones and take away all your tin' (Isa. 1:25).

D. "If judges end [in Israel], the rulers of thousands will come to an end [in Iran], as it is written, 'The Lord has taken away your judgments, he has cast out your enemy' (Zeph. 3:15)."

C.

A   Said R. Yohanan, "If you see a generation growing less and less, hope for him, as it is said, 'And the afflicted people will you save' (2 Sam. 22:28)."

B.   Said R. Yohanan, "If you see a generation over which many troubles flow like a river, hope for him, as it is written, 'When the enemy shall come in like a flood, the spirit of the Lord shall lift up a standard against him' (Isa. 59:19), followed by: 'And the redeemer shall come to Zion' (Isa. 59:20)."

C.   And said R. Yohanan, "The son of David will come to a generation that is either entirely righteous or entirely wicked.

D.   "A generation that is entirely righteous, as it is written, 'Your people also shall be all righteous, they shall inherit the land forever' (Isa. 60:21),

E.   "or a generation that is entirely wicked, as it is written, 'And he saw that there was no man and wondered that there was no intercessor' (Isa. 59:16), and it is written, 'For my own sake, even for my own sake I will do it' (Isa. 60:22)."

CI.

A.   Said R. Alexandri, "R. Joshua b. Levi contrasted verses as follows:

B.   It is written; "in its time [will the Messiah come]," and it is also written; "I [the Lord] will hasten it."

C.   [What is the meaning of the contrast?]

D.   "If [the Israelites] have merit, I will hasten it, if they do not, [the Messiah] will come in due course.

E.   "'It is written, "And behold, one like the son of man came with the clouds of heaven" (Dan. 7:13), and it is written, "Behold your king comes to you...lowly and riding upon an ass" (Zech. 9:7). [What is the meaning of the contrast?]

F.   "'If [the Israelites] have merit, it will be "with the clouds of heaven" (Dan. 7:13), and if they do not have merit, it will be "lowly and riding upon an ass" (Zech. 9:7).'"

CII.

A   Said King Shapur to Samuel, "You say that the Messiah will come on an ass [which is a humble way]. Come and I shall send him a white horse that I have."

B.   He said to him, "Do you have one of many colors?"

CIII.

A   R. Joshua b. Levi found Elijah standing at the door of the burial vault of R. Simeon b. Yohai. He said to him, "Am I going to come to the world to come?"

B.   He said to him, "If this master wants."

C.   Said R. Joshua b. Levi, "Two did I see, but a third voice did I hear."

D.   He said to him, "When is the Messiah coming?"

E.   He said to him, "Go and ask him."

F.   "And where is he sitting?"

G.   "At the gate of the city."

H.   "And what are the marks that indicate who he is?"

I.   "He is sitting among the poor who suffer illness, and all of them untie and tie their bandages all together, but he unties them and ties them one by one. He is thinking, 'Perhaps I may be wanted, and I do not want to be held up.'"

J. He went to him, saying to him, "Peace be unto you, my master and teacher."

K. He said to him, "Peace be unto you, son of Levi."

L. He said to him, "When is the master coming?"

M. He said to him, "Today."

N. He went back to Elijah, who said to him, "What did he tell you?"

O. He said to him, "'Peace be unto you, son of Levi.'"

P. He said to him, "He [thereby] promised you and your father the world to come."

Q He said to him, "But he lied to me. For he said to me, 'I am coming today,' but he did not come."

R. He said to him, "This is what he said to you, '"Today, if you will obey his voice" (Ps. 95:7).'"

CIV.

A His disciples asked R. Yosé b. Qisma, "When is the son of David coming?"

B. He said to them, "I am afraid [to answer], lest you ask an omen from me [that my answer is right]."

C. They said to him, "We shall not ask for an omen from you." He said to them, "When this gate falls and is rebuilt, falls and is rebuilt, and falls a third time. They will not suffice to rebuild it before the son of David will come."

D. They said to him, "Our master, give us an omen."

E. He said to them, "But did you not say to me that you would not ask for an omen from me?"

F. They said to him, "Even so."

G He said to them, "Then let the waters of the grotto of Banias turn to blood," and they turned to blood.

H When he died, he said to them, "Dig my bier deep into the ground, [98B] for there is not a palm tree in Babylonia on which a Persian horse has not been tied, nor is there a bier in the Land of Israel from which a Median horse will not eat straw."

CV.

A Said Rab, "The son of David will come only when the monarchy [of Rome] will spread over Israel for nine months,

B. "as it is said, 'Therefore will he give them up, until the time that she who travails has brought forth; then the remnant of his brethren shall return to the children of Israel' (Mic. 5:2)."

CVI.

A. Said Ulla, "Let him come, but may I not see him."

B. Said Rabba, "Let him come, but may I not see him."

C. R. Joseph said, "May he come, and may I have the merit of sitting in the shade of the dung of his ass."

D. Said Abbayye to Rabbah, "What is the reason [that some do not wish to see the coming of the Messiah]? Is it because of the turmoil of the Messiah?

E. "And has it not been taught on Tannaite authority:

F. "His disciples asked R. Eliezar, 'What should someone do to save himself from the turmoil of the Messiah?'

G.   "[He replied to them], 'Let him engage in study of the Torah and acts of loving kindness.'

H.   "And lo, the master [at hand] practices Torah study and acts of loving kindness. [So why not want to see him?]"

I.   He said to him, "Perhaps he fears sin will cause [him to suffer], in line with what R. Jacob bar Idi said."

J.   For R. Jacob bar Idi contrasted two verses of Scripture, as follows: "It is written, 'And behold, I am with you and will keep you wherever you go' (Gen. 28:15), and another verse states, 'Then Jacob was greatly afraid' (Gen. 32:8).

K.   "[Why the contrast between God's promise and Jacob's fear?] Jacob feared [and thought to himself,] 'Sin which I have done may cause [punishment for me instead].'"

L.   That accords with what has been taught on Tannaite authority:

M.   "Till your people pass over, O Lord, till your people pass over, that you have acquired" (Ex. 15:16).

N.   "Till your people pass over" refers to the first entry into the land [in Joshua's time].

O.   "Till your people pass over, that you have acquired" refers to the second entry into the land [in the time of Ezra and Nehemiah. Thus a miracle was promised not only on the first occasion, but also on the second. But it did not happen the second time around. Why not?]

P.   On the basis of this statement, sages have said, "The Israelites were worthy of having a miracle performed for them in the time of Ezra also, just as it had been performed for them in the time of Joshua b. Nun, but sin caused the miracle to be withheld."

CVII.

A.   So said R. Yohanan, "Let him come, but let me not see him."

B.   Said R. Simeon b. Laqish to him, "What is the scriptural basis for that view? Shall we say that it is because it is written, 'As if a man fled from a lion and a bear met him, or went into the house and leaned his hand on the wall and a serpent bit him' (Amos 5:19)?

C.   "Come and I shall show you an example of such a case in this world.

D.   "When a man goes out to the field and a bailiff meets him, it is like one whom a lion meets. When he goes into town and a tax collector meets him, it is like one whom a bear meets.

E.   "When he goes into his house and finds his sons and daughters suffering from hunger, it is like one whom a snake bit.

F.   "Rather, it is because it is written, 'Ask you now and see whether a man travails with child? Why do I see every man with his hands on his loins, as women in travail, and all faces are turned into paleness' (Jer. 30:6)."

G.   What is the sense of, "Why do I see every man..."?

H.   Said Raba bar Isaac said Rab, "It speaks of him to whom all [manly] power belongs [God]."

I.   And what is the sense of "all faces are turned into paleness"?

J.   Said R. Yohanan, "[It speaks of God's] heavenly family and his earthly family, at the moment at which God says, 'These are the creation of my hands, and those are the creation of my hands. How shall I destroy these [gentiles] on account of [what they have done to] those [Israelites] [Freedman, p. 667, n. 2: to avenge the wrongs suffered by the Jews? Because the suffering would be so great that even the Almighty would lament it, Yohanan desired to be spared the Messiah's coming.]"

K. Said R. Pappa, "This is in line with what people say: 'The ox runs and falls, so the horse is put in its stall.' [Freedman, p. 667, n. 3: Then it is hard to get the horse out. So the Israelites, having fallen, were replaced in power by the gentiles, but on their recovery, it will be difficult to remove the gentiles from their position without inflicting much suffering.]"

CVIII.

A. Said R. Giddal said Rab, "The Israelites are going to eat [and not starve] in the years of the Messiah."

B. Said R. Joseph, "That is self-evident. If not, then who will eat? Joe and Mo?! [Text: Hiliq and Bileq?]"

C. [The statement at hand] serves to exclude the view of R. Hillel, who has said, "There will be no further Messiah for Israel, for they already consumed him in the time of Hezekiah."

CIX.

A. Said Rab, "The world was created only for David."

B. And Samuel said, "For Moses."

C. And R. Yohanan said, "For the Messiah."

D. What is his name?

E. The house of R. Shila said, "His name is Shiloh, as it is said, 'Until Shiloh come' (Gen. 49:10)."

F. Members of the house of R. Yannai say, "His name is Yinnon, for it is written, 'His name shall endure forever, before the sun was, his name is Yinnon' (Ps. 72:17)."

G. Members of the house of R. Haninah said, "It is Haninah, as it is said, 'Where I will not give you Haninah' (Jer. 16:13)."

H. Others say, "His name is Menahem, son of Hezekiah, for it is written, 'Because Menahem that would relieve my soul, is far' (Lam. 1:16)."

I. Rabbis said, "His name is 'the leper of the schoolhouse,' as it is written, 'Surely he has borne our griefs and carried our sorrows, yet we did esteem him a leper, smitten of God and afflicted' (Isa. 53:4)."

CX.

A. Said R. Nahman, "If he is among the living, he is such as I, as it is said, 'And their nobles shall be of themselves and their governors shall proceed from the midst of them' (Jer. 30:21)."

B. Said Rab, "If he is among the living, he is such as our Holy Rabbi [Judah the Patriarch], and if he is among the dead, he is such as Daniel, the most desirable man."

C. Said R. Judah said Rab, "The Holy One, blessed be He, is destined to raise up for [Israel] another David, as it is said, 'But they shall serve the Lord their God and David their king, whom I will raise up for them' (Jer. 30:9).

D. "'Raised up' is not what is said, but rather, 'will raise up.'"

E. Said R. Pappa to Abbayye, "But lo, it is written, 'And my servant David shall be their prince forever' (Ezek. 37:25) [with the title for prince standing for less than the title for king]."

F. [He said to him,] "It is like a king and a viceroy [the second David being king]."

CXI.

A. R. Simlai interpreted the following verse: "What is the meaning of that which is written, 'Woe to you who desire the day of the Lord! To what end is it for you? The day of the Lord is darkness and not light' (Amos 5:18)?

B. "The matter may be compared to the case of the cock and the bat who were waiting for light.

C. "The cock said to the bat, 'I am waiting for the light, for the light belongs to me, but what do you need light for [99A]?'"

D. That is in line with what a *min* said to R. Abbahu, "When is the Messiah coming?"

E. He said to him, "When darkness covers those men."

F. He said to him, "You are cursing me."

G. He said to him, "I am merely citing a verse of Scripture: 'For behold, the darkness shall cover the earth, and great darkness the people, but the Lord shall shine upon you, and his glory shall be seen upon you' (Isa. 60:2)."

CXII.

A. It has been taught on Tannaite authority:

B. R. Eliezer says, "The days of the Messiah will last forty years, as it is said, 'Forty years long shall I take hold of the generation' (Ps. 95:10)."

C. R. Eliezer b. Azariah says, "Seventy years, as it is said, 'And it shall come to pass in that day that Tyre shall be forgotten seventy years, according to the days of one king' (Isa. 23:15).

D. "Now what would be a one [and singular] king? We must say that it is the Messiah."

E. Rabbi says, "Three generations, as it is said, 'They shall fear you with the sun and before the moon, a generation and generations' (Ps. 72:5)."

CXIII.

A. R. Hillel says, "Israel will have no Messiah, for they consumed him in the time of Hezekiah."

B. Said R. Joseph, "May R. Hillel's master forgive him. When did Hezekiah live? It was in the time of the first Temple. But Zechariah prophesied in the second Temple's time and said, 'Rejoice greatly, O daughter of Zion, shout, O daughter of Jerusalem, behold your king comes to you; he is just and has salvation; lowly and riding upon an ass and upon a colt the foal of an ass' (Zech. 9:9)."

CXIV.

A. A further teaching on Tannaite authority:

B. R. Eliezer says, "The days of the Messiah will last for forty years. Here it is written, 'And he afflicted you and made you hunger and fed you with manna' (Deut. 8:3), and elsewhere: 'Make us glad according to the days [forty years in the wilderness] in which you have afflicted us' (Ps. 90:15)."

C.   R. Dosa says, "Four hundred years. Here it is written, 'And they shall serve them and they shall afflict them four hundred years' (Gen. 15:13), and elsewhere: 'Make us glad according to the days wherein you have afflicted us' (Ps. 90:15)."

D.   Rabbi says, "Three hundred and sixty-five years, according to the number of days in the solar year, as it is said, 'For the day of vengeance is in my heart and the year of my redemption has come' (Isa. 63:4)."

E.   What is the meaning of "the day of vengeance is in my heart" (Isa. 63:4)?

F.   Said R. Yohanan, "I have revealed it to my heart, but I have not revealed it to my limbs."

G.   R. Simeon b. Laqish said, "To my heart I have revealed it, to the ministering angels I have not revealed it."

H.   Abimi, son of R. Abbahu, stated on Tannaite authority, "The days of the Messiah for Israel will be seven thousand years, as it is said, 'And as the bridegroom rejoices over the bride [a week], so shall your God rejoice over you' (Isa. 62:5)."

I.   Said R. Judah said Samuel, "The days of the Messiah are the same as the days that have passed from the day of the creation of the world even to now, as it is said, 'As the days of heaven upon earth' (Deut. 11:21)."

J.   R. Nahman bar Isaac said, "As the days from Noah to now, as it is said, 'For this is as the waters of Noah, which are mine, so I have sworn it' (Isa. 54:9)."

CXV.

A.   Said R. Hiyya bar Abba said R. Yohanan, "All of the prophets prophesied only concerning the days of the Messiah.

B.   "But as to the world to come [thereafter]: 'Eye has not seen, O Lord, beside you, what he has prepared for him who waits for him' (Isa. 64:3)."

C.   That statement differs from the view of Samuel.

D.   For said Samuel, "There is no difference between this world and the days of the Messiah except for [Israel's] subjugation to the rule of the empires alone."

E.   And said R. Hiyya bar Abba said R. Yohanan, "All of the prophets prophesied only concerning those who repent, but as to the perfectly righteous people [who have never sinned to begin with]: 'Eye has not seen, O God, beside you, what he has prepared for him who waits for him' (Isa. 54:3)."

F.   That statement differs from the view of R. Abbahu.

G.   For, said R. Abbahu, "In the place in which those who repent stand, the righteous cannot stand, for it is said, 'Peace, peace to him who is far off and to him that is near' (Isa. 57:19).

H.   "'To begin with, he was 'far off,' and then he repented and so became 'near.'

I.   "What is the sense of 'far off'? Originally far off [a sinner], and what is the sense of 'near'? Originally near and still near. [Freedman, p. 671, n. 3: Thus he assigns a higher rank to the repentant sinner than to the completely righteous.]"

J.	R. Yohanan said, "'To the one who was distant' because he was far from sin, and 'near' in that he was near sin but distanced himself from it."
K.	And said R. Hiyya bar Abba said R. Yohanan, "All of the prophets prophesied only concerning him who marries his daughter off to a disciple of sages, conducts business to the advantage of a disciple of a sage, and benefits a disciple of a sage from his wealth.
L.	"But as to disciples of sages themselves: 'Eye has not seen, O God beside you' (Isa. 64:3)."
M.	What is the meaning of the phrase, "Eye has not seen"?
N.	Said R. Joshua b. Levi, "This refers to wine that has been kept in the grapes from the six days of creation."
O.	R. Simeon b. Laqish said, "This refers to Eden, which no eye has ever seen.
P.	"And if you should say, 'Then where did Adam dwell?' the answer is, in the garden.
Q.	"And if you should say, 'But it was the Garden that was Eden,' Scripture says, 'And a river issued from Eden to water the garden' (Gen. 2:10)."

CXVI.

A.	*And he who says, "The Torah does not come from heaven"* [M. 11:1D]:
B.	Our rabbis have taught on Tannaite authority:
C.	"Because he has despised the word of the Lord and broken his commandment, that soul shall utterly be cut off" (Num. 15:31):
D.	This refers to one who says, *"The Torah does not come from heaven."*
E.	Another matter:
F.	"Because he has despised the word of the Lord": This refers to an Epicurean.
G.	Another matter:
H.	"Because he has despised the word of the Lord": This refers to one who is without shame in interpreting the Torah.
I.	"And broken his commandment": This refers to one who removes the fleshly marks of the covenant.
J.	"That soul shall utterly be cut off": "Be cut off" – in this world. "Utterly" in the world to come.
K.	On the basis of this exegesis, *said R. Eliezer the Modite, "He who treats Holy Things as secular, he who despises the appointed times, he who humiliates his companion in public, he who removes the signs of the covenant of Abraham, our father, and he who exposes aspects of the Torah not in accord with the law, even though he has in hand learning in Torah and good deeds, will have no share in the world to come"* [M. Abot 3:11].
L.	A further teaching on Tannaite authority:
M.	"Because he has despised the word of the Lord" (Num. 14:31): This refers to one who says, *"The Torah does not come from heaven."*
N.	And even if he had said, "The entire Torah comes from heaven, except for this one verse, which the Holy One, blessed be He, did not say, but which Moses said on his own," such a one falls under the verse, "Because he has despised the word of the Lord" (Num. 15:31).
O.	And even if he had said, "The entire Torah comes from heaven, except for one minor point, an argument a fortiori, an argument

based on analogy," such a one falls under the verse, "Because he
has despised the way of the Lord" (Num. 15:31).

CXVII.

    A.   It has been taught on Tannaite authority:

    B.   R. Meir would say, "He who studies the Torah but does not teach it
falls under the verse, 'Because he has despised the word of the
Lord' (Num. 15:31)."

    C.   R. Nathan says, "Whoever does not pay close attention to the
Mishnah."

    D.   R. Nehorai says, "Whoever has the possibility of taking up the
study of the Torah and does not do so."

    E.   R. Ishmael says, "This refers to one who worships an idol."

    F.   What provides the implication that such a one is subject to
discussion here?

    G.   It accords with what the Tannaite authority of the house of R.
Ishmael [said], "'Because he has despised the word of the Lord'
(Num. 15:31) refers to one who despises the statement that was
made to Moses at Sinai: 'I am the Lord your God. You shall have
no other gods before me' (Ex. 20:2-3)."

CXVIII.

    A.   **R. Joshua b. Qorhah says, "Whoever studies the Torah and does
not review it is like a man who sows seed but does not harvest it."**

    B.   **R. Joshua says, "Whoever learns the Torah and forgets it is like a
woman who bears and buries."**

    C.   **R. Aqiba says, "[99B] A song is in me, a song always" [T. Ah.
16:8H-I].**

    D.   Said R. Isaac b. Abudimi, "What is the pertinent prooftext? As it is
said, 'He who labors labors for himself, for his mouth craves it of
him' (Prov. 16:26).

    E.   "He labors in one place, and the Torah labors for him in a different
place."

CXIX.

    A.   Said R. Eleazar, "Every man was born to work, as it is said, 'For
man is born to work' (Job 5:7).

    B.   "I do not know whether it is for work done with the mouth that he
is created, or whether it is for labor done through physical work
that he was created.

    C.   "When Scripture says, 'For his mouth craves it of him' (Prov. 16:26),
one has to conclude that it is for work done with the mouth that he
was created.

    D.   "Yet I still do not know whether it was to labor in the Torah or to
labor in some sort of other conversation.

    E.   "When Scripture says, 'This book of the Torah shall not depart out
of your mouth' (Josh. 1:8), one must conclude that it is for labor in
the Torah that he is created."

    F.   That is in line with what Raba said, "All bodies serve to bear
burdens. Happy are those who have the merit of bearing the
burden of the Torah."

CXX.

    A.   "Whoever commits adultery with a woman lacks understanding"
(Prov. 6:32):

B. Said R. Simeon b. Laqish, "This refers to one who studies the Torah at occasional intervals.

C. "For it is said, 'For it is a pleasant thing if you keep them within you, they shall withal be fitted in your lips' (Prov. 22:18). [Freedman, p. 673, n. 11: One can keep the Torah only if its words are fitted always on his lips, not at rare intervals only.]"

CXXI.

A. Our rabbis have taught on Tannaite authority:

B. "But the soul that does anything presumptuously" (Num. 15:30):

C. This refers to Manasseh, son of Hezekiah, who would go into session and interpret tales seeking flaws in them, saying, "Did Moses have nothing better to do than to write such verses as 'And Lotan's sister was Timna' (Gen. 36:22). 'And Timna was concubine to Eliphaz' (Gen. 36:12). 'And Reuben went in the days of the wheat harvest and found mandrakes in the field' (Gen. 30:14)?"

D. An echo came forth and said to him, "'You sit and speak against your brother; you slander your own mother's son. These things you have done, and I kept silence, you thought that I was altogether such a one as yourself, but I will reprove you and set them in order before your eyes' (Ps. 50:20-21)."

E. Concerning him it is spelled out in tradition: "Woe to them who draw iniquity with cords of vanity and sin as it were with a cart rope" (Isa. 5:18).

F. What is the sense of "and sin as it were with a cart rope"?

G. Said R. Assi, "The inclination to do evil to begin with is like a spider's thread and ends up like a cart rope."

H. In any event, what is the meaning of, "And Lotan's sister was Timna" (Gen. 36:22)?

I. She was a princess, as it is written, "Duke Lotan, Duke Timna," and "duke" refers to a kid who has not yet got his crown.

J. She had wanted to convert to Judaism. She came to Abraham, Isaac, and Jacob, and they did not accept her. She went and became the concubine to Eliphaz, son of Esau, saying, "It is better to be a handmaiden to this nation and not a noble woman to any other nation."

K. From her descended Amalak, who distressed Israel.

L. What is the reason? It was because they should not have put her off [but should have accepted her].

M. "And Reuben went in the days of the wheat harvest [and found mandrakes in the field]" (Gen. 36:12).

N. Said Raba, son of R. Isaac, said Rab, "On the basis of this verse, we learn that righteous folk do not lay hands on what is stolen."

O. "And found mandrakes in the field" (Gen. 36:12):

P. What are these?

Q. Said Rab, "Mandrakes."

R. Said Levi, "Violets."

S. Said R. Jonathan, "Mandrake flowers."

CXXII.

A. Said R. Alexandri, "Whoever is occupied in study of the Torah for the sake of heaven brings peace to the family above and to the family below,

B. "as it is said, 'Or let him take hold of my strength that he may make peace with me, and he shall make peace with me' (Isa. 27:5)."

C. Rab said, "It is as if he built the palace above and the one below, as it is said, 'And I have put my words in your mouth and I have covered you in the shadow of my hand, that I may plant the heavens and lay the foundations of the earth, and say to Zion, You are my people' (Isa. 51:16)."

D. R. Yohanan said, "Also he shields the world, as it is said, 'And I have covered you in the shadow of my hand' (Isa. 51:16)."

E. Levi said, "Also he draws the redemption nearer, as it is said, 'And say to Zion, you are my people' (Isa. 51:16)."

CXXIII.

A. Said R. Simeon b. Laqish, "Whoever teaches Torah to the son of his neighbor is credited by Scripture as if he had made him,

B. "as it is said, 'And the souls which they had made in Haran' (Gen. 12:5)."

C. R. Eleazar said, "It is as though he had made the words of Torah, as it is said, 'Therefore keep the words of this covenant and make them' (Deut. 29:9)."

D. Raba said, "It is as though he had made himself, as it is said – 'And make them' (Deut. 29:9).

E. "Do not read 'them' but 'yourselves.'"

CXXIV.

A. Said R. Abbahu, "Whoever makes his neighbor carry out a religious duty is credited by Scripture as if he himself had done it, as it is said, 'The Lord said to Moses, Take...your rod, with which you hit the river' (Ex. 17:5).

B. "But did Moses hit the river? It was Aaron who hit the river.

C. "Rather, this shows, whoever makes his neighbor carry out a religious duty is credited by Scripture as if he himself had done it."

CXXV.

A. *An Epicurean [M. 11:1D]:*

B. Both Rab and R. Hanina say, "This refers to one who humiliates disciples of sages."

C. Both R. Yohanan and R. Joshua b. Levi say, "It is one who humiliates his fellow before a disciple of a sage."

D. Now from the viewpoint of him who says it is one who humiliates his fellow before a sage, it would also encompass a disciple of a sage himself, who *exposes aspects of the Torah not in accord with the law* [M. Abot 3:11] [acts impudently against the Torah (Freedman)].

E. But in the view of him who says that an Epicurean is one who humiliates a disciple of a sage himself, then what sort of person would fall into the category of one who *exposes aspects of the Torah not in accord with the law [M. Abot 3:11]*?

F. It would be someone of the sort of Manasseh b. Hezekiah.

G. There are those who repeat on Tannaite authority the dispute at hand in conjunction with the latter, rather than the former category, as follows:

H. *One who exposes aspects of the Torah [not in accord with the law] [M. Abot 3:11]:*

I.   Rab and R. Hanina say, "It is one who humiliates a disciple of sages."

J.   R. Yohanan and R. Joshua b. Levi say, "It is one who humiliates his fellow before a disciple of a sage."

K.   Now from the viewpoint of him who says it is one who humiliates a disciple of a sage himself, then one who reveals aspects of the Torah, one who humiliates his fellow before a disciple of a sage, would be an Epicurean.

L.   But from the viewpoint of him who says that it is one who humiliates his fellow before a disciple of a sage, with one who reveals aspects of the Torah [in an improper way] as an Epicurean, then who would fall into that latter category?

M.   Said R. Joseph, "It would, for example, be those who say, 'What good are the rabbis for us? It is for their own benefit that they study Scripture. It is for their own benefit that they repeat Mishnah teachings.'"

N.   Said Abbaye to him, "That, too, falls into the category of one who reveals aspects of the Torah in an improper way, for it is written, Thus says the Lord, But for my covenant [studied] day and night, I had not appointed the ordinances of heaven and earth' (Jer. 33:25). [Freedman, p. 676, n. 3: The world endures only because the Torah – 'my covenant' – is studied. To deny the utility of scholars therefore is to express disbelief of what is asserted in the Torah.]"

O.   Said R. Nahman bar Isaac, "The proof derives as well from the following, as it is said, Then I will spare all the place for their sakes' (Gen. 18:26)."

P.   Rather, it is one who, for example, was sitting before his master, and the topic of discussion moved to another subject, and he said, "This is what we said on the subject," rather than, "Master, you have said [on that topic]."

Q.   Raba said, "It would, for example, be like the members of the house of Benjamin, the physician, who say, 'What good are rabbis to us? They have never [100A] permitted us to eat a raven or forbidden us to eat a dove [but are limited to what the Torah itself states]."

R.   When people of the house of Benjamin brought Raba a problem involving the validity of a beast that had been slaughtered and that may or may not have been able to survive, if he found a reason to permit the matter, he would say to them, "See, I do permit the raven to you."

S.   When he found a reason to prohibit it, he would say to them, "See, I do forbid the dove to you."

T.   R. Pappa said, "It would be such as one who said, 'O, these rabbis!'"

U.   R. Pappa forgot himself and said, "O these rabbis!" He sat and fasted.

CXXVI.

A.   Levi bar Samuel and R. Huna bar Hiyya were fixing the mantles of the Torah scrolls of the house of R. Judah. When they got to the scroll of Esther, they said, "Lo, this scroll of Esther does not have to have a mantle at all."

B.   He said to them, "This sort of talk also appears to be Epicureanism."

CXXVII.

A.   R. Nahman said, "It is one who refers to his master by his name.

B.   For R. Yohanan said, "On what account was Gehazi punished? Because he called his master by name.

C.   "As it is said, 'My lord, O King, this is the woman, and this is her son whom Elisha restored to life' (2 Kgs. 8:5)."

CXXVIII.

A.   R. Jeremiah was in session before R. Zira and said, "The Holy One, blessed be He, by which there will be many kinds of delicious produce, as it is said, 'And by the river upon that bank thereof, on this side and on that side, shall grow all trees for meat, whose leaf shall not fade, neither shall the fruit thereof be consumed; it shall bring forth new fruit, according to his months, because their waters they issued out of the sanctuary, and the fruit therefore shall be for meat, and the leaf thereof for medicine' (Ezek. 47:12)."

B.   "Said to him a certain old man, 'Well said, and so did R. Yohanan say.'"

C.   Said R. Jeremiah to R. Zira, "Behavior of this sort [condescension to the master] likewise appears to be Epicureanism."

D.   He said to him, "But this represented a mere support for your position.

E.   "But if you have heard any tradition, this is the tradition that you heard:

F.   "R. Yohanan was in session and interpreting Scripture as follows: The Holy One, blessed be He, is destined to bring forth precious stones and jewels which are thirty cubits long and thirty cubits high, and engrave on them an engraving ten by twenty cubits, and he will set them up as the gates of Jerusalem, for it is written, "And I will make your windows of agates and your gates of carbuncles" (Isa. 54:12).

G.   "'A disciple ridiculed him, saying "Now if we do not find jewels the size of a dove's egg, are we going to find any that big?"

H.   "'After some time he took a sea voyage, and he saw ministering angels cutting precious stones and jewels. He said to them, "As to these, what are they for?"

I.   "'They said to him, "The Holy One, blessed be He, is destined to set them up as the gates of Jerusalem."

J.   "'When he came back, he found R. Yohanan in session and expounding Scripture. He said to him, "Rabbi, indeed give your exposition, for it is appropriate that you should expound Scripture. Exactly as you said, so I myself saw."

K.   "'He said to him, "Empty head! Had you not seen, would you not have believed me! You are one who ridicules teachings of sages." He set his eye on him and turned him into a hill of bones.'"

L.   An objection was raised [to the teaching of Yohanan]:

M.   "And I will make you go upright (Lev. 26:13)."

N.   R. Meir says, "It is the height of two hundred cubits, twice the height of Adam."

O.   R. Judah says, "A hundred cubits, the length of the Temple and its walls, as it is written, 'That our sons may be as plants grown up in their youth, that our daughters may be as cornerstones, fashioned after the similitude of the Temple' (Ps. 144:12)."

P.   What R. Yohanan meant was [Freedman]: the ventilation windows. [These would be ten by twenty, but the gates themselves would be much taller (Freedman, p. 678, n. 7)].

Q   What is the meaning of the phrase, "And the leaf thereof is for medicine" (Ezek. 47:12)?

R.   R. Isaac bar Abodimi and R. Hisda: one said, "It is to open up the upper mouth [and help the dumb to speak]."

S.   One said, "It is to open the lower mouth [and heal the barrenness of a barren woman]."

T.   It has been taught on Tannaite authority:

U.   Hezekiah said, "It is to open the mouth of the dumb."

V.   Bar Qappara said, "It is to open the mouth of the barren women."

W.   R. Yohanan said, "It serves as medicine, literally."

X.   What is the meaning of the statement, "Medicine"?

Y.   R. Ramual bar Nahmani said, "It is to improve the appearance of masters of mouths [disciples]."

CXXIX.

A   R. Judah b. R. Simon interpreted, "Whoever blackens his face [in fasting] on account of teachings of Torah in this world will find that the Holy One, blessed be He, polishes his luster in the world to come.

B.   "For it is said, 'His countenance shall be as the Lebanon, excellent as the cedars' (Song 5:15)."

C.   R. Ranhum bar Hanilai said, "Whoever starves himself for words of Torah in this world will the Holy One, blessed be He, feed to satisfaction in the world to come,

D.   "as it is said, 'They shall be abundantly satisfied with the fatness of your house, and you shall make them drink of the river of your pleasures' (Ps. 36:9)."

E.   When R. Dimi came, he said, "The Holy One, blessed be He, is destined to give to every righteous person his full pack load, as it is said, 'Blessed be the Lord, day by day, who loads us with benefits, even the God of our salvation, Selah' (Ps. 68:20)."

F.   Said Abbayye to him, "And is it possible to say so? Is it not said, 'Who has measured the waters in the hollow of his hand and measured out heaven with the span' (Isa. 40:12)?"

G   He said to him, "What is the reason that you are not at home in matters of lore? They say in the West in the name of Raba bar Mari, 'The Holy One, blessed be He, is destined to give each righteous person three hundred and ten worlds, as it is said, "That I may cause those who love me to inherit substance and I will fill their treasuries," (Prov. 8:21), and the numerical value of the word for substance is three hundred ten.'"

CXXX.

A.   It has been taught on Tannaite authority:

B.   *R. Meir says, "By the same measure by which a mate metes out, do they mete out to him [M. Sot. 1:7A],*

C. "For it is written, 'By measure in sending her away thou dost contend with her' (Isa. 27:8)."

D. Said R. Judah, "And can one say so? If a person gives a handful [to charity] to a poor man in this world, will the Holy One, blessed be He, give him a handful [of his, so much larger hand], in the world to come?

E. "And has it not been written, 'And meted out Heaven with a span' (Isa. 40:12)?"

F. [Meir replied] "But do you not say so? Which measure is greater? That of goodness or that of punishment? [100B]

G. "With regard to the measure of goodness it is written, 'And he commanded the clouds from above, and opened the doors of heaven and rained down manna upon them to eat' (Ps. 78:23-24).

H. "With regard to the measure of punishment it is written, 'And the windows of heaven were opened' (Gen. 7:11). [Freedman, p. 680, n. 5: 'Doors' implies a greater opening than windows; God metes out reward more fully than punishment.]

I. "In respect to the measure even of punishment it is written, 'And they shall go forth and look upon the carcasses of the men who have transgressed against me, for their worm shall not die, neither shall their fire be quenched, and they shall be a horror to all flesh' (Isa. 66:24).

J. "But is it not so that if a person put his finger into a fire in this world, he will be burned right away.

K. "But just as the Holy One, blessed be He, gives the wicked the power to receive their punishment, so the Holy One, blessed be He, gives the righteous the power to receive the goodness that is coming to them."

CXXXI.

A. R. Aqiba says, "*Also: He who reads in heretical books...*" [M. 11:1E]:

B. It was taught on Tannaite authority: That is the books of the *minim*.

CXXXII.

A. R. Joseph said, "It is also forbidden to read in the book of Ben Sira."

B. Said to him Abbayye, "What is the reason for that view?

C. Should I say that it is because it is written in it, 'Do not skin the fish, even from the ear, so that you will not go and bruise it, but roast it in the fire and eat two loaves with it'?

D. "In point of fact in the explicit view of Scripture it is also said, 'You shall not destroy the trees thereof' (Deut. 20:19). [Freedman, p. 681, ns. 1-2: A fish is fit for consumption even if baked or roasted with its skin and therefore it is wasteful to remove it. Likewise, one must not wantonly destroy what is fit for use.]

E. "And if it is a matter of exegesis [and not the literal sense], then the saying teaches us proper conduct, namely, that one should not have sexual relations in an unnatural way.

F. "Rather, might it be because it is written in it, 'A daughter is a worthless treasure for her father. For concern for her, he cannot sleep by night. In her childhood, it is lest she be seduced; in her girlhood, it is lest she play the whore; in her maturity, it is lest she not wed; once she is wed, it is lest she not have sons. In her old age it is lest she practice witchcraft'?

G. "But rabbis have also made the same statement: 'The world cannot exist without males and without females. Happy is he whose children are males, and woe is him whose children are females.'

H. "Rather, might it be because it is written in [Ben Sira]: 'Do not admit despair into your heart, for despair has killed many men'?

I. "Lo, Solomon made the same statement; 'Anxiety in the heart of man makes him stoop' (Prov. 12:25)."

J. R. Ammi and R. Assi: One said, "Let him banish it from his mind."

K. "The other said, "Let him tell it to others."

L. [Reverting to Abbayye's inquiry:] "Rather, might it be because it is written in [Ben Sira]: 'Keep large numbers of people away from your house, and do not let just anyone into your house'?

M. "Lo, Rabbi also made that statement.

N. "For it has been taught on Tannaite authority:

O. "Rabbi says, 'A person should never admit a great many friends into his house, as it is said, "A man who has many friends brings evil upon himself" (Prov. 18:24).'

P. "Rather, it is because it is written in it: 'A man with a thin beard is wise, a man with a thick beard is a fool; one who blows forth his beard is not thirsty. One who says, "What is there to eat with my bread" – take the bread away from him. [He, too, is not hungry.] He who parts his beard will overpower the world [being very clever.]' [This foolish statement, in point of fact, forms the basis for Joseph's judgment.]"

Q. Said R. Joseph, "But the excellent statements in the book [of Ben Sira] we do expound.

R. "[For example:] 'A good woman is a good gift, who will be put into the bosom of a God-fearing man. A bad woman is a plague for her husband. What is his remedy? Let him drive her from his house and be healed from what is plaguing him.

S. "'A lovely wife – happy is her husband. The number of his days is doubled.

T. "'Keep your eyes from a woman of charm, lest you be taken in her trap. Do not turn to her husband to drink wine with him, or strong drink, for through the looks of a beautiful woman many have been slain, and numerous are those who have been slain by her.

U. "'Many are the blows with which a peddler is smitten [for dealing with women]. Those who make it a habit of committing fornication are like a spark that lights the ember. "As a cage is full of birds, so are their houses full of deceit" (Jer. 5:27).

V. "'Keep large numbers of people away from your house, and do not let just anybody into your house.

W. "'Let many people ask how you are, but reveal your secret to one out of a thousand. From her who lies in your house keep protected the opening of your mouth.

X. "'Do not worry about tomorrow's sorrow, "For you do not know what a day may bring forth" (Prov. 27:1). Perhaps tomorrow you will no longer exist and it will turn out that you will worry about a world that is not yours.

Y. "'"All the days of the poor are evil" (Prov. 15:15). Ben Sira said, "So, too, his nights. His roof is the lowest in town, his vineyard on the topmost mountain. Rain flows from other roofs onto his and from his vineyard onto other vineyards.""'

CXXXIII.

A. Said R. Zira said Rab, "What is the meaning of the verse of Scripture, 'All the days of the afflicted are evil' (Prov. 15:15)?

B. "This refers to masters of Talmud.

C. "'But he that is of a good heart has a continuous banquet' (Prov. 15:15)? This refers to masters of the Mishnah."

D. Raba said, "Matters are just the opposite."

E. And that is in line with what R. Mesharshia said in the name of Raba, "What is the meaning of the verse of Scripture: 'Whoever removes stones shall be hurt with them' (Qoh. 10:9)?

F. "This refers to masters of the Mishnah.

G. "'But he who cleaves wood shall be warmed by it' (Qoh. 10:9)?

H. "This refers to masters of Talmud."

I. R. Hanina says, "'All of the days of the afflicted are evil' (Prov. 15:15) refers to a man who has a bad wife.

J. "'But he that is of a good heart has a continuous banquet' (Prov. 15:15) refers to a man who has a good wife.

K. R. Yannai says, "'All the days of the afflicted are evil' (Prov. 15:15) refers to one who is fastidious.

L. "'But he that is of a good heart has a continuous banquet' (Prov. 15:15) refers to one who is easy to please."

M. R. Yohanan said, "'All the days of the afflicted are evil' (Prov. 15:15) refers to a merciful person.

N. "'But he that is of a good heart has a continuous banquet' (Prov. 15:15) refers to someone who is cruel by nature [so nothing bothers him]."

O. R. Joshua b. Levi said, "'All the days of the afflicted are evil' (Prov. 15:15) refers to [101A] someone who is worrisome.

P. "'But he that is of a good heart has a continuous banquet' (Prov. 15:15) refers to one who is serene."

Q. R. Joshua b. Levi said, "'All the days of the afflicted are evil' (Prov. 15:15) – but [not] there are Sabbaths and festival days [on which the afflicted gets some pleasure]?"

R. The matter accords with what Samuel said. For Samuel said, "The change in diet [for festival meals] is the beginning of stomachache."

CXXXIV.

A. Our rabbis have taught on Tannaite authority:

B. He who recites a verse of the Song of Songs and turns it into a kind of love song, and he who recites a verse in a banquet hall not at the proper time [but in a time of carousal] bring evil into the world [cf. T. San. 12:10A].

C. For the Torah puts on sack cloth and stands before the Holy One, blessed be He, and says before him, "Lord of the world, your children have treated me like a harp which scoffers play."

D. He then says to her, "My daughter, when they eat and drink, what should keep them busy?"

E. She will say to him, "Lord of the world, if they are masters of Scripture, let them keep busy with the Torah, Prophets, and Writings; if they are masters of the Mishnah, let them keep busy with the Mishnah, law and lore; and if they are masters of the Talmud, let them keep busy on Passover with the laws of the Passover, with the laws of Pentecost on Pentecost, and with the laws of the Festival [of Tabernacles] on the Festival."

F. R. Simeon b. Eleazar gave testimony in the name of R. Simeon b. Hanania, "Whoever recites a verse of Scripture at the proper time brings good to the world,

G. "as it is said, 'And a word spoken in season, how good is it' (Prov. 15:23)."

CXXXV.

A. *And he who whispers over a wound [M. 1:1F]:*

B. Said R. Yohanan, "That is the rule if one spits over the wound, for people may not make mention of the Name of heaven over spit."

CXXXVI.

A. It has been stated on Amoraic authority:

B. Rab said, "Even 'When the plague of leprosy' (Lev. 1:1) [may not be recited]."

CXXXVII.

A. Our rabbis have taught on Tannaite authority:

B. People may anoint and massage the intestines on the Sabbath, and whisper to snakes and scorpions on the Sabbath, and place utensils on the eyes on the Sabbath.

C. Said Rabban Simeon b. Gamaliel, "Under what circumstances? In the case of a utensil that may be carried [on the Sabbath], but in the case of a utensil that may not be carried, it is forbidden."

D. And a question may not be addressed on a matter having to do with demons on the Sabbath.

E. R. Yosé says, "Even on a weekday it is forbidden to do so."

F. Said R. Huna, "The decided law accords with the view of R. Yosé."

G. And R. Yosé made that statement only on account of the danger involved in doing so.

H. This is illustrated by the case of R. Isaac bar Joseph, who got stuck in a cedar tree, and a miracle was done for him, so that the cedar tree split open and spit him out. [Freedman, p. 685, n. 5: He consulted a demon, which turned itself into a tree and swallowed him; it was only through a miracle that he escaped.]

CXXXVIII.

A. Our rabbis have taught on Tannaite authority:

B. People may anoint and massage the intestines on the Sabbath, so long as one does not do so as he does on a weekday.

C. How then should one do it?

D. R. Hama, son of R. Hanini, said, "One puts on some oil and then massages."

E. R. Yohanan said, "One puts on oil and massages simultaneously."

CXXXIX.

A. Our rabbis have taught on Tannaite authority:

B. As to the spirits of oil or eggs, it is permitted to address questions to them, except that they prove unreliable.

C. People whisper over oil that is in a utensil but not over oil that is held in the hand.

D. Therefore people apply oil by hand and not out of a utensil.

CXL.

A   R. Isaac bar Samuel bar Marta happened to stay at a certain inn. They brought him oil in a utensil, and he anointed himself.

B.   He broke out in blisters all over his face.

C   He went to a marketplace, and a certain woman saw him and said to him, "The blast of Hamath do I see here."

D.   She did something for him, and he was healed.

CXLI.

A   Said R. Abba to Rabba bar Mari, "It is written, 'I will put none of these diseases upon you, which I have brought upon the Egyptians, for I am the Lord who heals you' (Ex. 15:26).

B.   "But if he does not place those diseases, what need is there for healing anyhow?"

C   He said to him, "This is what R. Yohanan said, 'This verse of Scripture provides its own interpretation, since it is said, "And he said, If you will diligently obey the voice of the Lord your God" (Ex. 15:16). "If you obey, I shall not place those diseases upon you, and if you will not obey, I will do so."

D.   "'Yet even so: "I am the Lord who heals you"(Ex. 15:26).'"

CXLII.

A   Said Rabbah bar bar Hanah, "When R. Eliezer fell ill, his disciples came in to call on him.

B.   "He said to them, 'There is great anger in the world [to account for my sickness].'

C   "They began to cry, but R. Aqiba began to laugh. They said to him, 'Why are you laughing?'

D.   "He said to them, 'Why are you crying?'

E.   "They said to him, 'Is it possible that, when a scroll of the Torah [such as Eliezer] is afflicted with disease, we should not cry?'

F.   "He said to them, 'For that reason I am laughing. So long as I observed that, as to my master, his wine did not turn to vinegar, his flux was not smitten, his oil did not putrefy, and his honey did not become rancid,

G   "'I thought to myself, "Perhaps, God forbid, my master has received his reward in this world." But now that I see my master in distress, I rejoice [knowing that he will receive his full reward in the world to come].'

H   "[Eliezer] said to him, 'Aqiba, have I left out anything at all from the whole of the Torah?'

I.   "He said to him, '[Indeed so, for] you have taught us, our master, "For there is not a just man upon earth, who does good and does not sin" (Qoh. 7:20).'"

CXLIII.

A.   Our rabbis have taught on Tannaite authority:

B.   When R. Eliezer fell ill, four elders came to call on him: R. Tarfon, R. Joshua, R. Eleazar b. Azariah, and R. Aqiba.

C   R. Tarfon responded first and said, "You are better for Israel than a drop of rain, for a drop of rain is good for this world, but my master is good for this world and the world to come."

D. R. Joshua responded and said, "You are better for Israel than the orb of the sun, for the orb of the sun serves for this world, but my master serves for this world and the world to come."

E. R. Eleazar b. Azariah responded and said, "You are better for Israel than a father and a mother, for a father and a mother are for this world, but my master is for this world and the world to come."

F. R. Aqiba responded and said, "Suffering is precious."

G. He said to them, "Prop me up so that I may hear the statement of Aqiba, my disciple, who has said, 'Suffering is precious.'"

H. He said to him, "Aqiba, how do you know?"

I. He said to him, "I interpret a verse of Scripture: 'Manasseh was twelve years old when he began to reign, and he reigned fifty-five years in Jerusalem...and he did what was evil in the sight of the Lord' (2 Kgs. 21:1-2).

J. "And it is written **[101B]**, 'These are the proverbs of Solomon, which the men of Hezekiah, king of Judah, copied out' (Prov. 25:1).

K. "Now is it possible that Hezekiah, king of Judah, taught the Torah to the entire world, but to his son, Manasseh, he did not teach the Torah? [Obviously not!]

L. "But out of all the trouble that [his father] took with him, and with all the labor that he poured into him, nothing brought him back to the good way except for suffering.

M. "For it is said, 'And the Lord spoke to Manasseh and to his people, but they would not hearken to him. Therefore the Lord brought upon them the captains of the host of the king of Assyria, who took Manasseh among the thorns and bound him with chains and carried him to Babylonia' (2 Chr. 33:10-11).

N. "And it is written, 'And when he was in affliction, he sought the Lord his God and humbled himself greatly before the God of his fathers. And he prayed to him and he was entreated of him and heard his supplication and brought him again to Jerusalem to his kingdom, and Manasseh knew that the Lord is God' (2 Chr. 33:12-13).

O. "So you learn that suffering is precious."

CXLIV.

A. Our rabbis have taught on Tannaite authority:

B. Three came with a self-serving plea, and these are they: Cain, Esau, and Manasseh.

C. Cain, as it is written, "Is my sin too great to be forgiven?" (Gen. 4:13).

D. He said before him, "Lord of the world, is my sin any greater than that of the six hundred thousand who are destined to sin before you? And yet you will forgive them!"

E. Esau, as it is written, "Have you but one blessing, my father" (Gen. 27:38).

F. Manasseh: To begin with he called upon many gods and in the end he called upon the God of his fathers.

CXLV.

A. *Abba Saul says, "Also: he who pronounces the Divine Name as it is spelled out" [M. 11:1G].*

B. On Tannaite authority [it was stated]:

C. That is the rule in the provinces, and [when it is] in blasphemous language.

CXLVI.
A. *Three kings and four ordinary folk [have no portion in the world to come. Three kings: Jeroboam, Ahab, and Manasseh] [M. 11:2A-B]:*
B. Our rabbis have taught on Tannaite authority:
C. "Jerobam": for he treated the people as his sexual object.
D. Another matter: "Jeroboam": for he made strife in the people.
E. Another matter: "Jeroboam": for he brought strife between the people of Israel and their father in heaven.
F. Son of Nebat, a son who saw [a vision] but did not see [its meaning].

CXLVII.
A. On Tannaite [authority it was stated]:
B. Nebat is the same as Micah and Sheba son of Bichri.
C. Nebat: because he saw a vision but did not see [its meaning].
D. Micah: because he was [Freedman]: crushed in the building. [Freedman, pp. 688-689, n. 11: According to legend, when the Israelites in Egypt did not complete their tally of bricks, their children were built into the walls instead. On Moses' complaining thereof to God, He answered him that He was thus weeding out the destined wicked. As proof, he was empowered to save Micah, who had already been built into it, but only to become an idolator on his reaching manhood. Rashi also gives an alternative rendering: he became impoverished through building – presumably his idolatrous shrine.]
E. But what was his real name? It was Sheba, son of Bichri.

CXLVIII.
A. Our rabbis have taught on Tannaite authority:
B. There were three who saw [a vision] but did not see [its meaning], and these are they: Nabat, Ahitophel, and Pharaoh's astrologers.
C. Nabat saw fire coming forth from his penis. He thought that [it meant that] he would rule, but that was not the case. It was that Jeroboam would come forth from him [who would rule].
D. Ahitophel saw *saraat* spread over him and over his penis. He thought that it meant that he would be king, and that was not the case. It was Sheba, his daughter, from whom Solomon would come forth.
E. The astrologers of Pharaoh: In line with what R. Hama, son of R. Hanina, said, "What is the meaning of the verse of Scripture, 'These are the waters of rebellion, because they strove' (Num. 20:13)?
F. "These are the waters which the astrologers of Pharaoh foresaw, and about which they erred.
G. "They saw that the savior of Israel would be smitten because of water. So [Pharaoh] decreed, 'Every son that is born you shall cast into the river' (Ex. 1:22).
H. "But they did not know that it was on account of the water of rebellion that he would be smitten:"

CXLIX.
A. And how do we know that [Jeroboam] will not come into the world to come?

B.   As it is written, "And this thing became sin to the house of
       Jeroboam, even to cut if off and to destroy it from off the face of the
       earth" (1 Kgs. 13:34).

C.   "To cut it off" in this world.

D.   "And to destroy it" in the world to come.

CL.

A.   Said R. Yohanan, "On what account did Jeroboam have the merit to
       rule?

B.   "Because he reproved Solomon.

C.   "And on what account was he punished?

D.   "Because he reproved him publicly.

E.   "So it is said, 'And this was the cause that the lifted up his hand
       against the king: Solomon built Millo and repaired the breaches of
       the city of David his father' (1 Kgs. 11:27).

F.   "He said to him, 'David your father made breaches in the wall so
       that the Israelites might come up for the pilgrim festivals, but you
       have filled them in so as to collect a tax for the daughter of
       Pharaoh.'"

G.   And what is the meaning of the phrase, "That he lifted up his hand
       against the king" (1 Kgs. 11:27)?

H.   Said R. Nahman, "Because he took off his phylacteries in his
       presence."

CLI.

A.   Said R. Nahman, "The arrogance that characterized Jeroboam is
       what drove him out of the world.

B.   "For it is said, 'Now Jeroboam said in his heart, Now shall the
       kingdom return to the house of David. If this people go up to
       sacrifice in the house of the Lord at Jerusalem, then shall the heart
       of this people turn to their Lord, even to Rehoboam, king of Judah,
       and they shall kill me and go again to Rehoboam, king of Judah' (1
       Kgs. 12:27-26).

C.   "He said, 'We have a tradition that no one may sit down in the
       Temple courtyard except kings of the house of Judah alone. When
       the people see that Rehoboam is sitting down and I am standing,
       they will think that he is king, and I am merely a servant.

D.   "'But if I sit down, I shall be in the position of rebelling against the
       monarchy, and they will kill me and follow.'

E.   "Forthwith: 'Wherefore the king took counsel and made two calves
       of gold and said to them, It is too much for you to go up to
       Jerusalem. Behold your gods O Israel, who brought you up out of
       the land of Egypt, and he put one in Beth El and the other he put in
       Dan' (1 Kgs. 12:28)."

F.   What is the meaning of the phrase, "The king took counsel"?

G.   Said R. Judah, "That he sat a wicked person next to a righteous
       person. He said to them, 'Will you sign everything that I do.'

H.   "They said to him, 'Yes.'

I.   "He said to them, 'I want to be king.'

J.   "They said to him, 'Yes.'

K.   "He said to them, 'Will you do whatever I say?'

L.   "They said to him, 'Yes.'"

M.   "'Even to worship an idol.'

N. "The righteous one said to him, 'God forbid.'

O. "The wicked one said to the righteous one, 'Do you think that a person such as Jeroboam would really worship an idol? Rather, what he wants to do is to test us to see whether or not we shall accept his word **[102A]**.'"

P. "Even Ahijah the Shilonite made a mistake and signed, for Jehu was a very righteous man, as it is said, 'And the Lord said to Jehu, Because you have done well in executing what is right in my eyes and have done to the house of Ahab according to all that was in my heart, your children of the fourth generation shall sit upon the throne of Israel' (2 Kgs. 10:30).

Q. "But it is written, 'But Jehu took no heed to walk in the law of the Lord God of Israel with all his heart, for he did not depart from the sins of Jeroboam, which he had made Israel to sin' (2 Kgs. 10:31)."

R. What caused it?

S. Said Abbayye, "A covenant made orally, as it is said, 'And Jehu gathered all the people together and said to them, Ahab served Baal a little, but Jehu shall serve him much' (2 Kgs. 10:18). [Freedman, p. 691, n. 5: These words, though spoken guilefully, had to be fulfilled.]"

T. Raba said, "He saw the signature of Ahijah the Shilonite, and he erred on that account."

CLII.

A. It is written, "And the revolters are profound to make slaughter, though I have been a rebuke of all of them" (Hos. 5:2):

B. Said R. Yohanan, "Said the Holy One, blessed be He, 'They have gone deeper than I did. I said, "Whoever does not go up to Jerusalem for the Festival transgresses an affirmative requirement," but they have said, "Whoever does go up to Jerusalem for the festival will be stabbed with a sword."'"

CLIII.

A. "And it came to pass at that time, when Jeroboam went out of Jerusalem, that the prophet Ahijah the Shilonite found him in the way, and he had clad himself with a new garment" (1 Kgs. 11:20):

B. It was taught on Tannaite authority in the name of R. Yosé, "It was a time designated for punishment. [Freedman, p. 691, n. 9: On that occasion Ahijah prophesied the division of the kingdom as a punishment for Solomon's backsliding.]"

C. "In the time of their visitation they shall perish" (Jer. 51:18):

D. It was taught on Tannaite authority in the name of R. Yosé, "A time designated for punishment."

E. "In an acceptable time I have heard you" (Isa. 49:8):

F. It was taught on Tannaite authority in the name of R. Yosé, "A time designated for good."

G. "Nevertheless in the day when I visit, I will visit their sin upon them" (Ex. 32:34):

H. It was taught on Tannaite authority in the name of R. Yosé, "A time designated for punishment."

I. "And it came to pass at that time, that Judah went down from his brethren" (Gen. 38:1):

J.   It was taught on Tannaite authority in the name of R. Yosé, "A time designated for punishment."

K.   "And Rehoboam went to Shechem, for all Israel were come to Shechem to make him king" (1 Kgs. 12:1):

L.   It was taught on Tannaite authority in the name of R. Yosé, "A time designated for punishment. In Shechem men raped Dinah, in Shechem his brothers sold Joseph, in Shechem the kingdom of David was divided."

CLIV.

A.   "Now it came to pass at that time that Jeroboam went out of Jerusalem" (1 Kgs. 11:29):

B.   Said R. Hanina bar Pappa, "He went out of the realm of Jerusalem."

CLV.

A.   "And the prophet Ahijah the Shilonite found him in the way, and he clad himself with a new garment, and the two were alone in the field" (1 Kgs. 11:29):

B.   What is this "new garment"?

C.   Said R. Nahman, "It was as with a new garment: just as a new garment has no sort of blemish, so the Torah learning of Jeroboam had no sort of flaw."

D.   Another matter: "A new garment":

E.   It was that they said things so new that no ear had ever heard them.

F.   "And the two were alone in the field" (1 Kgs. 11:29): What is the meaning of this statement?

G.   Said R. Judah said Rab, "It is that all the disciples of sages were as grass of the field before them [and of no account]."

H.   And there is he who says, "It is that the reasons for the rulings of the Torah were revealed to them in the open as in a field."

CLVI.

A.   "Therefore shall you give parting gifts to Moresheth-gath, the houses of Achzib shall be a lie to the kings of Israel" (Mic. 1:14):

B.   Said R. Hanina bar Pappa, "An echo came forth and said to them, 'He who killed the Philistine and gave you possession of Gath – to his sons you will give parting gifts.'"

C.   "Therefore the houses of Achzib shall be a lie to the kings of Israel" (Mich. 1:14). [Freedman, p. 693, n. 2: "Since you deal treacherously with the house of David, preferring the rule of the kings of Israel, therefore you shall be delivered into the hands of the heathen, whose religion is false."]

CLVII.

A.   Said R. Hinnena bar Pappa, "Whoever derives benefit from this world without reciting a blessing is as if he steals from the Holy One, blessed be He, and the community of Israel.

B.   "For it is said, 'Who robs from his father or his mother and says, It is no transgression, is the companion of a destroyer' (Prov. 28:24).

C.   "'His father' is only the Holy One, blessed be He, as it is said, 'Is not [God] your father, who has bought you' (Deut. 32:6), and 'his mother' can mean only the congregation of Israel, as it is said, 'My son, hear the instruction of your father and do not forsake the Torah of your mother' (Prov. 1:8)."

D. "What is the sense of "He is the companion of a destroyer" (Prov. 28:24)?

E. "He is companion of Jeroboam, son of Nebat, who destroyed Israel for their father in heaven."

CLVIII.

A. "And Jeroboam drove Israel from following the Lord and made them sin a great sin" (2 Kgs. 17:21):

B. Said R. Hanin, "It was like two sticks that rebound from one another."

CLIX.

A. "[These are the words which Moses spoke to all Israel in the wilderness] and Di Zahab" (Deut. 1:1):

B. Said a member of the house of R. Yannai, "Moses said before the Holy One, blessed be He, 'Lord of the world, on account of the silver and gold which you showered on Israel until they said, "Enough," they were caused to make for themselves gods of gold.'

C. "It is comparable to the case of a lion, who does not tear and roar on account of what is in a basket containing straw, but because of what is in a basket of meat."

D. Said R. Oshaia, "Up to the time of Jeroboam, the Israelites would suck from a single calf [sinning on account of only one], but from that time on, it was from two or three calves."

E. Said R. Isaac, "You do not have any sort of punishment that comes upon the world in which is contained at least one twenty-fourth of part of the overweight of a *litra* of the first calf.

F. "For it is written, 'Nevertheless in the day when I visit, I will visit their sin upon them' (Ex. 32:34)."

G. Said R. Hanina, "After twenty-four generations this verse of Scripture will be exacted: 'He cried also in my ears with a loud voice, saying, cause the visitations of the city to draw near, even every man with his destroying weapon in his hand' (Ezek. 9:1)." [Freedman, p. 694, n. 4: The use of "visitations" suggests that this was the fulfillment of the doom threatened in Ex. 32:34. There were twenty-four generations from that of the wilderness, when the calf was made, to that of Zedekiah, in whose reign the state was overthrown and Judah was deported to Babylonia.]"

CLX.

A. "After this thing Jeroboam did not turn from his evil way" (1 Kgs. 13:33):

B. What is the sense of "after"?

C. Said R. Abba, "After the Holy One, blessed be He, seized Jeroboam by his garment and said to him, 'Repent, and you and the son of Jesse and I shall walk about in the Garden of Eden.'

D. "He said to him, 'Who will be at the head?'

E. "'The son of Jesse will be at the head.'

F. "'If so, I don't want it.'"

CLXI.

A. R. Abbahu would regularly give a public interpretation of the three kings [of M. 11:2A]. He fell ill and undertook not to give such an address [since he thought the illness was punishment for speaking about the king's sins].

B.   When [102B] he got better, he reversed himself and gave an
      address. They said to him, "You undertook not to speak about
      them."

C.   He said to them, "Did they repent, that I should repent!"

CLXII.

A.   At the house of R. Ashi, [the group] arose [from studying] at the
      teaching of the three kings. He said, "Tomorrow we shall open
      discourse with the topic of 'our colleagues' [M. 11:2, that is, the
      three kings, all of whom were held to be disciples of sages]."

B.   Manasseh came and appeared in a dream: "Do you call us 'your
      colleague' and 'your father's colleague'? [If you are as good as we
      are, then tell me] from what part of the bread do you take the piece
      for reciting the blessing, 'Who brings forth bread from the earth'?"

C.   He said to him, "I don't know."

D.   He said to him, "If you have not learned from what part of the
      bread do you take a piece for reciting the blessing, 'Who brings
      forth bread from the earth,' how can you call us 'your colleague'?"

E.   He said to him, "Teach me. Tomorrow I shall expound the matter
      in your name in the class session."

F.   He said to him, "One takes the part that is baked into a crust [and
      not the dough on the inside]."

G.   He said to him, "If you are so wise, then what is the reason that you
      worshiped an idol?"

H.   He said to him, "If you had been there, you would have picked up
      the hem of your garment and run after me."

I.   The next day he said to the rabbis, "Let us begin with our teacher."

CLXIII.

A.   The name 'Ahab' signifies that he was a brother to heaven (ah) but
      father of idolatry (ab).

B.   "He was brother to heaven, as it is written, 'A brother is born for
      trouble' (Prov. 17:17).

C.   "He was father to idolatry, as it is written, 'As a father loves his
      children' (Ps. 103:13)."

CLXIV.

A.   "And it came to pass, that it was a light thing for him to walk in the
      sins of Jeroboam, the son of Nebat" (1 Kgs. 16:31):

B.   Said R. Yohanan, "The lightest [sins] committed by Ahab were as
      the most severe ones that were committed by Jeroboam.

C.   "And on what account did Scripture blame Jeroboam? It was
      because he was the beginning of the corruption."

CLXV.

A.   "Yes, their altars are as heaps in the furrows of the fields" (Hos.
      12:12):

B.   Sad R. Yohanan, "You have no furrow in the whole of the Land of
      Israel in which Ahab did not set up an idol and bow down to it."

CLXVI.

A.   And how do we know that [Ahab] will not enter the world to
      come?

B.   As it is written, "And I will cut off from Ahab him who pisses
      against the wall, him that is shut up and forsaken in Israel" (1 Kgs.
      21:21).

C.   "Shut up" in this world.

D.   "Forsaken" in the world to come.

CLXVII.

A   Said R. Yohanan, "On what account did Omri merit the monarchy? Because he added a single town to the Land of Israel, as it is written, 'And he bought the hill Samaria of Shemer for two talents of silver and built on the hill and called the name of the city which he built after the name of Shemer, owner of the hill, Samaria' (1 Kgs. 16:24)."

B.   Said R. Yohanan, "On what account did Ahab merit ruling for twenty-two years? Because he honored the Torah, which was given with twenty-two letters [of the Hebrew alphabet], as it is said, 'And he sent messages to Ahab, king of Israel, to the city, and said to him, Thus says Ben-hadad, Your silver and your gold is mine, your wives also and your children, even the goodliest are mine....Yet will I send my servants to you tomorrow at this time and they shall search your house, and the houses of your servants, and it shall be, that whatsoever is pleasant in your eyes they shall put in their hand and take it away....Therefore he said to the messengers of Ben-hadad, Tell my lord the king, all that you send for to your servants at the first I will do, but this thing I may not do' (1 Kgs. 20:3, 6, 9).

C.   "What is the meaning of 'whatsoever is pleasant in your eyes'? Is it not a scroll of the Torah?"

D.   But could it not be an idol?

E.   "Let it not enter your mind, for it is written, 'And all the leader and all the people said to him, Do not listen to him or consent' (1 Kgs. 20:8) [the elders being sages]."

F.   And perhaps they were elders [who were identified with] the shame [of the idol itself]?

G.   Is it not written, "And the saying pleased Absalom well and all the elders of Israel" (2 Sam. 17:4)? On this passage, said R. Joseph, "They were elders [associated with] the shame."

H   "In that passage, it is not written, 'And all the people,' while here it is written, 'And all the people.' It is not possible that among them were no righteous men, for it is written, 'Yet have I left seven thousand in Israel, all the knees which have not bowed to Baal and every mouth which has not kissed him' (1 Kgs. 19:18)."

CLXVIII.

A   Said R. Nahman, "Ahab was right in the middle [between wickedness and righteousness], as it is said, 'And the Lord said, Who shall persuade Ahab, that he may go up and fall at Ramoth-gildean? And one said in this manner, and one said in that manner' (1 Kgs. 22:20). [Freedman, p. 697, n. 1: This shows that it was a difficult matter to lure him to his fate, and that must have been because his righteousness equalled his guilt.]"

B.   To this proposition R. Joseph objected, "We speak of one concerning whom it is written, 'But there was none like Ahab, who sold himself to work wickedness in the sight of the Lord, whom Jezebel his wife stirred up' (1 Kgs. 21:25),

C.   on which passage it was repeated on Tannaite authority, 'Every day she would weigh out gold sheqels for idolatry,' and can you say that he was right in the middle?"

D.   "Rather, Ahab was generous with his money, and because he gave benefit to disciples of sages out of his property, half of his sins were forgiven."

CLXIX.

A.   "And there came forth the spirit and stood before the Lord and said, I will persuade him. And the Lord said to him, With what? And he said, I will go forth and I will be a lying spirit in the mouth of his prophets. And he said, You shall persuade him and also prevail. Go forth and do so" (1 Kgs. 22:21-23):

B.   What spirit was it?

C.   Said R. Yohanan, "It was the spirit of Naboth the Jezreelite."

D.   What is meant by "go forth"?

E.   Said Rabina, "Go forth from my precincts, as it is written, 'He who lies will not tarry in my sight' (Ps. 101:7)."

F.   Said R. Pappa, "This is in line with what people say, 'He who exacts vengeance destroys his house.'"

CLXX.

A.   "And Ahab made a grove, and Ahab did more to provoke the Lord God of Israel to anger than all of the kings of Israel that were before him" (1 Kgs. 16:33):

B.   Sad R. Yohanan, "It was that he wrote on the gates of Samaria, 'Ahab has denied the God of Israel.' Therefore he has no portion in the God of Israel."

CLXXI.

A.   "And he sought Ahaziah, and they caught him for he hid in Samaria" (2 Chr. 22:9):

B.   Said R. Levi, "He was blotting out the mentions of the divine name [in the Torah] and writing in their place the names of idols."

CLXXII.

A.   Manasseh – [Based on the root for the word "forget"] for he forgot the Lord.

B.   Another explanation: Manasseh – for he made Israel forget their father in heaven.

C.   And how do we know that he will not come to the world to come?

D.   As it is written, "Manasseh was twelve years old when he began to reign, and he reigned fifty-five years in Jerusalem...and he made a grove as did Ahab, king of Israel" (2 Kgs. 21:2-3).

E.   Just as Ahab has no share in the world to come, so Manasseh has no share in the world to come.

CLXXIII.

A.   *R. Judah says, "Manasseh has a portion in the world to come, since it is said, 'And he prayed to him and he was entreated of him...' (2 Chr. 33:13)"* [M. 11:2C-D]:

B.   Said R. Yohanan, "Both authorities [who dispute the fate of Manasseh] interpret the same verse of Scripture, as it is said, 'And I will cause to be removed to all the kingdoms of the earth, because of Manasseh, son of Hezekiah, king of Judah' (Jer. 15:4).

C. "One authority takes the view that it is 'on account of Manasseh,' who repented, while they did not repent.

D. "The other authority takes the view **[103A]** that it is 'because of Manasseh,' who did not repent."

CLXXIV.

A. Said R. Yohanan, "Whoever maintains that Manasseh has no share in the world to come weakens the hands of those who repent."

B. For a Tannaite authority repeated before R. Yohanan, "Manasseh repented for thirty-three years, as it is written, 'Manasseh was twelve years old when he began to reign, and he reigned fifty-five years in Jerusalem and he made a grove as did Ahab, king of Israel' (2 Kgs. 21:2-3).

C. "How long did Ahab rule? Twenty-two years. How long did Manasseh rule? Fifty-five years. Take away twenty-two years, and you are left with thirty-three."

CLXXV.

A. Said R. Yohanan in the name of R. Simeon b. Yohai, "What is the meaning of the verse of Scripture, 'And he prayed to him and an opening was made for him' (2 Chr. 33:13)?

B. "It should say, 'and he was entreated of him'!

C. "It teaches that the Holy One, blessed be He, made a kind of cave for him in the firmament, so as to receive him in repentance, despite the [contrary will of] the attribute of justice."

D. And said R. Yohanan in the name of R. Simeon b. Yohai, "What is the meaning of the verse of Scripture, 'In the beginning of the reign of Jehoiakim, son of Josiah, king of Judah' (Jer. 26:1)?

E. "And it is written, 'In the beginning of the reign of Zedekiah, king of Judah' (Jer. 28:1).

F. "And is it the case that, up to that time there were no kings?

G. "Rather, the Holy One, blessed be He, planned to return the world to [its beginning condition of] chaos and formlessness on account of Jehoiakim. When, however, he took a close look at his generation, his anger subsided.

H. "[Along these same lines], the Holy One, blessed be He, planned to return the world to chaos and formlessness on account of the generation of Zedekiah. But when he took a close look at Zedekiah, his anger subsided."

I. But with regard to Zedekiah, also, it is written, "And he did that which was evil in the sight of God" (2 Kgs. 24:19)?

J. He could have stopped others but did not do so.

K. And said R. Yohanan in the name of R. Simeon b. Yohai, "What is the meaning of the verse of Scripture, 'If a wise man contends with a foolish man, whether rage or laughter, there is no satisfaction' (Prov. 29:9)?

L. "Said the Holy One, blessed be He, 'I was angry with Ahaz and I handed him over to the kings of Damascus and he sacrificed and offered incense to their gods, as it is said, 'For he sacrificed to the gods of Damascus who smote him, and he said, Because the gods of the kinds of Syria help them, therefore will I sacrifice to them that they may help me. But they were the ruin of him and of all Israel' (2 Chr. 28:23).

M   "I smiled upon Amaziah and delivered the kings of Edom into his
     power, so he brought their gods and bowed down to them, as it is
     said, 'Now it came to pass, after Amaziah was come from the
     slaughter of the Edomites, that he brought the gods of the children
     of Seir and set them up to be his gods and bowed down himself
     before them and burned incense to them' (2 Chr. 25:14)."

N   Said R. Pappa, "This is in line with what people say: 'Weep for the
     one who doe not know, laugh for the one who does not know. Woe
     to him who does not know the difference between good and bad.'"

O   "And all the princes of the king of Babylonia came in and sat in the
     middle gate" (Jer. 39:3):

P.   Said R. Yohanan in the name of R. Simeon b. Yohai, "It was the
     place in which laws were mediated."

Q   Said R. Pappa, "That is in line with what people say: 'In the place
     in which the master hangs up his sword, the shepherd hangs up his
     pitcher.' [Freedman, p. 700, n. 3: Where the Jews decided upon
     their laws, there Nebuchadnezzer issued his decrees.]"

CLXXVI.

A   Said R. Hisda said R. Jeremiah bar Abba, "What is the meaning of
     the following verse: 'I went by the field of the slothful and by the
     vineyard of the man void of understanding. And lo, it was all
     grown over with thorns and nettles had covered the face thereof,
     and the stone wall thereof was broken down' (Prov. 24:30-31)?

B.   "'I went by the field of the slothful' – this speaks of Ahaz.

C   "'And by the vineyard of the man void of understanding' – this
     speaks of Manasseh.

D.   "'And lo, it was all grown over with thorns' – this refers to Amon.

E   "'And nettles had covered the face thereof' – this refers to
     Jehoiakim.

F.   "'And the stone wall thereof was broken down' – this refers to
     Zedekiah, in whose time the Temple was destroyed.

G   And said R. Hisda said R. Jeremiah bar Abba, "There are four
     categories who will not receive the face of the Presence of God:

H.   "The categories of scoffers, flatterers, liars, and slanderers.

I   "The category of scoffers, as it is written, 'He has stretched out his
     hand against scorners' (Hos. 7:5).

J.   "The category of flatterers, as it is written, 'He who speaks lies shall
     not be established in my sight' (Job. 13:16).

K   "The category of liars, as it is written, 'He who speaks lies shall not
     be established in my sight' (Ps. 101:7).

L   "The category of slanderers, as it is written, 'For you are not a God
     who has pleasure in wickedness; evil will not dwell with you' (Ps.
     5:5). 'You are righteous, O Lord, and evil will not dwell in your
     house.' [Ps. 5 addresses slander.]"

M   And said R. Hisda said R. Jeremiah bar Abba, "What is the meaning
     of the verse, 'There shall nor evil befall you, neither shall any
     plague come near your dwelling' (Ps. 91:10)?

N   "'There shall not evil befall you' means that the evil impulse will
     not rule over you.

O   "'Neither shall any plague come near your dwelling' means that, when you come home from a trip, you will never find that your wife is in doubt as to whether or not she is menstruating."

P.   "Another matter: 'There shall not evil befall you' means that bad dreams and fantasies will never frighten you.

Q   "'Neither shall any plague come near your dwelling' means that you will not have a son or a disciple who in public burns his food [that is, teaches something heretical].'

R.   "Up to this point is the blessing that his father had given him.

S.   "From this point forward comes the blessing that his mother had given to him: 'For he shall give his angels charge over you, to keep you in all your ways. They shall bear you in their hands....You shall tread upon the lion and the adder' (Ps. 91:10).

T.   "Up to this point is the blessing that his mother gave him.

U.   "From this point onward comes the blessing that heaven gave him:

V.   "'[103B] Because he has set his love upon me, therefore will I deliver him. I will set him on high, because he has known my name. He shall call upon me, and I will answer him. I will be with him in trouble. I will deliver him and honor him. With long life will I satisfy him and show him my salvation' (Ps. 91:14-16)."

CLXXVII.

A   Said R. Simeon b. Laqish, "What is the meaning of the following verse of Scripture: 'And from the wicked their light is withheld, and the high arm shall be broken' (Job 38:15)?

B.   "Why is the letter *ayin* in the word for wicked suspended [in the text, being written above the level of the line, making it read 'poor,' rather than 'wicked' (Freedman, p. 701, n. 10)]?

C   "When a person becomes poor below, he is made poor above. [Freedman, p. 701, n. 11: Where one earns the disapproval of man, it is proof that he has earned the disapproval of God too.]"

D.   Then the letter should not be written at all?

E.   R. Yohanan and R. Eleazar: one said, "It is because of the honor owing to David."

F.   The other said, "It is because the honor owing to Nehemiah B. Hachaliah. [Freedman, p. 702, n. 1: Both had many enemies yet were truly righteous men.]"

CLXXVIII.

A.   Our rabbis have taught on Tannaite authority:

B.   Manasseh would teach the book of Leviticus from fifty-five viewpoints, corresponding to the years of his reign.

C.   Ahab did so in eighty-five ways.

D.   Jeroboam did so in a hundred and three ways.

CLXXIX.

A.   It has been taught on Tannaite authority:

B.   R. Meir would say, "Absalom has no share in the world to come,

C   "as it is said, 'And they smote Absalom and slew him' (2 Sam. 18:15).

D.   "'They smote him' in this world.

E.   "'And they slew him' in the world to come."

CLXXX.

A.   It has been taught on Tannaite authority:

B.   R. Simeon b. Eleazar says in the name of R. Meir, "Ahaz, Ahaziah, and all the kings of Israel concerning whom it is written, 'And he did what was evil in the sight of the Lord' will not live or be judged [in the world to come]."

CLXXXI.

A.   "Moreover Manasseh shed much innocent blood, until he had filled Jerusalem from one end to another, beside his sin wherewith he made Judah to sin, in doing that which was evil in the sight of the Lord" (2 Kgs. 21:16):

B.   Here [in Babylonia] it is explained that he killed Isaiah, [and that is the sin at hand].

C.   In the West they say that it was that he made an idol as heavy as a thousand men, and every day it killed them all.

D.   In accord with whose position is the following statement made by Rabbab b. b. Hana: "The soul of a righteous man is balanced against the whole world"?

E.   In accord with whom? With the position of him who has said that he had killed Isaiah.

CLXXXII.

A.   [It is written,] "And he set the graven image" (2 Chr. 33:7), and it is stated, "And the graves and the graven images which he had set up" (2 Chr. 33:19). [was there one image or were there many?]

B.   Said R. Yohanan, "In the beginning he made one face for it, and in the end he made four faces for it, so that the Presence of God should see it and become angry.

C.   "Ahaz set it up in the upper chamber, as it is written, 'And the altars that were on top of the upper chamber of Ahaz' (2 Kgs. 23:13).

D.   "Manasseh set it in the Temple, as it is written, 'And he set up a graven image of the grove that he had made in the house, of which the Lord said to David and to Solomon his son, in this house and in Jerusalem which I have chosen out of all tribes of Israel will I put my name forever' (2 Kgs. 21:7).

E.   "Amon put it into the Holy of Holies, as it is said, 'For the bed is shorter than that a man can stretch himself on it, and the covering narrower than that he can wrap himself in it' (Isa. 28:20)."

F.   What is the sense of, "For the bed is shorter than that one can stretch himself on it"?

G.   Said R. Samuel bar Nahmani said R. Jonathan, "This bed is too short for two neighbors to rule over it at one time."

H.   What is the sense of "And the covering is narrower"?

I.   Said R. Samuel bar Nahmani, "When R. Jonathan would reach this verse of Scripture, he would cry. 'He of whom it is written, "He gathers the waters of the sea together as a heap" (Ps. 33:7) – should a molten statue rival him!'"

CLXXXIII.

A.   Ahaz annulled the sacrificial service and sealed the Torah, for it is said, "Bind up the testimony, seal the Torah among my disciples" (Isa. 8:16).

B.   Manasseh blotted out the mentions of the divine Name and destroyed the altar.

C. Amon burned the Torah and let spiderwebs cover the altar.

D. Ahaz permitted consanguineous marriages.

E. Manasseh had sexual relations with his sister.

F. Amon had sexual relations with his mother, as it is said, "For Amon sinned very much" (2 Chr. 33:23).

G. R. Yohanan and R. Eleazar: one said that he burned the Torah.

H. The other said that he had sexual relations with his mother.

I. His mother said to him, "Do you have any pleasure from the place from which you came forth?"

J. He said to her, "Am I doing anything except to spite my creator?"

K. When Jehoiakim came, he said, "The ones who came before me really did not know how to anger him. Do we need him for anything more than his light? We have pure gold, which we use [for light], so let him take away his light."

L. They said to him, "But do not silver and gold belong to him, as it is written, 'Mine is the silver, and mine is the gold, saith the Lord of hosts' (Hag. 2:8)."

M. "He said to them, "He has already given them to us, as it is said, 'The heavens are the Lord's, and the earth he has given to the children of men' (Ps. 115:16)."

CLXXXIV.

A. Said Raba to Rabbah bar Mari, "On what account did they not count Jehoiakim [among those who do not get the world to come]?

B. "For it is written of him, 'And the remaining words of Jehoiakim and the abomination which he wrought and that which was found up upon him' (2 Chr. 36:8)."

C. What is the sense of "that which was found upon him" (2 Chr. 36:8)?

D. R. Yohanan and R. Eleazar: one said that he engraved the name of his idol on his penis.

E. The other said that he engraved the name of Heaven on his penis.

F. [Rabbah b. Mari] said to him, "As to the matter of kings, I have not heard any answer. But as to ordinary people, I have heard an answer.

G. "Why did they not count Micah? Because he made his bread available to travelers, for it is said, 'Every traveler turned to the Levites.'"

H. "And he shall pad through the sea with affliction and shall smite the waves in the sea" (Zech. 10:11).

I. Said R. Yohanan, "This speaks of the idol of Micah."

J. It has been taught on Tannaite authority:

K. R. Nathan says, "From Hareb to Shiloah is three *mils,* and the smoke of the pile and the smoke of the image of Micah mixed together. The ministering angels wanted to drive [Micah] off. The Holy One, blessed be He, said to them, 'Leave him alone, for his bread is made available to travelers.'"

L. And for the same matter those involved in the matter of the concubine at Gibeah (Judg. 19) were punished.

M. Said the Holy One, blessed be He, "On account of the honor owing to me you did not protest, and on account of the honor owing to a mortal you protested."

CLXXXV.

A   Said R. Yohanan in the name of R. Yosé b. Qisma, "Great is a mouthful of food, for it set a distance between two families and Israel,

B.   "as it is written, '[An Ammonite or Moabite shall not enter the congregation of the Lord]...because they did not meet you with bread and water in the way when you came forth from Egypt' (Deut. 33:4-5)."

C.   And R. Yohanan on his own said, "It creates distance among those who are close; it draws near those who are afar; it blinds the eye [of God] from the wicked; it makes the Presence of God rest even on the prophets of Baal, and it makes an unwitting offense appear to be deliberate [if it is performed in connection with care of the wayfarer]."

D.   [Now to spell out the foregoing:] "It creates distance among those who are close":

E.   [Proof derives] from [104A] the case of Ammon and Moab.

F.   "It draws near those who are afar":

G.   [Proof derives] from the case of Jethro.

H   For said R. Yohanan, "As a reward for saying, 'Call him that he may eat bread' (Ex. 2:20), [Jethro]'s descendants had the merit of taking seats [as authorities] in the chamber of the hewn stones, it is said, 'And the family of the scribes which dwell at Jabez, the Tirathites, the Shimeathites, and Suchathites. These are the Kenites that came of Hemath, the father of the house of Rechan' (1 Chr. 2:55).

I.   "And elsewhere it is written, 'And the children of the Kenite, Moses' father-in-law, went up out of the city of palm trees with the children of Judah into the wilderness of Judah, which lies in the south of Arab, and they went and dwelt among the people' (Judges 1:16). [Freedman, p. 705, n. 10: This shows that the Kenites were descended from Jethro and they sat in the hall of hewn stones as scribes and sanhedrin.]"

J.   "It blinds the eye [of God] from the wicked":

K.   [Proof derives] from the case of Micah.

L.   "It makes the Presence of God rest even on the prophets of Baal":

M   [Proof derives] from the friend of Iddo, the prophet, for it is written, "And it came to pass, as they sat at the table, that the word of the Lord came to the prophet that brought him back (1 Kgs. 13:20). [Freedman, p. 706, n. 2: He was a prophet of Baal, yet God's word came to him as a reward for his hospitality.]"

N.   "And it makes an unwitting offense appear to be deliberate":

O.   [Proof derives] from what R. Judah said Rab, said, "Had Jonathan only brought David two loaves of bread, Nob, the city of priests, would not have been put to death, and Doeg the Edomite would not have been troubled, and Saul and his three sons would not have been killed. [Freedman, p. 706, n. 4: For had he provided him with food, he would not have taken any from Ahimelech. Thus all this happened, though Jonathan's initial offense was due to an oversight.]"

CLXXXVI.

A.   Why did they not list Ahaz [at M. 11:2]?

B.   Said R. Jeremiah bar Abba, "Because he was positioned between two righteous men, between Hotham and Hezekiah."

C.   R. Joseph said, "Because he had the capacity to be ashamed on account of Isaiah, as it is said, 'Then said the Lord to Isaiah, Go forth now to meet Ahaz, you and Shear-jashub your son, at the end of the conduit of the upper pool in the highway of the field of the fuller's trough' (Isa. 7:3)."

D.   What is the source of "fuller's trough"?

E.   Some say, "He hid his face [using the same consonants] and fled."

F.   Some say, "He dragged a fuller's trough [the meaning of the word in general] on his head and fled."

CLXXXVII.

A.   Why did they not list Amon [at M. 11:2]?

B.   On account of the honor owing to Josiah.

C.   In that case, they also should not have listed Manasseh, on account of the honor owing to Hezekiah.

D.   The son imparts merit to the father, but the father does not give any merit to the son, for it is written, "Neither is there any one who can deliver out of my hand" (Deut. 32:39).

E.   Abraham cannot save Ishmael. Isaac cannot save Esau.

F.   If you go that far, then Ahaz also was omitted from the list on account of the honor owing to Hezekiah.

CLXXXVIII.

A.   And on that account did they not list Jehoiakim?

B.   It is on account of what R. Hiyya b. R. Abuyyah said.

C.   For R. Hiyya b. R. Abuyyah said, "It was written on the skull of Jehoiakim, 'This and yet another.'"

D.   The grandfather of R. Perida found a skull tossed at the gates of Jerusalem, on which was written, "This and yet another."

E.   He buried it, but it did not stay buried, and he buried it again but it did not stay buried.

F.   He said, "It must be the skull of Jehoiakim, for it is written in that connection, 'He shall be buried with the burial of an ass, drawn and cast forth beyond the gates of Jerusalem' (Jer. 22:19)."

G.   He said, "Still, he was a king, and it is not proper to treat him lightly."

H.   He wrapped the skull in silk and put it in a closet. His wife saw it. She thought, 'This is [the bone of] his first wife, whom he has not forgotten."

I.   She lit the oven and burned it up, and that is the meaning of what is written, "This and yet another." [Freedman, p. 707, n. 2: These indignities made sufficient atonement for him that he should share in the future world.]

CLXXXIX.

A.   It has been taught on Tannaite authority:

B.   R. Simeon b. Eleazar said, "On account of [Hezekiah's] statement, 'And I have done that which was good in your sight,' (2 Kgs. 20:3), [he had further to ask,] 'What shall be the sign [that the Lord will heal me]?' (2 Kgs. 20:9)."

C.   "On account of the statement, 'What shall be the sign?' (2 Kgs. 20:9), gentiles ate at his table.

D.   "On account of gentiles' eating at his table, (2 Kgs. 20:17-18), he made his children go into exile."

E.   That statement supports what Hezekiah said.

F.   For Hezekiah said, "Whoever invites an idolator into his house and serves him [as host] causes his children to go into exile, as it is said, 'And of your sons who will issue from you, which you shall beget, shall they take away; and they shall be eunuchs in the palace of the king of Babylonia' (2 Kgs. 20:18)."

G   "And Hezekiah was happy about them and showed them the treasure house, the silver and gold, spices and precious ointment" (Isa. 39:2):

H   Said Rab, "What is the sense of 'his treasure house'? It means, his wife, who served them drinks."

I.   Samuel said, "His treasury is what he showed them."

J.   R. Yohanan said, "His weapons, which had the capacity to consume other weapons, is what he showed them."

CXC.

A.   "How does the city sit solitary" (Lam. 1:1):

B.   Said Rabbah said R. Yohanan, "On what account were the Israelites smitten with the word 'how' [that begins the dirge]? [Since the numerical value of the letters of the word equals thirty-six], it is because they violated the thirty-six rules in the Torah that are penalized by extirpation."

C   Said R. Yohanan, "Why were they smitten [with a dirge that is] alphabetical?

D.   "Because they violated the Torah, which is given through the alphabet. [Freedman, p. 708, n. 6: Its words are formed from the alphabet.]"

CXCI.

A.   "Sit solitary" (Lam. 1:1):

B.   Said Rabbah said R. Yohanan, "Said the Holy One, blessed be He, 'I said, "Israel then shall dwell in safety alone, the foundation of Jacob shall be upon a land of corn and wine, also his heavens shall drop down dew" (Deut. 33:28) [so that sitting solitary was supposed to be a blessing (Freedman, p. 708, n. 8)], but now, where they dwell will be alone.'"

CXCII.

A.   "The city that was full of people" (Lam. 1:1):

B.   Said Rabbah said R. Yohanan, "For they used to marry off a minor girl to an adult male, or an adult woman to a minor boy, so that they should have many children. [But two minors would not marry.]"

CXCIII.

A.   "She is become as a widow" (Lam. 1:1):

B.   Said R. Judah said Rab, "Like a widow, but not actually a widow, but like a woman whose husband has gone overseas and plans to return to her."

CXCIV.

A   "She was great among the nations and princess among the provinces" (Lam. 1:1):

B.   Said R. Rabbah said R. Yohanan, "Everywhere they go they become princes of their masters."

CXCV.

A.   Our rabbis have taught on Tannaite authority:

B.   There is the case of two men who were captured on Mount Carmel. The kidnapper was walking behind them. [104B] One of them said to his fellow, "The camel that is walking before us is blind in one eye, it is carrying two skins, one of wine and one of oil, and of the two men that are leading it, one is an Israelite and the other is a gentile."

C.   The kidnapper said to them, "Stiff-necked people, how do you know?"

D.   They said to him, "As to the camel, it is eating from the grass before it on the side on which it can see, but on the side on which it cannot see, it is not eating.

E.   "And it is carrying two skins, one of wine and one of oil. The one of wine drips and the drippings are absorbed in the ground, while the one of oil drips, and the drippings remain on the surface.

F.   "And as the two men who are leading it, one is a gentile and one is an Israelite. The gentile relieves himself right on the road, while the Israelite turns to the side [of the road]."

G.   The man ran after them and found that things were just as they had said. He came and kissed them on their head and brought them to his house. He made a great banquet for them and danced before them, saying, "Blessed is he who chose the seed of Abraham and gave part of his wisdom to them, and wherever they go they become the princess over their masters."

H.   He sent them away and they went home in peace.

CXCVI.

A.   "She weeps, yes, she weeps in the night" (Lam. 1:2):

B.   Why these two acts of weeping?

C.   Said Rabbah said R. Yohanan, "One is for the first Temple and the other is for the second Temple."

D.   "At night":

E.   On account of things done in the night, as it is said, "And all the congregation lifted up their voice and cried, and the people wept that night [at the spies' false report]" (Num. 14:1).

F.   Said Rabbah said R. Yohanan, "That was the ninth of Ab. Said the Holy One, blessed be He, to Israel, 'You have wept tears for nothing. I now shall set up for you weeping for generations to come.'"

G.   Another interpretation of "At night":

H.   Whoever cries at night will find that his voice is heard.

I.   Another interpretation of "At night":

J.   Whoever cries at night finds that the stars and planets will cry with him.

K.   Another interpretation of "At night":

L.   Whoever cries at night finds that whoever hears his voice will cry along with him.

M.   That was the case of a woman in the neighborhood of Rabban Gamaliel, whose child died. She was weeping by night on account of the child. Rabban Gamaliel heard her voice and cried with her, until his eyelashes fell out. The next day, his disciples recognized what had happened and removed the woman from his neighborhood.

CXCVII.
- A. "And her tears are on her cheeks" (Lam. 1:2):
- B. Said Rabbah said R. Yohanan, "It is like a woman who weeps for the husband of her youth, as it is said, 'Lamentation like a virgin girded with sackcloth for the husband of her youth' (Joel 1:8)."

CXCVIII.
- A. "Her adversaries are the chief" (Lam. 1:5):
- B. Said Rabbah said R. Yohanan, "Whoever persecutes Israel becomes head [that is, comes to the fore],
- C. "as it is said, 'Nevertheless, there shall be no weariness for her that oppressed her. In the former time he brought into contempt the land of Zebulun and the land of Naphtali, but in the latter time he has made it glorious, by way of the sea, beyond Jordan, the circuit of the nations' (Isa. 8:23)."
- D. Said Rabbah said R. Yohanan, "Whoever oppresses Israel does not get tired."

CXCIX.
- A. "May it not happen to you, all passersby" (Lam. 1:12)."
- B. Said Rabbah said R. Yohanan, "On this basis we find in the Torah support for saying [when reciting woes], 'May it not happen to you.'"

CC.
- A. "All passersby" (Lam. 1:12):
- B. Said R. Amram said Rab, "They have turned me into one of those who transgress the law.
- C. "For in respect to Sodom, it is written, 'And the Lord rained upon Sodom and upon Gomorrah brimstone and fire' (Gen. 19:24). But in respect to Jerusalem it is written, 'From above he has sent fire against my bones and it prevails against them' (Lam. 1:13). [Freedman, p. 711, n. 4: Thus Jerusalem was treated as Sodom and Gomorrah.]"
- D. "For the iniquity of the daughter of my people is greater than the sin of Sodom" (Lam. 4:6):
- E. And is any sort of favoritism shown in such a matter [since Jerusalem was left standing, Sodom was wiped out]?
- F. Said Rabbah said R. Yohanan, "[Not at all, in fact] there was a further measure [of punishment] directed against Jerusalem but not against Sodom.
- G. "For with respect to Sodom, it is written, 'Behold, this was the iniquity of your sister, Sodom, pride, fullness of bread, and abundance of idleness was in her and in her daughters, neither did she strengthen the hand of the poor and the needy' (Ezek. 16:49).
- H. "With respect to Jerusalem, by contrast, it is written, 'The hands of merciful women have boiled their own children' (Lam. 4:10). [Freedman, p. 711, n. 8: Jerusalem suffered extreme hunger, which Sodom never did, and this fact counterbalanced her being spared total destruction.]"

CCI.

A. "The Lord has trodden under foot all my mighty men in the midst of me" (Lam. 1:15):

B. This is like a man who says to his fellow, "This coin has been invalidated."

C. "All your enemies have opened their mouths against you" (Lam. 2:16):

D. Said Rabbah said R. Yohanan, "On what account does the letter P come before the letter *ayin* [in the order of verses in the chapter of Lamentation, while in the alphabet, the *ayin* comes before the P]?

E. "It is on account of the spies, who said with their mouths [and the word for mouth begins with a P] what their eyes had not seen [and the word for eye begins with an *ayin*]."

CCII.

A. "They eat my people as they eat bread and do not call upon the Lord" (Ps. 14:4):

B. Said Rabbah said R. Yohanan, "Whoever eats the bread of Israelites tastes the flavor of bread, and who does not eat the bread of Israelites does not taste the flavor of bread."

CCIII.

A. "They do not call upon the Lord" (Ps. 14:4):

B. Rab said, "This refers to judges."

C. And Samuel said, "This refers to those who teach children."

CCIV.

A. Who counted [the kings and commoners of M. 11:2A]?

B. Said R. Ashi, "The men of the great assembly counted them."

CCV.

A. Said R. Judah said Rab, "They wanted to count yet another [namely, Solomon], but an apparition of his father's face came and prostrated himself before them. But they paid no attention to him. A fire came down from heaven and licked around their chairs, but they did not pay attention. An echo come forth and as said to them, 'Do you see a man diligent in his business? He shall stand before kings, he shall not stand before mean men' (Prov. 22:29).

B. "'He who gave precedence to my house over his house, and not only so, but built my house over a span of seven years, while building his own house over a span of thirteen years, "he shall stand before kings, he shall not stand before mean men."'"

C. "But they paid no attention to that either.

D. "An echo came forth, saying, 'Should it be according to your mind? He will recompense it, whether you refuse or whether you choose, and not I' (Job 34:33)."

CCVI.

A. Those who interpret signs [symbolically] would say, "All of them [listed at M. 11:2] will enter the world to come, as it is said, 'Gilead is mine, Manasseh is mine, Ephraim also is the strength of my head, Judah is my lawgiver, Moab is my washpot, over Edom will I cast my shoe, Philistia, you triumph because of me' (Ps. 60:9-10):

B. "'Gideon is mine' speaks of Ahab, who fell at Ramoth-gilead.

C. "'Manasseh' – literally.

D.   "'Ephraim also is the strength of my head' speaks of Jeroboam, who comes from Ephraim.

E.   "'Judah is my lawgiver' refers to Ahitophel, [105A] who comes from Judah.

F.   "'Moab is my washpot' refers to Gehazi, who was smitten on account of matters having to with washing.

G.   "'Over Edom will I cast my shoe' refers to Doeg the Edomite.

H   "'Philistia, you triumph because of me': the Ministering angels said before the Holy One, blessed be He, 'Lord of the world, if David should come, who killed the Philistine, and who gave Gath to them as an inheritance, what are you going to do to him?'

I.   "He said to them, 'It is my task to make them friends of one another.'"

CCVII.

A.   "Why is this people of Jerusalem slidden back by a perpetual backsliding" (Jer. 8:5):

B.   Said Rab, "The community of Israel answered the prophet with a lasting reply [a play on the words for backsliding and answer, using the same root].

C.   "The prophet said to Israel, 'Return in repentance. Your fathers who sinned – where are they now?'

D.   "They said to him, 'And your prophets, who did not sin, where are they now? For it is said, "Your fathers, where are they? and the prophets, do they live forever" (Zech. 1:5)?'

E.   "He said to them, 'They repented and confessed as it is said, "But my words and my statutes, which I commanded my servants the prophets, did they not take hold of your fathers? And they returned and said, like as the Lord of hosts thought to do unto us, according to our ways and according to our doings, so has he dealt with us" (Zech. 1:6).'"

F.   Samuel said, "Ten men came and sat before him. He said to them, 'Return in repentance.'

G.   "They said to him, 'If a master has sold his slave, or a husband has divorced his wife, does one party have any further claim upon the other? [Surely not.]' [Freedman, p. 714, n. 3: Since God has sold us to Nebuchadnezzar, he has no further claim upon us, and we have no cause to repent. This in Samuel's view was the victorious answer.]

H   "Said the Holy One, blessed be He, to the prophet, 'Go and say to them, "Thus says the Lord, where is the bill of your mother's divorcement, whom I have put away? Or which of my creditors is it to whom I have sold you? Behold for your iniquities you have sold yourselves, and for you transgressions is your mother put away" (Isa. 50:1).'"

I.   And this is in line with what R. Simeon b. Laqish said, "What is the meaning of what is written, 'David my servant [and] Nebuchadnezzar my servant' (Jer. 43:10)?

J.   "It is perfectly clear before him who spoke and brought the world into being that the Israelites were going to say this, and therefore the Holy One, blessed be He, went ahead and called him 'his servant.' [Why so?] If a slave acquires property, to whom does the slave belong, and to whom does the property belong?' [Freedman, p. 714, n. 7: Even if God had sold them to Nebuchadnezzar, they still belong to God.]'"

CCVIII.

A. "And that which comes into your mind shall not be at all, that you say, We will be as the heathen, as the families of the countries, to serve wood and stone. As I live, says the Lord God, surely with a mighty hand and with an outstretched arm, and with fury poured out, will I rule over you" (Ezek. 20:32-33):

B. Said R. Nahman, "Even with such anger may the All-Merciful rage against us, so long as he redeems us."

CCIX.

A. "For he chastises him to discretion and his God teaches him" (Isa. 28:26):

B. Said Rabbah bar Hanah, "Said the prophet to Israel, 'Return in repentance.'

C. "They said to him, 'We cannot do so. The impulse to do evil rules over us.'

D. "He said to them, 'Reign in your desire.'

E. "They said to him, 'Let his God teach us.'"

CCX.

A. *Four ordinary folk: Balaam, Doeg, Ahitophel, and Gehazi [M. 11:2F]:*

B. [The name] Balaam [means] not with [the rest of] the people [using the same consonants], [who will inherit the world to come].

C. Another interpretation: Balaam, because he devoured the people.

D. "Son of Beor" means that he had sexual relations with a cow [a play on the consonants of the word for Beor].

CCXI.

A. It was taught on Tannaite authority:

B. Beor, Cushan-rishathaim, and Laban, the Syrian, are one and the same person.

C. Beor: because he had sexual relations with a cow.

D. Cushan-rishathaim [two acts of wickedness], for he committed two acts of wickedness against Israel, one in the time of Jacob and one in the time of the Judges.

E. But what was his real name? It was Laban the Aramaean.

CCXII

A. It is written, "The son of Beor" (Num. 22:50), but it also is written, "His son was Beor" (Num. 24:3).

B. Said R. Yohanan, "His father was his son as to prophecy."

CCXIII.

A. Balaam is the one who will not come to the world to come. Lo, others will come.

B. In accord with whose view is the Mishnah passage at hand?

C. It represents the view of R. Joshua.

D. For it has been taught on Tannaite authority:

E. [In Tosefta's version:] **R. Eliezer says, "None of the gentiles has a portion in the world to come,**

F. **"as it is said, 'The wicked shall return to Sheol. All the gentiles who forget God' (Ps. 9:17).**

G. "'The wicked shall return to Sheol' – these are the wicked Israelites.

H. "'And all the gentiles who forget God' – these are the nations."

I. Said to him R. Joshua, "If it had been written, 'The wicked shall return to Sheol – all the gentiles' and then said nothing further, I should have maintained as you do.

J. "Now that it is in fact <u>written, 'All the gentiles who forget God,'</u> it indicates that there also are righteous people among the nations of the world who have a portion in the world to come" [T. San. 13:2E-J].

K. And that wicked man [Balaam] also gave a sign concerning his own fate, when he said, "Let me die the death of the righteous" (Num. 23:10).

L. [He said,] "If my soul dies the death of the righteous, may my future be like his, and if not, 'Then behold I go to my people'" (Num. 24:14)."

CCXIV.

A. "And the elders of Moab and the elders of Midian departed" (Num. 22:7):

B. It was taught on Tannaite authority:

C. There was never peace between Midian and Moab. The matter may be compared to two dogs who were in a kennel, barking at one another.

D. A wolf came and attacked one. The other said, "If I do not help him today, he will kill him, and tomorrow he will come against me."

E. So the two dogs went and killed the wolf.

F. Said R. Pappa, "This is in line with what people say: 'The weasel and the cat can make a banquet on the fat of the unlucky.'"

CCXV.

A. "And the princess of Moab abode with Balaam" (Num. 22:8):

B. And as to the princess of Midian, where had they gone?

C. When he said to them, "Lodge here this night and I will bring you word again [as the Lord shall speak to me]," (Num. 22:8), they said, "Does any father hate his son? [No chance!]"

CCXVI.

A. Said R. Nahman, "Hutzbah, even against heaven, serves some good. To begin with, it is written, 'You shall not go with them' (Num. 22:12), and then it is said, 'Rise up and go with them' (Num. 22:20)."

B. Said R. Sheshet, "Hutzbah is dominion without a crown.

C. "For it is written, 'And I am this day weak, though anointed king, and these men, the sons of Zeruiah, be too hard for me' (2 Sam. 3:39). [Freedman, p. 717, n. 1: Thus their boldness and impudence outweighed sovereignty.]"

CCXVII.

A. Said R. Yohanan, "Balaam had one crippled foot, for it is written, 'And he walked haltingly' (Num. 23:3).

B. "Samson had two crippled feet, as it is said, 'An adder in the path that bites the horses' heels' (Gen. 49:17). [Freedman, p. 717, n. 3: This was a prophecy of Samson. "An adder in the path' is taken to mean that he would have to slither along like an adder, being lame in both feet.]

C.   "Balaam was blind in one eye, as it is said, 'Whose eye is open' (Num. 24:3).

D.   "He practiced enchantment with his penis.

E.   "Here it is written, 'Falling but having his eyes open' (Num. 24:3), and elsewhere: 'And Haman was fallen on the bed whereon Esther was' (Est. 7:8)."

F.   It has been stated on Amoraic authority:

G.   Mar Zutra said, "He practiced enchantment with his penis."

H.   Mar, son of Rabina, said, "He had sexual relations with his ass."

I.   As to the view that he practiced enchantment with his penis it is as we have just now stated.

J.   As to the view that he had sexual relations with his ass:

K.   Here it is written, "He bowed, he lay down as a lion and as a great lion" (Num. 24:9), and elsewhere it is written, "At her feet [105B] he bowed, he fell" (Jud. 5:27)."

CCXVIII.

A.   "He knows the mind of the Most High" (Num. 24:16):

B.   Now if he did not know the mind of his own beast, how could he have known the mind of the Most High?

C.   What is the case of the mind of his beast?

D.   People said to him, "What is the reason that you did not ride on your horse?"

E.   He said to them, "I put it out to graze in fresh pasture."

F.   [The ass] said to him, "Am I not your ass" (Num. 22:30). [That shows he rode an ass, not a horse.]

G.   "[You are] merely for carrying loads."

H.   "Upon whom you rode" (Num. 22:30).

I.   "It was a happenstance."

J.   "Ever since I was yours, until this day" (Num. 22:30).

K.   [The ass continued,] "And not only so, but I serve you for sexual relations by night."

L.   Here it is written, "Did I ever do so to you" (Num. 22:30) and elsewhere it is written, "Let her serve as his companion." [The same word is used, proving that sexual relations took place as with David and the maiden in his old age.]

M.   Then what is the meaning of the statement, "He knows the mind of the Most High" (Num. 24:16)?

N.   He knew how to tell the exact time at which the Holy One, blessed be He, was angry.

O.   That is in line with what the prophet said to Israel, "O my people, remember now what Balak, king of Moab, consulted, and what Balaam the son of Beor answered him from Shittim to Gilgal, that you may know the righteousness of the Lord" (Mic. 6:5).

P.   What is the meaning of the statement, "That you may know the righteousness of the Lord" (Mic. 6:5)?

Q.   Said the Holy One, blessed be He, to Israel, "Know that I have done many acts of charity with you, that I did not get angry with you in the time of the wicked Balaam.

R. "For if I had become angry during all those days, there would not remain out of (the enemies of) Israel a shred or a remnant."

S. That is in line with what Balaam said to Balak, "How shall I curse one whom God has not cursed? Or shall I rage, when the Lord has not raged?" (Num. 23:8).

T. This teaches that for all those days the Lord had not been angry.

U. But: "God is angry every day" (Ps. 7:12).

V. And how long does his anger last? It is a moment, for it is said, "For his anger endures but a moment, but his favor is life" (Ps. 30:5).

W. If you wish, I shall propose, "Come, my people, enter into your chambers and shut your doors about you, hide yourself as it were for a brief moment, until the indignation be past" (Isa. 26:20).

X. When is he angry? It is in the first three hours [of the day], when the comb of the cock is white.

Y. But it is white all the time?

Z. All the other time it has red streaks, but when God is angry, there are no red streaks in it.

CCXIX.

A There was a *min* living in the neighborhood of R. Joshua b. Levi, who bothered him a great deal. One day he took a chicken and tied it up at the foot of his bed and sat down. He said, "When that moment comes [at which God is angry], I shall curse him."

B. When that moment came, he was dozing. He said, "What this teaches is that it is improper [to curse], for it is written, 'Also to punish is not good for the righteous' (Prov. 17:26) – even in the case of a *min*."

CCXX.

A A Tannaite authority in the name of R. Meir [said], "When the sun shines and the kings put their crowns on their heads and bow down to the sun, forthwith he is angry."

CCXXI.

A "And Balaam rose up in the morning and saddled his ass" (Num. 22:21):

B. A Tannaite authority taught in the name of R. Simeon b. Eleazar, "That love annuls the order of proprieties [we learn] from the case of Abraham.

C. "For it is written, 'And Abraham rose up early in the morning and saddled his ass' (Gen. 22:3) [not waiting for the servant to do so].

D. "And that hatred annuls the order of proprieties [we learn] from the case of Balaam.

E. "For it is said, 'And Balaam rose up early in the morning and saddled his ass' (Num. 22:21)."

CCXXII.

A Said R. Judah said Rab, "Under all circumstances a person should engage in study of Torah and practice of religious duties, even if it is not for their own sake, for out of doing these things not for their own sake one will come to do them for their own sake."

B. For as a reward for the forty-two offerings that Balak offered, he had the merit that Ruth should come forth from him.

C. Said R. Yosé bar Huna, "Ruth was the daughter of Egion, grandson of Balak, king of Moab."

CCXXIII.

A. Said Raba to Rabbah bar Mari, "It is written, '[And moreover the king's servants came to bless our lord king David, saying] God make the name of Solomon better than your name, and make his throne greater than your throne' (1 Kgs. 1:47).

B. "Now is this appropriate to speak in such a way to a king?"

C. He said to him, "What they meant is, 'as good as....' [Freedman, p. 720, n. 2: 'God make the name of Solomon illustrious even as the nature of your own and make his throne great according to the character of your throne.']

D. "For if you do not say this, then [take account of the following:] 'Blessed above women shall be Jael, the wife of Heber the Kenite, blessed shall she be above women in the tent' (Jud. 5:24).

E. "Now who are the women in the tent? They are Sarah, Rebecca, Rachel, and Leah.

F. "Is it appropriate to speak in such a way? Rather, what is meant is 'as good as...,' and here, too, the sense is, 'as good as....'"

G. That statement differs from what R. Yosé bar Honi said.

H. For R. Yosé bar Honi said, "One may envy anybody except for his son and his disciple.

I. "One learns the fact about one's son from the case of Solomon.

J. "And as to the case of one's disciple, if you wish, I shall propose, 'Let a double quantity of your spirit be upon me' (2 Kgs. 2:9).

K. "Or if you wish, I shall derive proof from the following: 'And he laid his hands upon him and gave him a charge' (Num. 27:23)."

CCXXIV.

A. "And the Lord put a thing in the mouth of Balaam" (Num. 23:5):

B. R. Eleazar says, "It was an angel."

C. R. Jonathan said, "It was a hook."

CCXXV.

A. Said R. Yohanan, "From the blessing said by that wicked man, you learn what he had in his heart.

B. "He wanted to say that they should not have synagogues and schoolhouses: 'How goodly are your tents, O Jacob' (Num. 24:5).

C. "[He wanted to say that] the Presence of God should not dwell on them: 'And your tabernacles, O Israel' (Num. 24:5).

D. "[He wanted to say] that their kingdom should not last [thus, to the contrary]: 'As the valleys are they spread forth' (Num. 24:6);

E. "...that they should have no olives and vineyards: 'As the trees of aloes which the Lord has planted' (Num. 24:6);

F. "...that their kings should not be tall: 'And as cedar trees beside the waters' (Num. 24:6).

G. "...That they should not have a king succeed his father as king: 'He shall pour the water out of his buckets' (Num. 24:6).

H. "...That their kingdom should not rule over others: 'And his seed shall be in many waters' (Num. 24:6).

I. "...That their kingdom should not be strong: 'And his king shall be higher than Agag' (Num. 24:6).

J.   "...That their kingdom not be fearful: 'And his kingdom shall be exalted' (Num. 24:6)."

K.   Said R. Abba b. Kahana, "All of them were [ultimately] turned into a curse, except for the one on the synagogues and schoolhouses, as it is said, 'But the Lord your God turned the curse into a blessing for you, because the Lord your God loved you' (Deut. 23:6).

L.   "'*The* curse' – not the [other] curses...."

CCXXVI.

A.   Said R. Samuel bar Nahmani said R. Jonathan, "What is the meaning of the verse of Scripture: 'Faithful are the wounds of a friend, but the kisses of an enemy are deceitful' (Prov. 27:6)?

B.   "Better was the curse with which Ahijah the Shilonite cursed the Israelites than the blessing with which the wicked Balaam blessed them.

C.   "Ahijah the Shilonite cursed the Israelites by reference to a reed, as it is said, 'For the Lord shall smite Israel as a reed is shaken in the water' (1 Kgs. 14:15).

D.   "Just as a reed stands in a place in which there is water, so its stem [106A] is renewed and its roots abundant, so that, even if all the winds in the world come and blow against it, they cannot move it from its place, but it goes on swaying with them. When the winds fall silent, the reed stands in its place. [So is Israel].

E.   "But the wicked Balaam blessed them by reference to a cedar tree [at 24:6].

F.   "Just as a cedar tree does not stand in a place in which there is water, so its roots are few, and its truck is not renewed, so that while, even if all the winds in the world come and blow against it, they will not move it from its place, when the south wind blows against it, it uproots it right away and turns it on its face, [so is Israel].

G.   "And not only so, but the reed has the merit that from it a quill is taken for the writing of scrolls of the Torah, prophets, and writings."

CCXXVII.

A.   "And he looked on the Kenite and took up his parable" (Num. 24:21):

B.   Said Balaam to Jethro the Kenite, "Were you not with us in that conspiracy [of Pharaoh, Ex. 1:22]? [Of course you were.] Then who gave you a seat among the mighty men of the earth [in the sanhedrin]?"

C.   This is in line with what R. Hiyya bar Abba said R. Simai said, "Three participated in that conspiracy [of Ex. 1:22, to destroy the Israelites in the river], Balaam, Job, and Jethro.

D.   "Balaam, who gave the advice, was slain. Job, who kept silent, was judged through suffering. Jethro, who fled, had the merit that some of his sons' sons would go into session [as judges] in the Hewn-Stone Chamber,

E.   "as it is said, 'And the families of scribes which dwelt at Jabez, the Tirathites, the Shemathites, the Sucathites. These are the Kenites that came of Hammath, the father of the house of Rehab' (2 Chr.

2:55). And it is written, 'And the children of the Kenite, Moses' father-in-law...' (Jud. 1:16)."

CCXXVIII.

A. "And he took up his parable and said, Alas, who shall live when God does this?" (Num. 24:23):

B. Said R. Yohanan, "Woe to the nation who is at hand when the Holy One, blessed be He, effects the redemption of his children!

C. "Who would want to throw his garment between a lion and a lioness when they are having sexual relations?"

CCXXIX.

A. "And ships shall come from the coast of Chittim" (Num. 24:24):

B. Said Rab, "[Legions will come] from the coast of Chittim" [cf. Freedman, p. 722, n. 12].

C. "And they shall afflict Assyria and they shall afflict Eber" (Num. 24:24):

D. Up to Assyria they shall kill, from that point they shall enslave.

CCXXX.

A. "And now, behold, I go to my people; come and I shall advise you what this people shall do to your people in the end of days" (Num. 24:24):

B. Rather than saying, "This people to your people," it should say, "Your people to this people." [Freedman, p. 723, n. 4: He advised the Moabites to ensnare Israel through uncharity. Thus he was referring to an action by the former to the latter, while Scripture suggests otherwise.]

C. Said R. Abba, "It is like a man who curses himself but assigns the curse to others. [Scripture alludes to Israel but refers to Moab.]

D. "[Balaam] said to [Balak], 'The God of these people hates fornication, and they lust after linen [clothing, which rich people wear]. Come and I shall give you advice: Make tents and set whores in them, an old one outside and a girl inside. Let them sell linen garments to them.'

E. "He made tents for them from the snowy mountain to Beth Hajeshimoth [north to south] and put whores in them, old women outside, young women inside.

F. "When an Israelite was eating and drinking and carousing and going out for walks in the market, the old lady would say to him, 'Don't you want some linen clothes?'

G. "The old lady would offer them at true value, and the girl would offer them at less.

H. "This would happen two or three times, and then [the young one] would say to him, 'Lo, you are at home here. Sit down and make a choice for yourself.' Gourds of Ammonite wine would be set near her. (At this point the wine of gentiles had not yet been forbidden to Israelites.) She would say to him, 'Do you want to drink a cup of wine?'

I. "When he had drunk a cup of wine, he would become inflamed. He said to her, 'Submit to me.' She would than take her god from her bosom and said to him, 'Worship this.'

J. "He would say to her, 'Am I not a Jew?'

K. "She would say to him, 'What difference does it make to you? Do they ask anything more from you than that you bare yourself?' But he did not know that that was how this idol was served.

L. "'And not only so, but I shall not let you do so until you deny the Torah of Moses, your master!'

M. "As it is said, 'They went in to Baal-peor and separated themselves unto that shame, and their abominations were according as they loved' (Hos. 9:10)."

CCXXXI.

A. "And Israel dwelt in Shittim" (Num. 25:1):

B. R. Eliezer says, "The name of the place actually was Shittim."

C. R. Joshua says, "It was so called because when there they did deeds of idiocy [STWT]."

D. "And they called the people to the sacrifices of their gods" (Num. 25:2):

E. R. Eliezer says, "They met them naked."

F. R. Joshua says, "They all had involuntary seminal emissions."

G. What is the meaning of Rephidim [Ex. 17:8: "Then came Amalek and fought with Israel in Rephidim"]?

H. R. Eliezer says, "It was actually called Rephidim."

I. R. Joshua says, "It was a place in which they weakened their [ties to] the teachings of the Torah, as it is written, 'The fathers shall not look back to their children for feebleness of hands' (Jer. 47:3)."

CCXXXII.

A. R. Yohanan said, "Any passage in which the word, 'And he abode' appears, it means suffering.

B. "So: 'And Israel abode in Shittim, and the people began to commit whoredom with the daughters of Moab' (Num. 23:1).

C. "'And Jacob dwelt in the land where his father was a stranger, in the land of Canaan' (Gen. 37:1). 'And Joseph brought to his father their evil report' (Gen. 37:3).

D. "'And Israel dwelt in the land of Egypt, in the country of Goshen' (Gen. 47:27), 'And the time drew near that Israel must die' (Gen. 47:29).

E. "'And Judah and Israel dwelt safely, every man under his vine and under his fig tree' (1 Kgs. 5:5). 'And the Lord stirred up an adversary to Solomon, Hadad the Edomite; he was the king's seed in Edom' (1 Kgs. 11:14)."

CCXXXIII.

A. "And they slew the kings of Midian, beside the rest of them that were slain....Balaam also, the son of Beor, they slew with the sword" (Num. 31:8):

B. What was he doing there anyhow?

C. Said R. Yohanan, "He went to collect a salary on account of the twenty-four thousand Israelites whom he had brought down' [Cf. Num. 25:1-9]."

D. Mar Zutra b. Tobiah said Rab said, "That is in line with what people say: 'When the camel went to ask for horns, the ears that he had they cut off him.'"

CCXXXIV.

A.   "Balaam also, the son of Beor, the soothsayer, [did the children of Israel slay with the sword]" (Josh. 13:22):

B.   A soothsayer? He was a prophet!

C.   Said R. Yohanan, "At first he was a prophet, but in the end, a mere soothsayer."

D.   Said R. Pappa, "This is in line with what people say: 'She who came from princes and rulers played the whore with a carpenter.'"

CCXXXV.

A.   [106B] "Did the children of Israel slay with the sword, among those who were slain by them" (Josh. 13:22):

B.   Said Rab, "They inflicted upon him all four forms of execution: stoning, burning, decapitation, and strangulation."

CCXXXVI.

A.   A *min* said to R. Hanina, "Have you heard how old Balaam was?"

B.   He said to him, "It is not written out explicitly. But since it is written, 'Bloody and deceitful men shall not live out half their days' (Ps. 55:24), he would have been thirty-three or thirty-four years old."

C.   He said to him, "You have spoken well. I saw the notebook of Balaam, in which it is written, "Balaam, the lame, was thirty-three years old when Pineas, the brigand, killed him.'"

CCXXXVII.

A.   Said Mar, son of Rabina, to his son, "In regard to all of those [listed as not having a share in the world to come], you should take up the verses relating to them and expound them only in the case of the wicked Balaam.

B.   "In his case, in whatever way one can expound the relevant passages [to his detriment], you do so."

CCXXXVIII.

A.   It is written, "Doeg" (1 Sam. 21:8) [meaning, "anxious" (Freedman, p. 726, n. 1)] and it is written, "Doeeg" (1 Sam. 22:18) [with letters indicating "woe" being inserted (Freedman, ad loc.)].

B.   Said R. Yohanan, "To begin with, the Holy One, blessed be He, sits and worries lest such a son one go forth to bad ways. After he has gone forth to bad ways, he says, 'Woe that this one has gone forth!'"

CCXXXIX.

A.   Said R. Isaac, "What is the meaning of the verse of Scripture, 'Why do you boast yourself in mischief, O mighty man? The goodness of God endures forever' (Ps. 52:3)?

B.   "Said the Holy One, blessed be He, to Doeg, 'Are you not a hero in Torah learning! Why do you boast in mischief? Is not the love of God spread over you all day long?'"

C.   And said R. Isaac, "What is the meaning of the verse of Scripture, 'But to the wicked God says, What have you to do to declare my statutes?' (Ps. 50:16)?

D.   "So the Holy One, blessed be He, said to the wicked Doeg, 'What have you to do to declare my statutes? When you come to the passages that deal with murderers and slanderers, what have you to say about them!'"

CCXL.

    A.   "Or that you take my covenant in your mouth?" (Ps. 50:16):

    B.   Said R. Ammi, "The Torah knowledge of Doeg comes only from the lips and beyond [but not inside his heart]."

CCXLI.

    A   Said R. Isaac, "What is the meaning of the verse of Scripture, 'The righteous also shall see and fear and shall laugh at him' (Ps. 52:8)?

    B.   "To begin with they shall fear [the wicked], but in the end they shall laugh at him."

    C   And said R. Isaac, "What is the meaning of the verse of Scripture: 'He has swallowed down riches and he shall vomit them up again, the God shall cast them out of his belly' (Job 20:15)?

    D.   "Said David before the Holy One, blessed be He, 'Lord of the world, let Doeg die.'

    E.   "He said to him, '"He has swallowed down riches, and he shall vomit them up again" (Job 20:15).'

    F.   "He said to him, '"Let God cast them out of his belly" (Job 20:15).'"

    G   And said R. Isaac, "What is the meaning of the verse of Scripture: 'God shall likewise destroy you forever' (Ps. 52:7)?

    H   "Said the Holy One, blessed be He, to David, 'Should I bring Doeg to the world to come?'

    I.   "He said to him, '"God shall likewise destroy you forever" (Ps. 52:7).'"

    J.   "What is the meaning of the verse: 'He shall take you away and pluck you out of the tent and root you out of the land of the living, *selah*' (Ps. 52:7)?

    K   "Said the Holy One, blessed be He, 'Let a tradition in the schoolhouse be repeated in his name.'

    L.   "He said to him, '"He shall take you away and pluck you out of the tent" (Ps. 52:7).'

    M.   "'Then let his children be rabbis.'

    N.   "'"And your root out of the land of the living, *selah*!"'"

    O.   And said R. Isaac, "What is the meaning of the verse of Scripture: 'Where is he who counted, where is he who weighed? Where is he who counted the towers' (Isa. 33:18)?

    P.   "'Where is he who counted all the letters in the Torah? Where is he who weighed all of the arguments a fortiori in the Torah?'

    Q   "'Where is he who counted the towers' – who counted the three hundred decided laws that concern the 'tower that flies in the air' [that is, the laws governing the status of the contents of a closed cabinet not standing on the ground]."

CCXLII.

    A   Said R. Ammi, "Four hundred questions did Doeg and Ahitophel raise concerning the 'tower flying in the air,' and they could not answer any one of them."

    B.   Said Raba, "Is there any recognition of the achievement of raising questions? In the time of R. Judah, all of their repetition of Mishnah teachings concerned the civil laws [of Baba Qamma, Baba Mesia, and Baba Batra], while, for our part, we repeat the Mishnah traditions even dealing with tractate Uqsin [a rather peripheral topic].

C. "When for his part R. Judah came to the law, '*A woman who pickles vegetables in a pot*' [M. Toh. 2:1], or some say, '*Olives which were pickled with their leaves are insusceptible to uncleanness*' [M. Uqs. 2:1], he would say, 'I see here all the points of reflection of Rab and Samuel.'

D. "But we repeat the tractate of Uqsin at thirteen sessions [having much more to say about it].

E. "When R. Judah merely removed his shoes [in preparation for a fast], it would rain.

F. "When we cry out [in supplication], no one pays any attention to us.

G. "But the Holy One, blessed be He, demands the heart, as it is written, 'But the Lord looks on the heart' (1 Sam. 16:7)."

CCXLIII.

A. Said R. Mesharsheya, "Doeg and Ahitophel did not know how to reason concerning traditions."

B. Objected Mar Zutra, "Can it be the case that one concerning whom it is written, 'Where is he who counted, where is he who weighed, where is he who counted the towers?' (Isa. 33:18) should not be able to reason concerning traditions?

C. "But it never turned out that traditions [in their names] were stated in accord with the decided law, for it is written, 'The secret of the Lord is with those who fear him' (Ps. 25:14)."

CCXLIV.

A. Said R. Ammi, "Doeg did not die before he forgot his learning, as it is said, 'He shall die without instruction, and in the greatness of his folly he shall go astray' (Prov. 5:23)."

B. Rab said, "He was afflicted with *saraat*, for it is said, 'You have destroyed all them who go awhoring from you' (Ps. 73:27), and elsewhere it is written, 'And if it not be redeemed within the span of a full year, then the house shall be established finally [to him who bought it]' (Lev. 25:30).

C. "[The word indicated as 'finally' and the word for 'destroyed' use the same letters]. And we have learned in the Mishnah: *The only difference between one who is definitely afflicted with saraat and one who is shut away for observation is in respect to letting the hair grow long and tearing the garment* [M. Meg. 1:7], [Freedman, p. 729, n. 6: which shows that the term at hand is used to indicate someone is afflicted with *saraat*. Hence the first of the two verses is to be rendered, 'You have smitten with definite leprosy all those who go awhoring from you.']"

CCXLV.

A. Said R. Yohanan, "Three injurious angels were designated for Doeg: one to make him forget his learning, one to burn his soul, and one to scatter his dust among the synagogues and schoolhouses."

B. And said R. Yohanan, "Doeg and Ahitophel never saw one another. Doeg lived in the time of Saul, and Ahitophel in the time of David.

C. "And said R. Yohanan, "Doeg and Ahitophel did not live out half their days."

D. It has been taught on Tannaite authority along these same lines:

E.   "Bloody and deceitful men shall not live out half their days" (Ps. 55:24):

F.   Doeg lived only for thirty-four years, Ahitophel for thirty-three.

G.   And said R. Yohanan, "At the outset David called Ahitophel his master, at the end he called him his friend, and finally he called him his disciple.

H.   "At the beginning he called him his master: 'But it was you, a man my equal, my guide and my acquaintance' (Ps. 55:14).

I.   "Then his companion: 'We took sweet counsel together and walked into the house of God in company' (Ps. 55:15).

J.   "Finally, his disciple: 'Yea, my own familiar friend, in whom I trusted [107A], who ate my bread, has lifted his heel against me' (Ps. 56:10). [Freedman, p. 729, n. 10: This is understood to refer to Ahitophel, and eating bread is a metaphor for 'who learned of my teaching.']"

CCXLVI.

A.   Said R. Judah said Rab, "One should never put himself to the test, for lo, David, king of Israel, put himself to the test and he stumbled.

B.   "He said before him, 'Lord of the world, on what account do people say, "God of Abraham, God of Isaac, and God of Jacob," but they do not say, "God of David"?'

C.   "He said to him, 'They endured a test for me, while you have not endured a test for me.'

D.   "He said before him, 'Lord of the world, here I am. Test me.'

E.   "For it is said, 'Examine me, O Lord, and try me' (Ps. 26:1).

F.   "He said to him, 'I shall test you, and I shall do for you something that I did not do for them. I did not inform them [what I was doing], while I shall tell you what I am going to do. I shall try you with a matter having to do with sexual relations.'

G.   "Forthwith: 'And it came to pass in an eventide that David arose from off his bed' (2 Sam. 11:2)."

H.   Said R. Judah, "He turned his habit of having sexual relations by night into one of having sexual relations by day.

I.   "He lost sight of the following law:

J.   "'There is in man a small organ, which makes him feel hungry when he is sated and makes him feel sated when he is hungry.'"

K.   "And he walked on the roof of the king's palace, and from the roof he saw a woman washing herself, and the woman was very beautiful to look upon" (2 Sam. 11:2):

L.   Bath Sheba was shampooing her hair behind a screen. Satan came to [David] and appeared to him in the form of a bird. He shot an arrow at [the screen] and broke it down, so that she stood out in the open, and he saw her.

M.   Forthwith: "And David sent and inquired after the woman. And one said, Is not this Bath Sheba, the daughter of Eliam, the wife of Uriah the Hittite? And David sent messengers and took her, and she came to him, and he lay with her; for she was purified from her uncleanness; and she returned to her house (2 Sam. 11:203).

N.   That is in line with what is written: "You have tried my heart, you have visited me in the night, you have tried me and shall find nothing; I am purposed that my mouth shall not transgress" (Ps. 17:3).

Q He said, "Would that a bridle had fallen into my mouth, that I had not said what I said!"

CCXLVII.

A. Raba interpreted Scripture, asking, "What is the meaning of the following verse: 'To the chief musician, a Psalm of David. In the Lord I put my trust, how do you say to my soul, Flee as a bird to your mountain?' (Ps. 11:1)?

B. "Said David before the Holy One, blessed be He, 'Lord of the world, Forgive me for that sin, so that people should not say, "The mountain that is among you [that is, your king] has been driven off by a bird."'"

C. Raba interpreted Scripture, asking, "What is the meaning of the following verse: 'Against you, you alone, have I sinned, and done this evil in your sight, that you might be justified when you speak and be clear when you judge' (Ps. 11:1)?

D. "Said David before the Holy One, blessed be He, 'Lord of the world. It is perfectly clear to you that if I had wanted to overcome my impulse to do evil, I should have done so. But I had in mind that people not say, "The slave has conquered the Master [God, and should then be included as 'God of David']."'"

E. Raba interpreted Scripture, asking, "What is the meaning of the following verse: 'For I am ready to halt and my sorrow is continually before me' (Ps. 38:18)?

F. "Bath Sheba, daughter of Eliam, was designated for David from the six days of creation, but she came to him through anguish."

G. And so did a Tannaite authority of the house of R. Ishmael [teach], "Bath Sheba, daughter of Eliam, was designated for David, but he 'ate' her while she was yet unripe."

H Raba interpreted Scripture, asking, "What is the meaning of the following verse: 'But in my adversity they rejoiced and gathered themselves together, yes, the abjects gathered themselves together against me and I did not know it, they tore me and did not cease' (Ps. 35:15)?

I. "Said David before the Holy One, blessed be He, 'Lord of the world, it is perfectly clear to you that if they had torn my flesh, my blood would not have flowed [because I was so embarrassed].'

J. Not only so, but when they take up the four modes of execution inflicted by a court, they interrupt their Mishnah study and say to me, "David, he who has sexual relations with a married woman – how is he put to death?"

K. "'I say to them, "He who has sexual relations with a married woman is put to death through strangulation, but he has a share in the world to come," while he who humiliates his fellow in public has no share in the world to come.'"'

CCXLVIII.

A. Said R. Judah said Rab, "Even when David was sick, he carried out the eighteen acts of sexual relations that were owing to his [eighteen] wives, as it is written, 'I am weary with my groaning, all night I make my bed swim, I water my couch with my tears' (Ps. 6:7)."

B. And said R. Judah said, Rab, "David wanted to worship idols, as it is said, 'And it happened that when David came to the head, where he worshiped God' (2 Sam. 15:32), and 'head' only means idols, as it is written, 'This image's head was of fine gold' (Dan. 2:32).

C. "'Behold, Hushai, the Archite came to meet him with his coat rent and earth upon his head' (2 Sam. 15:32):

D. "He said to David, 'Are people to say that a king such as you have worshiped idols?'

E. "He said to him, 'Will the son of a king such as me kill him? It is better that such a king as me worship an idol and not profane the Name of heaven in public.'

F. "He said, 'Why then did you marry a woman captured in battle?' [Freedman, p. 732, n. 7: Absalom's mother, Maachah, the daughter of Talmai, king of Geshur, was a war captive.]"

G. "He said to him, 'As to a woman captured in battle, the All-Merciful has permitted marrying her.'

H. "He said to him, 'You did not correctly interpret the meaning of the proximity of two verses. For it is written, "If a man has stubborn and rebellious son" (Deut. 21:18).'

I. "'[The proximity teaches that] whoever marries a woman captured in battle will have a stubborn and rebellious son.'"

CCXLIX.

A. R. Dosetai of Biri interpreted Scripture, "To what may David be likened? To a gentile merchant.

B. "Said David before the Holy One, blessed be He, 'Lord of the world, "Who can understand his errors?" (Ps. 19:13).'

C. "He said to him, 'They are remitted for you.'

D. "'" Cleanse me of hidden faults" (Ps. 19:13).'

E. "They are remitted to you.'

F. "'"Keep back your servant also from presumptuous sins" (Ps. 19:13).'

G. "They are remitted to you.'

H. "'"Let them not have dominion over me, then I shall be upright" (Ps. 19:13), so that the rabbis will not hold me up as an example.'

I. "They are remitted to you.'

J. "'"And I shall be innocent of great transgression" (Ps. 19:13), so that they will not write down my ruin.'

K. "He said to him, 'That is not possible. Now if the Y that I took away from the name of Sarah [changing it from Sarai to Sarah] stood crying for so many years until Joshua came and I added the Y [removed from Sarah's name] to his name, as it is said, "And Moses called Oshea, the son of Nun, Jehoshua" (Num. 13:16), how much the more will a complete passage of Scripture [cry out if I remove that passage from its rightful place]!'"

CCL.

A. "And I shall be innocent from great transgression: (Ps. 19:13):

B. He said before him, "Lord of the world, forgive me for the whole of that sin [as though I had never done it]."

C.   He said to him, "Solomon, your son, even now is destined to say in his wisdom, 'Can a man take fire in his bosom, and his clothes not be burned? Can one go upon hot coals, and his feet not be burned? So he who goes in to his neighbor's wife, whoever touches her shall not be innocent' (Prov. 6:27-29)."

D.   He said to him, "Will I be so deeply troubled?"

E.   He said to him, "Accept suffering [as atonement]."

F.   He accepted the suffering.

CCLI.

A.   Said R. Judah said Rab, "For six months David was afflicted with *saraat,* and the Presence of God left him, and the sanhedrin abandoned him.

B.   "He was afflicted with *saraat,* as it is written, 'Purge me with hyssop and I shall be clean, wash me and I shall be whiter than snow' (Ps. 51:9).

C.   "The Presence of God left him, as it is written, 'Restore to me the joy of your salvation and uphold me with your free spirit' (Ps. 51:14).

D.   "The sanhedrin abandoned him, as it is written, 'Let those who fear you turn to me and those who have known your testimonies' (Ps. 119:79).

E.   "How do we know that this lasted for six months? As it is written, 'And the days that David rules over Israel were forty years: **[107B]** Seven years he reigned in Hebron, and thirty-three years he reigned in Jerusalem' (1 Kgs. 2:11).

F.   "Elsewhere it is written, 'In Hebron he reigned over Judah seven years and six months' (2 Sam. 5:5).

G.   "So the six months were not taken into account. Accordingly, he was afflicted with *saraat* [for such a one is regarded as a corpse].

H.   "He said before him, 'Lord of the world, forgive me for that sin.'

I.   "'It is forgiven to you.'

J.   "'"Then show me a token for good, that they who hate me may see it and be ashamed, because you, Lord, have helped me and comforted me" (Ps. 86:17).'

K.   "He said to him, 'While you are alive, I shall not reveal [the fact that you are forgiven], but I shall reveal it in the lifetime of your son, Solomon.'

L.   "When Solomon had built the house of the sanctuary, he tried to bring the ark into the house of the Holy of Holies. The gates cleaved to one another. He recited twenty-four prayers [Freedman, p. 734, n. 4: in 2 Chr. 6 words for prayer, supplication and hymn occur twenty-four times], but was not answered.

M.   "He said, 'Lift up your head, O you gates, and be lifted up, you everlasting doors, and the King of glory shall come in. Who is this King of glory? The Lord strong and might, the Lord mighty in battle' (Ps. 24:7ff.).

N.   "And it is further said, 'Lift up your heads, O you gates even lift them up, you everlasting doors' (Ps. 24:7).

O.   "But he was not answered.

P.   "When he said, 'Lord God, turn not away the face of your anointed, remember the mercies of David, your servant' (2 Chr. 6:42), forthwith he was answered.

Q   "At that moment the faces of David's enemies turned as black as the bottom of a pot, for all Israel knew that the Holy One, blessed be He, had forgiven him for that sin."

CCLII.
A.   *Gehazi [M. 11:2F]:*
B.   As it is written, "And Elisha came to Damascus" (2 Kgs. 8:7).
C.   Where was he traveling [when he came to Damascus]?
D.   Said R. Yohanan, "He went to bring Gehazi back in repentance, but he did not repent.
E.   "He said to him, 'Repent.'
F.   "He said to him, 'This is the tradition that I have received from you: "Whoever has both sinned and caused others to sin will never have sufficient means to do penitence."'"
G.   What had he done?
H   Some say, "He hung a lodestone on the sin[ful statue built by] Jeroboam and suspended it between heaven and earth."
I.   Others say, "He carved on it the Name of God, so that it would say, 'I [am the Lord your God]....You shall not have [other gods...]' (Ex. 20:1-2)."
J.   Still others say, "He drove rabbis away from his presence, as it is said, 'And the sons of the prophets said to Elisha, "See now the place where we swell before you is too small for us"' (2 Kgs. 6:1). The sense then is that up to that time, it was not too small."

CCLIII.
A.   Our rabbis have taught on Tannaite authority:
B.   Under all circumstances the left hand should push away and the right hand should draw near,
C.   not in the manner of Elisha, who drove away Gehazi with both hands.
D.   What is the case with Gehazi?
E.   As it is written, "And Naaman said, 'Be pleased to accept two talents'" (2 Kgs. 5:23).
F.   And it is written, "But he said to him, 'Did I not go with you in spirit when the man turned from his chariot to meet you? Was it a time to accept money and garments, olive orchards and vineyards, sheep and oxen, menservants and maidservants'" (2 Kgs. 5:26).
G.   But did he receive all these things? He got only silver and garments.
H   Said R. Isaac, "At that moment Elisha was occupied with the study of the list of eight dead creeping things [M. Shab. 14:1, Lev. 11:29ff.]."
I.   Naaman, head of the army of the king of Syria, was afflicted with *saraat.* A young girl who had been taken captive from the Land of Israel said to him, "If you go to Elisha, he will heal you."
J.   When he got there, he said to him, "Go, immerse in the Jordan."
K.   He said to him, "You are making fun of me!"
L.   Those who were with him said to him, "Go, try it, what difference does it make to you?"
M.   He went and immersed in the Jordan and was healed.

N. He came and brought him everything that he had, but [Elisha] would not take it. Gehazi took leave of Elisha and went and took what he took and hid it.

O. When he came back, Elisha saw the marks of *saraat*, as they blossomed all over his head.

P. "He said to Gehazi, 'Wicked one! The time has come to receive the reward for the eight dead creeping things: "Therefore the leprosy of Naaman shall cleave to you and to your descendants forever" (2 Kgs. 8:27).'"

CCLIV.

A. "Now there were four men who were lepers [at the entrance to the gate]" (2 Kgs. 7:3):

B. R. Yohanan said, "This refers to Gehazi and his three sons."

C. It has been taught on Tannaite authority:

D. R. Simeon b. Eleazar says, "Also in one's natural impulse, as to a child or a woman, one should push away with the left hand and draw near with the right hand." [Freedman, p. 736, n. 2: The uncensored edition continues: What of R. Joshua b. Perahjah?– When King Jannai slew our Rabbis, R. Joshua b. Perahjah (and Jesus) fled to Alexandria of Egypt. On the resumption of peace, Simeon b. Shetach sent to him: "From me, (Jerusalem) the holy city, to thee, Alexandria of Egypt (my sister). My husband dwelleth within thee and I am desolate." He arose, went, and found himself in a certain inn, where great honor was shown him. "How beautiful is this Acsania?" (The word denotes both inn and innkeeper. R. Joshua used it in the first sense; the answer assumes the second to be meant.) Thereupon (Jesus) observed, "Rabbi, her eyes are narrow." "Wretch," he rebuked him, "dost thou thus engage thyself.' He sounded four hundred trumpets and excommunicated him. He (Jesus) came before him many times pleading, "Receive me!" But he would pay no heed to him. One day he (R. Joshua) was reciting the Shema, when Jesus came before him. He intended to receive him and made a sign to him. He (Jesus) thinking that it was to repel him, went, put up a brick, and worshiped it. "Repent," said he (R. Joshua) to him. He replied, "I have thus learned from thee: He who sins and causes others to sin is not afforded the means of repentance." And a Master has said, "Jesus the Nazarene practiced magic and led Israel astray."]

CCLV.

A. Our rabbis have taught on Tannaite authority:

B. Elisha bore three illnesses,

C. one because he brought the she-bears against the children, one because he pushed Gehazi away with both hands, and one on account of which he died.

D. For it is said, "Now Elisha had fallen sick of the ailment of which he died" (2 Kgs. 13:14).

CCLVI.

A. Until Abraham there was no such thing as [the sign of] old age. Whoever saw Abraham thought, "This is Isaac." Whoever saw Isaac thought, "This is Abraham."

B.   Abraham prayed for mercy so that he might have [signs of] old age, as it is said, "And Abraham was old, and well stricken in age" (Gen. 24:1).

C.   Until the time of Jacob there was no such thing as illness, so he prayed for mercy and illness came about, as it is written, "And someone told Joseph, behold, your father is sick" (Gen. 48:1).

D.   "Until the time of Elisha, no one who was sick ever got well. Elisha came along and prayed for mercy and got well, as it is written, "Now Elisha had fallen sick of the illness of which he died" (2 Kgs. 13:14). [Freedman: This shows that he had been sick on previous occasions too, but recovered.]

The important question at hand is self-evident: how has the compositor of this tractate of monstrous proportions arranged the materials at hand? The answer to the question is equally self-evident: he has laid out available materials, available in large blocks indeed, in accord with (1) the thematic program of the Mishnah, and (2) the further principles of agglutination and conglomeration dictated by the materials at hand. We have a Mishnah commentary; we also have subdivisions, which identify a theme and richly illustrate it; we furthermore have some units that are joined by reason of a common authority. In each major unit (signified in what follows by a Roman numeral), the ultimate redactor has taken up a fact – a topic, and allegation – of the Mishnah. Once he has dealt with that fact, he then drew upon materials that supplied a secondary expansion of it, and made use, further, of entire blocks of materials already arranged and joined together on the basis of principles of organization other than those deriving from Mishnah exegesis. That, in a single statement, accounts for the arrangement of everything at hand. So, as I suggested, not only is this enormous mass of materials not random or miscellaneous, but it follows simple rules of agglutination. Agglutinative discourse in the Bavli is, if not proposition, still entirely cogent and easy to follow, once you know the rules. And we do.

Let us proceed to test the thesis just now announced by reviewing an outline of the units of the immense construction at hand.

I.   The Life of the World to Come: When and why it is denied [M. 11:1A-D]

A.   Those who do not believe in it do not get it: I

B.   How on the basis of the Torah do we know that there will be resurrection of the dead: II-X

C.   Disputes with pagans on the resurrection of the dead: XI-XIV (Tradental construction based on Gebihah: XIV-XVII)

D.   Other disputes with pagan sages: XVIII-XXI

E.   Verses on the resurrection of the dead: XXII-XXV, XXVII-XXXV (Tradental construction based on Deut. 32:39: XXV-XXVI)

II.   Examples in Scripture of the Resurrection of the Dead

    A.   Daniel's Case: Hananiah, Mishael, and Azariah: XXXVI-XLIV, XLVII-XLIX (Further materials on Nebuchadnezzer: XLV-XLVI) (Tradental continuation of XLIX:L)

III.   Messianic Passages of Scripture. Sennacherib, Nebuchadnezzar

    A.   Isaiah and Hezekiah: LI-LXVII, LXXI-LXXXI

    B.   David: LXVIII-LXX

    C.   When will the Messiah come: LXXXII-CXV

IV.   He Who Says that the Torah Does Not Come from Heaven Will Not Enter the World to Come [M. 11:1D]:

    A.   Those who do not believe in it do not get it: CXVI

    B.   Importance of study of Torah: CXVII-CXXIV

V.   An Epicurean [M. 11:1D]:

    A.   Defined: CXXV-CXXX

VI.   Aqiba: Also He Who Read Heretical Books [M. 11:1E]:

    A.   Defined: CXXXIV

VII.   He Who Whispers over a Wound [M. 11:1F]:

    A.   Defined: CXXXV-CXLIV

VIII.   He Who Pronounces the Divine Name as it is Spelled Out [M. 11:1G]:

    A.   Defined: CXLV

IX.   Three Kings and Four Ordinary Folk [M. 11:2A-B]:

    A.   Stories about Jeroboam: CXLVI-CLXI, CLXIV

    B.   Stories about Manasseh: CLXII-CLXIII, CLXXII-CXXXV

    C.   Stories about Ahab: CLXVI-CLXXI

    D.   Those not listed who might have been: CXXXVI-CLXXXVIII (Excursus on the destruction of Jerusalem: CXC-CCIX)

X.   Four Ordinary Folk [M. 11:2F]:

    A.   Stories about Balaam: CCX-CCXXXVII

    B.   Stories about Doeg: CCXXXVIII-CCXLV

    C.   Those not listed who might have been (David): CCXLVI-CCLI

    D.   Gehazi: CCLII-CCLVI

We see, therefore, that the entire construction devotes itself to the exposition of the Mishnah. Two units, one on the resurrection of the dead, the other on messianic crises in Israelite history, complement unit I. Units I, IV-X, systematically work their way through the Mishnah's statements. Units II and III treat the resurrection of the dead, on the one hand, and the coming of the Messiah, on the other. Certainly any effort to expound the theme of the life of the world to come would have to deal with these other two topics, and, what the compositor has done is simply place into the correct context – namely, M. 11:1A-B – the available materials on these other two components of the principal congeries of ideas at hand. That is, once we take up the world to come, we deal also with the resurrection and the coming of the Messiah. Then, as is clear, the compositor simply proceeded on his way, generally defining the Mishnah's terms, often also greatly expanding on the themes introduced by the Mishnah. So the construction as a whole, seemingly vast and formless, turns out to follow rather simple rules of composition and organization, and we know precisely what those rules are.

11:3A-CC

A.   The generation of the flood has no share in the world to come,
B.   and they shall not stand in the judgment,
C.   since it is written, "My spirit shall not judge with man forever" (Gen. 6:3)
D.   neither judgment nor spirit.
E.   The generation of the dispersion has no share in the world to come,
F.   since it is said, "So the Lord scattered them abroad from there upon the face of the whole earth" (Gen. 11:8).
G.   "So the Lord scattered them abroad" – in this world,
H.   "and the Lord scattered them from there" – in the world to come.
I.   The men of Sodom have no portion in the world to come,
J.   since it is said, "Now the men of Sodom were wicked and sinners against the Lord exceedingly" (Gen. 13:13)
K.   "Wicked" – in this world,
L.   "And sinners" – in the world to come.
M.   But they will stand in judgment.
N.   R. Nehemiah says, "Both these and those will not stand in judgment,
O.   "for it is said, 'Therefore the wicked shall not stand in judgment [108A], nor sinners in the congregation of the righteous' (Ps. 1:5)
P.   "'Therefore the wicked shall not stand in judgment' – this refers to the generation of the flood.
Q.   "'Nor sinners in the congregation of the righteous' – this refers to the men of Sodom."
R.   They said to him, "They will not stand in the congregation of the righteous, but they will stand in the congregation of the sinners."
S.   The spies have no portion in the world to come,
T.   as it is said, "Even those men who brought up an evil report of the land died by the plague before the Lord" (Num. 14:37)
U.   "Died" – in this world.
V.   "By the plague" – in the world to come.

W. "The generation of the wilderness has no portion in the world to come and will not stand in judgment,

X. "for it is written, 'In this wilderness they shall be consumed and there they shall die' (Num. 14:35)," the words of R. Aqiba.

Y. R. Eliezer says, "Concerning them it says, 'Gather my saints together to me, those that have made a covenant with me by sacrifice' (Ps. 50:5)."

Z. "The party of Korah is not destined to rise up,

AA. "for it is written, 'And the earth closed upon them' – in this world.

BB. "'And they perished from among the assembly' – in the world to come," the words of R. Aqiba.

CC. And R. Eliezer says, "Concerning them it says, 'The Lord kills and resurrects, brings down to Sheol and brings up again' (1 Sam. 2:6)."

I.

A. Our rabbis have taught on Tannaite authority:

B. "The generation of the flood has no share in the world to come [M. 10:3A],

C. "nor will they live in the world to come,

D. "as it is said, And he destroyed every living thing that was upon the face of the earth (Gen. 7:23) in this world;

E. "and they perished from the earth in the world to come," the words of R. Aqiba.

F. R. Judah B. Betera says, "They will live nor be judged, as it is said, And the Lord said, My spirit shall not contend with man forever' (Gen. 6:3)

G. "It will not contend, nor will my spirit be in them forever."

H Another matter: "And the Lord said, My spirit shall not contend: – [Said the Omnipresent,] that their spirit will not return to its sheath.

I. R. Menahem b. R. Joseph says, [In T.'s version:] "It will not contend –

J. "Said the Omnipresent, 'I shall not contend with them when I pay the good reward which is coming to the righteous.'

K. "But the spirit of the evil is harder for them than that of all the others.

L. "as it is written, Their spirit is a fire consuming them (Isa. 33:11)'" [T. San. 13:6A-K].

II.

A. Our rabbis have taught on Tannaite authority:

B. The generation of the Flood acted arrogantly before the Omnipresent only on account of the good which he lavished on them, since it is said, "Their houses are safe from fear, neither is the rod of God upon them" (Job 21:9). "Their bull genders and fails not, their cow calves and casts not her calf" (Job 21:10). "They send forth their little ones like a flock, and their children dance" (Job. 21:11). "They spend their days in prosperity and their years in pleasures" (Job 36:11).

C.   That is what caused them to say to God, "Depart from us, for we do not desire knowledge of they ways. What is the Almighty, that we should serve Him, and what profit should we have, if we pray to him" (Job 21:14).

D.   They said, "Do we need Him for anything except a few drops of rain? But look, we have rivers and wells which are more than enough for us in the sunny season and in the rainy season, since it is said, And a mist rose from the earth (Gen. 2:6)."

E.   The Omnipresent then said to then, "By the goodness which I lavished on them they take pride before me? By that same good I shall exact punishment from them!"

F.   What does it say? "And I, behold, I bring a flood of water upon the earth" (Gen. 6:17)

G.   R. Yosé B. Durmasqit says, "The men of the Flood took pride only on account of [the covetousness of] the eyeball, which is like water, as it is said, 'The sons of God saw that the daughter of men were fair, and they took them wives from all which they chose' (Gen. 6:2).

H.   "Also the Omnipresent exacted punishment from them only through water, which is like the eyeball, as it is written, 'All the fountains of the great deep were broken up, and the windows of heaven were opened' (Gen. 7:11)" [T. Sot. 3:6-9].

III.

A.   Said R. Yohanan, "As to the generation of the flood, they corrupted their way 'greatly,' and they were judged 'greatly.'

B.   "They corrupted their way greatly, as it is said, 'And God saw that the wickedness of man was great in the earth' (Gen. 6:5).

C.   "They were judged greatly, as it is said, 'All the fountains of the great deep' (Gen. 7:11)."

D.   Said R. Yohanan, "Three [of those fountains remained, the gulf of Gaddor, the hot springs of Tiberias, and the great well of Biram."

IV.

A.   "For all flesh had corrupted its way upon the earth" (Gen. 6:12):

B.   Said R. Yohanan, "This teaches that [the men of the generation of the flood] made a hybrid match between a domesticated beast and a wild animal, a wild animal and a domesticated beast, and every sort of beast with man and man with every sort of beast."

C.   Said R. Abba bar Kahana, "And all of them reverted [to the right way] except for the Tartarian lark [Freedman, p. 740, n. 10]."

V.

A.   "And God said to Noah, the end of all flesh is come before me" (Gen. 6:13).

B.   Said R. Yohanan, "Come and take note of how great is the power of robbery.

C.   "For lo, the generation of the flood violated every sort of law, but the decree of punishment against them was sealed only when they went and committed robbery, for it is said, 'For the earth is filled with violence through them, and behold I will destroy them with the earth' (Gen. 6:13).

D. "And it is written, 'Violence is risen up into a rod of wickedness, none of them shall remain, nor of their multitude, nor any of theirs, neither shall there be wailing for them' (Ezek. 7:11)."

E. Said R. Eleazar, "The cited verse teaches that [violence] stood up straight like a staff and stood before the Holy One, blessed be He, and said to him, 'Lord of the world, Neither them, nor of their multitudes, nor of any thing belonging to them, nor will there be wailing for them.'"

VI.

A. A Tannaite authority of the house of R. Ishmael [said], "Also the decree of punishment for Noah was issued, but he pleased the Lord,"

B. "as it is said, 'I am sorry that I made them. But Noah found favor in the eyes of the Lord' (Gen. 6:7-8)."

VII.

A. "And the Lord was comforted that he had made man in the earth" (Gen. 6:6).

B. When R. Dimi came, [he said,] "The Holy One, blessed be He, said, 'I did well that I made graves for them in the earth [Freedman, p. 741, n. 6: since the wicked are thereby destroyed].'

C. "How is this indicated? Here it is written, 'And the Lord was comforted' (Gen. 6:6) and elsewhere: 'And he comforted them and spoke kindly to them' (Gen. 50:21)."

D. There are those who say, "[He said,] 'I did not do well that I made graves for them in the earth.'

E. "Here it is written, 'And the Lord regretted...' (Gen. 6:6) add elsewhere: 'And the Lord regretted the evil that he had thought to do to his people' (Ex. 32:14)."

VIII.

A. "These are the generations of Noah: Noah was a righteous man, perfect in his generations" (Gen. 6:9):

B. Said R. Yohanan, "By the standards of his generations, but not by the standards of other generations [was he perfect]."

C. R. Simeon b. Laqish said, "By the standards of his generations, and all the more so by the standards of other generations."

D. Said R. Hanina, "As to the view of R. Yohanan, one may propose a comparison. To what may the matter be compared? To the case of a keg of wine, stored in a wine cellar of vinegar."

E. "In its setting, its fragrance is noteworthy, but in any other setting, its fragrance would not be noteworthy."

F. Said R. Oshaia, "As to the view of R. Simeon b. Laqish, one may propose a comparison. To what may the matter be compared? To the case of a bottle of perfumed oil lying in a garbage dump."

G. "If it smells good in such a place, all the more so in a place in which there is spice!"

IX.

A. "And every living substance was destroyed which was upon the face of the ground, both man and beast" (Gen. 7:23):

B. While man sinned, what sin had beasts committed?

C. It was taught on Tannaite authority in the name of R. Joshua b. Qorha, "The matter may be compared to the case of a man who

made a marriage banquet for his son. He prepared all sorts of food
for the banquet. After some days the son died. The man went and
threw out [all the food he had prepared for] the banquet.

D. "He said, 'Did I do anything except for my son? Now that he is
died, what need have I for a marriage banquet?'

E. "So, too, the Holy One, blessed be He, said, 'Did I create
domesticated and wild beasts for any purpose other than for man?
Now that man has sinned, what need have I for domesticated
beasts or wild beasts?'"

X.

A. "All that was on the dry land died" (Gen. 7:22) –

B. But not the fish in the sea.

XI.

A. R. Yosé of Caesarea expounded as follows: "What is the sense of
the verse, 'He is swift as the waters, their portion is cursed in the
earth, [he does not behold the way of the vineyards]' (Job 24:18)?

B. "The verse teaches that Noah, the righteous man, rebuked them,
saying to [his generation], 'Carry out an act of repentance, for if not,
the Holy One, blessed be He, will bring upon you a flood and your
corpses will float on the water like gourds.'

C. "'So it is written, "He is light upon the waters" (Job 24:18).

D. "'And not only so, but people will take from your example a curse
for all who will pass through the world, as it is said, "Their portion
is cursed in the earth" (Job 24:18).'

E. "They said to him, 'And what is stopping him now?'

F. "He said to them, '[God] has one dear one to take away from your
midst.'

G. "[They replied], [108B] 'If so, we will not turn aside from the way of
the vineyards, [that is, we shall continue in our drunkenness].'"

XII.

A. Raba expounded as follows: "What is the meaning of the verse, 'He
that is ready to slip with his feet is as a stone despised in the
thought of him that is at ease' (Job 12:5)?

B. "This teaches that the righteous Noah rebuked them, saying to
them words as hard as stone, but they despised him, saying, 'Old
man, what is this ark for?'

C. "He said to them, 'The Holy One, blessed be He, is bringing a flood
on you.'

D. "They said to him, 'What sort of flood? If it is a flood of fire, we
have something called *alitha* [Freedman, p. 743, n. 7: a fire-
extinguishing demon].

E. "'And if he brings a flood of water, if it comes from the earth, we
have iron plates to cover up the earth [and keep the water down].

F. "'If it comes from heaven, we have *aqob* (others say, *aqosh*)
[Freedman, p. 743, n. 8: a legendary fungus, which when donned
on the head protects against rain].'

G. "He said to them, 'He will bring it from between your heels [legs,
that is, from your penis], as it is said, "He is ready for the steps of
your feet" (Job 12:5).'"

H. It has been taught on Tannaite authority:

I.   The water of the flood was as hard as semen, as it is written, "It is ready for the steps of his feet" (Job 12:5).

XIII.

A.   Said R. Hisda, "By hot fluid they corrupted their way in transgression, and by hot fluid they were judged.

B.   "Here it is written, 'And the water cooled' (Gen. 8:1), and elsewhere: 'Then the king's wrath cooled down' (Est. 7:10)."

XIV.

A.   "And it came to pass after seven days that the waters of the flood were upon the earth" (Gen. 7:10):

B.   Said Rab, "What is the meaning of these seven days?

C.   "These are the seven days of mourning for Methuselah, the righteous man. This teaches that lamentation for the righteous held back the retribution from coming upon the world.

D.   "Another matter: 'After seven days' teaches that the Holy One, blessed be He, changed the order of the world for them, so that the sun came up in the west and set in the east.

E.   "Another matter: It teaches that the Holy One, blessed be He, first set a long a time for them, and then a short time.

F.   "Another matter: It teaches that he gave them a taste of the world to come, so that they should know how much good he would withhold from them [T. Sot. 10:3C. 4]."

XV.

A.   "Of every clean beast you shall take by sevens, man and wife" (Gen. 7:2):

B.   Do beasts relate as man and wife?

C.   Said R. Samuel bar Nahmani said R. Jonathan, "It was to be from among those with whom no transgression had been committed."

D.   How did he know?

E.   Said R. Hisda, "He brought them before the ark. Any that the ark received could be known not to have been the object of a transgression, and any that the ark did not receive could be known to be those with whom a transgression had been committed."

F.   R. Abbahu said, "It was from among those who came on their won."

XVI.

A.   "Make an ark of gopher wood for yourself" (Gen. 6:14):

B.   What is gopher wood?

C.   Said R. Adda, "Members of the house of R. Shila say, 'It is a kind of cedar.'

D.   "Others say, 'It is a hard wood of cedar.'"

XVII.

A.   "A window [SHR] you shall make in the ark" (Gen. 6:16):

B.   Said R. Yohanan, "The Holy One, blessed be He, said to Noah, 'Put up in its precious stones and pearls, so that they will give light for you as at noon [using the root for window].'"

XVIII.

A.   "And in a cubit you shall finish the above" (Gen. 6:16):

B.   In what way will it stand firm [against the rain].

C.   "With lower, second, and third stories you shall make it" (Gen. 6:16)"

D.	It has been taught on Tannaite authority:
E.	The bottom for dung, the middle for beasts, the upper for man.

XIX.

A.	"And he set forth a raven" (Gen. 8:7):
B.	Said R. Simeon b. Laqish, "The raven gave Noah a victorious reply, saying to him, 'Your master [God] hates me, and you hate me.
C.	"'Your master hates me: "Of the clean, seven, of the unclean, two" [and the raven is unclean].
D.	"'You hate me, for you exempt the species of which you have seven, and send forth a species of which you have only two.
E.	"'If I should be injured by the prince of heat or cold, will the world not end up lacking one species?
F.	"'Or perhaps you need only to make use of my wife?'
G.	"He said to him, 'Wicked creature! Even sexual relations with one normally permitted to me are presently forbidden [since it was not permitted to have sexual relations in the ark. Is it not an argument a fortiori that I should not desire sexual relations with one who normally is forbidden to me [namely, a bird]?'"
H.	And how do we know that sexual relations were forbidden?
I.	As it is written, "And you shall enter the ark, you, your sons, your wife, and the wives of your sons with you" (Gen. 6:18).
J.	And elsewhere: "Go forth from the ark, you, your wife, your sons, and your sons' wives with you" (Gen. 8:16).
K.	And, said R. Yohanan, "On the basis of this statement they said that sexual relations were forbidden in the ark [and the instruction to go forth once more permitted sexual relations]."

XX.

A.	Our rabbis have taught on Tannaite authority:
B.	Three species had sexual relations in the ark, and all of them were smitten: the dog, raven, and Ham.
C.	The dog [was smitted by being condemned to be] tied up.
D.	The raven was smitted by having to spit [his semen into his mate's mouth].
E.	Ham was smitten in his skin.

XXI.

A	"Also he sent forth a dove from him to see if the waters had abated" (Gen. 8:8):
B.	Said R. Jeremiah, "On the basis of this verse [we learn] that the dwellings of the clean fowl was with the righteous man."

XXII.

A.	"And lo, in her mouth was an olive leaf as food" (Gen. 8:11):
B.	Said R. Eleazar, "The dove said before the Holy One, blessed be He, 'May my food be as bitter as an olive leaf but placed in our hand, and let it not be as sweet as honey but placed in the hand of mortals.'
C.	"What gives evidence that the word at hand means 'as food'?
D.	"From the following: 'Feed me [using the same root] with food convenient for me' (Prov. 30:8)."

XXIII.

A.	"After their families they went forth from the ark" (Gen. 8:19):

B. Said R. Yohanan, "'After their families' and not they [Freedman: alone]." [Freedman, p. 746, n. 6: While in the ark, copulation was forbidden. On their exit, it was permitted. That is the significance of "after their families," which denotes that mating was resumed and they ceased to be a group of single entities.]

XXIV.

A. Said R. Hana bar Bizna, "Said Eliezer [Abraham's servant] to Shem, the eldest [son], 'It is written, "After their families they went forth from the ark" (Gen. 8:19). How was it with you? [How did you take care of all the animals, given their diverse needs, while you were in the ark?]'

B. "He said to him, 'We had a great deal of trouble in the ark. A beast who usually was to be fed by day we fed by day. One that usually was to be fed by night we fed by night. As to the chameleon, father did not know what it ate.

C. "'One day he was sitting and cutting up a pomegranate, and a worm fell out of it. [The chameleon] ate it. From that point forth, he would mash bran for it. When it became maggoty, [the chameleon] ate it.'"

D. As to the lion, it was fed by a fever, for said Rab, "For no fewer than six days and no more than thirteen, fever sustains."

E. [Reverting to Shem's statement,] "'As to the phoenix, father found it lying in the hold of the ark. He said to it, "Don't you want food?"

F. "'It said to him, "I saw that you were occupied and thought not to bother you."

G. "'He said to it, "May it be God's will that you not die, as it is written, 'Then I said I shall die in the nest, but I shall multiply my days as the phoenix' (Job 29:18).'"'"

H. Said R. Hanah bar Livai, "Said Shem, the eldest [son] to Eliezer, 'When the kings of the east and the west came against you, what did you do?'

I. "He said to him, 'The Holy One, blessed be He, came to Abraham and set him at his right hand, and [God and Abraham] threw dirt, which turned into swords, and [they threw] chaff, which turned into arrows.

J. "'So it is written, "A Psalm of David. The Lord said to my master, Sit at my right hand until I make your enemies your footstool" (Ps. 110:1). And it is written, "Who raised up the righteous man from the east, called him to his food, gave the nations before him, and made him rule over kings? He made his sword as the dust and his bowl as driven stubble" (Isa. 41:2).'"

XXV.

A. Nahum of Gam Zo ["This Too"] was accustomed to say, on the occasion of anything that happened, "This, too, is for the good." One day, the Israelites wanted to end a gift to Caesar.

B. They said, "With [109A] whom shall we send it? Let us send it with Nahum of Gam Zo, for he is familiar with miracles."

C. When he got to an Inn, he wanted to lodge there. They said to him, "What do you have with you?"

D. He said to them, "I'm bringing a gift to Caesar."

E. They got up in the middle of the night and untied his box, took out everything in it, and filled the box with dirt. When he got there [to the capital], it turned out to be dirt. The [courtiers] said to him, "The Jews are ridiculing us."

F. They took him out to kill him. He said, "This, too, is for the good."

G. Elijah came and appeared to them as one of them. He said to them, "Perhaps this dirt comes from the dirt of Abraham, our father, who threw dirt that turned into swords and chaff that turned into arrows."

H. They looked, and that is what turned out. There was a province that they had not been able to conquer. They threw some of that dirt against it, and they conquered it. They brought [Nahum] to the treasury and said to him, "Take whatever you want."

I. He filled his box with gold. When he returned, those who were at the inn came and said to him, "What did you bring to the palace?"

J. He said to them, "What I took from here I brought there."

K. They took [dirt] and brought it there, and [the courtiers] put them to death.

XXVI.

A. *The generation of the dispersion has no share in the world to come [M. 10:3E]:*

B. What did they do wrong?

C. Said members of the house of R. Shila, "[They said], 'Let us build a tower and go up to the firmament and hit it with axes, so that the water will gush forth.'"

D. They ridiculed this in the West, "If so, they should have built it on a mountain!"

E. Said R. Jeremiah bar Eleazar, "They divided up into three parties. One said, 'Let us go up and dwell there.'

F. "The second said, 'Let us go up and worship an idol.'

G. "The third said, 'Let us go up and make war.'

H. "The party that said, 'Let us go up and dwell there – the Lord scattered them' (Gen. 11:9).

I. "The party that said, 'Let us go up and make war' turned into apes, spirits, devils, and night demons.

J. "The party that said, 'Let us go up and worship an idol' – 'for there the Lord did confound the language of all the earth' (Gen. 11:9)."

XXVII.

A. It has been taught on Tannaite authority:

B. R. Nathan says, "All of them [went up] intending to worship an idol.

C. "Here it is written, 'Let us make us a name' (Gen. 11:4), and elsewhere: 'And make no mention of the name of other gods' (Ex. 23:13).

D. "Just as in the latter passage [name stands for] idolatry, so here, too, 'name' stands for idolatry."

XXVIII.

A. Said R. Yohanan, "As to the tower, a third of it burned, a third of it sank into the earth, and a third is yet standing."

B. Said Rab, "The air of the tower makes people forget."

C.   Said R. Joseph, "Babylonia and Borsif are a bad sign for Torah study [because people there forget what they learn (Freeman, p. 748, n. 8)]."

D.   What is the sense of Borsif?

E.   Said R. Asi, "An empty pit [bor: pit: sif/shafi: empty]."

XXIX.

A.   *The men of Sodom have no portion in the world to come [M. 10:31]:*

B.   Our rabbis have taught on Tannaite authority:

C.   **The men of Sodom have no portion in the world to come [M. 11:31],**

D.   since it is said, **"And the men of Sodom were wicked sinners"** (Gen. 13:13) in this world.

E.   "Against the Lord exceedingly" – in the world to come. [T. San. 13:8A-C].

XXX.

A.   Said R. Judah, "'Wicked' – with their bodies.

B.   "And 'sinners' – with their money.

C.   "'Wicked' – with their bodies, as it is written, 'How then can I do this great wickedness and sin against God?' (Gen. 39:9).

D.   "'Sinners' – with their money, as it is written, 'And it be a sin unto you' (Deut. 15:9).

E.   "'Before the Lord' – this is blasphemy.

F.   "'Very much' – for they intended deliberately to sin."

G.   On Tannaite authority it was taught:

H.   "Wicked" – with their money.

I.   "And sinners" – with their bodies.

J.   "Wicked" – with their money, as it is written, "And your eye be wicked against your poor brothers" (Deut. 15:9).

K.   "And sinners" – with their bodies, as it is written, "And I will sin against God" (Gen. 39:9).

L.   "Before the Lord" – this is blasphemy.

M.   "Very much" – this refers to murder, as it is written, "Moreover, Manasseh shed innocent blood exceedingly" (2 Kgs. 21:16).

XXXI.

A.   Our rabbis have taught on Tannaite authority:

B.   The men of Sodom acted arrogantly before the Omnipresent only on account of the good which he lavished on them, since it is said, "As for the land, out of it comes bread....Its stones are the place of sapphires, and it has dust of gold. That path, no bird of prey knows....The proud beasts have not trodden it" (Job 28:5-8).

C.   Said the men of Sodom, "Since bread comes forth from our land, and silver and gold come forth from our land, and precious stones and pearls come forth from our land, we do not need people to come to us.

D.   "They come to us only to take things away from us. Let us go and forget how things are usually done among us."

E.   [Following T.'s version:] The Omnipresent said to them, "Because of the goodness which I have lavished upon you, you deliberately forget how things are usually done among you. I shall make you be forgotten from the world."

F.   What does it say? "They open shafts in a valley from where men
      live. They are forgotten by travelers. They hang afar from men,
      they swing to and fro (Job 28:4). In the thought of one who is at
      ease there is contempt for misfortune; it is ready for those whose
      feet slip. The tents of robbers are at peace, and those who
      provoke God are secure, who bring their god in their hand" (Job
      12:5-6).

G.   And so it says, "As I live, says the Lord God, your sister Sodom
      and her daughters have not done as you and your daughters have
      done. Behold, this was the guilt of your sister Sodom: she and
      her daughters had pride, surfeit of food, and prosperous ease, but
      did not aid the poor and needy. They were haughty and did
      abominable things before me. Therefore I removed them when I
      saw it" (Ezek. 16:48-50). [T. Sot. 3:11-2].

XXXII.
A.   Rabba expounded [the following verse]: "What is the sense of this
      verse: 'How long will you imagine mischief against a man? You
      shall be slain, all of you, you are all as a bowing wall and as a
      tottering fence' (Ps. 62:4)?

B.   "This teaches that the [Sodomites] would look enviously at wealthy
      men, so they would set such a man near a tottering fence and push
      it over on him and come and take away all his money."

C.   Raba expounded [the following verse]: "What is the meaning of
      this verse: 'In the dark they dig through houses, which they had
      marked for themselves in the daytime; they know not the light' (Job
      24:16)?

D.   "This teaches that the [Sodomites] would look enviously at wealthy
      men, so they would deposit with such a man valuable balsam. [The
      wealthy men] would put it into their treasure rooms. In the night
      [the others] would come and smell it out like a dog [and so know
      where there treasure was], as it is written, 'They return at evening,
      they make a noise like a dog, and go around the city' (Ps. 59:7).

E.   "They would then come and dig there and take away the money.

F.   "[As to the victim:] 'They cause him to go naked without clothing'
      (Job 24:10), 'that they have no covering in the cold' (Job 24:7). 'They
      lead away the ass of the fatherless, they take the widow's ox for a
      pledge' (Job 24:3). 'They remove the landmarks, they violently take
      away flocks and feed them' (Job 24:2). 'And he shall be brought to
      the grave and remain in the tomb' (Job 21:32)."

G.   R. Yosé interpreted the passage in this way in Sepphoris. That
      night three hundred houses in Sepphoris were broken into. They
      came and blamed him. They said to him, "You have shown the
      way to thieves."

H.   He said to them, "Did I know that thieves would come?"

I.   When R. Yosé died, the streets of Sepphoris ran with blood.

XXXIII.
A.   [The Sodomites] said, "Whoever has one ox must guard the herd
      one day, and whoever has no oxen must guard the herd two days."

B.   There was an orphan, son of a widow, the whom they gave the herd
      to pasture. He went and killed the [oxen]. He said to them, "He

who has one ox may take one hide. He who has no oxen may take two hides."

C. "Why so" they asked him?

D. He said to them **[109B]**, "The end of the matter must accord with its beginning. Just as, at the beginning, one who had an ox had to pasture the herd for one day and one who had none had to do it two days, so at the end, one who had an ox takes one hide, and one who has none takes two."

E. One who crosses a river [by a ferry] pays one *zuz*, and one who does not cross the river by a ferry [but crosses on his own] has to pay two.

F. If one had a row of bricks [drying in the sun], each one of them would take one, saying to him, "I only took one."

G. If one had garlic or onions drying [in the sun], each one of them would take one, saying to him, "I only took one."

XXXIV.

A. There were four judges in Sodom, named Liar, Big Liar, Forger, and Perverter of Justice.

B. If someone beat his neighbor's wife and made her abort, they say to him, "Give her to him, and he will make her pregnant for you."

C. If someone cut off the ear of his neighbor's ass, they say to him, "Give it to him, until it grows a new one."

D. If someone injured his neighbor, they say to [the victim], "Pay him the fee for letting blood from you."

E. One who crosses the river in a ferry pays four *zuz*, one who crosses through the water pays eight.

F. One day a washerman came by there. They said to him, "Pay four *zuz*."

G. He said to them, "I crossed in the water."

H. They said to him, "If so, pay eight, because you crossed through the water."

I. He would not pay, so they beat him up. He came before a judge, who said to him, "Pay the fee for his having let blood from you, as well as the eight *zuz* for crossing through the water."

J. Eliezer, Abraham's servant, happened to come there. Someone beat him up. He came before a judge, who said to him, "Pay him a fee for letting blood from you."

K. He took a stone and beat the judge. He said to him, "What's this?"

L. He said to him, "The fee that you now owe me give to this man, and my money will remain where it is."

M. They had beds, on which they would place guests. If someone was too long, they shortened him [by cutting off his legs], and if he was too short, they stretched him [on a rack].

N. Eliezer, Abraham's servant, happened by there. They said to him, "Come, lie down on the bed."

O. He said to the, "I took a vow from the time that my mother died never to sleep on a bed."

P. When a poor man came there, each one of them gave him a *denar*, on which he wrote his name. But they gave him no bread. When he would die, each one of them came and took back his *denar*.

Q   They made this stipulation among them: Whoever invited someone
       to a banquet will have to give over his cloak. There was a banquet,
       and Eliezer happened to come there, but they did not give him any
       bread. Since he wanted to eat, Eliezer came and sat down at the
       end of them all. They said to him, "Who invited you here?"

R.   He said to the one who sat nearby, "You were the one who invited
       me."

S.   He said, "Perhaps they will hear that I was the one who invited him
       and take away the cloak of that man [me]." He took off his cloak
       and ran away. And so they all did, until all of them were gone, and
       he ate the entire banquet.

T.   A certain girl brought out bread hidden in a pitcher to a poor man.
       The matter became known. They covered her with honey and put
       her on the parapet of the wall, and a swarm of bees came and ate
       her up.

U.   For it is written, "And the Lord said, The cry of Sodom and
       Gomorrah, because it is great" (Gen. 18:20).

V.   On this passage, said R. Judah said Rab, "It is on account of the girl
       [with the consonants for 'girl' and 'great' being the same]."

XXXV.

A   *The spies have no portion in the world to come, as it is said, "Even those*
       men who brought up an evil report of the land died by the plague before the
       Lord" (Num. 14:37). "Died" in this world. "By the plague" in the world
       to come.

B.   *"The party of Korah is not destined to rise up, for it is written 'And the*
       earth closed upon them' – in this world. 'And they perished from among
       the assembly' in the world to come," the words of R. Aqiba. And R.
       Eliezer says, "Concerning them it says, 'The Lord kills and resurrects,
       brings down to Sheol and brings up again' (1 Sam. 2:6)."

C.   Our rabbis have taught on Tannaite authority:

D.   "Korah and his company have no portion in the world to come
       and will not live in the world to come,

E.   "since it is said, 'And the earth closed upon them' (Num. 16:33) –
       in this world.

F.   "'And they perished from among the assembly' – in the world to
       come," the words of R. Aqiba [M. 11:3Z-BB].

G   R. Judah b. Petera says, "Lo, they are like something lost and
       searched for [T.: They will come to the world to come].

H   "For concerning them it is written, 'I have gone astray like a
       perishing sheep; seek your servant' (Ps. 119:176)

I.   [Following T.:] 'Perishing' is said here, and in the matter of Korah
       and his company, 'perishing' also is said.

J.   "Just as 'perishing' spoken of later on refers to that which is
       being sought, so 'perishing' spoken of here refers to that which is
       being sought" [T. San. 13:9C-I].

XXXVI.

A.   "Now Korah took..." (Num. 16:1):

B.   He took a bad deal for himself.

C.   "Korah" – for he was made a bald spot ["Korah" and "bald spot"
       using the same consonants] in Israel.

D. "Son of Izhar" – a son who turned the heat of the entire world against himself, as the heat of noon ["Izhar" and "noon" use the same consonants].

E. "Son of Kohath" – who set on edge [KHT] the teeth of those who gave birth to him.

F. "Son of Levi" – a son of the company of Gehenna ["Levi" and "company" use the same consonants].

G. Then why not say, "son of Jacob" – a son who followed to Gehenna [with the letters for "Jacob" and "follow" being shared]?

H. Said R. Samuel b. R. Isaac, "Jacob sought mercy for himself, [that he should not be listed here], as it is said, 'O my soul, come not into their secret, to their assembly my honor be not united' (Gen. 39:6).

I. "'O my soul, come not into their secret' – this refers to the spies.

J. "'Unto their assembly, my honor be not united' refers to the assembly of Korah."

K. "Dathan" (Num. 16:1) [colleague of Korah] – so-called because he transgressed the law [*dat*] of God.

L. "Abiram" (Num. 16:1) – so-called because he strengthened himself [using the consonants of the name] not to carry out an act of repentance.

M. "On" (Num. 16:1) [whose name means "lamentation"] – so-called because he sat and lamented [what he had done].

N. "Peleth [On's father]" (Num. 16:1) – so-called because wonders [using the same letters as the name] were done for him.

O. "The son of Reuben" (Num. 16:1) – who saw and understood [using the consonants of the name] [not to get involved].

XXXVII.

A. Said Rab, "As to On, son of Peleth, his wife saved him. She said to him, 'What do you get out of this matter? If one master is the greater, you are his disciple, and if the other master is the greater, you are still his disciple!'

B. "He said to her, 'What should I do? I was in their conspiracy and I took an oath to be with them.'

C. "She said to him, 'I know that they are all a holy congregation, for it is written, "Seeing all the congregation are holy, every one of them" (Num. 16:3).'

D. "She said to him, 'Stay here, and I'll save you.' She got him drunk on wine and laid him down in [the tent]. She sat down at the flap [110A] and loosened her hair. Whoever came and saw her turned back. [No one would gaze at her.]

E. "Meanwhile Korah's wife joined them, saying to them, 'See what Moses is doing! He is king. His brother made him high priest. His brother's sons he has made assistant priests. If heave-offering is brought, he says, "Give it to the priest." If tithe is brought, which you have every right to take [since it is for the Levites], he says, "Give a tenth of it to the priest."

F. "'Moreover, he has shaved off all your hair [as part of the purification rite, Num. 8:7], and ridicules you as if you were dirt, for he envied your hair.'

G. "He said to her, 'But he did the same thing to himself?'

H   "She said to him, 'It was because all the greatness was coming to him, he said also, "Let my soul die with the Philistines" (Jud. 16:30). [Freedman, p. 754, n. 5: This was used proverbially to denote readiness to suffer, so that others might suffer too. Moses, retaining all the greatness himself, did not mind shaving his own hair off, seeing that he had caused all the rest to do so, thus depriving them of their beauty.]

I   "'And furthermore he has said to you to make [fringes] of blue [on your garments] (Num. 15:38). But if you think that the blue [fringe] is a religious duty, then produce cloaks of blue and dress your entire academy in them.'

J.   "That is in line with what is written, 'Every wise woman builds her house' – referring to the wife of On, son of Peleth.

K.   "'But the foolish woman tears it down with her own hands' (Prov. 14:1) – referring to the wife of Korah."

XXXVIII.

A   "And they rose up before Moses, with certain of the children of Israel, two hundred and fifty" (Num. 16:2):

B.   They were the distinguished members of the community.

C.   "Chosen for the appointed times" (Num. 16:2):

D.   For they knew how to intercalate years and designate the beginnings of the new months.

E.   "Men of renown" (Num. 16:2):

F.   For they were known throughout the world.

XXXIX.

A.   "And when Moses heard, he fell on his face" (Num. 16:4):

B.   What did he hear?

C.   Said R. Samuel bar Nahmani said R. Jonathan, "That people suspected him of having sexual relations with a married woman, as it is said, 'And they expressed jealousy [as to sexual infidelity] of Moses in the camp' (Ps. 106:16)."

D.   Said R. Samuel bar Isaac, "This teaches that everyone expressed jealousy of his wife [M. Sot. 1:1] with respect to Moses, as it is said, 'And Moses took the tent and pitched it outside the camp' (Ex. 33:7). [Freedman, p. 755, n. 5: to avoid all ground of suspicion.]"

XL.

A   "And Moses rose up and went to Dathan and Abiram" (Num. 16:25):

B.   Said R. Simeon b. Laqish, "On the basis of this verse we learn that one should not hold on to a quarrel [but should be eager to end it, in the model of Moses, who modestly went out to the other side to seek a resolution]."

C.   For Rab said, "Whoever holds on to a quarrel [and does not seek to end it] violates a negative commandment, for it is said, 'And let him not be as Korah and as his company' (Num. 17:5)."

D.   R. Ashi said, "He is worthy of being smitten with *saraat*.

E.   "Here it is written, 'As the Lord said to him by the hand of Moses' (Num. 17:5), and elsewhere it is written, 'And the Lord said to him, Put your hand into your bosom [and when he took it out, behold, his hand was leprous as snow' (Ex. 4:6)."

XLI.
A Said R. Yosé, "Whoever contends with the kingdom of the house of David is worthy that a snake bite him.

B. "Here it is written, 'And Adonijah slew sheep and oxen and fat cattle by the stone of Zoheleth' (1 Kgs. 1:9), and elsewhere it is written, 'With the poison of serpents [using the same consonants as the word *Zoheleth*] of the dust' (Deut. 32:24)."

C. Said R. Hisda, "Whoever is contentious with his master is as if he were contentious with the presence of God, as it is said, 'When they strove against the Lord' (Num. 26:9). [Freedman, p. 755, n. 14: The reference is to Korah's rebellion; though against Moses only, it is stigmatized as being against God.]"

D. Said R. Hama b. R. Hanina, "Whoever undertakes to quarrel with his master is as if he had quarrelled with the Presence of God, as it is said, 'This is the water of Strife, because the children of Israel strove with the Lord' (Num. 20:13)."

E. Said R. Hanina bar Pappa, "Whoever complains against his master is as if he complains against the Presence of God, as it is said, 'Your murmurings are not against us but against the Lord' (Ex. 16:8)."

F. Said R. Abbahu, "Whoever murmurs against his master is as if he murmurs against the Presence of God, as it is said, 'And the people spoke against God and against Moses' (Num. 21:5)."

XLII.
A. "Riches kept for the owners to their hurt" (Qoh. 5:12):

B. Said R. Simeon b. Laqish, "This refers to the riches of Korah."

C. "And all the substance that was at their feet" (Deut. 11:6):

D. Said R. Eleazar, "This refers to the wealth of a man, that puts him on his feet."

E. And said R. Levi, "A load for three hundred white mules were made up by the keys of Korah's treasury, although all of them were made of leather, both keys and locks [and not metal]."

F. Said R. Hama b. R. Hanina, "Joseph hid three treasures in Egypt. One of them was revealed to Korah, one of them was revealed to Antoninus, son of Severus, and one of them is hidden away for the righteous in the world to come."

XLIII.
A And said R. Yohanan, "Korah was not among those who were swallowed up nor among those who were burned.

B. "He was not among those who were swallowed up, for it is written, 'And all the men that joined Korah' (Num. 16:32) – but not Korah.

C. "He was not among those who were burned, for it is written, 'When the fire devoured two hundred and fifty men' (Num. 16:10) – but not Korah."

D. In a Tannaite teaching it was repeated:

E. Korah was one of those who were burned up, and he was one of those who were swallowed up.

F. He was one of those who were swallowed up, for it is written, "And swallowed them up together with Korah" (Num. 16:10).

G. He was one of those who were burned, since it is written, "And there came up a fire from the Lord and consumed the two hundred fifty men" (Num. 16:35) – including Korah.

XLIV.

A. Said Raba, "What is the meaning of that which is written, 'The sun and the moon stood still in their *zebul*, at the light of your arrows they went' (Hab. 3:1)? [Freedman, p. 757, n. 1: There are seven heavens, of which *zebul* is one. What were they doing in *zebul*, seeing that they are set in the firmament, a lower heaven?]

B. "This teaches that the sun and the moon went up to the firmament called *zebul*. They said before the Holy One, blessed be He, 'Lord of the world, if you do justice with the son of Amram, we shall go forth, and if not, we shall not go forth.'

C. "He shot arrows at them and said to them, 'On account of the honor owing to me you never objected, but on account of the honor owing to a mortal man, you make a protest!'

D. "Nowadays they go forth only when they are driven out."

XLV.

A. Raba interpreted a verse of Scripture, "What is the meaning of what is written, 'But if the Lord make a new thing and the earth open her mouth' (Num. 16:30)?

B. "Said Moses before the Holy One, blessed be He, 'If Gehenna has been created, well and good, and if not, let the Lord now create it.'

C. "For what purpose? If we say that he was actually to create it then and there, [how can this be so, for] 'There is no new thing under the sun' (Qoh. 1:9)?

D. "Rather, it was to bring its mouth near [to the present place]."

XLVI.

A. "But the children of Korah did not die" (Num. 26:11):

B. A Tannaite authority taught in the name of our Master [Judah the Patriarch]: "A place was set aside for them in Gehenna, and they sat there and recited a song [for God]."

XLVII.

A. Said Rabbah bar bar Hana, "One time I was going along the way, and a Tai [Arab] said to me, 'Come, and I shall show you where the men of Korah were swallowed up.' I went and saw two crevasses, from which smoke came forth. He took a piece of wool, wet it down, and set it on the tip of his spear and passed it over the spot, and it was singed.

B. "I said to him, 'Listen to what you are going to hear.'

C. "And I heard him saying, 'Moses and his Torah are true, and they are liars.'

D. "[110B] He said to me, 'Every thirty days Gehenna turns them over like meat in a pot, and they say this: 'Moses and his Torah are true, and they are liars.'"

XLVIII.

A. *The generation of the wilderness has no portion in the world to come [M. 11:3 W]:*

B. Our rabbis have taught on Tannaite authority:

C. **"The generation of the wilderness has no portion in the world to come [M. 10:3W],**

D. **[T. adds:] "and will not live in the world to come,**

E. **"for it is said, 'In this wilderness they sall be consumed and there they shall die' (Num. 14:35),**

F. "'In this wilderness they shall be consumed' – in this world,

G. "and there they will die, ' in the world to come.

H "And it says, 'Of them I swore in my wrath that they should not enter into my rest' (Ps. 95:11)," the words of R. Aqiba.

I. R. Eliezer says, "They will come into the world to come,

J. "for concerning them it is said, 'Gather my saints together to me, those that have made a covenant with me by sacrifice' (Ps. 50:5) [M. 11:3Y] [T. San. 13:10].

K. "What does Scripture mean, 'I swore in my wrath'?

L. "'In my wrath I swore, but I retract it.'"

M R. Joshua b. Qorha says, "These things were spoken only regarding generations to come,

N as it is said, 'Gather my saints together to me' – these are the righteous of every generation [T.: because they did deeds of loving kindness to me];

O. "'Those that have made a covenant with me' – this refers to Hananiah, Mishael, and Azariah, who gave themselves up to the fiery furnace on my account.

P. "'By sacrifice' – this refers to R. Aqiba and his colleagues, who gave themselves over to the slaughter on account of the teachings of the Torah."

Q R. Simeon b. Menassia says, "They will come [into the world to come],

R. "and concerning them it is said, 'And the redeemed of the world shall return and come to Zion with gladness' (Isa. 35:10) [T. San. 13:11].

S. Said Rabbah bar bar Hannah said R. Yohanan, "R. Aqiba abandoned his love [of Israel, when he said that the generation of the wilderness will not enjoy the world to come].

T. "For it is written, 'Go and cry in the ears of Jerusalem, saying, thus says the Lord, I remember the loyalty of your youth, the love of your espousals, when you went after me in the wilderness, in an unsown land' (Jer. 2:2). [Freedman, p. 759, n. 1: Thus the merit of this act of faith on the part of the generation of the wilderness stood their descendants in good stead and conferred the privilege on them of a share in the world to come].

U. "Now if others will come on account of their merit [to the world to come,] how much the more so they themselves!"

The Talmud simply lays forth materials to complement the Mishnah's topics, item by item:

I. The generation of the flood [M. 11:3A]:
   I-XXV

II. The generation of the dispersion [M. 11:3E]:
   XXVI-XXVIII

III. The men of Sodom [M. 111:3I]:
   XXIX-XXXIV

IV. The spies [M. 11:3S]:
   XXXV

V.   The generation of the wilderness [M. 11:3W]:
       XLVIII
VI.   The party of Korah [M. 11:3Z]:
       XXXV-XLVII

The sole point of note is the change in the order of the Mishnah's topics at the final two items. Otherwise the sequence and topical unfolding are just as expected. So it appears that in my opening hypothesis I claimed not too much but too little. In fact, the miscellany forms a Mishnah commentary – but the purpose of the commentary is simply to extend, expand, illustrate a topic, rather than to analyze and criticize a proposition. But given the contents of the Mishnah paragraphs under study, we may hardly find that an inappropriate program. So, as I said, agglutinative discourse in the Bavli is, if not propositional, still entirely cogent and easy to follow, once you know the rules. And we do.

What I find surprising is that all of the analyses of this extended discussion of tractates Berakhot and Sanhedrin have been in hand for seven years, since my initial investigation of how the compositions we have examined form composites, and how these composites are held together and set in sequence, were complete when I did my translations of both tractates, published in 1984-1985. So the data were available. What was lacking was that I did not grasp, first, the distinction between composition and composite, and, second, the truly coherent character of the Bavli overall. It was only when I had grasped that the Bavli held together and, beginning to end, uses a few simple modes of discourse to make a few simple points, that I also began to find troubling what struck me as anomalous, even as recently as last year, when I worked on *The Bavli's One Voice*. Only when the anomalous character of the entire tractates absolutely demanded attention did I look again at the matter. And then, all of the foregoing discussions, in Chapters Four and Five of this book, were waiting for me. It is now possible to say very simply that, while merely topical, not propositional and assuredly not syllogistic, the miscellanies we have examined are so composed and also so arranged in sequence as to serve the Mishnah as commentaries of a particular kind – amplification on the subjects treated in the Bavli, and that alone.

6

Traits of Agglutinative Discourse in the Talmud of Babylonia

It is now very simple to define agglutinative discourse in the context of the Bavli. The Talmud of Babylonia makes use of two distinct principles for the formation of large-scale composites of distinct compositions, and the framers of the document very rarely set forth a composition on its own, standing without clear ties to a larger context. Ordinarily, they brought together distinct and free-standing compositions in the service of Mishnah exegesis and amplification of law originating in a Mishnah paragraph under analysis. For that purpose they would then draw upon already written compositions, which would be adduced as cases, statements of principles, fully exposed analyses, inclusive of debate and argument, in the service of that analysis. So all of the compositions in a given composite would serve the governing analytical or propositional purpose of the framer of the composite. Where a composition appears to shade over into a direction of its own, that very quickly is seen to serve as a footnote or even an appendix to the composite at hand.

We have now seen that in addition to propositional and even analytical composites, the framers of the Bavli also formed compositions into thematic composites, and on the face of it, this second type of composite presents the appearance of a miscellany. But far from forming a mere rubbish heap of this-and-that, this other type of composite proves not at all miscellaneous. Clear, governing, and entirely predictable principles allow us to explain how one composition is joined to another. Ordinarily, a sizable miscellany will tell us more about a subject that the Mishnah addresses or richly illustrate a principle that the Mishnah means to set forth through its cases and examples. In that sense, the miscellaneous kind of composite is set forth as Mishnah commentary of a particular kind. As we have seen, an agglutinative composite may be formed by appeal to a common theme, ordinarily stated by the Mishnah or at least suggested by its contents, and several closely related themes will then come under exposition in a massive miscellany. One common theme will be a passage of Scripture, systematically examined. A subordinate principle of agglutination will join composites attributed to the same authority or tradent, though it would be unusual for the compositions so joined to deal with entirely unrelated topics. So the principal point of differentiation between propositional composites and agglutinative ones is that the former analyze a problem, the latter illustrate a theme or even a proposition.

It follows that two modes of forming composites serve the framers of the Bavli, the paramount, propositional and analytical mode, and the subordinate, agglutinative sort. The one joins together a variety of distinct compositions into a propositional statement, commonly enriched with analytical initiatives, and frequently bearing a burden of footnotes and appendices. The other combines distinct compositions into a thematic composite, the proposition of which is ordinarily rather general and commonplace. A second principle of agglutinative composite making appeals to common attributions, though when two or more compositions are joined into a composite because they are assigned to the same authority or tradental chain, they very likely will also bear in common an interest in a single theme, if not in a uniform proposition in connection with that theme.

Since all of the miscellanies we have examined concern theological or exegetical subjects, none focusing upon a problem of law, we should be tempted to propose that agglutinative discourse governs the treatment of one type of subject matter, theology or exegesis, but not another, the more prominent, and generally held, normative one, of law. To demonstrate that the distinction between lore and law (*aggadah* and *halakhah*) makes no difference in whether or not compositions will be linked into composites by appeal to propositional analytical or merely agglutinative principles of formation, let me give a fine example of an agglutinative legal ("halakhic") passage, which shows beyond any doubt that there is no important point of distinction, so far as agglutinative discourse is concerned, between compositions and subcomposites of one kind and of the other. We find in both types of subject matter precisely the same literary traits of composite making. Here the compositions are joined agglutinatively, by reference to a common subject matter; but the composite that results does not make a point, for example, of proposition, analysis, or argument. Rather, it serves to illustrate a theme, very much the way the massive miscellanies in tractates Berakhot and

Sanhedrin illustrate a theme. We deal with Bavli Baba Batra Chapter Five.

5:11

A. Said Rabban Simeon b. Gamaliel, "Under what circumstances?
B. "In the case of liquid measures.
C. "But in the case of dry measures, it is not necessary."
D. [88B] And [a shopkeeper] is liable to let the scales go down by a handbreadth [to the buyer's advantage].
E. [If] he was measuring out for him exactly, he has to give him an overweight –
F. one part in ten for liquid measure,
G. one part in twenty for dry measure.
H. In a place in which they are accustomed to measure with small measures, one must not measure with large measures;
I. with large ones, one must not measure with small;
J. [in a place in which it is customary] to smooth down [what is in the measure], one should not heap it up;
K. to heap it up, one should not smooth it down.

III.1 A In a place in which they are accustomed to measure with small measures, one must not measure with large measures; with large ones, one must not measure with small; in a place in which it is customary to smooth down what is in the measure, one should not heap it up; to heap it up, one should not smooth it down:
B. *Our rabbis have taught on Tannaite authority:*
C. How on the basis of Scripture do we know that **in a place in which it is customary to smooth down what is in the measure, one should not heap it up; to heap it up, one should not smooth it down?** Scripture says, "A perfect measure" (Deut. 25:15). [Slotki: Deviating from the usual practice the buyer or the seller may defraud or mislead others.]
D. And how do we know that if one said, "Lo, where it is customary to heap up, I will level it off, and reduce the price, or, in a place where they level, I will heap it up, and raise the price," they do not listen to him [he may not do so]?
E. Scripture says, "A perfect and just measure you shall have" (Deut. 25:15).

III.2 A. *Our rabbis have taught on Tannaite authority:*
B. How on the basis of Scripture do we know that in a place where the practice is to allow an overweight, they do not give the exact weight, and in a place in which they give an exact weight, they do not give an overweight?
C. Scripture says, "A perfect weight" (Deut. 25:15).
D. And how on the basis of Scripture do we know that if one said in a place in which they give an overweight, "Lo, I shall give an exact weight and charge him less," or in a place in which they give an exact weight, "Lo, I shall give him an overweight and add to the price," they do not listen to him?
E. Scripture says, "A perfect weight and a just one" (Deut. 25:15).

F.   Said R. Judah of Sura, "'You shall not have anything in your house'
(Deut. 25:14). Why? Because of your 'diverse weights' (Deut.
25:13). But if you keep 'a perfect and just weight,' you shall have
things (Deut. 25:15), 'if a perfect and just measure, you shall
have....'"

There is no problem in explaining why No. 2 is tacked on to No. 1. The
proposition is the same, so is the form. But what follows is another
matter, since we are now going to entertain a different proposition
altogether.

III.3 A.   *Our rabbis have taught on Tannaite authority:*
       B.   "You shall have...": this teaches that they appoint market
supervisors to oversee measures, but they do not appoint market
supervisors to control prices.

No. 4 will now illustrate the foregoing.

III.4 A   *The household of the patriarch appointed market supervisors to oversee
measures and to control prices. Said Samuel to Qarna, "Go, repeat the
Tannaite rule to them:* They appoint market supervisors to oversee
measures, but they do not appoint market supervisors to control
prices.
       B.   *He went out and instructed them:* "They appoint market supervisors
to oversee measures and to control prices."
       C.   *He said to him, "What do they call you? Qarna [horn]? Let a horn grow
out of your eye." A horn grew out of his eye.*
       D.   *And as for Qarna, in accord with what authority did he reach this
conclusion?*
       E.   *It was in accord with what Rammi bar Hama said R. Isaac said, "They
appoint market supervisors to oversee measures and to control
prices, on account of crooks."*

Now we have a miscellany, meaning, a set of compositions, each
standing on its own foundation, all making clearly articulated points,
none related except in a shared theme to what stands fore or aft. What
we shall also observe is subsets, clearly joined to one another, but
connected to the larger context only by the general theme. These subsets
do not require explicit specification, being obvious on the face of it.

III.5 A.   *Our rabbis have taught on Tannaite authority:*
       B.   If somebody ordered a litra, he should measure out a litra; if he
ordered a half-litra, he should measure out for him a half-litra; a
quarter-litra, he should measure out a quarter.
       C.   *So what does that passage tell us?*
       D.   *It is that we provide weights in these denominations.*
III.6 A.   *Our rabbis have taught on Tannaite authority:*
       B.   If someone ordered three-quarters of a litra, he should not say to
him, "Weigh out for me three-quarters of a litra one by one," but

he should say to him, "Weight out a litra for me but leave out a quarter-litra with the meat" [Slotki: on the other scale].

III.7   A.   *Our rabbis have taught on Tannaite authority:*

      B.   If someone wanted to order ten litras, he should not say to him, "Weigh them out for me one by one and allow an overweight for each," but all of them are weighed together, with one overweight covering the whole order [cf. T. B.B. 5:9B-I].

III.8   A.   *Our rabbis have taught on Tannaite authority:*

      B.   [Slotki:] The hollow handle in which the tongue of the balance rests must be suspended in the air three handbreadths [removed from the roof from which the balance hangs], and it must be three handbreadths above the ground.

      C.   The beam and the rope that goes with it should be twelve handbreadths, and the balances of wool dealers and glassware dealers must be suspended two handbreadths in the air from the ceiling and two above the ground. The beams and ropes that go with them must be nine handbreadths in length. The balance of a shopkeeper and a householder must be suspended a handbreadth in the air from above and a handbreadth above the ground. The beam and ropes that go with them must be six handbreadths. A gold balance must be suspended three fingerbreadths in the air from above and three above the ground. I don't know the length of the beam and the cords.

      D.   *What kind of balance is the one mentioned first [before the specific rulings for those of the wool dealers, glassware dealers, and so on]?*

      E.   [89B] *Said R. Pappa, "The one used for heavy pieces of metal."*

III.9   A   Said R. Mani bar Patish, "Just as they have specified certain restrictions with regard to disqualifying balances for commercial purposes, so they have laid down disqualifications with regard to their constituting utensils for the purpose of receiving cultic uncleanness."

      B.   *What does he tell us that we do not learn from the following:* **The cord of the scales of the storekeepers and [or] of householders – [to be susceptible to uncleanness must be in length at least] a handbreadth. A handle of the ax at its front – a handbreadth. The projection of the shaft of a pair of compasses – a handbreadth. The shaft of a stonemason's chisel – a handbreadth A cord of the balances of wool dealers and of glass weighers – two handbreadths. The shaft of a millstone chisel – two handbreadths. The battle ax of the legions – two handbreadths. The goldsmith's hammer – two handbreadths. And of the carpenters – three handbreadths] [M. Kel. 29:5-6]!** [Slotki: Since this restriction has been applied to one kind of balance, are not the other kinds of balance to be implied?]

      C.   The statement that he made is necessary to deal with the sizes of the beam and cords [that are not dealt with at the parallel].

A subset now follows, Nos. 10-13, glossed by No. 14.

III.10 A.   *Our rabbis have taught on Tannaite authority:*

B.   They make weights out of neither tin or led or alloy but of stone or glass.

III.11   A.   *Our rabbis have taught on Tannaite authority:*
B.   They make the strike not out of a board, because it is light, nor out of metal, because it is heavy, but out of olive, nut, sycamore, or box wood.

III.12   A.   *Our rabbis have taught on Tannaite authority:*
B.   They do not make the strike thick on one side and thin on the other.
C.   They do not make the strike with a single quick movement, because striking in that way brings loss to the seller and advantage to the buyer, nor very slowly, since this is a loss to the buyer but a benefit to the seller.
D.   In regard to all of these shady practices, said Rabban Yohanan b. Zakkai, "Woe is me if I speak, woe is me if I do not speak. If I speak, then sharpers will learn from me, and if I don't speak, then the sharpers will say, 'The disciples of sages haven't got the slightest idea what we are doing.'"

III.13   A.   *The question was raised: "So did he speak of them or didn't he?"*
B.   Said R. Samuel bar R. Isaac, "He did speak of them: 'For the ways of the Lord are right, and the just walk in them; but transgressors stumble therein' (Hos. 14:10)."

III.14   A.   *Our rabbis have taught on Tannaite authority:*
B.   "You shall do no unrighteousness in judgment, in surveying, weight, or in measure" (Lev. 19:35):
C.   "In surveying": these refers to surveying the real estate, meaning, one should not measure for one party in the dry season and another in the rainy season.
D.   "Weight": one should not keep one's weights in salt.
E.   "In measure" (Lev. 19:35): one should not make the liquid form a head.
F.   And that yields an argument a fortiori: if with reference to a mere "measure" (Lev. 19:35), which is merely one sixth of a log, the Torah demanded meticulous attention, how much the more so must one give meticulous case in measuring out a hin, half a hin, a third of a hin, a quarter of a hin, a log, a half a log, a quarter of a log, a toman, half a toman, and an uqla.

III.15   A.   Said R. Judah said Rab, "It is forbidden for someone to keep in his house a measure that is either smaller or larger than the norm, even for the purpose of a piss pot."
B.   *Said R. Pappa, "But we have stated that rule only in a place where measures are not properly marked with a seal, but where they are properly sealed, they are permitted, since, if the purchaser sees no mark, he is not going to accept their use. And even in a place where measures are not properly marked with a seal, we have stated that rule only in a case in which they are not supervised [by administrative officers of the market], but if they are ordinarily supervised, we should have no objection."*
C.   *But that is not the case, for sometimes the buyer may come by at twilight and may happen to take a faulty measure. And so, too, that has been taught on Tannaite authority: It is forbidden for someone to keep in his house a measure that is either smaller or larger than the norm, even for the purpose of a piss pot. But he may make a seah*

measure, a tarqab, a half-tarqab, a qab, a half-qab, a quarter-qab, a toman, [90B] and an ukla measure. How much is an uqla measure? It is a fifth of a quarter of a qab. In the case of liquid measures, one may make a hin, a half-hin, third-hin, quarter-hin, log, half-log, quarter-log, eighth-log, and eight of an eighth, which is a qortob.

D. *So why shouldn't someone also make a double-qab measure?*

E. *It might be confused with a tarqab.*

F. *Therefore people may err by as much as a third.*

G. *If so, then a qab also people should not make, since they might confused it with a half-tarqab. Rather, as to a double-qab, this is the reason that one is not to make it, specifically, that one will confused it with a half-tarqab.*

H. *And this proves that one may err by a quarter.*

I. *If so, a half-toman and an ukla measure are things people should not make.* [Slotki: The difference between a half-toman, a sixteenth-qab, and an ukla, a twentieth-qab, is only one-eightieth of a qab, which is a fifth of the half-toman, less than a quarter, so that these two measures could certainly be mistaken for one another.]

J. *Said R. Pappa, "With small measures people are quite expert."*

K. *What about a third of a hin and a fourth of a hin — shouldn't people be forbidden to make these?*

L. *Since these were utilized in the sanctuary, rabbis made no decree in their regard.*

M. *Well, shouldn't there be a precautionary decree with respect to the sanctuary?*

N. *The priests are meticulous in their work.*

III.16 A. Said Samuel, "They may not increase the size of the measures [whether or not people concur] by more than a sixth, nor the coins by more than a sixth, and he who makes a profit must not profit by more than a sixth."

B. What is the operative consideration for the first of these three rulings?

C. *If we say that it is because the market prices will rise, then for that same consideration, it should not be permitted to increase the size of the measures even by a sixth. And if the operative consideration is overreaching, so that the transaction should not have to be annulled, did* not Raba say, "One can retract from an agreement that involves fraud in measure, weight, or number, even though it is less than the standard, a sixth, of overreaching." *And if the operative consideration is that the dealer may not incur any loss, then is the whole purpose of the law to guard him from loss? Is he not entitled to make a profit? But "buy and sell at no profit, merely to be called a merchant!"*

D. *Rather, said R. Hisda, "Samuel identified a verse of Scripture and interpreted it, 'And the sheqel shall be twenty gerahs, twenty sheqels, twenty-five sheqels, ten and five sheqels shall be your maneh' (Ezek. 45:12). [90B] Now was the maneh to be two hundred forty denars?* [But it is supposed to be twenty-five sheqels or a hundred denars (Cashdan).] *But three facts are to be inferred from this statement:* [1] The maneh used in the sanctuary is worth double what the maneh is usually worth; [2] they may not increase the size of the measures [whether or not people concur] by more than a sixth, and [3] the sixth is added over and above the original [so to add a sixth, the original is divided into five parts and another part of equal value, making a sixth one, then is added to it, so the maneh consisted of 240 denars (Cashdan, *Menahot*)]."

III.17 A   *R. Pappa bar Samuel ordained a measure of three qepizi. They said to him,* "Lo, said Samuel, 'They may not increase the size of the measures [whether or not people concur] by more than a sixth'!"

B   *He said to them, "What I am ordaining is an entirely new measure." He sent it to Pumbedita, and they did not adopt it. He sent it to Papunia and they adopted it, naming it the Pappa measure.*

Any doubt that we are dealing with a miscellany is removed by what follows, which in no way pertains to the foregoing in any detail. And yet it is introduced for a very clear purpose, which is to make a point about a common theme and proposition: fair dealing in the market, giving and getting true value.

III.18 A.   *Our rabbis have taught on Tannaite authority:*

B   Concerning those who store up produce, lend money on usury, falsify measures, and price gouge, Scripture says, "Saying, when will the new moon be gone, that we may sell grain, and the Sabbath, that we may set forth grain? Making the ephah small and the sheqel great and falsifying the balances of deceit" (Amos 8:5). And in their regard, Scripture states, "The Lord has sworn by the pride of Jacob, surely I will never forget any of their works" (Amos 8:7).

C.   *What would be an example of those who store up produce?*

D.   *Said R. Yohanan, "Like Shabbetai the produce hoarder."*

III.19 A   *The father of Samuel would sell produce at the early market price when the early market price prevailed [that is, cheap, so keeping prices down through the year (Slotki)]. Samuel his son held the produce back and sold it when the late market prices prevailed, but at the early market price.*

B   *They sent word from there, "The father is better than the son. How come? Prices that have been held down remain down."*

III.20 A   Said Rab, "Someone may store up his own produce" [but may not hoard for trading purposes (Slotki)].

B.   *So, too, it has been taught on Tannaite authority:*

C   [Following Tosefta's version:] They do not hoard in the Land of Israel things upon which life depends, for example, wine, oil, fine flour, and produce. But things upon which life does not depend, for instance, cummin and spice, lo, this is permitted. And they put things in storage for three years, the eve of the seventh year, the seventh year itself, and the year after the seventh year.

D.   Under what circumstances?

E.   In the case of that which one purchases in the market.

F.   But in the case of what one puts aside from what he himself has grown, even for a period of ten years it is permitted.

G   But in a year of famine even a qab of carobs one should not put into storage, because he brings a curse on the prices [by forcing them upward through artificial demand] [T. A.Z. 4:1A-G].

III.21 A   *Said R. Yosé b. R. Hanina to Puga his servant, "Go, store up fruit for me for the next three years: the eve of the Sabbatical Year, the Sabbatical Year, and the year after the Sabbatical Year."*

III.22 A.   *Our rabbis have taught on Tannaite authority:*

     B.   They do not export from the Land of Israel to Syria things upon which life depends, for example, wine, oil, and fine flour.

     C.   R. Judah b. Batera says, "I say that they export wine to Syria, because in doing so, one diminishes silliness [in the Land of Israel]."

     D.   Just as they do not export to Syria, so they do not export from one hyparchy to another.

     E.   And R. Judah permits doing so [91A] from one hyparchy to another [T. A.Z. 4:2].

III.23 A.   *Our rabbis have taught on Tannaite authority:*

     B.   They are not to make a profit in the land of Israel from the necessities of life, for instance, wine, oil, and flour.

     C.   They said concerning R. Eleazar b. Azariah that he would make a profit from wine and oil all his life [T. A.Z. 4:1H-J].

     D.   *In the matter of wine, he concurred with the view of R. Judah [b. Batera], and in the matter of oil, as it happens, in the place where R. Eleazar b. Azariah lived, oil was abundant.*

III.24 A.   *Our rabbis have taught on Tannaite authority:*

     B.   People are not to profit from eggs twice.

     C.   *Said Mari bar Mari, "There was a dispute between Rab and Samuel. One says, 'Two for one' [selling for two what was bought for one], and the other said, 'Selling by a dealer to a dealer' [making two profits on the same object]."*

III.25 A.   *Our rabbis have taught on Tannaite authority:*

     B.   They sound the alarm on account of a collapse in the market in trading goods even on the Sabbath.

     C.   Said R. Yohanan, "For instance, linen clothing in Babylonia and wine and oil in the Land of Israel."

     D.   *Said R. Joseph, "But that is the case when these are so cheap that ten go for the price of six."*

III.26 A.   *Our rabbis have taught on Tannaite authority:*

     B.   A person is not allowed to emigrate from the Land of Israel unless wheat goes at the price of two seahs for a sela.

     C.   Said R. Simeon, "Under what circumstances? Only in a case in which he does not find any to buy even at that price. But if he finds some to buy at that price, even if a seah of grain goes for a sela, he should not emigrate."

     D.   And so did R. Simeon bar Yohai say, "Elimelech, Machlon and Kilion were the great men of his time, and one of those who sustained the generation. But because he went abroad, he and his sons died in famine. But all the Israelites were able to survive on their own land, as it is said, 'and when they came to Bethlehem, the whole town was stirred because of them' (Ruth 1:19). This teaches that all of the town had survived, but he and his sons had died in the famine" [T. A.Z. 4:4A-H].

III.27 A   "And when they came to Bethlehem, the whole town was stirred because of them, and the women said, 'Is this Naomi'" (Ruth 1:19):

     B.   *What is the meaning of the phrase, "Is this Naomi"?*

     C.   Said R. Isaac, "They said, 'Did you see what happened to Naomi, who emigrated from the Land for a foreign country?'"

III.28 A   And said R. Isaac, "The day that Ruth the Moabite emigrated from the Land to a foreign land, the wife of Boaz died. *That is in line with what people say: 'Before a person dies, his successor as master of the house is appointed.'"*

III.29 A.   Said Rabbah bar R. Huna said Rab, "Isban is the same as Boaz."

   B.   *So what in the world does that mean?*

   C   *It is in line with what Rabbah b. R. Huna further said, for* said Rabbah bar R. Huna said Rab, "Boaz made for his sons a hundred and twenty wedding banquets: 'And Isban had thirty sons and thirty daughters he sent abroad, and thirty daughters he brought from abroad for his sons, and he judged Israel seven years' (Judg. 12:9). For each one of them he made two wedding feasts, one in the household of the father, the other in the household of the father in law. But to none of them did he invite Manoah, for he said, 'How will that barren mule ever repay my hospitality?' And all of them died in his lifetime. *That is in line with what people say, 'In your lifetime you begot sixty? What good are the sixty? Marry again and get another one, brighter than all sixty.'"*

III.30 A   Said R. Hanan bar Raba said Rab, "Elimelech and Salmon and 'such a one' (Ruth 4:1) and the father of Naomi were all sons of Nahshon b. Amminadab (Ex. 6:23, Num. 10:14)."

   B.   *So what in the world does that mean?*

   C   It is that even one who has a substantial store of unearned merit gained from his answers, it will serve him no good when he emigrates from the Land to a foreign land."

III.31 A   And said R. Hanan bar Raba said Rab, "*The mother of Abraham was named Amathelai, daughter of Karnebo; the name of the mother of Haman was Amatehilai, daughter of Orabti; and the mnemonic will be, 'unclean to the unclean, clean to the clean.' The mother of David was Nizbeth daughter of Adael, the mother of Samson was Zlelponit, and his sister was Nasyan.*"

   B.   *So what?*

   C.   For answering heretics.

III.32 A   And said R. Hanan bar Raba said Rab, "For ten years our father, Abraham, was kept in prison, three in Kuta, seven in Kardu."

   B.   *And R. Dimi of Nehardea repeats the matter in reverse order.*

   C   *Said R. Hisda, "The lesser Kuta is the same as Ur of the Chaldees (Gen. 11:31)."*

III.33 A   And said R. Hanan bar Raba said Rab, "The day on which our father, Abraham, died, all of the principal authorities of the nations of the world formed a line and said, 'Woe is the world that has lost [91B] its leader, woe to the ship that has lost its helmsman.'"

III.34 A.   "And you are exalted as head above all" (1 Chr. 29:11):

   B.   *Said R. Hanan bar Raba said Rab, "Even the superintendent of the water supply is appointed by Heaven."*

III.35 A   Said R. Hiyya bar Abin said R. Joshua b. Qorhah, "God forbid! Even if [Elimelech and his family] had found bran, they would never have emigrated. So why were they punished? Because they should have besought mercy for their generation but failed to do so: 'When you cry, let them that you have gathered deliver you' (Isa. 57:13)."

III.36 A Said Rabbah bar bar Hannah said R. Yohanan, "This [prohibition against emigration] has been taught only when money is cheap [and abundant] and produce expensive, but when money is expensive [and not to be found, there being no capital], even if four seahs cost only a sela, it is permitted to emigration."

B. *Said R. Yohanan, "I remember when four seahs of grain cost a sela and many died of starvation in Tiberias, not having an issar for bread."*

C. *And said R. Yohanan, "I remember when workmen wouldn't agree to work on the east side of town, where workers were dying because of the scent of bread [which they could not afford to buy]."*

III.37 A *And said R. Yohanan, "I remember when a child would break open a carob pod and a line of honey would run over both his arms."*

B. *And said R. Eleazar, "I remember when a raven would grab a piece of meat and a line of oil would run down from the top of the wall to the ground."*

C. *And said R. Yohanan, "I remember when boys and girls would promenade in the market at the age of sixteen or seventeen and not sin."*

D. *And said R. Yohanan, "I remember when they would say in the house of study, 'Who agrees with them falls into their power, who trusts in them — what is his becomes theirs.'"*

III.38 A It is written, "Mahlon and Chilion" (Ruth 1:2) and it is written "Joash and Saraph" (1 Chr. 4:22)!

B. Rab and Samuel —

C. One said, "Their names really were Mahlon and Chilion, and why were they called Joash? Because they despaired hope of redemption [the words for Joash and despair using the same letters], and Saraph? because they become liable by the decree of the Omnipresent to be burned."

D. And the other said, "Their names really were Joash and Saraph, but they were called Mahlon and Chilion, Mahlon, because they profaned their bodies [the words for Mahlon and profane using the same letters], and Chilion, because they were condemned by the Omnipresent to destruction [the words for destruction and Chilion using the same letters]."

E. *It has been taught on Tannaite authority in accord with the view of him who said that their names really were Mahlon and Chilion. For it has been taught on Tannaite authority:* What is the meaning of the verse, "And Jokim and the men of Cozeba and Joash and Saraph, who had dominion in Moab, and Jashubilehem, and the things are ancient" (1 Chr. 4:22)?

F. "Jokim": this refers to Joshua, who kept his oath to the men of Gibeon (Josh. 9:15, 26).

G. "And the men of Cozeba": these are the men of Gibeon who lied to Joshua [the words for lie and Cozeba using the same letters] (Josh. 9:4).

H. "And Joash and Saraph": Their names really were Mahlon and Chilion, and why were they called Joash? Because they despaired hope of redemption [the words for Joash and despair using the same letters], and Saraph? because they become liable by the decree of the Omnipresent to be burned.

I. "Who had dominion in Moab": they married wives of the women of Moab.

J.   "And Jashubilehem": this refers to Ruth of Moab, who had returned [using letters that are shared with Jashub] and remained in Bethlehem of Judah.

K.   "And the things are ancient": these things were stated by the Ancient of Days.

III.39 A.   "These were the potters and those that dwelt among plantations and hedges; there they dwelt occupied in the kings work" (1 Chr. 4:23):

B.   "These were the potters": this refers to the sons of Jonadab, son of Rahab, who kept the oath of their father (Jer. 35:6).

C.   "And those that dwelt among plantations": this speaks of Solomon, who in his rule was like a fecund plant.

D.   "And hedges": this refers to the Sanhedrin, who hedged in the breaches in Israel.

E.   "There they dwelt occupied in the kings work": this speaks of Ruth of Moab, who lived to see the rule of Solomon, her grandson's grandson: "And Solomon caused a throne to be set up for the king's mother" (1 Kgs. 2:19), in which connection R. Eleazar said, "For the mother of the dynasty."

III.40 A.   *Our rabbis have taught on Tannaite authority:*

B.   "And you shall eat of the produce, the old store" (Lev. 25:22) – without requiring preservatives.

C.   *What is the meaning of* without requiring preservatives?

D.   R. Nahman said, "Without grain worms."

E.   And R. Sheshet said, "Without blast."

F.   *It has been taught on Tannaite authority in accord with the view of R. Sheshet, and it has been taught on Tannaite authority in accord with the view of R. Nahman.*

G.   *It has been taught on Tannaite authority in accord with the view of R. Nahman:*

H.   "And you shall eat the old store" (Lev. 25:22) – might one suppose that the sense is that the Israelites will be eager for the new produce because last year's has been destroyed [by the grain worm]? Scripture says, "until her produce came in," that is, until the produce will come on its own [without an early, forced harvest (Slotki)].

I.   *It has been taught on Tannaite authority in accord with the view of R. Sheshet:*

J.   "And you shall eat of the produce, the old store" (Lev. 25:22) – might one suppose that the sense is that the Israelites will be eager for the new produce because last year's has been spoiled [Slotki: by the blast]? Scripture states, "until her produce came in," that is, until the new crop will come in the natural way.

III.41 A.   *Our rabbis have taught on Tannaite authority:*

B.   "And you shall eat old store long kept" (Lev. 26:10) – whatever is of an older vintage than its fellow is better in quality than its fellow.

C.   I know that that is so only of things that are ordinarily aged. What about things that are not ordinarily aged?

D.   Scripture is explicit: "old store long kept" (Lev. 26:10) – in all cases.

III.42 A.   "And you shall bring forth the old from before the new" (Lev. 26:10) –

B. This teaches that the storehouses will be full of last year's crop, and the threshing floors, this year's crop, and the Israelites will say, "How are we going to remove the one before the other?"

C. Said R. Pappa, *"Everything is better when aged, except for dates, beer, and fish hash."*

III.1, 2 provide a scriptural basis for the rule and principle of the Mishnah. The key verse of No. 2 accounts for the inclusion of No. 3, which carries in its wake No. 4. Further Tannaite thematic supplements are at Nos. 5-8. No. 8 is glossed by No. 9, and then Nos. 10-12+13, 14 continue the Tannaite supplement. Carrying forward the general theme at hand, Nos. 15-42 form a miscellany built around the general theme before us. I see no formal differences between the miscellany at hand and those we have already examined. The only difference is subject matter – but not *classification of subject matter*. Is it possible, then, to state the propositions of the subsets of the miscellany? These seem to me to state the paramount proposals:

1. People are to employ honest measures and when selling, to give accurate and honest measures: Nos. 5-17.

2. People are not to take advantage of shortages nor create shortages: Nos. 18-25.

3. If there are shortages, people are to try to remain in the Land of Israel if they possibly can: Nos. 26-28+29-36, 37-40.

One might argue that the combination of the set yields the syllogism that honesty in buying and selling the necessities of life is what makes possible Israel's possession of the Holy Land, but that does not seem to me a plausible proposal. I see here only a thematic composite, all the numbered items addressed to that single theme, perhaps, furthermore, with a number of cogent propositions joining some of compositions as well.

The conclusion may be stated very simply. We have now formed a hypothesis that quite random compositions, each with its own focus, will be formed into a composite on the basis of one of three theories of linkage: [1] topic, [2] attribution, or [3] sequence of verses of a passage of Scripture. The agglutination of topically coherent compositions predominates. And this leads to a further theory on the miscellany. The conglomerates of random compositions formed into topical composites ordinarily serve as an amplification of a topic treated in the Mishnah, or are joined to a composite that serves in that way, so that, over all, the miscellanies are made to extend and amplify the statements of the Mishnah, as much as, though in a different way from, the commonplace propositional, analytical, and syllogistic composite.

On the basis of that hypothesis, which has to be tested against the evidence of all of the other miscellanies of the Bavli, I should be prepared to propose the further hypothesis that the Bavli contains no important or sizable sequences of compositions that are entirely unrelated to one another, that is, nothing we should classify as a mere miscellany at all. Faced with three massive miscellanies, we have come to the conclusion that what appears to be a random hodgepodge of this and that and the other thing in fact forms a considered and even crafted composite, the agglutinative principles of which we may readily discern. In fact what we have in the miscellany is nothing more than a Mishnah commentary of a peculiar sort, itself extended and spun out, as the more conventional Mishnah commentaries of the Bavli tend to be extended and spun out. The miscellany may be defined, therefore, in a very simple way: it is, specifically, a composite that has been compiled so as to present for the Mishnah a commentary intending to provide information on topics introduced by the Mishnah – that, and not much more than that. True, the miscellany is not propositional, and it is certainly not analytical. But it is very much a composite in the sense in which I have defined that literary structure in the present context: purposeful, coherent, and I think, elegant. I do not claim that the pages of tractates Berakhot and Sanhedrin may compete in power and intellect with the pages of tractate Baba Qamma where we began. I do claim that what appears by contrast to those pages to be odd, incoherent, pointless, rambling, to the contrary attests in its own way to the single and definitive program of the Bavli's framers. Whatever those framers wished to say on their own account they insisted on setting forth within the framework of that received document upon the structure of which they made everything to depend. All the more reason to admire the remarkable originality and genuinely fresh perspective – and statement – that, in the guise of a commentary, the Bavli was to make. It is nearly time to say what that was.

Index

South Florida Studies in the History of Judaism